COLUMBIA SERIES IN REFORMED THEOLOGY

The Columbia Series in Reformed Theology represents a joint commitment of Columbia Theological Seminary and Westminster John Knox Press to provide theological resources for the church today.

The Reformed tradition has always sought to discern what the living God revealed in scripture is saying and doing in every new time and situation. Volumes in this series examine significant individuals, events, and issues in the development of this tradition and explore their implications for contemporary Christian faith and life.

This series is addressed to scholars, pastors, and laypersons. The Editorial Board hopes that these volumes will contribute to the continuing reformation of the church.

COLUMBIA SERIES IN REFORMED THEOLOGY

Reformed Confessions

Theology from Zurich to Barmen

JAN ROHLS

Translated by John Hoffmeyer

 Westminster John Knox Press
Louisville, Kentucky

Translated by John F. Hoffmeyer from *Theologie reformierter Bekenntnisschriften*, published 1987 by Vandenhoeck and Ruprecht.

© 1997 Vandenhoeck and Ruprecht

English translation © 1998 Westminster John Knox Press

Publisher's Note: The publication of this work was made possible through the assistance of INTER NATIONES, Bonn./Die Herausgabe dieses Werkes wurde aus Mitteln von INTER NATIONES, Bonn, gefördert.

Book and cover design by Drew Stevens

Published by Westminster John Knox Press
Louisville, Kentucky

This book is printed on acid-free paper that meets the American National Standards Institute Z39.48 standard. ⊖

PRINTED IN THE UNITED STATES OF AMERICA

98 99 00 01 02 03 04 05 06 07 — 10 9 8 7 6 5 4 3 2 1

Library of Congress Catloging in Publication Data

Rohls, Jan, date.
 [Theologie reformierter Bekenntnisschriften. English]
Reformed confessions : theology from Zurich to Barmen / Jan Rohls ; John Hoffmeyer, translator.
  p.   cm. — (Columbia series in Reformed theology)
 Includes bibliographical references and index.
 ISBN 0-664-22078-9 (alk. paper)

 1. Reformed Church—Doctrines. 2. Reformed Church—Doctrines—History. 3. Reformed Church—Creeds. I. Title. II. Series.
BX9428. A1R6413   1998
238'. 42—dc21   97-38079

For Herbishofen/Allgaü,
the oldest Reformed congregation in Germany,
and Munich II, the youngest congregation
of the Evangelical Reformed Church
in Bavaria

CONTENTS

INTRODUCTION:
CONFESSING AFTER BARMEN

The initial sentences of Professor Rohls's welcome book identify a characteristic of the Reformed tradition that sets it apart from another major
Reformation movement. He writes: "In Lutheranism the process of confessional development came to a conclusion with the Formula of Concord
(1577) and the Book of Concord (1580). On the Reformed side there is nothing that corresponds to this conclusion."

The Reformed sector of the Protestant Reformation is one that holds to
what can be called an "open" rather than a "closed" confessional tradition.
A closed tradition holds a particular statement of beliefs to be adequate for
all times and places. An open tradition anticipates that what has been confessed in a formally adopted confession takes its place in a confessional
lineup, preceded by statements from the past and expectant of more to
come as times and circumstances change. Thus, the Reformed tradition—
itself a wide river with many currents—affirms that, for it, developing and
adopting confessions is indeed an obligation, not an option. These contemporary confessions are recognized as extraordinarily important for a
church's integrity, identity, and faithfulness. But they are also acknowledged to be relative to particular times and places. This "occasional" nature of a Reformed confession is as well a reminder that statements of faith
are always subordinate in authority to scripture.

What constitutes a confessional "occasion"? The one continuing theological affirmation is that from time to time God through the Spirit calls the
church to say what it believes. Whether a confession is to be written and
adopted is itself a matter of thoughtful and prayerful discernment of God's
call. There are, however, certain typical occasions that provide settings for
the church to say in fresh ways what it believes. In one instance it may be
a perceived internal threat to the church's integrity, the issue of heresy. In
another it may be the coming together of diverse and previously separated
faith communities, now seeking a common voice to affirm their unity, a
unity which is a sign of the oneness Christ intends for the whole church.
Or it could be the sense that the church is threatened from without and
needs to articulate clearly the nature of that threat and what is to be done

about it. At the extreme, the setting may be one of a *"status confessionis,"* where a clear sense emerges that the church can no longer be the church of Jesus Christ without taking a risky but firm stand on what must be affirmed, what denied in church and/or world. In a less turbulent time the opportunity to rehearse what the church believes may arise from a felt need to articulate more adequately the good news of Jesus Christ for the church and for the world beyond the church.

In the text that follows, Professor Rohls has chronicled this dynamic tradition of Reformed confessing from the sixteenth through the first third of the twentieth centuries. He discusses theological themes and positions that have informed both the tradition in its entirety and also particular confessions. He concludes his account with the Declaration of Barmen in 1934, adopted by the Confessing Church in Germany. But true to their heritage, Reformed churches have continued to write and to adopt confessions. Indeed, there has been a significant outpouring of confessional statements during the last six decades. One evidence of that is the 1982 volume edited by Lukas Vischer entitled *Reformed Witness Today: A Collection of Confessions and Statements of Faith Issued by Reformed Churches.* In that collection Vischer has included twenty-six confessional statements from around the world, adopted by the church for various purposes and uses. This number is not exhaustive. But it is illustrative of the fact that Reformed theology continues to find expression in contemporary confessions of faith.

These post-Barmen confessions invite consideration of theological themes that are lodged within earlier confessions but that have taken on prominence since 1934. Questions such as these addressed to more recent confessions include: "What characterizes these confessions?" "Are there common emphases?" "Are there shared theological themes?" "Are there elements that set these confessions off from previous Reformed confessions?"

A survey of these more recent confessions reveals that there are several theological affirmations or themes that are not for the most part new but that have a certain common accent that reflects the past sixty years. More attention or emphasis is given to one in some documents than in others, but all are present in all. Some of these theological themes are: (1) an ecclesiology that affirms the unity of the church; (2) the centrality of Jesus Christ, human and divine, with more focus on the human; (3) a high view of scripture that incorporates the importance of critical tools for understanding the written Word; (4) social ethics; and (5) mission.

In the following paragraphs, primary references to these themes will be drawn from five statements of faith whose provenance is North America and Cuba. But other confessions from around the world will be referred to as they illumine the topic addressed. The five are: The Confession of 1967 (C67), adopted by the United Presbyterian Church in the U.S.A., the immediate occasion for which was the uniting of two denominations. Other propelling concerns were that no statement of faith had been adopted for three hundred years and that the turbulence of the 1960s cried out to be addressed. The Presbyterian Church in the United States in 1977 approved the Declaration of Faith (the Declaration) for study, liturgical use, and inspiration. This document, like C67, was a response to the need for a confession that would restate the faith in terms that would both express it in more accessible ways and open the confessional base of the denomination to other than the seventeenth-century Westminster Standards. While rejected as a confessional standard, A Declaration of Faith has been widely used. Our Song of Hope was approved by the Reformed Church in America in 1978. While, like the above Declaration, this statement was not approved as a standard equal to the sixteenth- and seventeenth-century confessions, it was commended and approved for use in the denomination in its teaching, witness, and worship. In 1977 the Presbyterian-Reformed Church in Cuba adopted its Confession of Faith. The context was the revolutionary change that had occurred in Cuba and the need of the Cuban church to establish its own identity as an autonomous body. A Brief Statement of Faith was adopted by the Presbyterian Church (U.S.A.) in 1991. The Articles of Agreement that formed the basis of the reunion of the Presbyterian Church in the United States and the United Presbyterian Church in the U. S. A. in 1983 called for such a document to be proposed to the new church.

Now we turn to a consideration of the theological themes indicated above.

1. *Ecclesiology, the unity of the church.* The gift of and the commitment to the unity of Christ's church are pervasive in the more recent confessions of faith. One reason for the importance of this emphasis is that many of the post-Barmen confessions have been elicited by and were instruments of the uniting of churches. For example, in 1941 the Basis of Union of the Church of South India focused on unity grounded in Christ and to be testified to by the life of the church. Confessional and practiced ecclesiology came together. Later in the century it is a sign of the power of the theological norm of unity that it becomes an assumption rather than a position requiring defense.

For instance, it is remarkable that C67 does not, though its occasion was the uniting of two denominations, feel the need to give extended or explicit attention to the oneness of the church. It does relate the theological claim of unity in Christ with institutional consequences. Under the section on Forms and Order (II, A. 2) the two are related. "The institutions of the people of God change and vary as their mission requires in different times and places. The unity of the church is compatible with a wide variety of forms, but it is hidden and distorted when variant forms are allowed to harden into sectarian divisions, exclusive denominations, and rival factions."

A Declaration of Faith of the Presbyterian Church in the United States, written in a narrative form, follows the order of the Apostles' Creed in locating the discussion of the church under the doctrine of the Holy Spirit. One section is devoted to the oneness of the church, with the title of "The Holy Spirit Unifies the Christian Church" (V, 6): "We know that the same Spirit (who gave unity to the early church) gives us a unity we cannot create or destroy." This unity does not dispel diversity but does impel the church to make the oneness of the church "visible to a divided world," while assuring the church that it shall be one.

A Brief Statement of Faith had its impetus in the reunion of the Presbyterian Church in the U.S. and the United Presbyterian Church in the U.S.A. in 1983. This eighty-line statement accepts the givenness of the unity of the church and affirms under the category of Holy Spirit these words: "[The Spirit] binds us together with all believers in the one body of Christ, the Church."

Our Song of Hope, received by the Reformed Church in America in 1978, affirms that the Spirit gives unity and compels Christians to learn from traditions other than their own, while striving for visible unity (VI, 18).

In these and other confessions from the second half of the twentieth century, the theme of unity in Christ and visible unity expressed in some institutional ways are given strong expression and form a backdrop for considering other convictions of the faith. What they also demonstrate is that the context for thinking about the unity of the church is one committed to working for and achieving institutional shape and form. If the nineteenth century can be characterized as the missionary century, as some would contend, then the twentieth century may justifiably be termed the ecumenical century. During this time churches at all levels have simultaneously opened their borders to allow for and encourage cross-migration of beliefs, rituals, and practices. Unity and diversity are now not seen as inevitably contradictory experiences, but as ecclesial norms to be incorporated into new expressions of oneness of the church. And while at the end of this century overt enthusiasm and support for ecumenical endeavors seems to have waned, the confessions serve as a continuing call to seek and to manifest the oneness of the church.

2. *Christology, the centrality of Jesus Christ, human and divine, with more focus on the human.* If the unity of the church is a backdrop for recent Reformed confessions, Christology is at center stage. C67 begins with the acclamation, "In Jesus Christ, God was reconciling the world to himself. Jesus Christ is God with man. He is the eternal Son of the Father, who became man and lived among us to fulfill the work of reconciliation. He is present in the church by the power of the Holy Spirit to continue and complete his mission" (9.07). This is immediately followed by the initiating section of the confession, entitled "The Grace of Our Lord Jesus

Christ," thus beginning with the second person of the Trinity. In the paragraphs on Jesus Christ, the humanity of Jesus is the starting point: "In Jesus of Nazareth, true humanity was realized once and for all. Jesus, a Palestinian Jew, lived among his own people and shared their needs, temptations, joys and sorrows" (I, A, 1). That statement is followed by other actions of Jesus Christ, leading to the confessing of his Lordship and to proclaiming Jesus Christ as savior and judge.

As with the Barmen Declaration, so C67 moves from the second person of the Trinity to Creator and Spirit. But it is a christomorphic perspective that rules. It is Jesus Christ who gives shape and content to God's love. It is Jesus Christ whose cross and resurrection become personal crisis and present hope for humankind (9.21). It is Jesus Christ whose living points the way to true life for humans. "The new life finds its direction in the life of Jesus, his deeds and words, his struggles against temptation, his compassion, his anger, and his willingness to suffer death"(9.32). Again, "The life, death, resurrection and promised coming of Jesus Christ has set the pattern for the church's mission" (9.32).

Similarly, though with far less specific content, A Brief Statement of Faith follows the order of both Barmen and C67. Using the Apostolic Benediction as the ordering principle, its opening section, following the introduction, begins with these words: "We trust in Jesus Christ, fully human, fully God" (7). The sentences that follow rehearse the life and ministry of Jesus: preaching, teaching, blessing the children, healing, eating with outcasts, forgiving sinners, and calling all to repent and believe the gospel. It goes on to assert that the crucifixion was a rejection of the way that Jesus lived and taught, and therefore of God. Resurrection, then, has as one of its many meanings the vindication of Jesus' sinless life as a model to be followed.

Perhaps the recent confession most centered on Christology and with special focus on the humanity of Jesus Christ is the Confession of Faith of the Presbyterian-Reformed Church in Cuba. There the human nature of Jesus Christ is addressed in the first section, entitled "The Centrality of the Human Being Given in Jesus Christ." The opening sentence reads, "The Church believes in God because it believes in the human being, and it believes in the human being because it believes in Jesus Christ, the 'Son of God,' our older brother." Jesus Christ is named as the center of the church's interest, a Son of God thoroughly embedded in history. Through him God calls all Christians "to fulfill ourselves as human beings through concrete historical projects of redemption" (I, A).

The Cuban confession emphasizes the historical location for situating and following Jesus, in contrast to an otherworldly and privatized Christ. It testifies to its own occasional setting as it identifies "projects of redemption" as including adopting the goals of the socialist revolution, with the working class as its standard bearer. "The 'creation' of a 'new man' means the establishment of a new community life in the new society" (III, C). At the center of that life is Jesus Christ.

Christology is, as might be expected, a controlling theme for all the confessions noted above, as well as many others. It is affirmation of Jesus Christ as both human and divine. But the weight of attention, not importance, is on the human.

3. *Scripture*. A common thread in the more recent Reformed confessions is a treatment of scripture that reflects the struggle in the church over how one is to understand and therefore read and be instructed by it. In contrast to a position loosely identified as inerrancy, a perspective that proposes that the very words of the Bible have been dictated directly by God and are not to be doubted as to their full truth, the recent Reformed confessions adopt and therefore consolidate a different view. They specifically make a place for critical reading and interpretation of the scriptures. In doing so, they legitimate the use of such interpretive tools as historical and literary criticism as important instruments for understanding how the Bible is to be read and understood. This focus is not one intended to discount or to deny the uniqueness of scripture as a book of and for the church, and its authority. Rather the intention is to make for a written Word that yields richer and clearer ways of understanding both written Word and Word made flesh.

The recent Reformed confessions also shift the theological category for approaching scripture. They turn from inspiration as the model for affirming scriptural authority to revelation. Revelation becomes a dynamic interaction between the self, the church, the Bible, and, most important, the Word of God. It is Jesus Christ who is confessed as the Word of God. Scripture is the written Word. In the section on the Bible in C67 there is a "high" view of that scripture. "The one sufficient revelation of God is Jesus Christ, the Word of God incarnate, to whom the Holy Spirit bears unique and authoritative witness through the Holy Scriptures, which are received and obeyed as the Word of God written. The Scriptures are not a witness among others, but the witness without parallel" (I, C, 2).

This affirmation of the scriptures as written Word, witness by the Holy Spirit to the living Word, is held together with the affirmation that the Bible is also a very human document. In C67 the words of scripture are ". . . the words of men, conditioned by the language, thought forms, and literary fashions of the places and times in which they were written." "The church, therefore, has an obligation to approach the Scriptures with literary and historical understanding" (I, C, 2).

In a similar way A Declaration of Faith treats scripture as part of the category of the Word of God, following a paragraph entitled "Jesus Christ is the Living Word of God." The Bible is identified as the written Word of

God (VI, 3). It is necessary, sufficient, and reliable as witnessing to Jesus Christ, the living Word. Indeed, scripture is the touchstone for testing whether what is said in church or world is authentic and truthful. Such an understanding of scripture does not guarantee that there will be agreement about what God is saying to the people. But it locates the critical determination of what God is saying in an interpretation of that scripture as witness to Jesus Christ.

A Declaration of Faith underscores the importance of using the "... best available methods of understanding them [scriptures] in their historical and cultural settings and the literary forms in which they are cast." Yet, finally, the appeal is to the Word made flesh. "When we encounter apparent tensions and conflicts in what Scripture teaches us to believe and do, the final appeal must be to the authority of Christ" (VI, 3).

These two confessions are reflective of all recent Reformed statements of belief. The uniting of Authority (the Word of God) and Subordinate Authority (the written Word) does not negate in any way the authority of either written or living Word. Rather it addresses the issue of appropriate authority and the relationship between diverse authorities that are essential for human life.

The recent Reformed confessions maintain a "high" view of scripture while embracing a variety of instruments for understanding the Word made flesh. Such a view of scripture also reflects a "higher" view of Jesus Christ, to whom scriptures themselves bear witness and testimony. And it is to these scriptures that the church turns as it seeks to discern what faithfulness to Christ means in the society.

4. *Social ethics.* Social ethics has to do with responsibility not only for persons and interpersonal relationships but also for social structures. It is a commitment to provide for social, economic, and political institutions that maintain and advance justice and well-being for all people, no matter what their religious commitment, or if any. It would be inaccurate to say that there are no social ethics in earlier Reformed confessions. But it is accurate to note that the social context for the church and for the individual Christian has shifted dramatically from the sixteenth and seventeenth centuries when so many Reformed confessions blossomed. For example, the separation of church and state is a phenomenon that was unanticipated and unknown until late in the eighteenth century. And the relationship between religious and political bodies in a secular society, where no special status or privilege is accorded to religious bodies, is a matter of intense debate and action throughout the world today. Under such conditions the church is one political unit among many. Another feature of the setting of the church in relation to the society is the expansion of the little worlds for whom responsibility was to be exercised to one world. As the world has expanded,

the church's confessed responsibility has been broadened and extended. The landscape of church and society has changed dramatically in the last three to four hundred years. The commitment to social responsibility endures.

One characteristic of recent Reformed confessions is their specifying of broad issues that the church must address for the sake of its own integrity and for the health of the world. And while the church is called to bring critical words of judgment and hope to bear on human issues, the particularities of a social ethic will vary greatly from time to time and from place to place, as will be illustrated later.

A Declaration of Faith includes references to the social and political responsibility of the church. It does so in a section on "The Christian Church" and in one that is titled "The Christian Mission." In the former the continuing issue of the church's faithfulness is recognized. "Throughout its history the church has struggled to be faithful to God in political situations: under persecution, or as an established arm of the state, or in separation from it" (VII, 5). What must be affirmed in every situation is that the state is not God and the church is not the state, despite temptations by both to believe otherwise. Whatever the relationship between church and state, there is a perennial temptation to make Caesar god or to identify the role of the church as exercising rule as a state.

The section on "The Christian Mission" in the Declaration moves toward more explicitness about social responsibility. A section on "God sends us to strive for justice" details the necessity of the faithful church to "labor to change customs and structures that enslave and oppress human beings"(VIII, 3). It proceeds to identify in broad strokes issues that require the church's attention. These include working with others to overcome the "growing disparity between rich and poor nations and to root out prejudice and racism in personal attitudes and in institutions." This portion of the Declaration also includes a full section on the church's working for peace (VII, 5). While remaining at a high level of generality, the direction for the church to follow is clearer here than in other places. Written in the midst of a cold war where all residents of the world were threatened by the possibility of a nuclear holocaust, the Declaration refers specifically to the need to perceive the threat of annihilation as a condition of modern life and calls the church, with others, to find alternative ways of resolving international disputes.

C67 also includes references to broad arenas of social concern that call the church to faithfulness. Dealt with under the category of the ministry of reconciliation, the confession puts its social ethic into proper context. "In each time and place, there are particular problems and crises through which God calls the church to act. The church, guided by the Spirit, humbled by its own complicity and instructed by all attainable knowledge,

seeks to discern the will of God and learn how to obey in these concrete situations. The following are particularly urgent at the present time" (II, A,
4). The specific issues then addressed are race, peace, poverty, and sexual-
ity. When it comes to race, C67 gives more explicit targets of concern. They
include provision for equal access for all without regard to race or ethnicity in housing, education, and employment, to cite three.

The second issue to be confronted and dealt with is the church's commitment to seek peace in the world. Written in a time of nuclear standoff
and the temptation to uncritical nationalism, C67 called for fresh relations
between nations, ". . . even at risk to national security." The latter phrase
was the subject of great disagreement in the denomination, revealing
perhaps the reality that "occasional" confessions are charged with the en-
ergy of disagreement. What seems today to be a truism took on different
coloration in the days of the Vietnam War and the background of a cold
war with the Soviet Union and its client states.

The third area considered is that of economic justice. This issue is ap-
proached through the question of poverty. "The reconciliation of man
through Jesus Christ makes it plain that enslaving poverty in a world of
abundance is an intolerable violation of God's good creation. Because
Jesus identified himself with the needy and exploited, the cause of the
world's poor is the cause of his disciples. The church cannot condone
poverty, whether it is the product of unjust social structures, exploitation
of the defenseless, lack of national resources, absence of technological understanding or rapid expansion of populations"(II, A, 4). In a context of a
national war on poverty in the United States, this is an example of a claim
on the church that had its roots in Jesus Christ's life and ministry and had
political consequences for the life of the church at that time.

The final issue addressed is not one that is technically a social ethic. It
calls for no reformation of institutions and social structures. It does, however, speak to the ongoing social issue of sexual relations, an issue very
much on people's minds during the so-called sexual revolution of the
1960s. Calling the time one of sexual anarchy, the confession called for responsible freedom, urging the development and demonstration of a "life
together in families and by individuals."

The two previous confessions cited locate the basis of a social ethic in
sections on ministry and mission. Another tack is taken by the Reformed
Church in America in its Our Song of Hope. Here the injunction to the
church to hear the cry of the oppressed and to deal with new discoveries
of science and technology comes under "Our Hope in God's Word," related immediately to scripture. In "A Brief Statement of Faith" the enlist-
ment of the church in addressing issues of justice and peace is under the
category of the work of the Holy Spirit.

Other recent confessions elevate the social ethic dimension of the gospel. None is more explicit, however, than the Cuban confession. There a specific political program is endorsed as a "project of redemption." The confession, in a section on salvation, affirms that in "the stability of the Government—in spite of all its necessary ambiguities—we can find a guarantee for the administration of Justice and the maintenance of Peace when it is a case of 'non-classist' societies, where the power of the state is not in the hands of exploiting and oppressing classes, but in the hands of the workers." It continues: "The Church lives in the same measure in which each one of its members works for the social-economical reconstruction of the human being within the Socialist State; because of all the forms of State known and experienced to this day, it is the society organized with such (socialist) structures which offers the most concrete possibilities for making workable a more and more fairly distributive justice, which progressively reaches all citizens with greater efficiency"(III, C).

In this Cuban confession one sees clearly the "occasionalism" of confessions, their inevitable risky character as they move toward specificity in social ethics, and yet their venturesomeness in seeking to witness to the concrete love of God in Jesus Christ. All recent confessions join in placing issues of social justice on the agenda of their churches. The justice sought is recognized by all to be at best an approximation and a sign of God's universal rule in the world.

5. *Mission.* The early confessions of the Reformed communities of faith for the most part assumed a world where a church's boundaries were coterminous with political units. Each church and state was neighbor to another Christian country. So one grew up Christian by growing up English, Scottish, Danish, etc. Churches identified as state churches held positions of privilege and power in the society. There was, however, little attention given to the mission of the church beyond its boundaries. Mission as a category of the church's constitutional documents was absent. There was at best only brief reference to the church's reaching out beyond itself. Confessions from early in the Reformed heritage are oriented more internally than externally.

In the recent Reformed confessions the missiological assumptions shift. Now mission is assumed as a topic to be included in confessions. Now the church as mission and the church as an instrument of mission are brought to the forefront. The marks of the authentic church stated early on in the Reformed tradition were preaching and hearing of the word, proper administration of the sacraments, and church order or discipline. Now, without setting aside these essential characteristics, a fourth emerges—the mission of the church. A quick comparison of older and more recent confessions persuades one that mission has become "de facto" if not "de jure" one of the four marks of the faithful church.

C67 has three sections, the middle of which is entitled "The Ministry of

Reconciliation." The first subsection is "The Mission of the Church." It holds up the "sending" of the church into the world, overcoming enmities between God and people and among peoples. "Christ has called the church to this mission and given it the gift of the Holy Spirit. The church maintains continuity with the apostles and with Israel by faithful obedience to his call" (II, A, 1). The continuity of the church is not assured by a particular ecclesiastical office or confessional tradition. Continuity is given as the church down through the ages engages in mission, going into the world to evangelize and do justice.

A Brief Statement of Faith put the matter concisely. "In a broken and fearful world the Spirit gives us courage to pray without ceasing, to witness among all peoples to Christ as Lord and Savior, to unmask idolatries in church and culture, to hear the voices of peoples long silenced, and to work with others for justice, freedom, and peace." Our Song of Hope shares this perspective. Paragraph 16 reads: "The Spirit sends His church to call sinners to repentance, to proclaim the good news that Jesus is personal Savior and Lord. He sends it out in ministry to preach good news to the poor, righteousness to the nations and peace among humankind." A Declaration of Faith manifests a common approach. Its section on "The Christian Mission" underscores the sending of the church into the world to proclaim the gospel, to strive for justice, to exercise compassion, and to work for peace.

In all these and other recent Reformed confessions mission encompasses a commitment to both evangelism and social responsibility. Both are integrated by being grounded in the church's mission and ministry. The theological background is that the mission of the church is derivative from the mission of God, which is revealed in and through Jesus Christ and by the Holy Spirit. As the body of Christ the church by grace participates in that mission, proclaiming and enacting in the world the message of God's love and justice. Mission is of the essence of the church.

* * *

The survey above of certain theological and ecclesial characteristics of recent Reformed confessions is not to suggest that the themes used are inclusive of all emphases and perspectives. The documents are far too rich to be captured by these categories alone. A further lack is that one type of confession that sprang forth in the last two decades is of a different order of urgency and is more pointed than others in its nature. It is a statement of faith that addresses what was referred to earlier as a "*status confessionis.*" This state occurs when the church draws a clear line between affirming what it believes and in rejecting what some in the world or church would have it say and do. These occasions are rare, or at least are perceived as being unusual in their occurrence. The theologian Robert McAfee Brown writes of these times: "Every now and then the issues become so clear and the stakes so high, that the privilege of amiable disagreement must be superceded by clear-cut decisions. And the choice must move from both/and to either/or. Such a time is called a *'status confessionis,'* a 'confessional situation.'"(Brown, p. 7). That was the setting of the Barmen Declaration.

Among recent Reformed confessions one stands out as addressing a *"status confessionis."* It is the Theological Declaration adopted in 1979 in South Africa. The setting was this: The minority white government adopted and imposed a policy and accompanying practices labeled "apartheid" or separate development. The state's policy and practices were such that a minority population in South Africa—whites—defined people by race or ethnicity and imposed on the nonwhites living conditions that required different racial groups to live apart and to be subject to the oppressive rule of the government. The dominant white Dutch Reformed Church provided theological legitimation for this ideology and its consequential practices. It mirrored the government's policy by requiring the nonwhite churches of the Dutch Reformed community to set up separate denominations.

It was to reject such ecclesiastical and governmental policies that a group of nonwhite pastors of the separated Dutch Reformed Churches gathered in 1974, organizing themselves and later others, including laity, under the name of the Broederkring. The Broederkring adopted a five-point theological statement. Included was the call for all churches to affirm the unity of the churches in Jesus Christ and to commit themselves to a visible unity that could not be divided into separate racial/ethnic churches. A second affirmation was of the Kingship of Christ, a reign that should and would triumph over the ideology of apartheid. There was as well the call to advance the liberation of the oppressed from the pervasive violence and structural injustice of the state. These and other positions clearly drew a line in the sand between those opposed to and those supportive of apartheid. There was no longer a neutral ground.

Some five years later the annual conference of the Broederkring adopted the Theological Declaration of September 5, 1979. This document affirmed God's persistent work to "break the power of injustices" and the responsibility of the peoples of God to live as one undivided body of Christ. The concluding paragraph is a ringing challenge, affirmation, and source of comfort. "In our South African situation this [obedience to Christ over Caesar] means that we as part of the church of Christ in this world should unflinchingly persevere for establishing God's justice. The Church may, in faithful allegiance to its Head, Jesus Christ, come into conflict with human authorities. If the church has to suffer in the process we know that this is part of the way of God's people through history and that the word of Christ remains in force, 'I will never leave you or forsake you.' "

The context in which this Theological Declaration was forged and adopted left no room for misunderstanding. Those who theologically and ecclesiastically supported apartheid in church or nation were named as heretical. Later the World Alliance of Reformed Churches would endorse this position, brand the white Dutch Reformed Church as heretical, and expel it from its membership.

The Theological Declaration is a confession standing with others in loyalty to Christ and its own tradition. It represents a position of risky truthfulness, riskier than many of its contemporaries. It may also be useful to note that it weaves together theological themes that are characteristic of recent Reformed confessions, namely, an emphasis on the oneness of the church, the centrality of Jesus Christ, the claim to speak from scripture, social ethics and mission.

* * *

Continuity and discontinuity mark the Reformed confessional tradition. Theologies and events in church and world will continue to raise the questions of when confessions are to be written and adopted next and what they will say. The Reformed churches of the world will give answer only as concrete conditions require or call for such responses to God. One thing is clear, however. When such confessional occasions arise, those who draft, debate, and adopt statements of contemporary belief will be instructed by the confessions of their forebears, both those discussed by Professor Rohls in this book and those in more recent times.

—JACK L. STOTTS

BIBLIOGRAPHY

Brown, Robert McAfee, ed. *KAIROS*. Grand Rapids: Wm. B. Eerdmans Publishing Co., 1990.

Dowey, Edward A., Jr. *A Commentary on the Confession of 1967 and An Intoduction to "The Book of Confessions."* Philadelphia: Westminster Press, 1968.

Eberts, Harry W., Jr. ed. *We Believe: A Study of the Book of Confessions for Church Officers.* Rev. ed. Louisville, Ky.: Westminster/John Knox Press, 1994.

Leith, John H. *Creeds of the Churches.* 3d ed. Atlanta: John Knox Press, 1982.

Placher, William C., and David Willis-Watkins. *Belonging to God: A Commentary on "A Brief Statement of Faith."* Louisville, Ky.: Westminster/John Knox Press, 1992.

Rogers, Jack. *Presbyterian Creeds.* Philadelphia: Westminster Press, 1985.

Reformed Confessions

PREFACE

A theology of Reformed confessional writings is confronted with several problems not shared by its Lutheran counterpart. First, there is no official corpus, but only various private collections of Reformed symbols. Second, there is no critical edition of confessional texts that would attain the compass of older editions. Most of the documents are found in E. F. K. Müller's *Die Bekenntnisschriften der reformierten Kirche* (Leipzig: Deichert, 1903). This can be supplemented with the editions and translations of H. A. Niemeyer, P. Schaff, W. Niesel, and P. Jacobs.[1] Jacobs is also the source of what has been until now the only *Theologie reformierter Bekenntnisschriften in Grundüzgen* (Neukirchen: Moers, 1959). Jacobs's work, though, is based on a narrow selection of confessions, chosen from the perspective of historical dissemination and theological value. A theology of Reformed confessional writings that wishes to take account of the entire compass of the tradition will need to free itself from this limitation. By contrast, this work follows Jacobs in limiting itself to the older Reformed confessions from the period of the Reformation and Reformed Orthodoxy in order not to blur the distance, with respect to the history of dogma, between older and newer Reformed confessions, and not to have the latter appear to be merely a Neo-Orthodox repristination of the heritage of the Reformation.

In presenting the theological contents of the older Reformed confessional writings, it quickly becomes clear that one can speak of a theology only in the sense of a plurality of theological conceptions. The individual confessions stem from diverse tendencies and schools. For the sake of historical order it is therefore necessary to start by sketching the development of older Reformed confessional formation from the beginnings of the Zurich Reformation until the end of Reformed Orthodoxy. One can dispense with a more detailed treatment of the historical and systematic connections because there are a number of studies of the history and content of Reformed dogma. One should name here A. Schweizer's *Die Glaubenslehre der reformierten Kirche dargestellt und aus den Quellen belegt* (Zurich: 1844–47), and those works that engage Schweizer's position in critical detail: F. C. Baur, "Über Princip und Charakter des Lehrbegriffs der

3

reformierten Kirche" (*Theologische Jahrbücher:* 1847); M. Schneckenburger, "Die reformierte Dogmatik mit Rücksicht auf Schweizers Glaubenslehre" (*Studien und Kritiken:* 1848); J. H. A. Ebrard, *Das Verhältnis der reformierten Dogmatik zum Determinismus* (Zurich: 1849). There is also from A. Schweizer *Die protestantischen Central-Dogmen in ihrer Entwicklung innerhalb der reformierten Kirche* (Zurich: 1854–56). M. Schneckenburger provides a *Vergleichende Darstellung des lutherischen und reformierten Lehrbegriffs* (1855), and E. Bizer offers a historical sketch of the dogmatic work of Reformed Orthodoxy in his new edition of H. Heppe's *Die Dogmatik der evangelisch-reformierten Kirche* (Neukirchen: 1958). An evaluation of the treatment of Reformed doctrine in the recent history of theology is found in W. Neuser, "Dogma und Bekenntnis in der Reformation: Von Zwingli und Calvin bis zur Synode von Westminster" (in C. Andresen, ed., *Handbuch der Dogmen- und Theologiegeschichte,* vol. 2 [Göttingen: 1980], 165–66).

In the context of posing the question of theological mediation and inquiring after the principles of Protestantism, the problem of a particular Reformed principle was immediately posed, without its finding a satisfying solution. When the issue was confessional particularity over against Lutheranism, one thought such a Reformed principle could be seen, instead of in the doctrine of justification, in the doctrine of predestination, insofar as the latter brings to expression the absoluteness of God and the absolute dependence of human beings. As a student of Schleiermacher, Schweizer thus sees Reformed Christianity as essentially directed not against "Judaistic" works righteousness but against the pagan divinization of the creature. For Schneckenburger, on the contrary, the difference between Lutheranism and Reformed Christianity lies in the fact that the former is passively oriented because of the centrality of justification to its faith, while the latter is actively oriented—namely, toward the sanctification made possible by the forgiveness of sins—and thus represents teleological piety as a type. It is this psychological definition of the Reformed principle which is then transported by K. B. Hundeshagen and E. Troeltsch into the sociological domain.

The impossibility of maintaining the thesis that the doctrine of predestination is the Reformed principle was already emphasized by Ebrard. The treatment of the doctrine of predestination is too diverse, as is the place granted to it in the confessions. Admittedly, on one occasion it is characterized as the fundamental article of the Christian faith. But in this one case it is explicitly conceived as the doctrine of gracious election: that is, as the result of projecting back from the doctrine of justification. Therefore, the present theology of Reformed confessional writings will not proceed analytically by developing theological contents out of a presupposed Reformed principle. Instead it will proceed synthetically in presenting theological contents. One point of support for this method is the structure of most of the confessions themselves, which, arising primarily from the time of Reformed Orthodoxy, often give the impression of being a dogmatic compendium. At the same time, the individual dogmatic loci are presented in a way that I hope neither levels the theological differences between the various confessional writings nor fails to take account of their historical succession.

The primary intention of the present work is to present the theological contents of the old Reformed confessional writings. This intention is not tied to an interest in repristinating the old Reformed doctrinal tradition. Instead the very aim of the concluding section is to show how the end of the confessional era and the beginning of modernity bring with them the dissolution of that tradition. The confessional doctrinal systems collapse under the storm of Enlightenment criticism, and the Reformed churches adjust themselves to this development by either totally abandoning their confessions, reworking them, or formulating new ones. In this way the critique of confessional dogma introduced by the Enlightenment is ultimately acknowledged even where one condemns the entire epoch of Neo-Protestantism introduced by the Enlightenment, and demands a return to Orthodoxy.

I am particularly grateful to my friends and colleagues Dorothea Wendebourg, who provided me access to the manuscript of her work *Reformation und Orthodoxie* (Göttingen: 1986), and Gunther Wenz, who put at my disposition the typescript of his *Einführung in die evangelische Sakramentenlehre* (Darmstadt: 1987).

ABBREVIATIONS

The following abbreviations are used for the collections of confessional writings from which the source references in the text are taken.

BC   T. G. Tappert, trans. and ed., *The Book of Concord: The Confessions of the Evangelical Lutheran Church* (Philadelphia: Fortress, 1959)

BSLK *Die Bekenntnisschriften der evangelisch-lutherischen Kirche* (Göttingen: Vandenhoeck and Ruprecht, 1982)

C   A. C. Cochrane, ed., *Reformed Confessions of the Sixteenth Century* (Philadelphia: Westminster Press, 1966)

CC   A. C. Cochrane, *The Church's Confession under Hitler* (Philadelphia: Westminster Press, 1962)

CT   J. F. Clarkson et al., trans., *The Church Teaches: Documents of the Church in English Translation* (St. Louis, Mo.: B. Herder, 1955)

DS   H. Denzinger and A. Schönmetzer, eds., *Enchiridion Symbolorum,* 33d ed. (Freiburg: Herder, 1965)

J   P. Jacobs, *Reformierte Bekenntnisschriften und Kirchenordnungen in deutscher Übersetzung* (Neukirchen: Moers, 1949)

M   E. F. K. Müller, ed., *Die Bekenntnisschriften der reformierten Kirche in authentischen Texten mit geschichtlicher Einleitung und Register* (Leipzig: Deichert, 1903)

N   H. A. Niemeyer, *Collectio confessionum in ecclesiis reformatis publicatarum* (Leipzig: Klinkhardt, 1840)

Ni   W. Niesel, *Bekenntnisschriften und Kirchenordnungen der nach Gottes Wort reformierten Kirche* (Zurich: Zollikon, 1938)

S   P. Schaff, ed., *The Creeds of Christendom, with a History and Critical Notes,* vol. 3 (New York: Harper & Brothers, 1882)

T   T. F. Torrance, trans. and ed., *The School of Faith: The Catechisms of the Reformed Church* (New York: Harper & Brothers, 1959)

Z   S. M. Jackson, trans., *The Latin Works of Huldreich Zwingli,* vol. 2, ed. W. J. Hinke (Philadelphia: Heidelberg, 1922)

1.

THE DEVELOPMENT OF THE OLD REFORMED CONFESSIONAL WRITINGS

In Lutheranism the process of confessional development came to a conclusion with the Formula of Concord (1577) and the Book of Concord (1580). On the Reformed side there is nothing that corresponds to this conclusion. The Book of Concord represents at least the attempt to introduce a body of doctrine (*corpus doctrinae*) as a unitary norm of proclamation and doctrine for all of Lutheranism. The Book of Concord developed in connection with the struggle with Cryptocalvinism, and was supposed to replace the Philippist body of doctrine—authored in the battles against the Gnesiolutherans—and thereby exclude Philippism as heterodox. To be sure, the Reformed churches have not lacked for attempts to establish a common confession or a universally binding collection of confessional writings. It was precisely the consolidation of Concordistic Lutheranism that gave rise to these undertakings. After all, the Formula of Concord understood itself to be the only valid interpretation of the Augsburg Confession. In doing so it necessarily awakened on the Reformed side the fear of losing the protection granted by the 1555 Peace of Augsburg. The Formula of Concord offered a specifically anti-Reformed interpretation of that confession and excluded the altered Augsburg Confession of 1540 as an independent interpretation.

It is against this background that one must regard the failed attempt of Count Palatine Johann Casimir to have all the Reformed churches of Europe commit to a common confession at an assembly convened in Frankfurt in 1577. The Reformed "works of union," occasioned by the publication of the Book of Concord, fared no better than Casimir's undertaking at achieving an extensive and lasting success. The *Harmony of Confessions of Faith of the Orthodox and Reformed Churches* (*Harmonia confessionum fidei, orthodoxarum et reformatarum ecclesiarum*), produced by Jean François Salvard with the collaboration of Beza, Daneus, Goulart, and de Chandieu, was published in Geneva in 1581. This text sought to present the confessional unity of the various Reformed churches and their agreement with genuine Lutheranism. This unionistic purpose was served by the inclusion of two confessions stemming from Melanchthon—the altered Augsburg Confession and the Saxon Confession (1551)—and of the Wurttemberg Confession (1552), authored by Brenz. Zurich and Geneva, which had kept their distance from the Frankfurt assembly, gave their joint approval to the *Harmony*. It did not, however, receive official recognition until the Huguenot national synod meeting in Vitré in 1583.

Yet even this work of Reformed union is not a closed body of doctrine comparable to the Book of Concord. In its new edition of 1612 under the title *Ordered Body of Confessions of Faith* (*Corpus et syntagma confessionum fidei*) it was extended by seven additional confessions. The 1654 edition contained still three more. In this edition the unionistic goal led even to the inclusion of the private confession of the Orthodox Patriarch Cyril Lukaris (1631). By contrast, all the confessions directly influenced by Zwingli were left out of consideration, as was the entire German Reformed and Puritan confessional tradition. While the first private collection of Reformed confessions, that of J. C. W. Augusti (1827), adds several German Reformed texts to the selection, H. A. Niemeyer's *Collection of Confessions Published in the Reformed Churches* (*Collectio confessionum in ecclesiis reformatis publicatarum*) (1840) also includes Zwinglian and Puritan confessions. The latter could claim to be the most comprehensive collection of older Reformed confessions until 1903, when E. F. K. Müller published an edition that suggested completeness: *The Confessional Writings of the Reformed Church*.

The development of the Old Reformed confessions begins with Zwingli in the 1520s and ends in the last third of the seventeenth century, at a time when confessional consciousness together with Reformed Orthodoxy goes into decline. Zwingli's Articles (1523), which introduced the Zurich Reformation, count as the first of these confessions. The Helvetic Consensus Formula (1675), which gave fixed formulation to Orthodox doctrine, marks the concluding point. Like the beginning and ending of the development themselves, the confessional writings that arose between them belong to various theological traditions. By simplifying, we can divide the development of the Old Reformed confessions into six phases. The confessions of the German-speaking Swiss—confessions influenced above all by Zwingli—constitute the beginning. In a second phase a Geneva tradition develops with Calvin. Under Bullinger, the Geneva tradition is combined with the Zurich tradition, but without the latter fully surrendering its own particularity. The spread of Calvinism in Western and Eastern Europe characterizes the third phase. In a fourth phase Calvinism and Philippism fuse to found a specifically German Reformed confessional tradition. The fifth phase is marked by the doctrinal decrees of the Dordrecht Synod, which signify the victory of strict Calvinism over Arminianism. A sixth phase is marked by Puritanism and its separation from the established Anglican state church. At the end, finally, stands the Helvetic Consensus Formula, which again defends Calvinist Orthodoxy, this time against above all the innovations arising from the school of Saumur.

ZWINGLI AND GERMAN-SPEAKING SWITZERLAND

In German-speaking Switzerland the Reformation was carried out by civil authority. The city councils invited the representatives of the contending religious parties to public disputations, in which the councils accorded scripture the role of a criterion of truth. The confessional writing that stands at the beginning of the development, Zwingli's Articles, is a number of summary propositions that were prepared for the First Zurich Disputation (1523). Scripture, with Christ as its center, is regarded here as the only authority able to legitimate a critique. Following the First Disputation, the council could accordingly judge that no one had been able to overcome Zwingli with scripture, and that therefore from that point on nothing should be preached that was not in accord with scripture. The Second Zurich Disputation, which took place in the same year and was dedicated to the question of images and to the sacrifice of the Mass, then led to carrying through the Reformation. Zwingli's "Short Introduction" grounded the removal of images and of the sacrifice of the Mass. In doing so it grounded the purist shape of the Reformation movement in Zurich and the areas influenced by that city. The Reformation was carried out by the city council, which regarded Zwingli as the legitimate representative of the church community. The relation between the magistrate and Christian community is thus defined in the sense of a state church arrangement.

As in Zurich, in Berne the resolution of disputed religious questions was considered a task of the state. The council accordingly invited participation in a disputation (1528). Besides the Zurich and Basle representatives Zwingli and Johannes Oecolampadius, representatives from the South German centers of the Reformation (Strassburg, Cologne, Memmingen, Lindau, Ulm, Augsburg) attended. The Theses of Berne, authored by the local Reformers Berthold Haller and Franz Kolb, and edited by Zwingli, served as the doctrinal basis of the disputation. The acceptance of the Theses laid the groundwork for the Berne Reformation.

Luther and Zwingli were of one mind in preserving infant baptism, and thus in rejecting the Anabaptist movement. And they both wanted to restrict the sacraments to Baptism and the Lord's Supper. But with regard to the Supper, dissension arose between the two Reformers, and the Wittenberg and Zurich Reformations took divergent paths. Luther, struggling against the spiritualism of the Enthusiasts, insisted more and more on the real presence. By contrast, from 1524 onward Zwingli was led by the teaching letter of the Dutch humanist Cornelius Hoenius to a symbolic interpretation of the words of institution—an interpretation that fit with his spiritualistic concept of God. In order to be able to unite all the Protestant powers into a great anti-Hapsburg coalition after the Diet of Speyer, Philip of Hesse convened in Marburg a colloquy on religion that was supposed to serve the goal of laying to rest the controversy concerning the Lord's Supper. The Wittenberg delegates, the Swiss, and the South Germans were able to agree on all points except that of the real bodily presence. The Marburg Articles thus record dissension on this point. This dissension became manifest at the Diet of Augsburg. The Augsburg Confession excluded a Zwinglian interpretation of the Lord's Supper, so that the South Germans (Strassburg, Memmingen, Constance, Lindau) saw themselves compelled to present a confession of their own, the Tetrapolitan Confession. For reasons of time, Zwingli could submit only the Account of Faith (*Fidei ratio*), a private confession clarifying the Swiss position.

The Tetrapolitan Confession mediates between the Swiss and the Wittenbergers in the way typical of the South Germans under the leadership of Bucer and Capito. The confession is based on various preliminary works and proposals that leave open several possible courses of action. Strassburg attained the agreement of the Swabian cities only by shortening the long article on the Lord's Supper. In sum, the Tetrapolitan Confession represents the attempt by the South Germans to approximate the Augsburg Confession. However, the former confession is distinguished from the latter not only in the question of the Lord's Supper but also in its ethics, which ties together justification and love as tightly as possible, and in its biblicism. At any rate, though, the article on the Lord's Supper avoided Swiss radicalism. In so doing it laid the basis for the South German cities linking up with the Wittenberg Reformation and the Augsburg Confession—a connection that was sealed when Luther and Bucer signed the Wittenberg Concordat (1536). From then on Switzerland and Germany went their separate ways in the development of the Reformation.

Zurich tried to carry out the Reformation—even resorting to military means—in the cantons that had continued in the old faith. Following the failure of that attempt and after Zwingli's death, the Second Peace of Kappel (1531) gave fixed formulation to the confessional division of German-speaking Switzerland. In the meantime Basle, Berne, Schaffhausen, and St. Gall had aligned themselves on the side of Zurich in this division. In Basle the Reformation was carried out by the humanistically inclined Johannes Oecolampadius. Oecolampadius's critique of state church form and his engagement in favor of separating civil punishment from church discipline—that is, in favor of separating state from church—distinguished him from Zwingli. Working from the draft of Oecolampadius's Synod Confession (1531), his successor Oswald Myconius authored the First Confession of Basle (1534). This confession draws upon Zwingli in its doctrine of the sacraments and of the Lord's Supper, as well as in its Christology.

After Zwingli's death the influence of the Strassburg theologians gained strength in Switzerland, and along with their influence the tendency toward a unification with the Wittenberg Reformation also gained strength. Only after the formulation of the Wittenberg Concordat was this tendency definitively abandoned. When conflicts arose in Berne between the government and the preachers, Haller sought support in Strassburg. Thus it was that Capito authored the Synodical Declaration of Berne (1532), which contains the convened synod's decisions concerning questions of doctrine and church order. The Synodical Declaration is distinguished by a unionistic understanding of the Lord's Supper and by a push for a stronger separation of church and state, but above all by its Christocentric antinomianism.

As in the Synodical Declaration of Berne, Strassburg's unionistic efforts also find expression in the Second Confession of Basle, the First Helvetic Confession (1536). This confession arose as a reaction to the announcement of a council to be convened in Mantua. In the First Helvetic Confession all the German-speaking Swiss cities that had gone over to the Reformation (Zurich, Basle, Berne, Schaffhausen, St. Gall, Muhlhausen, Biel) present their common faith. Myconius, Grynaeus, Megander, Capito, Bucer, Bullinger, and Leo Judae all collaborated in this confession. Leo Judae is also the source of the German version, which eliminates the unionistic elements of the Latin original. The First Helvetic Confession forms the apex in the confessional development of Zwinglianism. As a result of the circumstances that occasioned its writing, the question of doctrinal authority comes to the fore in a way that had not been the case in the previous confessional writings. For the first time, the question of doctrinal authority is answered with the formal principle of scripture. Previously, references to scripture or the word of God were always made with regard to particular contents. At any rate, the unionistic intentions of the Strassburg theologians were definitively disappointed. Although Luther, to whom the confession had been sent, regarded it as being correct in itself, he required that the Swiss sign the Wittenberg Concordat.

CALVIN, BULLINGER, AND
THE AGREEMENT BETWEEN
ZURICH AND GENEVA

The First Helvetic Confession arose in Basle at the same time as the first version of Calvin's *Institutes*. Calvin's appearance on the scene marks the beginning of a new stage in the development of the Reformation and in confessional formation. The Geneva Reformation was at first limited to

French-speaking Switzerland and was influenced not by Zwingli but by Luther. But after the shared way with Wittenberg broke off, the Geneva Reformation sought ties with Zurich and thus contributed to the Reformed consensus in Switzerland.

In 1536 Calvin was constrained by William Farel to remain in Geneva as a coworker. In the same year Calvin participated in the Lausanne Disputation, convened by the Council of Berne, which had previously conquered and reformed Vaud. The foundation for the Lausanne Disputation was the Lausanne Articles (1536) authored by Farel. In Geneva Calvin himself composed a sort of catechism for the instruction of the citizenry concerning the foundations of Reformation belief. An extract from this composition is the First Geneva Confession (1536), which was elevated to the level of a fundamental politico-religious law of the republic, and to which the entire citizenry subscribed under oath. Of course, after Calvin was driven out of Geneva the Confession lost its significance.

As leader of the French refugee congregation in Strassburg, Calvin came into contact with Bucer and met Melanchthon at the colloquies of Hagenau, Worms, and Regensburg. Following this period Calvin returned to Geneva and directed the work of reform there into its decisive phase. In this work he was supported by two documents. One was the Geneva Catechism (1545), which, although it was not elevated to the status of a confession in the juridical sense, was used as a basis of instruction, and subordinated the entire body of doctrinal material to the idea of glorifying God. The other document, and of greater importance to Calvin's work, was the Ecclesiastical Ordinances (1541). These church ordinances, modified by the Council, separated church and state and adopted a doctrine of ministerial offices that was influenced by Strassburg and Basle. It is precisely ecclesiology that formed an ongoing point of difference between Zurich and Geneva.

By contrast, with the Zurich Consensus (1549) a settlement was reached in the question of the Lord's Supper. When this settlement became known, it unleashed the second great conflict concerning the Supper, this time between Calvin and the Gnesiolutherans, and made an agreement with Lutheranism completely impossible. In reaction to Luther's "Short Confession of the Holy Sacrament" (1545), Bullinger had in the same year composed, in the name of the Zurich clergy, the baldly Zwinglian Zurich Confession. But this confession never achieved official validity, and in any case soon was made superfluous by the consensus between Bullinger and Calvin concerning the sacramental question. Bullinger had reacted with self-critique to Calvin's objections to the bald Zwinglianism. An occasion for Zurich and Geneva to reach an agreement was then presented by the ecclesiastical conflict in Vaud. Although the Calvinist spirit predominated there, under the influence of Berne the church was organized along the lines of the Zurich state church model. Calvin worked up a presentation of the doctrine of the Lord's Supper for the Synod of Berne. This presentation then served as the draft for the consensus between Zurich and Geneva. By taking a conciliatory position on the question of the Supper, Calvin was able to gain acceptance for congregationally controlled church discipline, and thereby to loosen the strict state church structure in Vaud.

The first conflict concerning the Lord's Supper had been the controversy between Luther and the German-speaking Swiss. The second such conflict had as its participants on the Reformed side Calvin, Bullinger, Beza, Jan Laski, and Valérand Poullain. This conflict arose in connection with the spread of Calvinism in Western Europe. The extent of this spread came to the awareness of the Lutherans in part through their contact with the Dutch refugee congregation that had to leave its London refuge after the Catholic Queen Mary ascended the throne. Under the leadership of Laski and Poullain, this refugee congregation finally found acceptance for a while in Frankfurt. When he returned from England, Laski authored the Emden Catechism (1554). This stood alongside the Augsburg Confession as doctrinal norms of the church of East Friesland, and replaced various earlier confessions, including Laski's Large Catechism and the purely Zwinglian East Friesland Confession (1528). To defend itself against the reproach of being Sacramentarians, the foreign congregation in Frankfurt conceived its own confession (1554). As the pastor of this congregation, Poullain even declared himself prepared to subscribe the Saxon Confession (1551), composed by Melanchthon for the Council of Trent and conceived as a reiteration of the Augsburg Confession. To be sure, like the pastor of the Dutch refugee congregation in Wesel, François Perucelle, Poullain insisted as a Zwinglian on the removal of the term "substantially" (*substantialiter*) from the article on the Lord's Supper. Laski, by contrast, had distanced himself from the Zwinglianism of his youth and had drawn nearer to Calvin.

Calvin and Laski attempted to bring about a union with the Lutherans on the basis of the Augsburg Confession's article on the Lord's Supper. In this attempt they worked from the altered Augsburg Confession (1540). Commissioned by the Schmalkaldic League, Melanchthon had produced this version as the official new edition of the Augsburg Confession for the impending doctrinal discussions. In this edition he had altered the original article on the Lord's Supper in accordance with the Wittenberg Concordat. However, the attempts to reach a union on the basis of the Augsburg Confession ultimately failed. This failure was due in part to the unyielding posture of the Gnesiolutherans, who were willing to permit only the unaltered Augsburg Confession as the text of reference. And in part the failure was due to the Zwinglians, who wished to eliminate the concept of substance from the article on the Lord's Supper.

The second controversy concerning the Lord's Supper had the effect, though, that the Palatinate, one of the theaters of the controversy, decided in favor of Calvinism. The controversy also led to the disappearance of Zwinglianism in its original form. From then on it lived only in the modification it had experienced at the hands of Bullinger. As such it nevertheless preserved its particularity over against Calvinism insofar as it:

> held fast to Zwingli's Neoplatonic-Augustinian concept of God as the highest good and to Zwingli's defense of a state church;
> continued to share his sacramental dualism, at least in an altered form, after the union with Geneva; and
> developed, on the basis of his concept of God, a Christocentric doctrine of predestination together with its understanding of covenant in terms of salvation history.

The classic document of this modified Zwinglianism is the Second Helvetic Confession (1561), which was originally written by Bullinger as a private confession, and then adopted by all the Reformed German-speaking Swiss cities except Basle—which was at the time taking a Lutheranizing direction—and by Geneva. This confession then replaced the First Helvetic Confession as a pan-Swiss confession.

THE SPREAD OF CALVINISM IN
WESTERN AND EASTERN EUROPE

In the second half of the sixteenth century, Genevan Calvinism began to spread in Western and Eastern Europe. This means that, along with a theological system that is built on the idea of glorifying God, at the same time a specific ecclesiology was adopted—one which emphasizes the sovereignty of the church over against the state, and the church's self-regulation by means of church ordinances. The purpose of this ecclesiological emphasis was to differentiate Calvinism from the Zwinglianism of Zurich.

It was in France that for the first time congregations that had previously been only loosely connected with each other were bound together into a national church on a Calvinist basis. A dispute that broke out in Poitiers concerning the doctrine of predestination provided the occasion for Antoine de la Roche-Chandieu to introduce the idea of the Huguenot congregations sharing a common confession and a unitary church order. The

Geneva model had only a pastoral colloquium along with the consistory, which encompassed the various offices. By contrast, the Huguenot church order (1559) further developed the presbyterial conception into a presbyterial-synodical one. In France, unlike Geneva, the state authority did not treat the Reformed church favorably. So the Reformed church in France went a step further in the direction of a separation of church and state. Against Calvin's wish, although not without taking into account his draft statement, the constituting national synod in Paris formulated, besides the church order, a confession, the French Confession (1559). In contrast to Calvin's proposal, this confession intensifies biblicism in the sense of a formal scriptural principle. Just as in the *Institutes,* the doctrine of predestination does not follow the doctrine of God immediately. Instead it finds its place between the doctrine of sin and the doctrine of justification. In Poissy's and St. Germain's negotiations of a union among the French churches, the French Confession served as a shared Huguenot confession. In a revised version it was declared authentic at the Seventh National Synod at La Rochelle (1571). Since then it has also carried the name of the "Confession of La Rochelle." Later synodical additions concern chiefly the article on the Lord's Supper, defending its substantialist language against the critique brought against it by the school of Petrus Ramus, with that school's rejection of theological Aristotelianism.

The attempt to wipe out the Huguenots in the St. Bartholomew's Day Massacre (1572) heightened the politicization of French Protestantism. This politicization is reflected in conceptions of the state that concentrated power in the hands of the monarch. After eight wars the Edict of Nantes (1598) under Henry IV, although underscoring the state-church character of Catholicism, also recognized the independent Huguenot church, and thus recognized confessional difference on a national level. The Edict granted religious toleration and permitted public worship, the building of schools and academies (Montauban, Sedan, Saumur), and extensive civil parity.

The Belgic Confession (1561), drafted by Guido de Brès and revised numerous times, followed closely the French Confession. In the Belgic Confession the biblicistic scriptural principle took an even more intensified form. Originally conceived as an apology of the evangelical faith over against Philipp II, the Belgic Confession ultimately became the standard confession of the church in the Netherlands. It was first adopted by the Synod of Wesel (1568) and the Synod of Emden (1571). These synods were held by the congregations that had fled to England, France, and Germany from the Netherlands in the face of the Alba's Spanish governorship. The Synod of Emden is to be reckoned as the actual founding synod of the Dutch Reformed Church, which there adopted its presbyterial-synodical order. However, while the freedom struggle of the newly founded

Republic of the United Netherlands was still going on, the question of church order provided the spark for the conflict between the adherents of the presbyterial-synodical system and the adherents of the state church system. With the support of the theologians of the recently constituted universities (Leiden, Franeker, Groningen), this conflict ultimately turned into a battle between, on the one hand, a Calvinism marked by the doctrine of predestination and, on the other hand, an Arminianism that integrated humanism within itself.

The introduction of Calvinism into Scotland by John Knox was of the greatest historical import. During the reign of Mary Stuart, Knox had fled to Geneva. There, as well as in Frankfurt, he had served as leader of the English refugee congregation. When he returned to Scotland he was able to have an act of Parliament bestow state authority on the Scottish Confession of Faith (1560), which he had drafted. The first General Assembly of the Scottish church passed a church order, the First Book of Discipline (1560), which was sharply antipapal and marked by a biblicistic rigorism that even Calvin himself found unsettling. However, the First Book of Discipline was not yet able to bring the Presbyterian goals to complete realization. Only with the Second Book of Discipline (1581), conceived by Melville, were all accommodations to the episcopal system removed. This Second Book of Discipline, with its thesis of the divine right of the presbyteria-synodical system, ignited the struggle between Episcopalians and Presbyterians. In order to assure itself concerning the king, who continued to be under suspicion of belonging to the Papists, the Scottish nobles compelled James VI to swear to God's covenant with the Scottish people, which was designated the Second Scottish Confession (*Confessio Scotica posterior*). Through acts of Parliament, the Presbyterian church had become the Scottish state church, whose influence was soon to extend to England as well.

In Western Europe Calvinism was able to spread primarily in France, Scotland, and the Netherlands. In Eastern Europe it took root particularly in Hungary and Poland. In Hungarian Transylvania Calvinism had to assert itself primarily over against Antitrinitarianism, which Giorgio Biandrata had here recognized for the first time as a confession alongside Catholicism, Lutheranism, and Calvinism (1568). Picking up on the thought of Lelio Sozzini and Michael Servetus, but without adopting the pantheistic tendencies of the latter's Logos Christology, Unitarianism understood itself to be the actual fulfillment of the Reformation. The first Reformed confession in Hungary was the Erlauthal Confession (1562), which carried two official names: either the Catholic Confession (*Confessio catholica*) or the Confession of the Church of Debreczin (*Confessio ecclesiae debrecienensis*). This confession was written by Peter Melius, a Wittenberg student of Melanchthon and the first Bishop of Debreczin. Strongly influenced by Scholastic Aristotelianism and even according a positive evaluation to the Council of Trent's decree concerning justification, this confession wavered between Philippist, Flacian, and Calvinist ideas. The confession's lack of unity made it seem necessary to replace it at the Synod of Tarczal with the Hungarian Confession (1562). This latter confession itself represented a revision of Theodor Beza's Confession of the Christian Faith (*Confessio Christianae fidei*) (1559). Out of consideration for the nobility the Hungarian Confession eliminated the antipapal polemic and the articles concerning presbyterial church order. The Hungarian Confession remained in force until the Synod of Debreczin (1567) adopted the Second Helvetic Confession. This same Synod also condemned Antitrinitarianism—prior to the Synod there had been antagonistic debates with Antitrinitarianism's representative Franz David.

As in Hungarian Transylvania, so too in Poland the nobility aided the establishment of the Reformation and of religious toleration. In Poland this development was helped along by the weakness of the elected monarchy there. The Warsaw Confederation (1573) extended religious toleration to all four Reformation confessions. Besides the Lutherans, the Calvinists, and the Bohemian Brethren, who had fled persecution by the Hapsburgs, the humanistic Antitrinitarians also enjoyed freedom of religion. Especially influenced by the critique directed by Matteo Gribaldi, Giovanni Gentile, and Lelio Sozzini against the Reformed reception of Christology and of the doctrine of the Trinity, the representatives of the Antitrinitarian "Lesser Church" (*Ecclesia minor*) broke away from the Reformed confession in 1565. Under the direction of Gregor Pauli, formerly a Reformed pastor, they founded their church center in Rakow. With Fausto Sozzini, the critique of dogma began shifting from Christology and the doctrine of the Trinity to the doctrine of sin and soteriology: that is, Antitrinitarianism was turning into Socinianism. This development found its conclusion in the Rakow Catechism (1605).

Although the Bohemian Brethren had already joined with the Calvinists in the Union of Koźminek (1555), Laski, returned to his homeland, did not live to see the ultimate success of his efforts for a union between Lutherans and Reformed. This union occurred in the Sendomir Consensus (1570) when Lutherans, Calvinists, and Bohemian Brethren mutually permitted pulpit and table fellowship. The document, composed by the Reformed side, recognized the Second Helvetic Confession as the Reformed Confession valid in Poland. The importance of the Consensus declined as Concordistic Lutheranism made inroads. The latter found it impossible to approve the Saxon Confession's Philippist doctrine of the Lord's Supper as the basis of comparison.

PHILIPPISM AND
GERMAN REFORMED THEOLOGY

The Palatinate's move into the Reformed camp (1560) was of decisive importance for the progress of Reformed Christianity in Germany. Although the Peace of Augsburg (1555), which gave religious primacy to the princes of the individual lands, placed the adherents of the Augsburg Confession under imperial protection, it explicitly excluded the "Sacramentarians" from that protection. Frederick III thus had to prove that he had not abandoned the foundation of the Augsburg Confession in joining the Reformed side. To this end he was able to appeal to his agreement with the Augsburg Confession, including its article on the Lord's Supper, as interpreted by the altered Augsburg Confession. The Heidelberg Catechism (1563) served as means of instruction and as doctrinal norm in the Palatinate. The catechism was the work of a commission. Zacharias Ursinus, who had been a student of Melanchthon, Kaspar Olevian, whose thought had been shaped by Calvin, and other members of the Heidelberg faculty and the Church Council participated in creating the Catechism. This fact explains the Catechism's integration of very diverse doctrines. Rather than following the method of synthetically placing the material into a succession based on relative proximity, the work is an analytical catechism, treating the instructional material under a determinate aspect—in this case the communion of human beings in Christ. The tripartite division adopted from Melanchthon—law, gospel, new obedience—is filled out *à la Calvin*, insofar as the law is first presented in the third part under the aspect of the "third use of the law" (*tertius usus legis*). The doctrine of the sacraments oscillates between Zwinglianism and Calvinism. Whether for the sake of the unity of the commission itself or for unionistic reasons, any treatment of predestination was wholly omitted. In addition to Ursinus's writings, almost all catechisms that were accessible at that time served as working papers for drafting the Heidelberg Catechism. After the Council of Trent's decree on the sacrifice of the Mass became public knowledge, the Catechism was twice expanded by question 80, which treats the Mass and transubstantiation. The Catechism was finally published as part of the church order, in which it came to take a place between the treatment of Baptism and the treatment of preparation for the Lord's Supper. It was adopted not only in those German territories that soon followed the Palatinate's movement into the Reformed camp, but also in the church of the Netherlands, which ultimately went so far as to raise the Heidelberg Catechism to confessional status.

Already Melanchthon himself in his later years, in the dispute about the Lord's Supper in Bremen and Heidelberg, had come closer to the Calvinist doctrine. After his death the Wittenberg faculty developed into a bastion of Philippism, which was increasingly branded Cryptocalvinism by the Gnesiolutherans. The leader of the Cryptocalvinists was Christoph Pezel, who both in the doctrine of the Lord's Supper and in Christology represented Melanchthon's mediating position, which was primarily directed against the doctrine of ubiquity developed by Brenz. In the Wittenberg Catechism (1571) Pezel insists in the interest of soteriology on the integrity of the human nature of Christ. Count Palatine Johann Casimir's demonstration of an agreement between the Wittenberg and the Heidelberg Catechisms, combined with the Gnesiolutherans' critique, eventually resulted in the Philippists—Pezel and Cruciger among them—being forced to leave Saxony. They found a reception in those German territories which, under the influence of the Counter-Reformation directed by the Jesuits, wanted to carry out a reformation following the Palatine model primarily in ceremonial matters. Pezel, who first carried out this "second Reformation" in Nassau-Dillenburg-Siegen, elaborated the Confession of Nassau (1578) for this purpose. This confession was received by the Synod of Dillenburg, along with the Church Order of the Palatinate and the Heidelberg Catechism. The Synod assumed the ongoing validity of the Augsburg Confession as a matter of course.

The Bremen Consensus (1595), also written by Pezel, expands the Confession of Nassau, and signals by its reception of the Geneva doctrine of predestination the turn from Philippism to Calvinism. The Consensus was initially signed only by the ministerium; only later (1644) did the Council declare it to be a valid confessional writing. The "second Reformation" met a swift demise in Baden-Durlach, where the Margrave Ernst Friedrich made it his personal cause and attempted to provide a grounding for it by publishing the Book of Staffort (1599), directed against Concordistic Lutheranism. After Friedrich's death Baden-Durlach returned to Lutheranism. By contrast, in Anhalt the Philippistic Anhalt Repetition (*Repetitio anhaltina*) (1579) paved the way for the successful carrying out of the "second Reformation" by the secular authority. Landgrave Moriz of Hesse-Kassel also succeeded in introducing the Reformed movement after the General Synod of Kassel (1607) accepted the Hessian "Points of Improvement," which treated the communication of properties (*communicatio idiomatum*), the numbering of the commandments, the rite of the Lord's Supper, and the prohibition of images. In addition, the Synod approved a reworking of Luther's Small Catechism that brought it into line with Reformed doctrine. The transition of the County of Bentheim to the Reformed movement is attested to by the Bentheim Confession (1613), produced under Count Arnold Jobst.

Already in 1614 the Sigismund Confession, commissioned by the Elector of Brandenburg and authored by Füssel, the superintendent of Zerbst, presents a different kind of confession. Here we no longer have a confession that is promulgated and used by the authority, exercising his episcopal right and his responsibility for the first table of the Decalogue, to bring about the transition of his land into the Reformed movement. Instead the Sigismund Confession is a private confession in which the Elector attests to his decision, conditioned by his own study and the model of the Palatinate, to change confessional allegiance, but without requiring such a change of his subjects as well. To be sure, the confessional difference between the ruling house of Brandenburg and the majority of its Prussian subjects also explains the Elector's efforts to bring about a balance between Lutherans and Reformed.

The Leipzig Colloquy (1631) and the Colloquy of Thorn (1645) both served that end. The former was convened under pressure of the imperial Edict of Restitution, and attended by representatives of Brandenburg, Hesse, and Saxony. After the collapse of Socinianism and the strengthening of the Counter-Reformation, the Colloquy of Thorn was supposed to prepare the way for an understanding to be reached between Catholicism, Lutheranism, and Calvinism. The Helmstadt theologian Georg Calixt participated in the Colloquy on the Reformed side after the Lutherans had not accepted the irenic syncretist as their representative. Despite a series of points of comparision, neither the Leipzig Colloquy nor the Colloquy of Thorn led to a rapprochement. Nevertheless, the Elector of Brandenburg accepted both the minutes of the Colloquy and the Declaration of Thorn as confessional writings and united them with the Sigismund Confession in the *Corpus constitutionum marchicarum*.

THE DORDRECHT SYNOD AND
THE THEOLOGY OF THE NETHERLANDS

Pointing to his private confession, Johann Sigismund also declined to participate in the Dordrecht Synod (1618), the international council of Reformed churches convened by the church of the Netherlands in order to bring an end to the conflict between Orthodox Calvinists and Arminians. Besides the States General themselves, the Palatinate, Nassau, Hesse, East Friesland, Bremen, England, Scotland, and Switzerland were represented in Dordrecht. While the participation of the French was forbidden by Louis XIII, Anhalt was not even invited on account of deficient orthodoxy. The Synod confirmed the Belgic Confession and the Heidelberg Catechism as confessional writings of the church of the Netherlands. The validity of these texts had been cast into doubt by the Arminians. At the heart of the disputes, however, stood the doctrine of predestination. The doctrine of predestination had already increasingly surged to the fore in the conflict with Lutheranism, joining there the doctrine of the Lord's Supper and Christology.

The doctrine of predestination first acquired interest on its own account in Calvin's dispute with Bolsec. The result of this dispute was the Geneva Consensus, which gave fixed form to the strict version of the doctrine, and to which all Geneva clergy were required to subscribe. Although this was not yet true in Calvin himself, in his follower Beza the doctrine of predestination occupies the center in such a way that the doctrine of predestination is anchored in the doctrine of God and God's eternal decrees. This a priori construction of the doctrine of predestination, which when developed to its logical consequences requires supralapsarianism, was defended in the Strassburg predestination controversy by Hieronymus Zanchi against the Lutheran Johann Marbach. Nevertheless, within the Reformed movement it was shared only by a strictly Calvinist wing. Although a student of Beza, Jacob Arminius took a decisive position against an a priori construction of the doctrine of predestination. In the interest of human responsibility, he instead argued for a christological universalism, which uses God's foreknowledge of faith as the ground of election. In response to Orthodox accusations, the Remonstrance of the Arminians was written in 1610. They supplemented this text before the Dordrecht Synod with explanatory additions (1618), which strengthened the suspicion of synergism. In spite of foreign theologians who inclined toward a Christocentrically shaped doctrine of predestination, the Dordrecht Synod condemned Arminianism, and the Synod's Canons (1619) carried out the sanctioning of the particularistic doctrine of predestination. However, a decision in favor of the supralapsarianism represented by Franciscus Gomarus was consciously left open. The condemnation of Arminianism also signified a rejection of the state church organization favored by the Remonstrants. It would be improper, though, to say that in the subsequent period the secular authority did not intervene in internal church affairs. The state maintained the right to be represented by political commissioners at church assemblies. And the fact that the Reformed church was given privileged but not exclusive recognition ensured that a comprehensive toleration of other confessions would result.

The Canons of the Dordrecht Synod are a doctrinal statement essentially determined by the theology of the high Orthodoxy of the Netherlands. Old Reformed Orthodoxy shared the emphasis on the formal authority of scripture, the development of the metaphysical concept of God, and the predestination controversy. But precisely with regard to the last point, there were strong differences between the various schools. The particularistic, supralapsarian, and a priori version of predestination was the achievement of the Geneva Academy (1559), which stood under the immediate influence of Calvin. Leading figures of the Academy were Lambert Daneus, Mattaeus Virellus, and Theodor Beza. Beza was a Calvinist Aristotelian who developed the Scholastic formulas for supralapsarianism, for the syllogism, and for the Calvinist "extra" (*extra Calvinisticum*). Although linked to the Geneva Academy with regard to the doctrines of predestination and the sacraments, Petrus Martyr Vermigli and Hieronymus Zanchi presented an independent line, with Zanchi developing his theology from the Thomist conception of God as pure act (*actus purus*) and primary cause (*prima causa*).

A movement opposed to this Aristotelianism arose in the form of Ramism. In its practical-humanistic orientation, its limitation of dialectic to formal logic, and the high status it accorded to rhetoric and grammar, Ramism tended toward Zwinglianism. As had been the case earlier with Zwingli himself and with Bullinger, in Ramism an idea of covenant conceived in terms of salvation history took the place of predestinarian particularism. This resulted in preference being given to the a posteriori analytical method over the a priori synthetic method. As members of the Heidelberg School (1561), to which Boquin and Zanchi also belonged, Ursinus and Olevian had already been oriented toward covenant theology. The most prominent instance of Ramistic influence was the School of Herborn (1584), to which Johannes Piscator and Johann Heinrich Alsted contributed, in addition to Olevian. Piscator was the origin of the conception, directed against Beza, that only the passive obedience of Christ made satisfaction, while the active obedience to the law belonged to the perfection of Jesus' human nature. Amandus Polanus and his student Johannes Wolleb were both Ramistic Aristotelians, who belonged to the School of Basle (1586).

Bartholomäus Kekkerman, who taught at the Illustrious Gymnasium of Danzig (1580), defined theology as a practical science: that is, as a science conceived with respect to the goal of appropriating salvation. In this definition Kekkerman considered himself to be picking up the analytical method of the Heidelberg Catechism. Of decisive importance for the further development of covenant theology and for the softening of the rigid doctrine of predestination were the infralapsarian conceptions represented by the Philippistically colored School of Marburg (1604), and by Matthias Martini and Ludwig Crocius at the Illustrious Gymnasium of Bremen (1610).

The covenant theology and infralapsarian ideas of these German Reformed distinguished them from the representatives of the Orthodoxy of the Netherlands. The supralapsarianism of the latter was represented at the Dordrecht Synod by Franciscus Gomarus, who taught at the University of Leiden (1575). His student Gisbert Voetius, who taught at the School of Utrecht (1634), attempted once more to defend Calvinist Aristotelianism against the inroads of Cartesianism. By contrast, John Cocceius, a student of Martini and Crocius and an instructor in Franeker (1585) and Leiden, developed covenant theology to include an understanding of salvation history that made an essential contribution to dissolving the doctrine of predestination. The idea of covenant entailed the unity and difference of the Old and New Testaments. Cocceius used the idea of different stages of the abrogation of the covenant of works to interpret this unity and difference. The covenant of works, which forms the basis for natural theology, was instituted in the original estate of creation. After the Fall, that covenant was replaced by the covenant of grace. This covenant in turn rests upon God's innertrinitarian pact (*pactum*) with the Son: that is, upon an eternal decree of salvation. The covenant of grace is realized in various stages until the reign of God. Cocceius's stronger emphasis on the difference between the individual stages led him to oppose Old Testament nomism with a New Testament interpretation of the commandment to honor the Sabbath. This led to the Sabbath controversy, in which Voetius was his opponent. Jacob Alting and Abraham Heidanus rejected as unbiblical the idea of a covenant of works, but Herman Witsius gave it further elaboration in the interest of emphasizing the independence of human beings as covenant partners. The law that is given to human beings in the covenant of works is the natural law that is anchored in their conscience and identical with the Decalogue. The covenant of grace is nothing other than the mere restitution of the covenant of works broken by the Fall.

As Cocceius overcame the doctrine of predestination with his covenant theology, so too did his teacher William Amesius, who was active in Franeker, overcome Orthodoxy's intellectualization of the faith with the empirico-practical orientation of his theology. The Ramistic inheritance shows itself when Amesius defines theology as "doctrine of the living God" (*doctrina Deo vivendi*) that is not, however, exhausted in ethics, but that is also dogmatics, since faith itself is an act of the will and not only of the intellect. This voluntaristic understanding of faith thus leads to a turning away from scriptural dogmatism and to a turning toward self-reflection. In self-reflection the believing individual makes certain of his or her election. The doctrine of predestination is interpreted and defined empirically in this form of early pietistic precisianism.

ENGLISH PURITANISM

Amesius himself was a student of William Perkins in Cambridge, who laid the foundations of Puritanism with its pietistic leanings. With Thomas Cartwright and William Whitacker, Cambridge had developed into a bastion of Presbyterian Calvinism. Cartwright opposed Episcopalianism's proposition that the episcopacy was divinely instituted, claiming for his part that only the presbyterial church polity was in accordance with divine law (*iure divino*). Whitacker presented the Archbishop of Canterbury with the Cambridge theologians' Lambeth Articles (1595) without their ever having been approved by Elizabeth I. The articles were conceived as an addition to the Anglican Articles, which had originally been drafted under Edward VI by Cranmer (1553), then revised and reduced to thirty-nine (1563) by the queen as supreme governor of the English state church.

The Anglican confession had adhered closely to the Augsburg and Wittenberg Confessions, except in the doctrine of the Lord's Supper, where it was influenced by Bucer and Calvin. It mentioned only predestination to eternal life, thus allowing an Arminian interpretation as well as a Calvinist one. The Lambeth Articles aimed to replace the seventeenth article with theses on double predestination. This strict doctrine of predestination, which nevertheless left open the alternative of supralapsarianism or infralapsarianism, also made its way into the Irish Articles of Religion (1615). Written by Archbishop Usher, these articles were approved by the Stuart King James I, who also joined Scotland to the rest of the island kingdom. However, hopes that the Stuarts would take a Presbyterian outlook in confessional politics were soon disappointed. The linking of absolutism and episcopal uniformity ultimately led to conflict between king and Parliament, Episcopalianism and Puritanism.

Already in 1638 Scotland had signed the Covenant to Maintain Presbyterian Doctrine in answer to the attempt to bring its state church into conformity. Now with the convocation of the Long Parliament in England the Puritan Revolution erupted, leading to the Civil War. In order to carry out the true reformation of the English church, the Westminster Assembly was entrusted with the revision of the Anglican Articles and the elaboration of a church polity. After the unification with the Scots sealed in the Solemn League and Covenant, the Presbyterian influence gained strength to implement uniformity in polity, catechism, liturgy, and confession. Instead of concluding the reworking of the Anglican Articles, the Westminster Assembly, with an eye on the Irish Articles, authored a completely new confession, the Westminster Confession (1647). This confession was supplemented by both Westminster Catechisms (1647), the larger of which was based on Johannes Wolleb's Compendium of Theology (*Compendium theologiae*). In its ecclesiology the Westminster Confession is strictly Presbyterian, while in its reflection on the individual's perfection and state of salvation it is Puritan. The confession thus breathes the air of a mitigated Calvinist Orthodoxy that clearly subordinates the doctrine of decrees to covenant theology. For the English state church the confession was in fact of no significance, due to the restoration that soon followed. However, the confession was received by the Scottish state church and replaced the Scottish Confession.

The Presbyterian influence was heavy on the Westminster Assembly, and was strengthened still more by the presence of the Scots. By contrast, after the execution of Charles I and during the Republic and Cromwell's Protectorate, Independent Congregationalism predominated for a time. It-self anti-episcopalian and thus Puritan, Congregationalism differed from Presbyterianism with regard to polity. The place of the one church of the state and people is assumed by the many local congregations, which consist of actual believers. The congregations are not subordinated to any synod as a superior authority, but rather are independent. The rejection of uniformity of Episcopalian and Presbyterian provenance led Congregationalists to criticize an understanding of confessions as doctrinal laws. It thus also led them to develop the idea of toleration. Having fled to Holland to escape persecution by Elizabeth I, the English Congregationalists hoped to return under James I and sent him a presentation of the Congregationalist Points of Difference (1603). The lack of prospects for return ultimately led them to the decision to emigrate to North America as "Pilgrims" (1620).

As the influence of the English Independents began to climb under Cromwell, they decided to meet in synod in London's Savoy Palace to demarcate themselves over against the Presbyterians. Actually assembling only after the death of the Protector, the Congregationalists revised the articles of the Westminster Confession that dealt with presbyterial polity. Otherwise, with the exception of some modifications informed by covenant theology, the Congregationalists adopted the Westminster Confession in their Savoy Declaration (1658). Appended to the Declaration was a platform that specified congregationalist church order. Like the Westminster Confession, the Savoy Declaration lost significance after the restoration of the absolutist kingship and the Episcopal state church in England. But both documents were received by the Puritan immigrants to North America, where they were able to develop their far-reaching influence.

THE SCHOOL OF SAUMUR AND THE HELVETIC CONSENSUS FORMULA

After the particularistic doctrine of predestination was approved at the Dordrecht Synod, the need developed in France to mitigate the severity of that particularism. Attempts to do so were proffered primarily in the

Academy of Saumur, specifically by the Scot John Cameron and his students. Their point of departure was the idea that God wills the salvation of all human beings in Christ, but that this salvation occurs on condition of faith, which God does not grant to all. In this way real particularism was connected with ideal universalism. The resulting hypothetical universalism (*universalismus hypotheticus*), elaborated by Moyse Amyraut, was approved by the national synods in Alençon (1637) and Charenton (1644/45), despite the critique of Pierre du Moulin.

Amyraut's successor Claude Pajon turned his attention to the question of how grace and the divine Spirit really operate. Pajon arrived at the Occasionalist understanding—which helped prepare the way for Deism—that the Spirit never acts without mediation, but only through the means of the word, and through the circumstances and occasional causes foreordained by the Spirit. As Amyraut and Pajon attempted to modify the severity of particularistic predestination, Josué de la Place tried to modify the Orthodox doctrine of original sin, which vitiated the responsibility of the individual. De la Place rejected any direct imputation of Adam's actual sin to his descendants, accepting only an indirect imputation of Adam's guilt on the basis of the original sin inhering in individuals.

De la Place, and especially Amyraut, were sharply criticized by Geneva and Zurich, who had battled for strict predestinationism at the Dordrecht Synod. By contrast, Louis Cappel's demonstration of the relatively recent origin of the pointing of Hebrew scriptures—a demonstration that called into question the integrity of scripture and thus the basis of the Orthodox doctrine of inspiration—first met with protest at the hands of the two Buxtorfs of Basle. Appealing to the Zurich Consensus, the Genevan Orthodoxy under Franz Turretini demanded a general Swiss formula of unity against the heterodox doctrines of the Saumur school. The resulting Helvetic Consensus Formula (1675) was elaborated by the Zurich covenant theologian Johann Heinrich Heidegger, the preeminent teacher in the twilight of Orthodoxy. The Formula also blocked the wish of Zurich's Antistes Müller, who wanted to go further and condemn Cocceianism and its connected Cartesianism. A confessional symbol born in the eleventh hour, the Formula was accepted almost everywhere in the Swiss churches as an appendix and explanation of the Second Helvetic Confession, although only clergy, professors, or ordinands needed to subscribe it. In Vaud it was even subscribed only "insofar as it agrees with Sacred Scripture" (*quatenus S. Scripturae consentit*). Yet when Huguenot refugees streamed into Vaud after the lifting of the Edict of Nantes (1685), confessional Orthodoxy reared its head one last time and demanded that the symbol be subscribed unconditionally "*purement et simplement.*"

2.

THE THEOLOGICAL CONTENTS OF THE OLD REFORMED CONFESSIONAL WRITINGS

REVELATION, GOD'S WORD, AND TRADITION

REVELATION BY WORKS AND REVELATION BY WORD

All confessional writings agree that human beings are able to know God only because of God's self-revelation to them. God's revelation is accordingly the condition for the possibility of human knowledge of God. The fact that God reveals God's self to us can also be expressed in a figurative sense by the statement that God speaks to us. One thus arrives at an identification of revelation and God's word. This could give the impression that revelation was to be identified with scripture. Yet this is not the case, at least in the early confessions. There the word of God has not yet been equated with scripture. The early confessions admittedly speak of God's word as doctrine, but what they mean by "doctrine" is first of all a historical event. For example, the Synodical Declaration of Berne propounds the thesis that "the only Christ is the sum of doctrine" (M 34, 6). In this way the *sum* of doctrine is identified with "saving doctrine": that is, the gospel. This saving doctrine is after all nothing other "than the only Word of God, the fatherly kindness and goodness that God has communicated to us through Christ, which is nothing other than Christ Jesus himself, who was crucified for the sake of our sin and raised from the dead for the sake of our righteousness, that we might be justified" (M 34, 8–12).

This identification of God's word or self-revelation and the gospel categorically excludes a revelation of God besides and outside the revelation in Christ, the *only* Word of God. This does not entail doubting that independently of the revelation in Christ people also speak of God and claim to possess knowledge of God. But the Synodical Declaration does not conclude from these two facts that besides and outside the revelation in Christ there is another revelation of the God who is manifest in Jesus Christ. Indeed, the Synodical Declaration energetically contests the idea that God is manifest *at all* to those to whom God is not manifest "in the face of Christ." The Synodical Declaration can thus say of the heathen that they are simply "without God in the world." Admittedly they have "heard and talked

29

a lot of prattle about a natural God." But this natural God, who supposedly can be known independently of the revelation in Christ, cannot be identical with God at all, since God is *eo ipso* the God who is manifest in Christ, and thus can be known only "in the face of Jesus Christ . . . and not outside or without Christ." A knowledge of God independent of Christ is unmasked as an impossibility. There is no access to God that exists independently of God's revelation in Christ, such that valid statements could be made about the existence and essence of God *an sich*. Admittedly, people want "to talk a lot about the omnipotent God without Christ, but that is fruitless" (M 35, 24ff.). If one is not ready to deny not only heathen but also Jews any knowledge of God, the thesis of the exclusivity of God's self-revelation in Christ compels a thoroughgoing interpretation of the Old Testament as a witness to Christ. The events and objects of the history of the Old Testament people of God thus become as a whole "figures, shadows, and prefigurations of Christ Jesus." The assertion that Jesus Christ is the only Word of God ineluctably entails the exclusively christological interpretation of the Old Testament. For the Synodical Declaration of Berne we thus can conclude that God's revelation in Jesus Christ is God's *only* self-revelation, so that God communicates God's self to us *only* in the gospel: that is, in the "course of grace."

However, this understanding of the exclusivity of the revelation in Christ propounded by the Synodical Declaration of Berne, and the attendant contestation of a general self-revelation of God independent of the revelation in Christ, is not common property of the Reformed confessions. Instead it is a position put forward only by the aforementioned document. By contrast, the other confessions share with Lutheran and Roman theology the assumption of a twofold knowledge of God that is grounded in a twofold revelation of God. The French Confession begins with the statement that there is only one God: that is, "one sole and simple essence, spiritual, eternal, invisible, immutable, infinite, incomprehensible, ineffable, omnipotent; who is all-wise, all-good, all-just, and all-merciful" (S 359–60; cf. 383–84). According to the second article of this same confession, the God who is characterized by these properties "reveals himself" (*se manifeste*) "as such" (*tel*) to human beings. God not only reveals God's self, but reveals God's self as defined by the properties listed above. According to the French Confession, this revelation occurs in a twofold way: "firstly, in his works (*oeuvres*), in their creation, as well as in their preservation and control. Secondly, and more clearly, in his Word . . ." (S 360). There is thus a double revelation of God. Prior to God's self-revelation through God's word there is a general revelation of God in God's works. This means that, independently of the revelation by the word, God already reveals God's self to every human being, through the creation and preservation of the world, as the Being who is characterized by the properties listed at the outset.

To be sure, the thesis of God's double revelation is not present in Calvin's draft for the French Confession. But we do find in the Geneva Catechism, which also stems from Calvin, the following clear statement: "Because He [sc. God] has manifested Himself to us (*per opera se nobis patefecit*) by works (Ps. 104; Rom. 1:20) we ought to seek Him in them. Our mind cannot comprehend His essence. But the world is for us like a mirror (*speculum*) in which we may contemplate Him in so far as it is expedient for us to know Him" (T 8).

Calvin thus does not contest the idea of revelation through God's works. Rather he admits that we can know God through the divine works, in which God reveals God's self to us. It is thus also not the case that although God reveals God's self through the divine works, we are *totally unable* to know God through those works. For while the French Confession speaks exclusively of a double *revelation*, the Belgic Confession, which is dependent upon the French Confession, speaks of a double *knowledge of God*: "We know (*connaissons*) him (sc. God) by two means: first, by the creation, preservation, and government of the universe. . . . Secondly, he makes himself more clearly and fully known to us by his holy and divine Word" (S 384). There is thus, corresponding to God's self-revelation *in* God's work and word, a knowledge of God *through* that work and word. In this context the work itself is understood as word. The created world assumes a place beside the Holy Scriptures, for the former "is before our eyes as a most elegant book, wherein all creatures, great and small, are as so many characters leading us to contemplate the invisible things of God, namely, his eternal power and Godhead, as the Apostle Paul saith (Rom. 1:20)" (S 384).

The thesis of the double self-revelation and knowledge of God is thus developed as a theory of two books. Creation is the book that is accessible to everyone and that gives a sufficient testimony to God. In creation God reveals the divine goodness, wisdom, and power in such a way that they can be known by the light of nature (*lumen naturae*) alone (S 600). Accordingly, the Westminster Larger Catechism can take the following approach in answering the question of the source of our knowledge that God exists. The Catechism refers to the light of nature proper to human beings as creatures, and to the works of God (*opera Dei*), which are accessible to that light. The Catechism insists that these works *clearly* (*luculenter*) reveal God's existence (M 612, 30–32). "The light of nature showeth that there is a God, who hath lordship and sovereignty over all; is good, and doeth good unto all; and is therefore to be feared, loved, praised, called upon, trusted in, and served with all the heart, and with all the soul, and with all the might" (S 646).

The assertion of a double—namely, a general and a special—revelation and knowledge of God raises the question of how the two relate to each other. For the French Confession, special revelation is distinguished from general revelation solely by the former's greater degree of clarity (*clairement*) (S 360). By contrast, the Belgic Confession characterizes the special knowledge of God not only as clearer (*plus manifestement*), but also as fuller (*pleinement*) (S 384). General and special knowledge of God are distinguished not only by their degree of clarity, but also by their compass. In general there is no interest in assigning to general revelation an exceptional roll in the genesis of the knowledge of God. Instead general revelation is treated from the perspective of its function in securing the universal possibility of the knowledge of God. On the basis of God's general revelation every human being can know God, however rudimentary this knowledge of God might be. It is at least sufficient "to convince human beings, and leave them without excuse" (S 384). "The light of nature, and the works of creation and providence, do so far manifest the goodness, wisdom, and power of God, as to leave men inexcusable," we read in the Westminster Confession, with references to Rom. 2:14–15; Rom. 1:19–20; and Rom. 1:32–2:1 (S 600). The function of the general knowledge of God is accordingly very limited. Its only function is to ground the inexcusability of every human being. This is guaranteed only when every human being has at his or her disposition an at least rudimentary knowledge of God. If a human being could not possess such knowledge at all, the possibility of presenting her as guilty before God would be excluded. A human being's guilt before God presupposes that she has at least some sort of knowledge of God's will (cf. M 267, 13ff.).

As early as the Second Helvetic Confession one finds the assertion, made for the sake of the universality of the knowledge of the divine law, that this law is "written in the hearts of men by the finger of God (Rom. 2:15), and is called the law of nature" (C 247). Knowledge of the law is mediated not only to the Jews by scripture but also to the Gentiles through the light of natural reason. Accordingly, the Canons of the Dordrecht Synod declare that even after the Fall "there remain . . . in man . . . the glimmerings of natural light (*lumen naturae*), whereby he retains some knowledge (*notitias*) of God, of natural things, and of the difference between good and evil" (S 588, 565).

Although universal knowledge of God and of the divine will ground the inexcusability of human beings before God, natural reason and nature in general "are not sufficient to give that knowledge of God, and of his will, which is necessary unto salvation" (S 600). The universal knowledge of God does not lead to the knowledge of salvation; no soteriological quality inheres in the former. Only of the word, and not of the work, can it be said that it reveals God "sufficiently and efficaciously unto salvation" (*sufficienter ac efficaciter ad salutem*) (M 612, 33). In this context—as the Synodical Declaration of Berne shows—the word of God is by no means initially identified with scripture, but primarily with God's saving historical action in Jesus Christ. God's word is "the fatherly kindness and goodness that God has communicated to us through Christ, which is nothing other than Christ Jesus himself" (M 34, 8–10). One likewise finds this historical under-standing of God's word in Zwingli. In his Sixty-seven Articles he confesses that he has preached "on the basis of the Scripture which is called *theopneustos* (i.e., inspired by God)," but he shows that he is interested not in scripture as such but in its historical content. He defines God's word pri-marily as gospel, the sum of which is "that our Lord Jesus Christ, the true Son of God, has made known to us the will of His heavenly Father, and by his innocence has redeemed us from death and reconciled us unto God" (C 36). The gospel is not the written word of the Bible, but "God's gracious action" (M 13, 20) as the "glad Word of God" (M 18, 10).

In turning to Orthodoxy, though, the confessional writings soon turned away from this understanding of the word of God in terms of salvation his-tory. Now the word of God is conceived first as the oral word that "long ago God spoke to our ancestors in many and various ways by the prophets, but in these last days . . . has spoken to us by a Son" (Heb. 1:1–2). However, "for the better preserving and propagating of the truth, and for the more sure establishment and comfort of the Church against the corruption of the flesh, and the malice of Satan and of the world" (S 600–601), God has com-mitted this oral word to writing. Scripture as the fixed form of God's oral word is thus the concluded revelation of the divine will, "those former ways of God's revealing his will unto his people being now ceased" (S 601). God's word thus identified with scripture encounters human beings not only as gospel, but also as law (M 405, 10ff.). But scripture's reason for con-taining the law is not that we would otherwise possess no knowledge of it. Rather it is given fixed written form in the Decalogue, with the latter's ex-planations and supplements, for the sake of greater clarity. It is one and the same law that, on the one hand, God has written in the hearts of all hu-man beings, and that, on the other hand, has been "inscribed by his finger on the two Tables of Moses, and eloquently expounded in the books of Moses" (C 247; cf. M 405, 17ff.). The knowledge of God made possible by the law, however, is knowledge of God only as the righteous judge who rewards with eternal life those who fulfill the law and punishes with eter-nal death those who transgress the law (M 267, 19ff.).

But that means, as the Heidelberg Catechism puts it, that from the law of God I know only my misery (S 308), and that this knowledge is the pre-condition for the knowledge of salvation through the gospel (S 313), which on this basis can be characterized as the "only comfort" (S 307). This only comfort in life and in death consists of the certain knowledge that "I, with body and soul, both in life and in death, am not my own, but belong to my faithful Saviour Jesus Christ, who with his precious blood has fully satisfied for all my sins, and redeemed me from all the power of the devil; and so preserves me that without the will of my Father in heaven not a hair can fall from my head; yea, that all things mayst work together for my salvation. Wherefore, by his Holy Spirit, he also assures me of eternal life, and makes me heartily willing and ready henceforth to live unto him" (S 307–8).

Even though for the sake of greater clarity the law that is accessible to the natural light of reason is also a component of scripture, the knowledge of that law is not yet the knowledge that is necessary for salvation. Instead the Canons of the Dordrecht Synod assert that "what is true of the light of nature is also true of the law of the Decalogue, delivered by God to his peculiar people the Jews, by the hands of Moses. For though it discovers the greatness of sin, and more and more convinces man thereof, yet as it neither points out a remedy nor imparts strength to extricate him from misery, and thus being weak through the flesh, leaves the transgressor under the curse, man can not by this law obtain saving grace" (S 588). The only knowledge of God that is necessary for salvation is that which provides the basis for my knowing that God is not only just, but merciful. I come to know God as merciful by knowing the word of God not as law, but as gospel. "What, therefore, neither the light of nature nor the law could, that God performs by the operation of his Holy Spirit through the word or ministry of reconciliation: which is the glad tidings concerning the Messiah, by means whereof it hath pleased God to save such as believe, as well under the Old as under the New Testament" (S 588–89). Through the gospel as a form of the word of God that is different from the law I am given knowledge of God not as a righteous judge but as merciful and gracious (M 267, 31ff.; 405, 26). It is this knowledge that is necessary for salvation. We attain this knowledge only by means of scripture because, in contrast to the law, the gospel is not an object of natural human reason, but transcends it (M 406, 14ff.).

The gospel is not identical with the New Testament. The Heidelberg Catechism speaks of the gospel "which God himself first revealed in Paradise, afterwards proclaimed by the holy Patriarchs and Prophets, and foreshadowed by the sacrifices and other ceremonies of the law, and finally fulfilled by his well-beloved Son" (S 313). The story of Jesus of Nazareth is the story of the fulfillment of the gospel that was already revealed in Paradise. For that reason the story of Jesus, like the apostolic proclamation of Christ, is "gospel" in a preeminent sense. "Therefore, the history delineated by the four Evangelists and explaining how these things were done or fulfilled by Christ, what things Christ taught and did, and that those who believe in him have all fulness, is rightly called the Gospel. The preaching and writings of the apostles, in which the apostles explain for us how the Son was given to us by the Father, and in him everything that has to do with life and salvation, is also rightly called evangelical doc-trine" (C 250).

GOD'S WORD AND SCRIPTURE

The Synodical Declaration of Berne still understands the word of God as a player in salvation history when the Synodical Declaration identifies God's word with the goodness of God communicated to us in Christ: that is, when it identifies God's word with Christ himself (M 34, 8ff.). As early as the First Helvetic Confession, however, we find a departure from this historical specification of God's word. For the First Helvetic Confession, the "holy, divine, Biblical Scripture" is identical with the "Word of God" (C 100). God's word is not only *contained* in scripture and *attested* to by scripture, but as "inspired by the Holy Spirit and delivered to the world by the prophets and apostles," it *is* scripture. The identification of God's word with scripture leads to God's word no longer being conceived pri-marily as gospel in the sense of a divine saving action, but in the sense of a doctrine as "the most ancient, most perfect and loftiest teaching" (C 100), which contains all that is necessary for true knowledge and worship of God. This fundamentally doctrinal understanding of scripture is not al-tered by pointing out that the purpose of all of scripture is that human be-ings "understand that God is kind and gracious" to them (C 101).

The identification of God's word with scripture makes necessary a pre-cise demarcation of scripture. The type of formal demarcation that is to be found in several Reformed confessional writings can be understood as a reaction to two different tendencies. On the one hand, the understanding of the word that arose out of a strict concentration on the Christ-event sug-gested disputing the identity of God's word and scripture. Disputing this identity led to a devaluation of certain New Testament writings (Revela-tion, James, 2 Peter, Jude, 2 and 3 John), and on the Lutheran side led to a distinction between protocanonical and deuterocanonical writings. The Zurich Confession opposes this distinction when, after enumerating all the New Testament writings, it declares that "in the assembled books of the New Testament no difficult passage leads us astray. Nor do we hold that anything in them is of straw, nor that any parts are jumbled together in a disorderly way. And if the human spirit does not want to betake itself to Revelation or other books, we esteem that the question of where to betake ourselves is not ours to answer. For we certainly know that we human be-ings are to direct ourselves in accordance with Scripture, and not Scripture in accordance with us" (M 155, 19–25).

This type of formal demarcation of scripture is to be understood not only as a reaction to the distinction within the churches of the Reformation between God's word and scripture—a distinction made on the basis of content. It is also to be understood as a reaction to the Council of Trent's decree "On the Reception of Sacred Books and of Traditions" (*De libris sacris et de traditionibus recipiendis*). In this decree the apocryphal writings are counted among the books of the Old Testament and are recognized as sacred and canonical (DS 1501–1504, CT 95–96). The lists of the canonical books of the Old and New Testaments provided by many Reformed confessions differ from the list of Trent precisely by their omission of the apocryphal writings. These are valued, to be sure, by the French Confession as certainly "useful" ecclesiastical books, but no "article of faith" can be founded on them (S 361–62). The Belgic Confession lists the apocryphal books individually, and says that "the Church may read and take instruction from" them (S 387). But they must be in agreement with the canonical books. They thus have no "power and efficacy as that we may from their testimony confirm any point of faith or of the Christian religion; much less to detract from the authority of the other sacred books" (S 387; cf. 226–27). The apocryphal books are not renounced. Rather the admission is clearly made that they contain "many worthy things for example of life and instruction of manners" (S 527; cf. 490–91). However, they are denied any canonical authority (S 602). The precise delineation of the canonical scriptures is a consequence of this removal of the apocryphal writings from the list of sacred books approved at Trent.

Because the word of God is identified with scripture, formally determining what counts as Holy Scripture by listing the canonical books has the consequence that ultimately the word of God is no longer determined with respect to content, but purely with respect to form. The Westminster Larger Catechism can answer the question, "What is the word of God (*verbum Dei*)?" with the response, "the Holy Scriptures of the Old and New Testaments" (M 612, 34ff.). In this context it is explicitly asserted that the Old Testament does not contradict the New Testament, but that already in the Old Testament eternal life is promised in Christ to the human race, so that the trust of the fathers of the Old Covenant was not confined to merely transitory promises (S 491–92). God's word is thus the entire formally demarcated canon: "We believe and confess the canonical Scriptures of the holy prophets and apostles of both Testaments to be the true Word of God" (C 224). In defining God's word, reference to content is left out of the picture. This position ultimately fully distances its adherents from the genuine understanding of God's word in terms of salvation history, or from the conception of God's word as law and gospel.

When the canonical scriptures of the Old and New Testaments are identified with God's word, so that the latter is collapsed into the canon, then it is necessary to advance the thesis, appealing to 2 Tim. 3:16, that scripture itself is inspired by God. The identification of God's word with scripture entails the assertion of the inspiration of scripture. "We confess that this Word of God was not sent nor delivered by human will, but that holy people of God spake as they were moved by the Holy Ghost, as the Apostle Peter saith. And that afterwards God, from a special care he has for us and our salvation, commanded his servants, the Prophets and Apostles, to commit his revealed Word to writing" (S 384–85; cf. 362, 463, C 224). As identical with the canon, the word of God is "given by inspiration of God" (S 602).

As early as the Belgic Confession we find the declaration with respect to the Decalogue that God "himself wrote with his own finger the two tables of the law" (S 385). In this way the manner of inspiration is specified more precisely. What is described is not a mere inspiration of biblical authors sunk to the level of mere secretaries. Instead God's very self is now named as author of all canonical writings. "The authority of the holy Scripture, for which it ought to be believed and obeyed, dependeth . . . wholly upon God (who is truth itself), the Author thereof" (S 602). The ante is raised, with the thesis of the divine inspiration of scripture turning into the thesis of God's authorship. Moreover, God is named specifically as the author of scripture in its original textual forms. The Westminster Confession, appealing to Matt. 5:18, thus arrives at the assertion that "the Old Testament in Hebrew (which was the native language of the people of God of old), and the New Testament in Greek (which at the time of the writing of it was most generally known to the nations), being immediately inspired by God, and by his singular care and providence kept pure in all ages, are therefore authentical" (S 604). Authenticity is attested for the canonical scriptures only in the original text, since only the original text has God as its author. The claim of divine authorship for the original texts of the canonical books, and thus the claim of *verbal* inspiration, ultimately leads to a literal application of Matt. 5:18 to the original biblical texts.

The terminal point of this path is marked by the Helvetic Consensus Formula. Over against the literary criticism of the Saumur school, it characterizes the Jewish canon of the Old Testament ("the book that we received from the tradition of the Jewish assembly"—*codex quem ex traditione Ecclesiae Judaicae . . . accepimus*) as "God-breathed." The canon is inspired not only with respect to content (*res*) or to words (*verba*). The quality of being inspired is extended to the consonants and vowels, whether that be with regard to the signs or only with regard to their meaning ("the vowels, whether the points themselves or at any rate the force of the points"— *vocalia, sive puncta ipsa, sive punctorum saltem potestatem*) (M 862, 42–46). The Masoretic text as such thus counts as inspired, so that every attempt to treat the Codex Hebraicus as a collection of writings that rests upon a voluntary human decision, every attempt to measure it against other textual traditions or to examine it with the help of rational criticism, is rejected. The Masoretic text itself is confirmed as the ultimate criterion.

CANONICITY AND INTERPRETATION

When on the basis of the identification of God's word with biblical scripture the divine authorship of the canonical writings is *asserted*, one must ask how the canonicity of these writings comes to be *recognized* in the first place. What are the reasons for the acceptance of the biblical canon? The concept of canon entails that the books contained in it are treated as a measuring rod. They are treated as the measuring rod not only of faith (S 361) but of life. The canon is—as the Westminster Confession confirms— "the rule of faith and life" (S 602). However, the church did not give itself this rule or measuring rod. It is precisely not the case that the church fixed the expanse of the canon in such a way that the canon exists on the basis of—that is, by the grace of—a decree made by the church. Instead, the French Confession declares: "We know these books to be canonical, and the sure rule of our faith, not so much by the common accord and consent of the Church" (S 361). The reason for the acceptance of the biblical canon is not the ecclesiastical reception and approval (*reçoit et approuve*) of certain writings as canonical (S 386). In taking this position one distances oneself from what is at least one possible interpretation of the Tridentine decree "On the Reception of the Sacred Books and of Traditions" (DS 1501ff., CT 95–96). This decree's recognition of biblical writings as "holy and canonical" can, after all, be understood as if the church *grounded* the canonicity of these writings by the power of its decree.

If one does strictly reject the option of having biblical canon grounded by the church, the question is again posed: What reason or ground can then be named for the canonicity of the biblical writings? The assertion that their authority results from their divine authorship does not yet give us any criterion for knowing the truth of this state of affairs. This is not in any way to exclude the possibility that the church's testimony is a reason for our high evaluation of scripture. "We may be moved and induced by the testimony of the Church to an high and reverent esteem of the holy Scripture" (S 602–3). Nor does the Westminster Confession refuse to give a series of external criteria. Ultimately "the Heavenliness of the Matter, the Efficacy of the Doctrine, the Majesty of the Stile, the Consent of all the Parts, the Scope of the Whole (which is to give all Glory to God), the full Discovery it makes of the only Way of Man's Salvation, the many other incomparable Excellencies, and the intire Perfection thereof" are all arguments by which the biblical writings suggest their identity with God's word: that is, their canonicity. But in the last analysis the properties listed, which have to do in part with content and in part with form, are able to ground only the *preeminence* of the biblical books over other books with regard to content and form, not the *canonicity* of the biblical books. What recourse to such external, literary qualities of the Bible does show, at any

rate, is that one seeks the criterion for knowing the canonicity of the biblical books not in a decree of the church, but in scripture itself. It is not the
church that is able to guarantee the identity of scripture with God's word.
Instead scripture "doth abundantly evidence itself" as identical with the
word of God (S 603; cf. M 386–87).

If the literary qualities of the biblical writings are also unable to ground
the canonicity of those writings, by what means can we know that scripture is the canonical word of God? The French Confession picks up on
Calvin's model by responding that one recognizes as canonical the previously named books not so much on the basis of ecclesiastical testimony,
but more so "by the testimony and inward illumination of the Holy Spirit,
which enables us to distinguish them from other ecclesiastical books" (S
361). The decisive criterion for the recognition of the canonicity of the biblical writings is neither ecclesiastical testimony nor the literary quality of
the books, but rather the "testimony of the Holy Spirit" (*testimonium Spiritus Sancti*), "the internal testimony and persuasion of the Holy Spirit"
(*le temoignage et persuasion intérieur du Saint-Esprit*) in our hearts (S 361,
386–87).

Accordingly the Westminster Confession says that "our full persuasion
and assurance of the infallible truth, and divine authority thereof [sc. the
Bible], is from the inward work of the Holy Spirit, bearing witness by and
with the Word in our hearts" (S 603; cf. M 613, 1ff.). What persuades us of
the biblical writings' identity with God's word is the testimony of the Holy
Spirit. On the basis of this testimony—an internal testimony that occurs in
our hearts—it is evident to us that God's word and the biblical writings are
identical. To be sure, the thesis of the "internal testimony of the Holy
Spirit" or the "secret testimony of the Holy Spirit" (*testimonium Spiritus
Sancti internum* or *testimonium Spiritus Sancti arcanum*) would be question-
able if it amounted to the introduction of a judge or criterion *independent*
of scripture itself. But this is precisely not what is intended. Instead the internal work of the Holy Spirit and scripture as the external word are related to each other such that the Holy Spirit's testimony occurs exclusively
"*by*, and *with* the Word (*per verbum et cum verbo*) in our Hearts" (M 545,
7–8). This means that, while the fact of scripture's identity with God's
word becomes evident and manifest only on the basis of the working of
the Holy Spirit, there is no revelation of the Holy Spirit that occurs outside
of and disjunct from scripture. The role of the Spirit is limited to making
the identity of scripture and God's word evident, without adding anything
new to scripture. The thesis of the "inward Work of the Holy Spirit" is only
legitimate when it goes hand in hand with the rejection of the spiritualistic claim of "new Revelations of the Spirit" (M 545, 19–20). There is no immediacy of the Spirit. The Holy Spirit works in us only mediately through
scripture and with scripture.

The thesis that the divine authority of scripture becomes evident to us on the basis of the internal testimony of the *Holy Spirit* is directed primarily against the view that testimony of the *church* could make their divine authority evident. Not only this view, though, is disputed, but also the assertion of an ecclesiastical monopoly of interpretation. Such a monopolistic position is attributed to the church by the Tridentine decree "On the Manner of Interpreting Sacred Scripture" (*De modo interpretendi s. Scripturam*), when it declares "that no one should dare to rely on his own judgement in matters of faith and morals affecting the structure of Christian doctrine and to distort Sacred Scripture to fit meanings of his own that are contrary to the meaning that holy Mother Church has held and now holds; for it is her office to judge about the true sense and interpretation of Sacred Scripture" (DS 1507, CT 98; cf. DS 1863, CT 9; DS 3007). To be sure, it is at first still an open question who is the "holy Mother Church" (*sancta mater Ecclesia*) and thus who alone has responsibility for judging "the true sense and interpretation of Scripture" (*de vero sensu et interpretatione Scripturae*). After all, this question first receives a conclusive answer from Vatican I with its assertion that the Roman Pope possesses an infallible magisterium.

In any case, the confessions take a position fundamentally opposed to every interpretive authority of the *church,* however that authority might be more precisely defined. They can only do this, though, because they are of the view that scripture, on the basis of its clarity, is able to interpret *itself.* As early as the First Helvetic Confession we read that "this holy, divine Scripture is to be interpreted in no other way than out of itself" (C 100). It is to self-interpreting scripture alone that infallibility is attributed. It is not the ecclesiastical magisterium, however that might be understood, which interprets scripture in a binding manner. Instead scripture infallibly interprets itself. "The infallible rule of interpretation of Scripture is the Scripture itself" (S 605). To be sure, the Second Helvetic Confession, appealing to 2 Peter 1:20 and in apparent agreement with the Tridentine decree, declares "that the Holy Scriptures are not of private interpretation" (C 226). But what counts as a private interpretation is not every interpretation of scripture undertaken by an individual, as opposed to the interpretation authorized by the church. Instead what is attacked as private is precisely the interpretation that "is called the conception (*sensus*) of the Roman Church, that is, what the defenders of the Roman Church plainly maintain should be thrust upon all for acceptance" (C 226). Private interpretation of scripture is arbitrary interpretation of scripture, to which is contrasted an orthodox and genuine interpretation that is based not on external authorities but exclusively on scripture itself. Those external authorities could be the magisterium of the Roman church or the bearer of an ecclesiastical office or a so-called layperson. "The interpretation of Scripture, we confess, does not belong to any private or public person, nor yet to any Kirk for preeminence or precedence, personal or local, which it has above others, but pertains to the Spirit of God by whom the Scriptures were written" (C 177).

But how is an interpretation of scripture possible for which scripture alone is responsible? The condition of the possibility of scripture's self-interpretation is scripture's clarity. The thesis that scripture does not allow any other interpretive authority besides itself, but instead interprets itself, entails the assumption of a fundamental clarity of scripture. This does not mean that the meaning of all scriptural passages is equally clear. It does mean, as the Irish Articles put it, that "all things necessary to be known unto everlasting salvation are clearly delivered therein: and nothing of that kind is spoken under dark mysteries in one place, which is not in other places spoken more familiarly and plainly, to the capacity both of learned and unlearned" (S 527). The assertion of a fundamental clarity of scripture by no means wishes to call into question the existence of obscure—that is, incomprehensible—passages, but only to confirm the comprehensibility of those matters the knowledge of which is necessary for salvation (S 604). In the words of the Westminster Confession, these matters are asserted so clearly "in some Place of Scripture or other" that everyone, "not only the learned, but the Unlearned, in a due Use of the ordinary Means," can attain a sufficient knowledge of them. Against this background, the interpretive principle that scripture can be interpreted only "with itself" means that the sense of obscure passages must be interpreted with the help of clear passages of scripture. "Self-interpretation of Scripture" means that the passages of scripture that are comprehensible on first inspection interpret the passages that are incomprehensible on first inspection.

Along with this the thesis of the clarity of scripture entails the rejection of the manifold sense of scripture and the limitation to the literal sense (*sensus litteralis*). "When there is a question about the true and full sense of any Scripture (which is not manifold, but one), it must be searched and known by other places that speak more clearly" (S 605). Accordingly the Second Helvetic Confession also understands as orthodox and genuine only that interpretation of scripture "which is gleaned from the Scriptures themselves (from the nature of the language in which they were written, in accordance both with the context and with the understanding of like and unlike passages, especially of clear passages)" (C 226, translation altered; cf. 177). The original Hebrew or Greek text is thus to serve as the foundation of correct interpretation of scripture. Only the original language text possesses that authenticity that makes scripture the rule of faith and life. Specifically, the Vulgate is not authentic—contrary to the assertion of Trent (DS 1506, CT 97). The necessity of translating the original biblical texts into the vernacular results from the right and duty of every believer to read and study scripture "because these Original Tongues are not known to all the People of God" (M 546, 17ff.; cf. 526, 28ff.).

SCRIPTURE AND TRADITION

If the asserted clarity of scripture is portrayed as the clarity not of *all* matters asserted in scripture but only of those matters that are necessary for salvation, an internal distinction has been made in scripture—the same scripture that is identified with the word of God. To be sure, on the basis of this identification the Westminster Confession says that scripture *as a whole* is "most necessary." But this necessity of scripture as such is not synonymous with necessity for salvation. The latter necessity is limited to certain contents asserted in scripture. "The holy Scriptures contain all things necessary to salvation, and are able to instruct sufficiently in all points of faith that we are bound to believe, and all good duties that we are bound to practice" (S 527–28; cf. 489). Scripture is in any case said to be sufficient only insofar as it *contains* everything that must be known for salvation. For this reason it does not need any supplement, whether from other revelations of the Spirit, as spiritualism claims, or by tradition, as the Roman doctrine asserts. "The whole counsel of God concerning all things necessary for his own glory, man's salvation, faith, and life, is either expressly set down in Scripture, or by good and necessary consequence may be deduced from Scripture: unto which nothing at any time is to be added, whether by new revelations of the Spirit, or traditions of men" (S 603). On the basis of the sufficiency of scripture—that is, because scripture contains everything necessary for our salvation—"it is not lawful for human beings, nor even for angels, to add to it, to take away from it, or to change it" (S 362; cf. 388). Scripture is in no way in need of being supplemented.

This assertion of the complete sufficiency of scripture is directed against the dogma, sanctioned by the Council of Trent, that the gospel, understood as the source of all saving truth and order, is contained "in written books *and* in unwritten traditions" (*in libris scriptis et sine scripto traditionibus*) (DS 1501, CT 95). Of course, the oral traditions named here together with scripture are intended to be exclusively the *apostolic* traditions, not the *ecclesiastical* ones (DS 1863, CT 9). These traditions concerning faith and morals are qualified as apostolic because the apostles received them from Christ, or because at the command of the Holy Spirit they were passed on by the apostles from hand to hand, as it were, and preserved in the church in unbroken succession (*continua successione*). But the Council of Trent says that the church "accepts and venerates" these traditions "with the *same* (*pari*) sense of loyalty and reverence with which it accepts and venerates all the books both of the Old and the New Testatment" (DS 1501, CT 95). The equal degree of loyalty and reverence with which scripture and apostolic tradition are accepted and venerated makes it possible to draw the conclusion that both carry the same weight. Oral tradition is thus not subordinated to scripture, but placed alongside it. This at least suggests a two-source theory, according to which the gospel is contained partly (*partim*) in scripture and partly (*partim*) in oral tradition.

The confessional writings reject this assumption of an oral tradition whose status is on a par with scripture's. The traditions are summarily denigrated as "traditions of *men*" (S 603). This is not to say that the difference between human and apostolic tradition is ignored. There is definitely an awareness that a difference of that sort is *asserted* on the Roman side. What is contested is precisely the *legitimacy* of this assertion. The Second Helvetic Confession rejects "human traditions, even if they be adorned with high-sounding titles, as though they were divine and apostolical, delivered to the Church by the living voice of the apostles, and, as it were, through the hands of apostolical men to succeeding bishops" (C 227; cf. 388). Admittedly, this rejection applies only to those traditions, supposedly apostolic but in truth human, which "when compared with the Scriptures, disagree with them; and by their disagreement show that they are not apostolic at all." Freedom from contradiction is thereby attributed to the apostolic doctrine contained in scripture, so that there can be no oral tradition that contradicts that doctrine. "It would be wicked to assert that the apostles by a living voice delivered anything contrary to their writings."

Of course one can hardly portray the Roman view as saying that tradition contains something that contradicts scripture. Tradition should receive recognition and honor equal to that of scripture precisely because *the same* gospel is contained in tradition as in scripture. However, the confessional writings dispute this ground of parity in the treatment of scripture and tradition. The confessional writings not only reckon with the possibility that certain parts of the supposedly apostolic tradition contradict scripture, they accept it as fact. The discovery of such a contradiction presupposes a distance over against tradition—a distance made possible on the basis of the thesis of the sufficiency of scripture. This does not mean that tradition in general is rejected. It does mean, though, that tradition is fundamentally subordinated to scripture. Tradition cannot be regarded as having equal authority with scripture in deciding matters of faith. Instead "we do not admit any other judge than God himself, who proclaims by the Holy Scriptures what is true, what is false, what is to be followed, or what to be avoided" (C 227). Scripture is the only, clear, and sufficient rule of faith. As such it decides which traditions are in agreement with the faith. Tradition itself thus cannot be elevated to the status of an authority that gives a binding interpretation of scripture.

The Council of Trent advanced the thesis that no one should dare "to distort Sacred Scripture to fit meanings of his own that are contrary to the meaning that holy Mother Church has held and now holds . . . [or] to interpret Sacred Scripture contrary to the unanimous agreement of the Fathers" (DS 1507, CT 98). Over against this thesis we find the admonition that one should "not despise the interpretations of the holy Greek and Latin fathers . . . *as far as* they agree with the Scriptures" (C 226). This means that instead of tradition being the authority that decides the correctness of scriptural interpretation, scripture, which interprets itself, is the authority that decides the correctness of tradition. The validity of tradition, unlike that of scripture, is not unconditional, but conditional. Tradition is valid only on condition of agreeing with scripture. Whether or not tradition agrees with scripture can be known only from scripture, without appealing to tradition for assistance.

A fundamentally different estimation of ecclesiastical tradition results from this definition of the relation between scripture and tradition. The Second Helvetic Confession states that "we do not permit ourselves, in controversies about religion or matters of faith, to urge our case with only the opinions of the fathers or decrees of councils; much less by received customs, or by the large number of those who share the same opinion, or by prescription of long time" (C 227). In this way ecclesiastical traditions, including conciliar decisions about doctrine, are robbed of that authority conceded to them by the Tridentine specification of tradition's relation to scripture. The Westminster Confession declares: "The Supreme Judge, by which all controversies of religion are to be determined, and all decrees of councils, opinions of ancient writers, doctrines of men, and private spirits, are to be examined, and in whose sentence we are to rest, can be no other but the Holy Spirit speaking in the Scripture" or "holy Scripture delivered by the Spirit" (S 605–6; M 547, 44; cf. S 362). Conciliar decisions about doctrine can of course be accepted, but their acceptance presupposes that one has, with the help of self-interpreting scripture, tested them for agreement with scripture, and has arrived at a positive result. Because the conciliar definitions and canons (*definitiones* and *canones*) are given a rank ordering similar to that of the church fathers, it is also true of them that they are accepted "*as far as* they agree with the Scriptures" (C 226).

When specific confessions and decrees of the early church are in fact recognized, the implication is *that* these do agree with scripture. The Tetrapolitan Confession explains its agreement with Trinitarian and christological dogma, as well as with the Apostles' Creed, on the basis of their being in accord with scripture (C 56–57). The French Confession accepts "the three creeds, to wit: the Apostles', the Nicene, and the Athanasian, because (*parce que*) they are in accordance (*conformes*) with the Word of God" (S 362). The Anglican Articles name the same three creeds with the rationale that their truth can be proved (*probari possunt*) by scripture—although one should note that the Athanasian Creed is omitted from the American Revision (S 492). The Irish Articles, picking up on the Anglican Articles, state that "all and every the Articles contained in the Nicene Creed, the Creed of Athanasius, and that which is commonly called the Apostles' Creed, ought firmly to be received and believed, *for* they may be proved by most certain warrant of holy Scripture" (S 528). Because ecclesiastical dogma and creeds are only valid *as far as* they agree with scripture, it must be proved *that* they agree with scripture before they can be accepted. Accordingly, the creeds named above are accepted in the belief that they are in such agreement. To the question of why they are to be accepted the answer must be: *"because* they agree with Scripture."

The thesis that scripture is the only rule of faith has as its consequence a fundamental relativization of tradition, and thus of creeds and dogma. The only infallible interpretive authority for scripture is scripture itself, not, for instance, the ecclesiastical magisterium. What is decisive is not the form of this magisterium, but the very assertion that an ecclesiastical authority is infallible in questions of faith. In this way the creeds and dogma of the church would attain a dignity characterized by immunity to reform. But such a dignity belongs to scripture alone, not to them. It is totally beside the point whether the creeds and dogma attain this dignity on the basis of the infallibility of the pope or a council. Neither the pope as the highest teacher of the church as a whole nor the creeds and dogma agreed upon by a council are beyond reform. For this reason the Scottish Confession declares that, without testing the material in question against scripture, it is not prepared to accept "whatever has been declared to men under the name of the General Councils, for it is plain that, being human, some of them have manifestly erred, and that in matters of great weight and importance" (C 178). This disputes the position that general councils have the prerogative of being unable to err (*praerogativa . . . ut errare non possent*) (S 466). Instead it is the case, as the Westminster Confession puts it, that "all synods or councils since the apostles' times, whether general or particular, may err, and many have erred; therefore they are not to be made the rule of faith or practice, but to be used as a help in both" (S 670, cf. 539–40).

DIVINITY AND TRINITY

GOD'S ESSENCE AND PROPERTIES

God is the subject and the object of revelation "in his works . . . and more clearly, in his Word." It is God who reveals *God's self* in the divine work and word. To the revelation in God's works belongs the function of guaranteeing that human beings are without excuse in the face of God's claim. The French Confession, which speaks in this double way about God's self-revelation, precedes its statements about revelation with a definition of God's essence and properties. Indeed, the text begins with the confession "that there is but one God, who is one sole and simple essence, spiritual, eternal, invisible, immutable, infinite, incomprehensible, ineffable, omnipotent; who is all-wise, all-good, all-just, and all-merciful" (S 359–60). The Belgic Confession likewise begins with a definition of the meaning of the word *God*. According to the Belgic Confession, *God* is a synonym for "one single and simple spiritual essence" (*une seule et simple essence spirituelle*) (S 383, trans. altered). A singularity is already implied in the definition of God. Unlike a material object, but also unlike the created nonmaterial objects, which are invisible and spiritual, God is a spiritual essence characterized by simplicity. God is simple Spirit (C 120; M 643, 19–20).

This definition gives only the most general meaning of the word *God*. This meaning is then further specified by additional properties. These properties *result* in part from God's spirituality and simplicity. This is true primarily of those properties that designate the exclusion of a property of created objects. Thus the definition of God as a simple spiritual essence entails that God is invisible, incorporeal, indivisible (*impartibilis*), immutable, incomprehensible, and ineffable (cf. C 166; S 487, 528; M 547, 12ff.). This definition of God's essence remains exclusively within the framework of the philosophical concept of God received from Patristic and Scholastic theology. At least in its basic features, one views this concept of God as identical to the biblical one (M 658, 11ff.). It is also true of several of the positive properties that they have their origin in the general philosophical doctrine of God.

The Second Helvetic Confession heads up its list of properties by describing God as "subsisting in himself" (*per se subsistentem*) and "all sufficient in himself" (*sibi ad omnia sufficientem*) (C 228, S 240). God is "eternal self-subsistent Spirit without beginning or end" (*spiritus aeternus ex se subsistens absque principio, fine carens*) (M 658, 12–13). This means, first, that God is "infinite in being" (S 606) in the sense that God exists eternally. There is no beginning or ending point of God's existence. The statement "God exists" has always been true and always will be true. But second, it also means that God does not owe God's existence or life to any other object. There is no cause that effects God's existence. Therefore there is no causal explanation for the fact that God exists. Instead, in the words of the Westminster Confession, God has the divine life "in Godself" (*in sese*) and "from Godself" (*a seipso*) (S 607). God is self-existent (*a se*), "and is alone in and unto himself all-sufficient, not standing in need of any creatures which he hath made" (ibid.). This is because God is the only "fountain of all being, of whom, through whom, and to whom are all things" (ibid., trans. altered).

God as simple spiritual essence is thus defined as the cause, characterized by aseity and sufficiency, of the existence of all things. This is implied in the statement that God creates, quickens, and preserves all visible and invisible objects (C 228, 166). As cause of the existence of all things, God is their maker (*creator*) and preserver (*conservator*) (S 487). Further properties of God can be named that are gained neither by the way of negation (*via negationis*) nor by the way of causality (*via causalitatis*), but by the way of eminence (*via eminentiae*). Among these properties are omnipresence, omnipotence, and omniscience (M 613, 18). Unlike a material object, God does not exist at a specific point in time only at a specific location. Instead God is simultaneously present at all locations. Nor is the divine power limited in such a way that God would possess only the capacity to perform a limited number of actions. Instead, God is able to do everything. Finally, God's wisdom does not apply only to a limited number of true states of affairs. Instead, it applies to all true states of affairs, including those that concern the future, and whose truth for us is thus not yet fixed, but remains contingent. "In his sight all things are open and manifest; his knowledge is infinite, infallible, and independent upon the creature; so as nothing is to him contingent or uncertain" (S 607).

Finally, besides all the properties already named, God also possesses all virtues (M 658, 14). Chief among these virtures are wisdom (*sapientia*), goodness (*bonitas*), righteousness (*iustitia*), holiness (*sanctitas*), and mercy (*misericordia*) (cf. C 120, 228, S 359–60, 383–84; M 613, 19–20). God is—as summarized in the Westminster Confession—"most wise, most holy, most free, most absolute, working all things according to the counsel of his own immutable and most righteous will, for his own glory; most loving, gracious, merciful, long-suffering, abundant in goodness and truth, forgiving iniquity, transgression, and sin; the rewarder of them that diligently seek him; and withal most just and terrible in his judgments; hating all sin, and who will by no means clear the guilty" (S 606–7). God is defined not only as the most perfect being (*perfectione infinitus*) (S 606) but also as the "overflowing fountain of all good" (*source très-abondante de tous biens*) (S 384).

When the Second Helvetic Confession speaks of God as the "highest good" (*summum bonum*) (S 240), it is picking up the Platonic-Augustinian concept of God, which Zwingli ties together with the pantheistically inclined ontological speculation of Renaissance philosophy. Zwingli's Account of Faith begins with the confession "that God is one and He alone is God, and that He is by nature *good*, true, powerful, just, wise, the Creator and Preserver of all things, visible and invisible" (Z 36). If all beings are either created or uncreated, there can only be a single uncreated essence, which we call "God." The reason for this is that what is uncreated is exclusively that which is eternal and thus infinite. "Because the infinite can be only one (as soon as we admit two infinite substances, each of them is limited), it is thereby clear that only God is uncreated." There can be nothing besides God that does not owe its existence to God. If this were not the case and something could exist whose existence were not caused by God, God would not be infinite: "God would not extend to where that other one was, for it would exist without God." As this uncreated source, characterized by infinity, of the existence of all other objects, God is good. Because whatever God is, God is by nature, God is by nature good. "But that which is good is what is gentle and just. Deprive gentleness of justice and it ceases to be gentleness, but becomes indifference or fear. On the other hand, if you do not temper justice with kindness and patience, it degenerates in a moment into the greatest injustice and the most severe force. When we recognize that God is by nature good, we confess that God is kind, gentle and benevolent, but also holy, just and inviolable."

The definition of God as simple spiritual essence—a definition developed within the framework of the general doctrine of God—entails that God cannot be represented. Many confessions emphasize this in their interpretation of the prohibition of images, which, in connection with the supposedly original numbering of the Ten Commandments, appears in its own right as the Second Commandment. The preparation of images to represent God is rejected because there is no similarity between, on the one hand, God as eternal, incomprehensible Spirit and, on the other hand, a material, transitory, and dead object (M 130, 5ff.; 370, 4ff.). According to the Second Helvetic Confession, images that purport to represent God are violations of God's majesty. "Since God as Spirit is in essence invisible and immense, he cannot really be expressed by any art or image. For this reason we have no fear pronouncing with Scripture that images of God are mere lies. Therefore we reject not only the idols of the Gentiles, but also the images of Christians" (C 229). The fact that God cannot be represented follows from God's spirituality and infinity (S 343; M 791, 45ff.). The Westminster Catechism applies the thesis that God cannot be represented not only to external images of God, that is, paintings or sculptures, but also to internal images of God, that is, conceptions of God in the human imagination (M 627, 35ff.). If God cannot be externally represented (*dargestellt*), this presupposes that God also cannot be internally imagined (*vorgestellt*).

THE DOCTRINE OF THE TRINITY

It is characteristic of most of the confessional writings that they begin with a general doctrine of God's essence and properties, and only then proceed to the doctrine of the Trinity. The two pieces "On the One God" (*De deo uno*) and "On the Triune God" (*De deo trino*) are thus separated from each other. The French Confession says of the God who is defined as simple spiritual essence and who is qualified by the properties listed: "*As such* this God reveals himself to human beings; firstly, in his works, in their creation, as well as in their preservation and control. Secondly, and more clearly, in his Word" (S 360). This means that already in the divine works, God makes God's self known not only as spiritual, simple, eternal, invisible, immutable, infinite, omnipotent, omniscient, and obiquitous essence, but also as the wise, holy, righteous, good, and merciful creater and preserver of all things. The Geneva Catechism, which asserts that true and right knowledge of God is the chief goal (*praecipius finis*) and highest good of human life (*summum bonum hominis*), names as the central element of this knowledge our placing our entire trust (*fiducia*) in God. This happens when, on the basis of God's revelation in the divine works (M 118, 50ff.), we recognize God "as almighty and perfectly good" (T 6). But that is not enough, because "we are unworthy that He should show us His power in helping us, or employ His goodness toward us." In addition we must "be certain that He loves us, and desires to be our Father, and Savior" (ibid.). But that we recognize only through scripture, for in it God "declares His mercy to us in Christ, and assures us of His love toward us" (ibid.).

As the Erlauthal Confession emphasizes, God is thus known in a twofold way (*dupliciter cognoscitur*) (M 267, 13). On the one hand, knowledge of God arises "in a general way from creatures" (*ex creaturis communiter*) (M 267, 14): that is, through the "contemplation of the things of nature" (*contemplatio rerum naturalium*) (M 376, 24). But the *general* knowledge of God acquired in this way does not lead to salvation: *haec cognitio non salvat* (M 267, 14–15). Only the *special* knowledge of God saves. This latter knowledge is acquired not "from creatures" (*ex creaturis*) through mere contemplation, but by faith "from the word made manifest" (*ex verbo patefacto*) in Christ through the action and revelation of the Holy Spirit for salvation (M 267, 15ff.). God can be known in a saving way (*salutariter*) only in the Son through the Holy Spirit, because only thus do we experience God's grace toward us (M 658, 7ff.).

In this way we are led to a special knowledge of God as Father, Son, and Holy Spirit. The saving knowledge of God is the knowledge of God as triune. In its interpretation of the Apostles' Creed, the Heidelberg Catechism makes clear that the point of departure is the economic Trinity: that is, the action of Father, Son, and Holy Spirit in salvation history. The Heidelberg Catechism differentiates the individual articles of the creed in the following way: "The first is of God the Father and our creation; the second, of God the Son and our redemption; the third, of God the Holy Ghost and our sanctification" (S 315). Father, Son, and Holy Spirit appear as subjects of externally directed actions that are different from each other: salvation, redemption, and sanctification. These external works (*opera ad extra*) are attributed to different agents. At the same time, the subject of creation is identical with the subject of redemption and sanctification, insofar as these three subjects are not three gods, but one and the same God. The assertion of three agents is not intended to call into question God's singularity and unity. Because "there is but one Divine Being" (S 315), the Father, Son, and Holy Spirit cannot be three gods. Making reference to the Shema Israel (Deut. 6:4) and the First Commandment (Ex. 20:2–3), the Second Helvetic Confession explicitly rejects polytheism (C 228). Instead the Basle Confession declares: "We believe in God the Father, God the Son, God the Holy Spirit, one holy, divine Trinity, three *Persons* and one single, eternal, almighty God, in essence and *substance,* and not three gods" (C 91). God is "one in *essence,* threefold according to the persons" (C 101; cf. M 376, 28ff.). In the divine word (Matt. 3:16–17; 28:19; 1 John 5:7) "God has so revealed himself . . . that these three distinct Persons are the one, true, eternal God" (S 315). The thesis of the unity of the Three, differentiated among themselves by the attribution of specific events in salvation history, is confirmed by reference to the testimony of scripture.

To express the differentiation within that unity—a differentiation that is also attested by scripture—the confessional writings make use of the classical concepts "substance" and "person." In the process, though, the meaning of the term "person" in particular remains unclear. Zwingli's confessions give the impression that Father, Son, and Holy Spirit are ultimately only modes of one and the same substance. For these confessions Father, Son, and Holy Spirit are "not creatures or different gods, even though, as we see, they are individually called God in holy Scripture. Instead these three are one: one essence, one *ousia;* one power and one might, one wisdom and one providence, one goodness and one favor, three *names or persons* (*nomines sive personae*), but all and each one and the same God." The equation of the two concepts "person" and "name" at least suggests a Sabellian-modalistic understanding of the Trinity, which the Belgic Confession excludes when it declares that the three persons are from eternity really and truly distinct by virtue of their incommunicable properties (S 389). The Son and the Spirit are not merely appearances (*affectiones*) and properties (*proprietates*) of the Father as the monarchical divine subject, but Father, Son, and Spirit are three different hypostases, and as such individual subjects of properties (S 389–90; cf. C 229 and M 173, 45ff.).

This differentiation, though, is only personal or hypostatic. It implies no plurality of gods and thus no division of the divine essence. Instead the three persons are the one and only God. This means that the *distinction* does not have as a consequence a *division* of the individual persons. According to the Second Helvetic Confession, there are not three gods, but three consubstantial hypostases, who are so bound together with each other on the basis of their nature or essence that they are one God. In interpreting the action of Father, Son, and Holy Spirit in salvation history, only the simultaneous assertion of the singularity of God's essence and the plurality of consubstantial divine persons avoids either opening the door to polytheism or falling into Arianism or subordinationism. A Jewish or Islamic understanding of God's singularity—an understanding that allows no plurality of consubstantial divine persons—is rejected in view of its Antitrinitarianism (C 229, S 392–93). Also rejected is the Arian thesis "that the Son and the Holy Spirit are God in name only, and also that there is something created and subservient, or subordinate to another in the Trinity, and that there is something unequal in it, a greater or a less, something corporeal or corporeally conceived, something different with respect to character or will, something mixed or solitary" (C 229).

Scripture attests not only to God's singularity (Deut. 6:4; Ex. 20:2–3; Isa. 45:5, 21) but also to the plurality of persons in God. The Belgic Confession refers to the classic Old Testament proof texts from the creation account (Gen. 1:27; 3:22) in order then to adduce the New Testament statements about the saving action of Father, Son, and Spirit (Matt. 3:16–17; 28:19; Luke 1:35; John 14:26; 2 Cor. 13:13; 1 John 5:7–8): "In all which places we are fully taught that there are three persons in one only divine essence" (S 392; cf. C 228–29). Of course, if these persons are consubstantial, one must ask how they differ from each other at all. The traditional answer is that they are "really, truly, and eternally distinct, according to their incommunicable properties" (S 389). "We believe and teach that the same immense, one and indivisible God is in person inseparably and without confusion distinguished as Father, Son and Holy Spirit so, as the Father has begotten the Son from eternity, the Son is begotten by an ineffable generation, and the Holy Spirit truly proceeds from them both, and the same from eternity and is to be worshipped with both" (C 228).

According to the Second Helvetic Confession, Father, Son, and Spirit are eternally distinct by means of specific properties that already belong to them on the basis of their relation to each other, and that do not first arise with their relation to the world. The immanent differentiation of three divine persons is constituted not by their external works (*opera ad extra*) but by their internal works (*opera ad intra*). It is a basic truth about the internal works that they cannot be attributed to all persons, but only in each particular case to one of the Trinitarian persons. As the Westminster Confession puts it: "The Father is of none, neither begotten nor proceeding: The Son is eternally begotten of the Father; the Holy Ghost eternally proceeding from the Father and the Son" (S 608). Father, Son, and Spirit are eternally distinct by virtue of the fact that only the Father has the relational property of begetting (*gignere*), only the Son has the relational property of being begotten (*gigni*), and only the Spirit has the relational property of proceeding (*procedere*) (M 266, 1ff.). The subjects of these relational properties are exclusively the consubstantial persons, but not the one substance or essence itself. Otherwise Father, Son, and Spirit would differ not only personally but also by a difference in their essence. Identity of essence must be preserved for the sake of God's singularity and to avoid subordinationism.

The Fourth Lateran Council had already declared that "each of the persons is that reality, namely, the divine substance, essence, or nature. . . . That reality does not beget, nor is it begotten, nor does it proceed; but it is the Father who begets, the Son who is begotten, the Holy Spirit who proceeds" (DS 804, CT 307). The Irish Articles are only reiterating these statements when they assert that "the essence of the Father doth not beget the essence of the Son; but the person of the Father begetteth the person of the Son, by communicating his whole essence to the person begotten from eternity" (S 528; cf. DS 805, CT 307). The Father is Father through his relation to Christ as the eternal Son begotten of the Father. The first reason for calling the first person of the Trinity "Father" is not that he is *our* Father. The fact that this person of the Trinity is our Father is mediated by his being the Father of the eternal Son (M 118, 35ff.). In the words of the Geneva Catechism, *we* "are the children of God not by nature, but only by adoption and by grace, in that God wills to regard us as such (Eph. 1:5). But the Lord Jesus who was begotten of the substance of His Father, and is of one essence with Him, is rightly called the only Son of God" (John 1:14; Heb. 1:2) (T 12).

Christ is God's Son according to his divine nature. He does not first become God's Son when he becomes human; he is God's Son from eternity, insofar as the Son already functions as mediator of creation (John 1:1, 3; Col. 1:16). According to the Belgic Confession, "it must needs follow that he—who is called God, the Word, the Son, and Jesus Christ—did exist at that time when all things were created by him" (S 394).

The Son is distinct from the Father and the Spirit by virtue of the fact that only the Son is begotten of the Father. Because we are talking here about differences in God *an sich*—that is, from eternity—the begetting of the Son must be an eternal begetting. The Spirit, in turn, is distinct from the Father and the Son by virtue of the fact that only the Spirit eternally proceeds from the Father and the Son. Because the majority of the confessional writings also appeal to the Athanasian Creed as a creed in accordance with scripture, they propound the view mediated to the West by Augustine that the Spirit eternally proceeds "from the Father and the Son" (*ex patre filioque*). This view of course also was incorporated into the Western text of the Niceno-Constantinopolitan Creed (DS 150, CT 3). The Athanasian Creed propounded the Filioque with the words: "The Holy Spirit is not made nor created nor generated, but proceeds from the Father and the Son" (DS 75, CT 6; cf. DS 527, CT 301). Finally the Florentine Decree for the Jacobites explained the Filioque as follows: "All that the Father is, and all that he has, he does not have from another, but of himself, he is the principle that has no principle. All that the Son is, and all that he has, he has from the Father; he is a principle from a principle. All that the Holy Spirit is and all that he has, he has from the Father and equally from the Son. Yet the Father and the Son are not two principles (*duo principia*) of the Holy Spirit, but one principle (*unum principium*)" (DS 1331, CT 312). This Filioque is accepted across the board by the confessional writings. For instance, the Irish Articles say that "the Holy Ghost, proceeding from the Father and the Son, is of one substance, majesty, and glory with the Father and the Son, very and eternal God" (S 528; cf. 489).

With their reception of the Filioque the Reformed confessional writings place themselves, along with the entire Western tradition, in a certain opposition to Orthodox Christianity. In the case of Orthodoxy, adherence to the original text of the Niceno-Constantinopolitan Creed is combined with the dogmatic thesis that the Father is the sole cause of the Spirit's procession—that is, with the rejection of the Filioque. The Greeks see the Filioque as threatening the monarchy of the Father in the immanent Trinity. By contrast, the Latins see in the denial of the Filioque a challenge to the essential identity of the Father and the Son. If in the eternal begetting of the Son the Father imparts the Father's entire essence to the Son, then the assertion that the Spirit proceeds from the Father and the Son is merely the logical conclusion (DS 526, CT 300; DS 805, CT 307). Since in the eternal begetting of the Son the Father gives the Son everything that the Father possesses, with the exception of the Father's being the Father, it is also eternally true that the Spirit proceeds from the Son (DS 1301). The Spirit receives the Spirit's essence eternally from the Father and the Son, through whom the Spirit proceeds as from one principle and through one action (*tamquam ex uno principio et unica spiratione procedit*) (DS 1300).

This means that, although on the one hand the consubstantiality of the persons is asserted all the way to drawing the conclusion of the Filioque, on the other hand a certain ordering among the essentially identical persons is affirmed. Speaking of the persons "with respect to order (*ordine*)," the Second Helvetic Confession describes "the one preceding the other yet without any inequality. For according to the nature or essence they are so joined together that they are one God, and the divine nature is common to the Father, Son and Holy Spirit" (C 228). The Erlauthal Confession, though, declares that the externally directed works of the Trinity, unlike the Trinity's internally directed actions, can be attributed to all persons in common: "The external works of the Trinity are undivided" (*opera Trinitatis ad extra sunt indivisa*) (M 265, 36; cf. 377, 36ff.). In this view the immanent difference between persons would be grounded exclusively in their internal works. The subject of the externally directed actions would not be a specific person from case to case, but each and every person: that is, God *an sich*, independently of the divine personal differentiation. In matters concerning the external works, the Trinity would disappear behind the one divine essence. This would amount to forgetting that it is the attribution of God's saving historical action to different divine persons that provides the basis for the construction of the immanent Trinity. The point of departure is formed by the biblical testimony to the divine economy carried out by Father, Son, and Spirit. In order to ground the immanent Trinity, therefore, the Belgic Confession recurs to the "offices" (*offices*) and "operations" (*effets*) of the persons "toward us" (*envers nous*) as the ground of our knowledge of them (S 390–92). The immanent Trinity is known exclusively through God's saving action—that is, the economic Trinity—and is thematized only insofar as the former is the presupposition of the latter.

By no means do Father, Son, and Holy Spirit differ from each other only by their internal works. Rather, the differences constituted by the external works form the eternal presupposition for the differing relations of the individual persons to God's saving action. "For the Father hath not assumed the flesh, nor hath the Holy Ghost, but the Son only" (S 390). Even when the external works are ascribed to the whole Trinity, the relations of the individual persons to these works—relations grounded in the way in which the persons relate to each other within the divinity—are different. According to the Erlauthal Confession, the persons differ from each other not only by their internal works, but also by the "properties of their offices" (*officiales proprietates*), which result from their external works (M 266, 1ff.). "The Father is called our Creator by his power; the Son is our Saviour and Redeemer by his blood; the Holy Ghost is our Sanctifier by his dwelling in our hearts" (S 392). This differentiation of the divine persons, conditioned as it is by the external works, has as its presupposition an eternal differentiation within the Trinity, according to which the Father is "first cause, principle, and origin of all things"; "the Son, his Word and eternal wisdom"; "the Holy Spirit, his virtue, power, and efficacy" (S 363). The economic Trinity is thus the ground of our knowledge of the immanent Trinity, while the immanent Trinity is the ground of the reality of the economic Trinity.

CREATION AND PROVIDENCE

CREATION AND PRESERVATION OF THE WORLD

Insofar as God is the triune God, all externally directed works of God are actions of the whole Trinity. It is impossible to speak of an external work of God (*opus Dei ad extra*) in which only one of the Trinitarian persons would participate. The Augustinian axiom holds true: "The external works of God are undivided." To be sure, the Apostles' Creed ascribes the various external works to the different persons of the Trinity, so that the Father appears as creator, the Son as redeemer, and the Spirit as sanctifier. But this ascription cannot mean dissolution of the unity of the triune God in God's externally directed works. All persons of the Trinity participate in each instance of saving action, so that every saving action of *God* is a saving action of the whole *Trinity.* For this reason it is impossible to understand the designation of the Father as creator in an exclusive sense, so that the Son and the Spirit would not have a part in the creation of the world.

According to the Erlauthal Confession, creation is a "work of the Trinity" (*opus Trinitatis*) (M 269, 12; 377, 36ff.). As early as the First Confession of Basle we read "that God has created all things by His eternal Word, that is, by His only-begotten Son, and preserves and strengthens all things by His Spirit" (C 91). As an externally directed work of God, creation is carried out by the Father through the Son and Spirit (M 377, 20ff.). "We believe that God, in three co-working persons, by his power, wisdom, and incomprehensible goodness, created all things" (S 363). The Father is admittedly the primary subject of creation (Gen. 1:1). But the Son functions as mediator of this action. The thesis of the mediator role of the Word—that is, of the *Son*—in creation excludes the possibility of regarding creation as the work of the *Father* alone. Creation must be understood as a process that is not merely a one-time past event, but applies to every moment of time. Creation is not something over and done with. Preservation is also an essential part of creation. Because the creation (*creatio*) entails preservation (*conservatio*), it is continuous creation (*creatio continua*). As continuous, creation is a work of the *whole* Trinity, and thus also of the *Spirit.* The Second Helvetic Confession explains that "God created all things. This good and almighty God created all things, both visible and invisible, by his co-eternal Word, and preserves them by his co-eternal Spirit" (C 234).

The Father creates and preserves through the Son and Spirit. The object of the creation of the triune God, that which the triune God creates, the confessions call "all things, both visible and invisible." This characterization of the project of creation is to be understood as an interpretation of the biblical assertion that God has created heaven and earth along with all that is in them (Gen. 1:1; Acts 17:24; Rev. 4:11). The Scottish Confession ties the two together when it confesses that "all things in heaven and earth, visible and invisible," have been created and preserved by God (C 166). Creation is thus not identical with the empirical world, the world available to sense perception. Creation encompasses not only that which is visible, but also that which is invisible. Nevertheless one cannot say that *everything* invisible has been created by God. The fact that God is the creator of all things, both visible and invisible, *in heaven and on earth,* does not mean that God has created *everything,* period. For it is true neither of God's self nor of any one of the Trinitarian persons that they are created by God. God is not God's own creator. God has created only that which is not identical to God's self. That is precisely all things, both visible and invisible, *in heaven and on earth*. This of course raises the question of what is meant by all things invisible, whether in heaven or on earth. The French Confession declares that God created "not only the heavens and the earth and all that in them is, but also invisible spirits" (S 363). Admittedly this passage seems to be talking about something invisible that exists *outside* of that which is invisible in heaven and on earth. But in this case heaven and earth, together with all that is in them, are understood as only the *visible* world (*mundus aspectabilis*), not as the entirety of visible *and invisible* creation (M 377, 26ff.). That which is created and invisible is in fact the invisible spirits (S 363), which means angels.

If the triune God is regarded as the subject of creation, and all things visible, together with the invisible angels, are regarded as the object of creation, the first characteristic of creation is that it happens out of nothing. Creation is "out of nothing" (*creatio ex nihilo*). "The work of creation is God's making all things of nothing," according to the Westminster Shorter Catechism (S 677; cf. 611; M 614, 5ff.; S 315). The fact that the world is created out of nothing does not mean, though, that in the divine act of creation "nothingness" functions as matter out of which the world is formed. The addition "out of nothing" (*ex nihilo*) entails, rather, the negation of any matter given prior to the act of creation. There existed nothing out of which God created the world. God created the world "in the beginning of time, when no creature had any being" (S 529). Specifically, God created "by his word alone" (ibid.), which can thus be characterized as "the word of his *power*" (M 643, 37). Creation out of nothing is an expression of divine *omnipotence*. Within the six-day work of creation, the Erlauthal Confession further distinguishes the creation of matter (*abyssum*)—a one-time event that occurred at the beginning—from the formation of the individual creatures and the establishment of the order of creation, processes that were divided over the individual days (M 269, 12ff.). God created all creatures out of nothing, "giving unto every creature its being (*être*), shape (*figures*), form (*forme*), and several offices (*divers offices*)" (S 395).

Creation is not necessary, but issued from God's free decision. God created heaven and earth and all that is in them only because it pleased God to reveal God's self. "It pleased God the Father, Son, and Holy Ghost, for the manifestation of the glory of his eternal power, wisdom, and goodness, in the beginning, to create or make of nothing the world, and all things therein, whether visible or invisible, in the space of six days, and all very good," declares the Westminster Confession (S 611). God created the world "on God's own account" (*propter semet ipsum*) (M 614, 8). From the perspective of the Erlauthal Confession, the goal and end (*finis*) of the works of creation is to serve as "mirrors of God's wisdom, goodness, power and divinity" (*specula sapientiae, bonitatis, potentiae et divinitatis Dei*), praising God's glory and in this way making God present (M 269, 15ff.). The Geneva Catechism accordingly interpets the confession of God as creator of heaven and earth in the following way: "Because He has manifested Himself to us by works (Ps. 104; Rom. 1:20) we ought to seek Him in them. Our mind cannot comprehend His essence. But the world is for us like a mirror in which we may contemplate Him in so far as it is expedient for us to know Him" (T 8). If creation is understood as a mirror of God's power, wisdom, and goodness, it follows that creation must be good. "As Scripture says, everything that God had made was very good" (C 234). As mirror of God's goodness, creation as a whole is oriented toward human beings. All the rest of the creatures were created "for the service of mankind" (S 395). Their task is the "profit (*utilitas*) and use (*usus*) of man" (C 234). Creation is thus understood primarily in a functional manner. Creation serves human beings, and to that extent is "subject" to them. Yet in this functional orientation of the creatures to humankind the responsibility of human beings with regard to the creatures is also implied. The creatures are created "for the service of mankind, to the end that man may serve his God" (S 395). Sovereignty over the other creatures belongs to human beings not by nature, but because in exercising this sovereignty, human beings function as God's authorized representatives.

PROVIDENCE AND FREEDOM

The statement that the triune *God* created all things visible and invisible in heaven and earth is a fundamental protection against a Marcionite or Manichaean dualism. The world can be traced back to a single cause (*principium*) (S 246). The Second Helvetic Confession condemns the Manichaeans and Marcionites, "who impiously imagined two substances and natures, one good, the other evil; also two beginnings and two gods contrary to each other, a good and an evil one" (C 234). Over against dualism of every stripe, the Christian belief in creation insists that there is only a single free cause of all things visible and invisible, which is itself good, and whose creation is a mirror of this goodness.

Since creation is to be understood not only as the world's coming into being, but also as its preservation (*conservatio*), another view in addition to dualism must be rejected. This is the view that, although God is the cause of the world's coming into being, God is not the world's creator, since God is not the cause of the world's preservation. The Belgic Confession declares "that the same God, after he had created all things, did not forsake them, or give them up to fortune (*fortune*) or chance (*l'aventure*)" (S 396). The contrary view is decisively rejected as a "damnable error of the Epicureans, who say that

God regards nothing, but leaves all things to chance" (S 398). The confession of God as creator is incompatible with the thesis that "God is busy with the heavens and neither sees nor cares about us and our affairs" (C 233). An opposition is erected between the heathen belief in "*blind* fortune" (ibid.) and the Christian belief in divine "providence," through which all that has been created is preserved (*conservare*) and governed (*gubernare*) (C 232). In the Deist conception of God, God is the cause of the world's coming into being, but not of its preservation. The Geneva Catechism regards this conception as nothing less than a denial of divine omnipotence, since "it is much more to uphold and preserve creatures in their state, than to have once created them" (T 9). The designation of God as "Creator" thus does not mean "that God brought His works into being at a single stroke, and then left them without a care for them. We ought rather to understand, that as the world was made by God in the beginning, so now it is preserved by Him in its estate, so that the heavens, the earth and all creatures do not continue in their being apart from this power. Besides, seeing that He holds all things in His hand, it follows that the government and lordship over them belongs to Him. Therefore, in that He is Creator of heaven and earth, it is His to rule the whole order of nature by His goodness and power and wisdom" (T 9).

God's *providence* must not be immediately identified with God's *foreknowledge*, although the two are closely connected. God's providence entails God's foreknowledge, as the Westminster Confession emphasizes: "God . . . doth uphold, direct, dispose, and govern all creatures, actions, and things, from the greatest even to the least, by his most wise and holy providence, according to his infallible foreknowledge and the free and immutable counsel of his own will" (S 612). As in all confessions influenced by the strict Calvinist doctrine of divine decree, here providence entails not only God's infallible foreknowledge, but also God's decree (*decretum Dei*): that is, the "free and immutable counsel" of God's will (*voluntatis consilium liberum ac immutabile*) (ibid.). Providence has a cognitive and a volitional aspect. By no means may providence be reduced to the former. It is, rather, the second aspect that is decisive.

The Heidelberg Catechism accordingly defines "providence" as the "almighty and every where present power of God, whereby, as it were by his hand, he still upholds heaven and earth, with all creatures, and so governs them" (S 316; cf. 753, 25ff.). God infallibly knows everything in advance, and can preserve and govern everything on the basis of a free and immutable decision of the will. God's providence consists in this preservation (*conservatio*) and governance (*gubernatio*) of creation. "God's work of providence are His most holy, wise, and powerful preserving and governing all His creatures and all their actions" (M 644, 5–6; cf. 528, 24ff.). Once the world has come into being, it needs God for both its preservation and its governance. It cannot preserve itself, for without an external cause it would cease to exist. Nor is it a self-ordering system, and in this sense a self-governing one. Since the cause of its preservation and governance must lie outside itself, that cause can only be God, who is also the cause of the world's coming into being, and whose glorification is the purpose of its coming into being. The Scottish Confession thus declares: "We believe and acknowledge one God . . . by whom we confess and believe all things in heaven and earth, visible and invisible, to have been created, to be retained in their being, and to be ruled and guided by His inscrutable providence for such end as His eternal wisdom, goodness, and justice have appointed, and to the manifestation of His own glory" (C 166).

God's providence encompasses the preservation and governance of the world: that is, the goal-oriented and purposeful order of the world. But in doing so God's providence applies not just to creation in *general* but also to the *individual* creature. It is this orientation to the individual that first allows the idea of divine providence to emerge as a source of great comfort. The central point is not that God preserves and governs the world as such, and as part of the package preserves and governs humanity as a species. The Heidelberg Catechism interprets the first article of the Apostles' Creed as the basis of a trust in God such "as to have no doubt that he will provide me with all things necessary for body and soul; and further, that whatever evil he sends upon me in this vale of tears, he will turn to my good; for he is able to do it, being Almighty God, and willing also, being a faithful Father" (S 315–16). Only insofar as God's providence extends to every individual can we draw from the knowledge of that providence the benefit "that we may be patient in adversity, thankful in prosperity, and for what is future have good confidence in our faithful God and Father that no creature shall separate us from his love" (S 316). This is because all creatures are subject to divine providence in such a way that without that providence they "can not so much as move" (ibid.). The primary goal of the assertion of God's all-encompassing preservation and governance is the comfort that the individual human being can draw from that assertion. That assertion "affords us unspeakable consolation, since we are taught thereby that nothing can befall us by chance, but by the direction of our most gracious and heavenly Father, who watches over us with a paternal care, keeping all creatures so under his power that not a hair of our head (for they are all numbered), nor a sparrow, can fall to the ground, without the will of our Father" (S 397).

When in this way the conclusion is drawn from the idea of providence that God is the cause of *all* events and actions, human beings' freedom of decision does indeed seem to be threatened. After all, apart from the will of God human beings "can not so much as move." Since God governs and directs all things, there is evidently no remaining place for human freedom. This suggests the view of those whom the Second Helvetic Confession cites with the statement: "If all things are managed by the providence of God, then our efforts and endeavors are in vain. It will be sufficient if we leave everything to the governance of divine providence, and we will not have to worry about anything or do anything" (C 233).

The confessions, however, take a decisive stand aginst fatalism of this sort. Like the Epicurean thesis of contingency, they also strictly reject the opposing Stoic thesis of the necessity of all that happens (M 278, 41ff.). In no way does the assertion of a providence that extends to the actions of the individual do away with the human will. According to the Westminster Confession, one must carefully distinguish between God as primary cause (*prima causa*) and the secondary causes (*causae secundae*) (S 612). God is indeed the primary cause of all that happens, but God works through intermediate causes, among which is the human will. For the Second Helvetic Confession the secondary causes are "means (*media*) by which divine providence works. . . . For God who has appointed to everything its end (*finis*), has ordained the beginning (*principium*) and the means (*media*) by which it reaches its goal" (C 233). In realizing the divine will, which is the first cause of all that happens, God makes use of the human will as a secondary and intermediate cause, so that there can be no question of appealing to divine omnicausality as a basis for not making one's own decision. At the same time, though, this does not mean that God is in any way dependent on these instrumental causes and could neither preserve nor govern the world without them. On the contrary, "God, in his ordinary providence, maketh use of means, yet is free to work without, above, and against them, at his pleasure" (S 612–13). God's freedom and omnipotence are in no way limited by God's making use of intermediate causes.

Pointing out that God makes use of intermediate causes in upholding and governing creation does not, of course, completely answer the question of human freedom of decision. In the final analysis the fatalist could declare that, if God indeed makes use of the human will as a secondary cause, but God's self is the primary cause, then the possibility of human beings *freely* willing anything is excluded. On the contrary, they are *compelled* to will that which God ordains them to will. Fatalism, though, seems to be not just a consequence of asserting an all-comprehensive divine providence but already implied in the presupposition of God's foreknowledge. If from all eternity God has a knowledge of all that is to come, then it seems to be settled in advance which of two contradictory statements about future things is true. Everything that will happen evidently happens out of necessity, so that contingency is excluded across the board.

It is the relation between the necessity and contingency of events, on the one hand, and divine providence and foreknowledge, on the other hand, that especially the Bremen Consensus and the Westminster Confession seek to clarify. Their treatment gives decisive importance to the relation in which an individual event is considered: Is it considered in relation to its primary cause or in relation to its secondary cause? The Westminster Confession declares: "Although in relation to the foreknowledge and decree of God, the first cause, all things come to pass immutably and infallibly, yet by the same providence he ordereth them to fall out, according to the nature of second causes, either necessarily, freely, or contingently" (S 612). The modality that is proper to a specific state of affairs—whether it is necessary or contingent—must be decided according to the rule "that each and every thing is to be named according to its proximate cause" (*id est, secundem proximas et immediatas causas*) (M 755, 13–15). An event is designated as contingent with regard to its *immediate* cause: that is, the secondary cause and not the primary one. The modality ascribed to an event is always determined by the event's relation to the secondary cause, not by its relation to God as primary cause. "Therefore all things, when one regards them for themselves and in their nature, happen in a manner that is natural or free or contingent, and thus also mutable. Thus it is not incorrect that in such a way one posits a contingency and grants the Philosophers that much happens which according to its nature either might not have happened or might have happened otherwise. This is because God as well as the angels and human beings are free-willed natures" (M 755, 15–22). Statements such as "Adam fell away from God" or "Joseph was sold by his brothers" are contingent propositions. For Adam could just as well have not fallen away from God and Joseph's brothers could just as well have not sold him. Because the things that happened in a natural or arbitrary or contingent manner, and that in or for themselves could well have happened otherwise, are nevertheless subject to divine providence, Scripture often says that a particular thing had to happen necessarily "with respect to the divine ordering" (*respectu ordinationis divinae*). One gives these the name of "necessary propositions" (*propositiones necessarias*) (M 755, 30–35).

While statements about human actions, when these actions are related to their immediate causes, are seen as contingent, the same statements, when the actions to which they refer are related to God as their primary cause, are seen as necessary. The necessity in question here is by no means *absolute* necessity (*necessitas absoluta*), but rather necessity "of consequence" (*necessitas consequentiae*) (M 755, 35–36; cf. 279, 23ff.). What is at issue is a conditional necessity, not an unconditional one. An absolute or unconditional necessity would be incompatible with the contingency of events.

Conditional necessity is another matter. Every human action considered in itself is contingent; it is necessary only on condition that God wills for the action to be carried out. By no means is it absolutely necessary that human beings act as they do. It is thoroughly possible that they act otherwise. However, all human action is conditionally necessary insofar as it is necessary that, if God wills human beings to act in a certain way, they do indeed act in that way. The fact that God wills human beings to act in that certain way, though, is contingent. Consequently, the fact that they act in that way is also contingent.

Those who demonstrated that divine providence in no way calls into question the contingency of human actions believed that they had also thereby proved that the human will is free in deciding on specific actions. God's providence thus does not contradict the volitional freedom of human actions. To be sure, when God wills that a human being act in a certain way, then it is necessary that the human being act in that way. But that does not make it necessary that she act in that way, and *when* God wills that a human being act in a certain way of her own free will, *then* she acts in that way of her own free will.

GOD AND EVIL

One may think that the distinction between absolute and hypothetical necessity avoids a contradiction between, on the one hand, God's providence as it extends to everything that happens and, on the other hand, the contingency of events within the world and freedom of volition in human action. But a further question still remains open: How is the assertion of an all-encompassing divine providence compatible with the fact of evil? The confessions are united in their rejection of dualism. The thesis of God's all-encompassing providence is the ultimate consequence of precisely this rejection. But when nothing happens without God willing it, God seems also to will the evil that is undisputedly present. Consequently, God seems to be the cause of evil.

However, the confessions sound a resounding no to precisely this assertion. Admittedly, the French Confession declares that God "governs and directs [all things], disposing and ordaining by his sovereign will all that happens in the world." But at the same time it denies "that he is the author of evil, or that the fault of it can be imputed to him, as his will is the sovereign and infallible rule of all right and justice" (S 364). Evil cannot be traced back to God in the sense of declaring God to be the highest efficient cause not only of all that is good, but also of all that is evil. For although "nothing happens in this world without his appointment . . . God neither is the author of, nor can be charged with, the sins which are committed" (S 396).

How then is the relation between God's all-encompassing providence and the reality of evil to be defined? The Bremen Consensus again draws a Scholastic distinction here between that which God works or effects and that which God permits. God rules creation in such a way "that Godself *works* in all creatures all that which is good, but from God's righteous judgment freely *permits* the evil that is done by evil men and angels" (M 753, 34–37). In this case evil is to be understood as the evil acts of human beings—that is, sin as *malum culpae,* culpable evil—and not *malum poenae,* the punishment of sin, which God decrees as a righteous judgment upon sin. However, it cannot rightly be said of sin that God is its primary cause in the sense of creating or effecting it. At the same time, to treat sin as something outside of God's providence would be to deny the universality of that providence. Yet to relate providence to sin in such a way that one presented sin as something created and effected by God would amount to disputing the goodness of God. One must avoid both paths if one does not wish to call into question either God's goodness or the universality of God's providence. Instead of either of those two paths, the Bremen Consensus argues the thesis that God *permits* sin. "God does not ordain evil in the same way that God ordains good—that is, as something pleasing to God—but as something that God hates, yet knowingly and willing decrees, allows to be in the world, and in a wonderful way uses for good" (M 754, 15–18). God creates good and allows evil to be in the sense that God's self forbears to do evil, but at the same time permits evil to be done. Good must therefore be regarded as God's own proper work; evil, as God's alien work. "God thus appoints good such that God, by divine action, does good and carries it out as God's own work in the creatures themselves. Evil, though, as an alien work—namely, of the devil and of perverted human beings . . . is appointed by God in such a way and to such an extent that God does not hinder evil, as God certainly could, but allows it to happen and directs it toward the divinely appointed goal" (M 754, 22–29).

The only way that the fact that God permits evil can be harmonized with divine providence as the preservation and governance of creation is to regard evil as oriented toward a specific goal, thereby giving a meaning to evil. Otherwise the goodness of creation would have to be doubted. The existence of evil in the good creation thus does not permit any ultimate explanation. On the presupposition of divine providence the only thing that can be said is that although God does not work evil, God has permitted it. This permission calls the goodness of God into question, and can only be brought into agreement with that goodness if one joins the French Confession in assuming that God has "wonderful means of so making use of devils and sinners that he can turn to good the evil which they do, and of which they are guilty" (S 364). God "even constrains them to execute His will, although it is against their own intention and purpose" (T 9; cf. S 397). Evil therefore must not be seen as independent in the sense that it would be located outside of divine providence and thus viewed as unforeseen by God. The existence of evil admittedly calls God's goodness and power into question. Yet the thesis of God's all-encompassing providence has the function of providing an answer to this question. For if God permits evil, this permission is incomprehensible to us and its reasons are concealed from us. Consequently "we humbly bow before the secrets which are hidden to us, without questioning what is above our understanding" (S 364). We only attain comfort and consolation if we never exceed the limits set for our curiosity by Christ's statement—asserting God's all-encompassing providence—that "nothing can befall us by chance, but by the direction of our most gracious and heavenly Father . . . in whom we do entirely trust; being persuaded that he so restrains the devil and all our enemies that, without his will and permission, they can not hurt us" (S 397). "It would go ill with us if devils and wicked men had power to do anything in spite of the will of God. Moreover we could never be at rest in our minds if we were exposed to them in danger, but when we know that they are curbed by the will of God, so that they can do nothing without His permission, then we may rest and breathe again, for God has promised to protect and defend us" (T 9–10). Although God hates evil, God permits it. The existence of this evil is bearable only if we believe that the same God who has permitted evil is the good and almighty Father proclaimed by Christ—the Father who by his providence takes care that not a single hair falls from our head.

This is the only way of providing effective protection against a dualistic worldview that gives evil an independence such that evil appears to be an autonomous principle opposed to God. The Belgic Confession thus rejects the Manichaean worldview that "the devils have their origin of themselves, and that they are wicked of their own nature, without having been corrupted" (S 396). Instead the Belgic Confession treats the devils as creatures of God, specifically as those invisible angels whom God created and ordained to serve as messengers to human beings, but who "are fallen from that excellency, in which God created them, into everlasting perdition . . . are enemies of God and every good thing to the utmost of their power, as murderers watching to ruin the Church and every member thereof, and by their wicked stratagems to destroy all" (S 395–96; cf. 363). As evil powers they work evil, which can appear in a variety of ways. For everything that obviously contradicts God's goodness and thus calls God's goodness into question is to be considered evil.

HUMAN BEINGS AND SIN

THE IMAGE OF GOD AND
THE ORIGINAL ESTATE OF CREATION

Human beings were the culmination of God's creation of the world, insofar as all creatures are appointed "for the service of mankind" (S 395). Therefore creation is understood appropriately only when it is viewed anthropocentrically in this sense. There are no other creatures whom human beings would be allowed to serve in a way that took primacy over service to their fellow human beings. On the contrary, all the other creatures are subject to humanity. The words of the Second Helvetic Confession apply to all of them when it says that they were created "for the profit and use of man" (C 234). Among creatures human beings have preeminent standing by virtue of the fact that the entire rest of creation is oriented toward them (M 659, 49ff.). This subordination of the entire rest of creation to human beings receives expression in God's charge to have dominion. "Now concerning man, Scripture says . . . that God placed him in Paradise and made all things subject to him" (C 234–35). With appeals to Gen. 1:26ff., Gen. 2:15, and Ps. 8:7, "dominion among creatures" (*dominium in creaturas*) is attributed to human beings (S 612; M 614, 20; S 677–78). Human beings are thus the center of creation.

This preeminence of human beings does not imply, however, that they have limitless independence. Although the other creatures are subordinate to human beings, the latter are by no means the measure of all things. While it is indeed true that all remaining creatures stand in "the service of mankind," that service is "to the end that man may serve his God" (S 395). The final purpose of creation is not humanity, toward which all other creatures are oriented, but God. For in the words of the Westminster Confession it pleased the triune God to create the world for one chief reason: "for the manifestation of the glory of his eternal power, wisdom, and goodness" (S 611). The manifestation of God's power, wisdom, and goodness culminates in the creation of human beings. The latter therefore correspond to their essence only when they not only lay claim to the service of the other creatures but also place themselves in the service of God. As the rest of creation fulfills its purpose only in the service of humanity, so do human beings fulfill their purpose only in the service of God. The Frankfurt Confession thus states that God has revealed the divine goodness, wisdom, and care in a stronger and better way in human beings than in other creatures, which God turns over to human beings for their use and benefit. And, the Frankfurt Confession says, God created human beings in order that God might be honored and glorified (*coleretur et glorificaretur*) by them (M 659, 49ff.).

The Westminster Shorter Catechism accordingly gives the following answer to the question of the chief goal and purpose of human life: "Man's chief end is to glorify God, and to enjoy him forever" (S 676). The glorification of God is named as the "highest goal" (*finis summus*) toward which human existence is directed: that is, human beings are ordained to glorify God (M 612, 28–29). All things are to happen "to the honor of God and His holy Word" (C 50). God is glorified by the knowledge of God (*cognitio Dei*). This knowledge is the highest good of human beings (*summum bonum*

hominis): that is, their chief end (*humanae vitae praecipuus finis*) (M 117, 7ff.).
God has created us in order to be glorified by us, and we glorify God by
knowing God. The true knowledge of God is thus a knowledge by which
God is glorified. In response to the question, "How do we honour Him
aright?" the Geneva Catechism answers: "We put our reliance entirely on
Him, by serving Him in obedience to His will, by calling upon Him in all
our need, seeking salvation and every good thing in Him, and acknowledging with heart and mouth that all our good proceeds from Him" (T 6).
The goal of human beings, that which they are ordained to do as part of
creation, is to know (*cognoscere*) God according to the divine essence and
will, to delight (*delectari*) in God, to honor (*celebrare*) God, to call on God
(*invocare*), to act (*laborare*) in accord with God's word, and thus to be a mirror of the divine virtues (M 269, 44–M270, 2).

Among the properties that distinguish human beings as sexually
differentiated beings (S 611), the distinction between body and soul is primary. Along with this distinction the confessions adopt the psychophysical dualism bound up with the idea of immortality. Human beings
are not just bodies like other material bodies. In the words of the Westminster Confession, God created human beings "with reasonable and immortal souls" (M 553, 25–26; cf. 270, 2ff.). Human beings possess immortal
rational souls, which distinguish them from other bodies. It is this rational
soul which constitutes the personhood of human beings. In this sense the
soul has priority over the body. Thus "man consists of two different substances in one person: an immortal soul which, when separated from the
body, neither sleeps nor dies, and a mortal body which will nevertheless
be raised up from the dead at the last judgment, in order that then the
whole man, either in life or in death, abide forever" (C 235). The Second
Helvetic Confession here understands body and soul as two different substances that together constitute the whole human being: that is, the person.
At the same time, one of these substances, the soul characterized as spirit
(M 660, 6), is seen as the element that constitutes the person, so that the
body is subordinate to the soul.

Immortality is proper to the soul by the latter's very essence. This does
not mean, though, that the soul itself is a part of God (C 235). Like the body,
the soul is a creature of God. It is immortal, but its existence has a temporal
beginning (M 660, 6–7). Unlike God, the soul is not eternal, but only of end-
less duration. Yet in spite of the fundamental dualism of body and soul, and
in spite of the primacy of the soul understood as that part of human beings
which constitutes them as persons, it is not the human soul that constitutes
the culmination of creation, but the entire human being, consisting of soul
and body. God created the human person as an ensouled body.

Just like every other creature, human beings were "made righteous and
good" by God (C 102). But only of human beings is it said that they were

created "in the image of God" (M 95, 20), "according to the image and likeness of God" (C 234). That which distinguishes human beings from all
other creatures is the former's qualification as "the most perfect image of
God on earth and among visible creatures the most excellent and eminent"
(C 102). Only human beings did God create "good, *and* after his own image" (S 309). Human beings are the image of God *as creatures,* so that the
removal of their status as bearers of the image of God would also be the removal of their status as creatures. It is certainly possible that the image or
likeness of God (*imago* or *similitudo Dei*) can be corrupted. But at the same
time the possibility of its being removed is excluded. It belongs to the
essence of human beings as God's creatures to bear God's image. Against
the background of psychophysical dualism, the image of God is related not
to the body, but to the soul. The Frankfurt Confession grounds this by appealing to the fact that human beings are ordained within creation to
honor and glorify God. For the sake of this ordination God created human
beings "in the divine image and likeness" (*ad imaginem et similitudinem
suam*) in that God, who is Spirit, gave human beings a soul as a spiritual
principle (M 660, 5ff.). Insofar as the soul is immortal, human beings can
not totally lose the image of God, since the subject of whatever other properties belong to bearing the image of God is indestructible. The Frankfurt
Confession names goodness (*bonitas*), power (*potentia*), wisdom (*sapientia*),
holiness (*sanctitas*), and righteousness (*iustitia*) as perfect properties and
gifts of the soul. However, it is not simply as creatures that human beings
possess these perfections. If they did, then these perfections, like the soul,
could not be destroyed without also doing away with the creaturehood of
human beings. But actual human beings are distinguished precisely by the
fact that they are no longer who they were, and who they are supposed to
be, as God's image. The current condition of humanity no longer corresponds to its original estate. The conception of an original estate serves to
make clear the difference between, on the one hand, the inability of human
beings in their current condition to fulfill by their own power the role appointed for them within creation and, on the other hand, the abilities to fulfill this role—abilities that, with those perfections, were given to human
beings as creatures.

Thus we read in the Second Helvetic Confession: "In the beginning,
man was made according to the image of God, in righteousness and true
holiness, good and upright" (C 235). "We believe that God created man . . .
and made and formed him after his own image and likeness, good, righteous, and holy" (S 398; cf. M 379, 20ff.). God created human beings "in
righteousness and true holiness" (S 309). In their original estate human beings, on the basis of their spiritual nature, were not merely God's image in
the sense that they still are that image as God's creatures. The soul had at
its disposition certain cognitive and volitional advantages. These consisted

"especially in the Wisdom of his mind and the true Holiness of his free will" (S 530). God created human beings "endued with knowledge (*cognitio*), righteousness (*iustitia*), and true holiness (*sanctitas*), after his own image" (S 611; cf. M 614, 18f.; S 564). Human beings in their original estate are distinguished not only by virtue of the fact that as spirit—that is, as beings endowed with knowledge and will—they are God's image. Rather, the knowledge and will of these human beings are also of a specific quality, which allows the human beings themselves to be characterized as good, righteous, and holy. Originally human beings possessed not only the spiritual nature that constituted their bearing of the image of God, but in addition the original righteousness (*iustitia originalis*) that constituted their original manner of bearing the image of God.

COVENANT OF WORKS AND FALL

To define the relation between, on the one hand, human beings' creator and, on the other hand, human beings themselves existing in the image of God, the Westminster Confession and the Westminster Catechisms, under the influence of covenant theology, took recourse to the concept of covenant and endowed it with the systematic function that it had received especially in the works of Ursinus, Olevian, and Perkins. From this perspective God's relation to human beings is always a covenantal relation. Only because God makes a covenant with human beings is God accessible to them. The covenant is thus an expression of God's condescension. God comes down to meet human beings. "The distance between God and the creature is so great that although reasonable creatures do owe obedience unto him as their Creator, yet they could never have any fruition of him as their blessedness and reward but by some voluntary condescension on God's part, which he hath been pleased to express by way of covenant" (S 616). But when the relation between God and human beings is defined exclusively as a covenantal relation, such a relation must also be presupposed in the original estate of creation. The Irish Articles, which constitute the basis for the Westminster Confession, characterize this covenant that existed between God and human beings in the original estate of creation as a covenant of law and works (*foedus legale* and *operum*). This covenant is God's first covenant with human beings and thus also the first expression of God's condescension (S 530; 616–17; M 615, 44; 869, 20; S 678).

The first covenant is called a covenant of law, because the law gives the covenantal conditions that human beings are obligated to fulfill. It is called a covenant of works, because the works of the law are the achievements that human beings must perform in order to attain the enjoyment of that which the covenant promises. For this covenant is one "whereby God did promise unto him everlasting life, upon condition that he performed active and perfect obedience unto his Commandments, according to that measure of strength wherewith he was endued in his creation, and threatened death unto him if he did not perform the same" (S 530). On account of the promise that God connected with the fulfillment of the divine law, the first covenant is also called a covenant of life (S 678). For according to the Heidelberg Catechism, "God created man good, and after his own image—that is, in righteousness and true holiness; that he might rightly know God his Creator, heartily love him, and live with him in eternal blessedness, to praise and glorify him" (S 309). The original destiny of human beings is right knowledge of God and love of God, along with life in eternal blessedness, earned by this fulfillment of the law. Already in the first covenant human beings are promised everlasting communion with God, on condition of complete obedience (M 864, 17ff.). In contrast to the Saumur school, the Helvetic Consensus Formula rejects the position that the promise attached to the covenant of law is merely a continuation of the life lived in humanity's original estate of an *earthly* paradise and a continuation of the happiness felt therein. The promised eternal and heavenly life of the entire human person in communion with God is distinct from the life already lived in humanity's original estate. There is a qualitative difference, not merely a quantitative one, between the life of the original human being and the life promised on the presupposition of complete obedience (M 864, 20ff.).

In the first covenant God requires obedience to the law, and this obedience alone brings with it the fulfillment of the promise of eternal life. This required obedience presupposes that the original human being already knows God's law. Human beings must know what is good and what is evil in order to be able to earn eternal life by good action. They know what is good and what is evil by means of the divine law (*lex divina*). Appealing to Rom. 2:14–15, the Westminster Confession declares that God created human beings "having the law of God written in their hearts" (S 611). The law as the universal ethical authority is known to every human being insofar as it has been engraved in every human being as a creature. The divine law is identical with the moral law (*lex moralis*); its content is the same as that of the Decalogue (S 640; M 624, 20; 625, 11ff.). In their original estate human beings have knowledge of God's law, whose content is defined by the Decalogue. Obeying this law is the condition laid down by the first covenant, and this condition can be met.

The Irish Articles content themselves with mentioning the universally valid moral laws summarized in the Decalogue. By contrast, the Westminster Confession uses a literal interpretation of the biblical story of the Fall to unfold the idea of the covenant of law in baroque intricacy. Here the covenant of works no longer rests on the universal moral law, but on a particular prohibition. "Besides this Law written in their Hearts, they received a Command, not to eat of the Tree of the Knowledge of Good and Evil, which while they kept, they were happy in their Communion with God, and had Dominion over the Creatures" (M 553, 34–41; cf. 581, 14ff.). If one sees in the refusal to transgress this particular prohibition the reason for the fulfillment of the promise, the question arises, What is the relation of this *particular* prohibition to the *universal* moral law? The transgression of the *particular* divine law is viewed as disobedience to God, and thus as a violation of the moral law's command to love God. The violation of the particular law breaks the unconditional obedience toward God that is required by the moral law written in the heart. Contravening the duty of obedience has as its consequence not only exclusion from eternal life, which is qualitatively distinct from the original estate, and which was promised to the first human being on condition of fulfilling this duty. In addition, the penalty connected with the transgression of the particular command is bodily and spiritual death (S 640; M 614, 41–42; S 678).

By means of the literal interpretation of the biblical narrative of the Fall, the covenant of works is, to be sure, understood as a covenant that God made with Adam. But as God's covenantal partner, Adam is not a private person, but the representative of humanity. Therefore the Westminster Confession states that "the first covenant made with *man* was a covenant of works, wherein life was promised to *Adam, and in him* to his posterity" (S 616–17). "God gave to *Adam* a law, as a covenant of works, by which he bound *him and all his posterity* to personal, entire, exact, and perpetual obedience" (S 640). God makes the first covenant with Adam as "public person" (*persona publica*), in the name not only of Adam, but of all Adam's descendants. To that extent the covenant of works is a covenant made with the entire human race as it descends from Adam (M 614, 49ff.; S 679; M 864, 36ff.). Adam fulfills or transgresses the conditions of the covenant not as a private person but as the representative and head of humanity in its entirety, just as God also made the covenant with Adam as the representative and head of humanity in its entirety.

On the presupposition that already in the original estate of humanity God made a covenant with Adam that linked the gift of perfect eternal life to the condition of observing the divine commandments, sin appears as Adam's fall. Adam fails to fulfill that condition insofar as he transgresses the particular prohibition against eating from the tree of knowledge. In doing so Adam also violates the duty of obedience imposed on him by the Decalogue as the natural moral law ingraved in Adam's heart. "Our first parents . . . sinned in eating the forbidden fruit" (S 615). "The sin whereby our first parents fell from the estate wherein they were created, was their eating the forbidden fruit" (S 678–79). By failing to observe the particular prohibition, personally given to him as the first human being, Adam violates the moral law and thus breaks the covenant of works that God made with him in the original estate of creation. By his own conduct Adam renounces the covenant of works.

Adam's fall—which is a fall of the human race, since Adam functions as representative of all humanity—presupposes that Adam or the original human being can fall. Adam must possess the ability or the capacity to fall. For this reason the confessions ascribe to Adam, in addition to the perfections of the soul already mentioned, a free will. For example, the Scottish Confession declares that "God has created man, i.e., our first father, Adam, after His own image and likeness, to whom He gave wisdom, lordship, justice, free will, and self-consciousness, so that in the whole nature of man no imperfection could be found" (C 167). The original human being is distinguished by a free will (*liberum arbitrium*). According to the Second Helvetic Confession, in the original estate of humanity human freedom is defined by the fact "that he could both continue in goodness and decline to evil" (C 237). Freedom of volition (*libertas voluntatis*) consists in human beings' ability to choose between two alternative actions and to decide for one or the other. "God hath indued the will of man with that natural liberty (and power of acting upon choice), that (it) is neither forced nor by any absolute necessity of nature determined to do good or evil. . . . Man, in his state of innocency, had freedom and power to will and to do that which is good and well-pleasing to God" (S 623; M 564, 3–4). The freedom of volition proper to human beings before the Fall is thus the will's natural freedom from every coercion and every absolute necessity to carry out a specific action. This means that human beings before the Fall could *will* good as well as evil. But not only could they *will* to do the one or the other, they could also *do* the one or the other. Before the Fall human beings could both will and do good as well as evil. They possessed both freedom of the will and freedom of action. This assertion excludes every form of determinism. Human beings in their original estate were fundamentally free with regard to their willing and their acting.

It is indeed true that God created the original human being as an ensouled body whose will was distinguished by holiness and righteousness. Adam possessed "the true holiness of his free will" (S 530). But at the same time he was characterized by the fact that "he could both *continue* in goodness and decline to evil" (C 237). This means that the will of the original human being was *mutable*. Adam possessed the freedom to will evil also, and thus to change his originally holy will. To be sure, Adam at first willed the good, "but yet mutably, so that he might fall from it" (S 623). The original human beings could fulfill God's law, but possessed this ability "under a possibility of transgressing, being left to the liberty of their own will, which was subject unto change" (S 611). It is not the freedom as such of human beings that provides the reason for their acting contrary to the divine command, but only the mutability that distinguishes their free will. For human beings are also to possess freedom of the will "in the state of glory" (*in statu gloriae*), but the will then will only be a will to do what is good, and consequently will be distinguished by immutability. "The Will of Man is made perfectly and immutably free to do Good alone, in the State of Glory only" (M 565, 5–8).

The assumption that the original human beings were distinguished by freedom of the will serves to characterize the Fall as a free act of human beings. In their original estate human beings had the ability either to fulfill God's law or not to fulfill it. The fact that they decided not to fulfill it can be attributed only to their free will. The Fall is human beings' own fault, even if, picking up on the biblical story of the Fall, the confessions often talk about the serpent leading the human beings astray. The serpent's leading them astray must not be conceived in such a way as to limit the original human beings' freedom of the will. Admittedly, we read in the Westminster Confession that Adam violated God's law, "being seduced by the subtilty and temptation of Satan" (S 615; cf. M 614, 44ff.). The "instigation of the serpent" (C 235) played an essential role in sin's coming into being, so that the Erlauthal Confession can designate the devil (*Diabolus*), along with the will of Eve and Adam (*voluntas Evae et Adae*), as the cause of sin (*causa peccati*) (M 268, 45). But the temptation by the Evil One must not be understood in such a way that Adam would be *compelled* to fall by the pressure of external circumstances. Rather it is asserted that Adam gave in to temptation *of his own free will and without compulsion* (*sua sponte et nullo penitus cogente*) (M 379, 27–28). Adam turned away from God of his own free will. He "wilfully" fell into sin (M 95, 22). Because he was purely right and free, "so that he could both continue in goodness and decline to evil" (C 237), "by his own fault (*sua culpa*) he abandoned goodness and righteousness" (C 235).

To be sure, all this does not give an ultimate reason why the original human beings fell away from the good. If there were a sufficient reason for this contingent fact, that would in any case remove the freedom of those human beings to will and then to do either the one or the other. On the presupposition of indeterminism, the ultimate reason for the Fall can only be the free will of the original human beings themselves. Adam "was capable in all things to will agreeably to the will of God. But being in honor, he understood it not, neither knew his excellency, but willfully subjected (*volens subiecit*) himself to sin, and consequently to death and the curse, giving ear to the words of the devil" (S 398).

As representative of all of humanity in its original estate, Adam is endowed by the confessions with a free will. In so doing the confessions want to trace the fact of sin back to the free activity of the original human being. As free action, the Fall has its sufficient cause exclusively in the spontaneity of the human will. Human being spontaneously falls victim to self-love—or, as Zwingli puts it, "self-serving" (M 9, 38). In the process the human will changes. The good will characterized by love of God changes into a bad will characterized by self-love. Because of this God's covenant of works and of law collapses. For in the covenant of works human beings are declared righteous by virtue of their works in accordance with the law. But through the fall of Adam as representative of the human species this covenant of law has become powerless. Not only have human beings lost the promised heavenly blessedness through the fall of Adam as the head of humanity; the transgression of the law also brings with it eternal death.

SIN AND FREEDOM OF THE WILL

Through the fall into sin human beings have, in the formulation of the French Confession, "alienated" themselves from God. Alienation from God is alienation from "the fountain of justice and of all good" (S 365). The extent of this alienation only becomes fully visible when one understands it as the total corruption of human nature. The fallen human being is alienated from God in such a way that, according to Gen. 6:5, "his nature is totally corrupt. And being blinded in mind, and depraved in heart, he has lost all integrity, and there is no good in him" (S 365). Sin destroys human beings not merely outwardly, but alters their nature. Not just a part of the human person is corrupted, but the whole person. "Nous recongnoissons l'homme en sa nature estre du tout aveugle en ténèbres d'entendement, et plain de corruption et perversite de cueur" (M 112, 8–9). Sin must be defined as "internal corruption of the *whole* human being" (*interior corruptio totius hominis*) (M 830, 5; cf. 38ff.). Sin would be misunderstood if one wanted to characterize it as an evil deed and action. To be sure, *action* that breaks the moral law as the essence of ethical norms is also sin, but it presupposes the sinfulness of the *subject* of action.

Therefore the Hungarian Confession distinguished three types of sin. Only the last of these three is the execution of an intended evil action. Besides it not being possible to limit sin to evil action, it is also impossible to limit it to an evil will that yields to inclinations and affects. Sin, rather, is every inclination and every thought, even when the will neither yields to inclination nor assents to the thought. For God wills that we love God "with all our heart, and with all our soul, and with all our mind" (Matt. 22:37), but this is just what we are incapable of doing because of our sinfulness (M 380, 38ff.).

After naming the command to love God and neighbor as the sum of the divine law, the Heidelberg Catechism answers the question, "Canst thou keep all this perfectly?" with the words, "No; for I am *by nature prone* to *hate* God and my neighbor" (S 309). Sin begins not with volition, still less with the intended action, but with inclination. It is this sinful inclination that determines our volition and action in such a way "that we are wholly unapt to any good" (S 310). We are not merely partially affected by sin, so that there would be certain abilities and capacities in us that would be untouched by sin. Rather we are completely "depraved," "prone to all evil" in such a way that we cannot free ourselves from this inclination. Instead it totally dominates us. According to the Second Helvetic Confession sin is a fundamental corruption (*corruptio*) of the human being, "by which we, immersed in perverse desires (*concupiscentiae*) and averse to all good (*a bono aversi*), are inclined to all evil. Full of all wickedness, distrust, contempt and hatred of God, we are unable to *do* or even to *think* anything good of ourselves (*ex nobis ipsis*)" (C 235, S 247).

The concept of sin would be misunderstood from the outset if one sought to apply it only to actions, but to treat volition and thought as not fundamentally subject to sin. Sin is first fully grasped in its radicality when it is understood as the depravity and corruption of the *entire* human being. This happens where sin is characterized as the inability not only to do the good, but also to will it and to think it. The "understanding (*intellectus*) is darkened, and the will (*voluntas*) which was free has become an enslaved will" (C 237, S 249). As a consequence "reason does not judge rightly of itself concerning divine things" (C 238). Since reason is the guide (*dux*) of the will, the will's lack of freedom follows from the blindness of reason. "Wherefore, man . . . has no free will for good, no strength to perform what is good" (C 238, S 250). The sinfulness of the human person entails that "he can in nowise approach [God] by his intelligence and reason"; moreover, the will "is altogether captive to sin, so that he [sc. the human being] has no other liberty to do right other than that which God gives him" (S 365). Human beings have become "slaves to Satan, and servants to sin" (C 167). The human being "has nothing of himself unless it is given him from heaven" (S 399). Through sin "our nature was enfeebled and became so inclined to sin that, unless it is restored by the Spirit of God, man neither does nor wants to do anything good of himself" (C 91). The human will is no longer free, but enslaved. The *servum arbitrium* replaces the *liberum arbitrium* (M 274, 29ff.). We are no longer free to do good. We can only will what is evil, and not also what is good. Insofar as we lack this ability, we are deprived of freedom of the will. For the will as free is the ability or capacity to will *either* what is evil *or* what is good (M 380, 24ff.). On the basis of sin as "corruption of nature" we are "utterly indisposed, disabled, and made opposite to all good, and wholly inclined to all evil" (S 615). As beings who *cannot* will to love God, we find ourselves in a continuous rebellion against God (M 660, 24ff.; cf. S 564).

Accordingly, sin is first grasped in its radicality when one understands it as the loss of freedom of the will. Such a concept of sin leads to misunderstandings, however, if one does not indicate the sphere of action to which this loss of freedom of the will applies. The thesis of the enslaved will is not to be understood as though sinful human beings no longer possessed the natural ability of the free will "with respect to natural and civil matters" (*quoad Naturalia et Civilia*) (N 672). One must carefully distinguish here between, on the one hand, divine and spiritual things, and on the other hand, worldly and earthly things. It is certainly granted that sinners, too, are free with respect to the latter. This means that sinners possess an external civil freedom (*libertas externa ac civilis*) "in mediate matters, in natural matters, in the external discipline to be followed" (*in rebus mediis, in rebus naturalibus, in externa disciplina facienda*) (M 274, 40–42). For "no one denies that in external things (*in externis*) . . . the unregenerate enjoy free will (*liberum arbitrium*) . . . to will some things and not to will others. Thus he is able to speak or to keep silent, to go out of his house or to remain at home, etc." (C 239, S 251).

The Canons of the Dordrecht Synod declare that even sinful human beings still have at their disposition a natural light (*lumen naturae*), whereby they retain "some knowledge of God, of natural things, and of the difference between good and evil, and [discover] some regard for virtue (*virtus*), good order in society, and for maintaining an orderly external deportment (*disciplina externa*)" (S 588, 565). It is immediately conceded that human beings do not use this natural light in the right way "even in things natural and civil" (*naturalibus ac civilibus*) (ibid.). Yet the fact that even the sinner possesses it is not thereby called into question. With regard to freedom of the will in external matters, it is a shared insight of the Reformation when the Augsburg Confession declares "that man possesses some measure of freedom of the will which enables him to live an outwardly honorable life and to make choices among the things that reason comprehends" (BC 39). Pseudo-Augustine is cited to the effect that "in the outward acts of this life" even sinful human beings "have freedom to choose good or evil. By good I mean what they are capable of by nature: whether or not to labor in the fields, whether or not to eat or drink or visit a friend, whether to dress or undress, whether to build a house, take a wife, engage in a trade, or do whatever else may be good and profitable" (ibid., 40). The disputing of the will's freedom thus must not be understood in the sense of a Stoic-Manichaean fatalism. The thesis that, in things external, sinful human beings definitely have the ability to will and to do either what is good or what is evil, is intended to be a defense against the opinion "that everything happens of necessity" (*ex necessitate*), which would ultimately imply that, on the basis of an enslaved will, the human person "also does evil, such as robbery, indecency, murder, theft and similar deeds, out of compulsion" (M 800, 4–7).

What is disputed, though, is not this freedom of the will in things *external* but the freedom of the will in things *spiritual*. Sinners have "no capacity or power in spiritual matters" (M 799, 32–33). Although sinful human beings still possess a free will "with respect to natural and civil matters," they no longer possess freedom to know, to will, or to do "the supernatural and natural good" (*bonum Supranaturale et Spirituale*) (N 672–73). For "in regard to goodness and virtue man's reason does not judge rightly of itself concerning divine things," so that one must deny that "we of ourselves are capable of thinking anything good" (C 238). To be sure, "in things earthly fallen human beings are not without reason" (ibid.). In mercy God permitted human beings to retain their mental faculty and enjoined them to develop it. But with regard to things spiritual, the Westminster Confession's statement holds that "Man, by his fall into a state of sin, hath wholly lost all ability of will to any spiritual good accompanying salvation" (S 623).

The thesis that the will of the sinful human being is enslaved means that on our own we are incapable of *willing* what is good in things spiritual—but not in matters concerning the external observation of civil laws: that is, in matters concerning legality. Our incapacity to will what is good in things spiritual ultimately means that our will in itself is not free to love God. Consequently, we cannot even *will* to love God. This excludes the possibility that sinful human beings on their own would remove their self-incurred alienation from God, and with the help of their natural powers and good works would repent and turn to God "by means of their natural powers and good works" (*naturalibus suis viribus et bonis operis*) (S 493). "Man . . . as a natural man . . . is not able, by his own strength, to convert himself, or to prepare himself thereunto" (S 623). Human beings do possess on their own the ability to operate within the framework of legality and to observe externally the norms of the divine laws summed up in the double commandment of love. But human beings are unable to fulfill these norms in such a way that they could in fact love or will to love God with all their heart, all their soul, all their mind, and all their strength, and their neighbor as themselves. Insofar as doing what the double commandment requires of us is alone that which is good, on our own we can only will its opposite, that which is evil.

This makes clear that the thesis that the will is enslaved does not deny the will's existence itself. Sinful human beings are still human beings and thus God's creatures, and as such good. The possession of reason and will belongs to the essence of being human. It is precisely by the possession of reason and will that human beings are distinguished from plants, animals, and inanimate objects. Sin entails the corruption and depravity of human beings, but not the removal of their essence, and thus not the removal of their reason and will. The Erlauthal Confession's Flacian assertion that as sinners human beings are like sticks or stones (M 274, 35ff.; 275, 35ff.) is an exception and only that. Speaking precisely with regard to freedom of the will as a matter that "has always produced many conflicts in the Church," the Second Helvetic Confession declares: "To be sure, his [i.e., 'man's'] reason was not taken from him, nor was he deprived of will, and he was not entirely changed into a stone or a tree. But they were so altered and weakened that they no longer can do what they could before the fall. For the understanding is darkened, and the will which was free has become an enslaved will" (C 237).

Although sin is a corruption of human nature, the essence of being human is not removed by sin in such a way that one could no longer speak of human beings *qua* sinners as individuals endowed with reason and will. What sin effects is the *obscuring* of reason and the *bondage* of the will. Yet reason and will belong to human beings as creatures. They thus are possessions of human beings as sinners, since the latter have not been deprived of their creaturehood, although they can no longer make adequate use of reason and will. For although the sinful human being "can still discern good and evil, we say, notwithstanding, that the light he has becomes darkness when he seeks for God, so that he can in nowise approach him by his intelligence and reason. And although he has a will that incites him to do this or that, yet it is altogether captive to sin, so that he has no other liberty to do right than that which God gives him" (S 365). Only because human beings as sinners still have a will at their disposition can it be asserted that human beings not only *do* evil but *will* it. Their sinfulness does not ultimately entail that they are *compelled* to do evil. Rather their sinfulness effects a bondage of the *will*. It is not the human *will* that is removed, but the *freedom* of that will. "We ascribe freedom of choice to man because we find in ourselves that we do good and evil knowingly and deliberately. We are able to do evil of ourselves but we can neither embrace nor fulfill the good" (C 102).

The Hungarian Confession explicitly maintains that human beings as sinners are not deprived of their natural faculties such as reason, judgment, and will. On the contrary, they still have a free will (*liberum arbitrium*) at their disposition. Yet what is here designated as free will is precisely not the natural faculty to will and to do either what is good or what is evil. Sinners' inability to will on their own what is good is given with the fact of sin. The free will in the sense used here is the uncompelled will (*voluntas non coacta*), which nevertheless wills only what is evil (M 380, 24ff.). What is expressed here—admittedly in a way that is open to misunderstanding—is the fact that sinners are characterized by the fact that they *will* to sin. It is not the case that although they *do* evil, they do not *will* it. Rather they do evil willingly: that is, without being compelled to do so. In the words of the Second Helvetic Confession, "it [i.e., the will] serves sin, not unwillingly (*nolens*) but willingly (*volens*). And indeed, it is called a will (*voluntas*), not an unwill(ing) (*noluntas*)" (C 237, S 249). Human beings sin willingly, not against their will or unwillingly. This means that human beings do evil of their own accord. "Therefore, in regard to evil or sin, man is not forced by God or by the devil but does evil on his own initiative (*sua sponta*), and in this respect he has a most free will (*liberrimum arbitrium*)" (C 237, S 249–50; trans. altered). One must carefully distinguish between two things. Sin does indeed entail the loss of the will's freedom, so that sinners cannot will what is good. But this does not mean that sinners do not will the evil that they do, and do it willingly. The evil actions that they perform are not done under coercion.

SIN AND THE IMAGE OF GOD

But if human beings are created as the image of God (*imago Dei*), the question arises, How does the sinfulness of human beings relate to their bearing the image of God? The French Confession declares its belief "that man was created pure and perfect in the image of God (*conforme à l'image de Dieu*), and that by his own guilt (*par sa propre faute*) he fell from the grace which he received (*la grâce qu'il avait reçue*)" (S 365). Does this also mean that the image of God in human beings has been "utterly defaced" (*penitus obliterata*), as the Scottish Confession asserts (C 167, S 441)? Must one even join the Frankfurt Confession in agreeing with Flacius and saying that sin effects not merely a qualitative change, but a change affecting nature, a substantial change, in the sense that human beings are transformed from the image of God to the image of the devil (*imago diaboli*) (M 660, 31ff.)?

On the Roman side a distinction is made, on the basis of Gen. 1:26–27, between the "image of God" (*imago Dei*) and the "likeness of God" (*similitudo Dei*) in the sense that although human beings as sinners no longer possess the likeness of God, they continue to be the image of God. While human beings are created as the image of God and cannot lose this image, since they would then cease to be human beings, the likeness of God is not something that belongs to human nature, but rather is a supernatural gift of grace. Although human beings in their original estate are distinguished by this gift, they can lose it without ceasing to be human beings (cf. DS 1926, 2435). That which Adam lost through the Fall is "the holiness and righteousness in which he had been *established* (*in qua constitutus fuerat*)" (DS 1511, CT 372). This avoids saying that human beings were *created* in holiness and righteousness, since these properties are such as do not belong to the nature of human beings as creatures, but are imparted as supernatural gifts of grace to human beings. This Roman thesis, that even sinful human beings are and remain the image of God, although they have lost holiness and righteousness, forms the foil to the thesis that we find in the Scottish Confession and the Frankfurt Confession, that the image of God in human beings has been completely defaced and that the image of the devil has taken its place.

However, this second thesis constitutes an exception within the Reformed confessions. In general the position is not disputed that, in spite of the corruption and depravity of the entire human being effected by sin, human beings continue to be the image of God. Since human beings are creatures of God, even as sinners they remain the image of God. Sin does not have the result of transforming human beings from being the image of God to being the image of the devil. The view defended by Flacius, that sin has become the *substance* of human beings, is thereby rejected. Nevertheless, only the Anhalt Repetition, standing as it does under the influence of Melanchthon, declares explicitly that sin is an *accident* of human beings (N 618). If sin were the substance of human beings, then God, as creator of all substances, would also have to be the cause of sin, and Christ, as a human being, would also be a sinner. If one wishes to avoid this consequence, one must surrender the view that sinfulness is either the substance of human beings or a property (*idioma, seu proprium*) of their substance. The rejection of the Flacian thesis is admittedly also contained in the French Confession's statement that "by his own guilt ['man'] fell from the *grace* which he received" (S 365). As the Belgic Confession puts it, "being thus become wicked, perverse, and corrupt in all his ways, he hath lost all his excellent *gifts* which he had received from God" (S 398). These statements distinguish between, on the one hand, human beings as creatures, and on the other hand, the gifts imparted to human beings or the particular graces received by human beings.

This distinction seems to accommodate the Roman thesis that, although human beings as sinners lack the supernatural gifts of grace, their nature is not harmed by sin. In this view that which human beings lose through sin would be only the likeness, while the image of God would remain untouched. However, this view cannot be harmonized with the view that identifies the image of God with original righteousness (*iustitia originalis*). Presupposing the latter view, the loss of original righteousness would indeed entail the loss of the image of God, so that one would in fact have to join the Scottish Confession in saying that the image of God has been utterly defaced by sin. When the Belgic Confession declares that God created human beings "in God's image and likeness" (*ad suam imaginam et similitudinam*), *namely* (*nempe*) good, righteous, and holy (M 237, 43–45), it collapses the difference between "image" and "likeness" and identifies the condition of bearing the image of God with the goodness, righteousness, and holiness of human beings in their original estate. "God created man good, and after his own image—that is, in righteousness and true holiness" (S 309). In a strict sense, identifying the condition of bearing the image of God with the righteousness of the original estate allows only the conclusion that the image of God was lost when the original righteousness was lost. Nor can one then say that a remnant of the image of God is still present. For on the presupposition of identity this would mean that one could likewise still encounter a *remnant* of the righteousness of the original estate. But precisely that possibility is what is to be excluded. If human beings as sinners are inclined to hate God and their neighbor, this signifies a *total* loss of those properties which distinguish human beings in their original estate: that is, goodness, righteousness, and holiness.

If one wishes to maintain that even sinful human beings, who totally lack these properties, are still the image of God, one must step back from letting the condition of bearing the image of God be absorbed into the righteousness of the original estate. Such a step back is presupposed wherever one sees the sinfulness of human beings not in the loss of the image of God but in the loss of all *gifts* that distinguish human beings in their original estate. According to the French Confession, human beings have "lost all integrity, without remainder" (S 365, trans. altered). Moreover, the loss of the "state of integrity" (*status integritatis*) means that human beings lose the goodness, righteousness, completeness, and holiness with which they were originally equipped. They are incapable of willing anything good in things spiritual.

Admittedly, according to Rom. 2:15, in spite of the loss of the properties distinguishing human beings in their original estate, they "retained a few remains thereof, which . . . are sufficient to leave man without excuse" (S 399). Even as sinners human beings can still differentiate between good and evil, and still possess a will and some knowledge of God (S 365, 588). Nevertheless "the light he has becomes darkness when he seeks for God," and the human will "is altogether captive to sin, so that he has no other liberty to do right than that which God gives him" (S 365). Even as sinners human beings still bear the image of God, insofar as they are individuals who are endowed with reason and will and who not only, as moral beings, can distinguish between good and evil, but also, as religious beings, possess some knowledge of God, whatever the character of that knowledge might be. "There remain, however, in man since the fall, the glimmerings of natural light (*lumen naturae*), whereby he retains some knowledge (*notitias*) of God, of natural things, and of the difference between good and evil, and discovers some regard for virtue, good order in society, and for maintaining an orderly external deportment. But so far is this light of nature from being sufficient to bring him to a saving knowledge of God, and to true conversion, that he is incapable of using it aright even in things natural and civil. Nay farther, this light, such as it is, man in various ways renders wholly polluted, and holds it [back] in unrighteousness, by doing which he becomes inexcusable before God" (S 588, 565).

Although one must distinguish the image of God from original righteousness if one wants to avoid claiming that human beings have lost the image of God, this distinction cannot mean that human *nature* remains untouched by sin, on the grounds that the loss of original righteousness is the loss of a *supernatural* gift of grace. To be sure, sin does not do away with human beings' substance, since even as sinners human beings are still human beings and bear God's image. But in losing the gifts imparted to them, human beings lose the ability to fulfill on their own a *natural* specification of their being: that is, the purpose for which they were created. For the human person was created "that he might rightly know God his Creator, heartily love him, and live with him in eternal blessedness, to praise and glorify him" (S 309). Sin does not do away with the human beings' humanity, but it is a corruption of human nature insofar as it causes human beings continually to fall short of the natural goal of their life.

Zwingli expresses this falling short or missing the mark when he characterizes sin as self-love (*philautia* or *amor sui*) (M 82, 20ff.). Sin consists in the fact that human beings, instead of being directed toward God, are curved back into themselves and thus characterized by selfishness and self-love. "Every human being is selfish, appropriates to himself achievement, honor, reputation, power, riches and fame, and is more pleased with himself than he deserves to be" (M 9, 23–24). Human beings try to excuse themselves by pointing to the instinctual behavior of animals: "Why shouldn't I first look out for myself? That is what nature teaches me. The irrational animals provide for themselves first" (M 9, 40–42). But human beings are distinguished from irrational creatures precisely by the fact that human life does not exhaust itself in the satisfaction of self-interest, but is directed toward God. For "as you are rational, you should readily note that without a doubt your thoughts and undertakings should be very different from those of irrational animals" (M 10, 2–4). Sin can thus be defined as a perversion of life orientation. Human beings are characterized by this perversion prior to any individual action. In this sense the Second Helvetic Confession compares human beings to bad trees. For "full of all wickedness, distrust, contempt and hatred of God, we are unable to do or even to think anything good of ourselves. Moreover, even as we grow older, so by wicked thoughts, words and deeds committed against God's law, we bring forth corrupt fruit worthy of a bad tree" (C 235, trans. altered). The human person is characterized by the fact that self-love "produceth in man all sorts of sin, being in him as a root thereof" (S 400). This fundamental sin of human beings, which Zwingli characterizes as self-interest and self-love, is designated by other confessions as concupiscence (cf. S 492–93). Concupiscence is a corruption of human nature, "whereby the flesh always lusteth against the spirit, and can not be made subject to the law of God" (S 530).

Self-love or concupiscence is the fundamental sin or original corruption of human nature. From this fundamental sin arise all sinful individual actions. These are grounded in concupiscence as the inclination and tendency toward evil. "From this original corruption, whereby we are utterly indisposed, disabled, and made opposite to all good, and wholly inclined to all evil, do proceed all actual transgressions" (S 615). This position presupposes the definition of sin as transgression of the law and as assault on God's honor: "Every sin, both original and actual, being a transgression of the righteous law of God" (S 616; cf. M 615, 7ff.; S 679). The corruption of human nature as the fundamental dispositional sin has as its consequence actual sins in the sense of sinful actions. These actions can in turn be distinguished from one another, "whether mortal, venial or that which is said to be the sin against the Holy Spirit which is never forgiven" (C 236). The Second Helvetic Confession grants that these sins are definitely not equal. On the contrary, in spite of their common source in the one fundamental sin some are more weighty than others. The Irish Articles also state that "all sins are not equal, but some far more heinous than others" (S 531). But unlike the Second Helvetic Confession, the Irish Articles do not continue the tradition of differentiating mortal from venial sins. Instead, despite the difference between individual sins, the text declares that "the very least is of its own nature mortal, and, without God's mercy, maketh the offender liable unto everlasting damnation" (S 531).

ORIGINAL SIN AND PUNISHMENT OF SIN

That assertion already broaches the topic of the relation between sin and punishment. On the basis of sin—that is, "by our own deserts"—we are "subject to the wrath of God" and "liable to just punishment" (C 235). Through this sin human beings make themselves guilty before God, and thus bring just punishment upon themselves. "Every sin, both original and actual . . . doth, in its own nature, bring guilt upon the sinner, whereby he is bound over to the wrath of God and curse of the law, and so made subject to death, with all miseries spiritual, temporal, and eternal" (S 616). As sinners human beings are liable to death as their just punishment. This means not only bodily death (*mors corporalis*) but primarily eternal death (*mors aeterna* or *sempiterna*) (C 235; 167; M 660, 39). For God "is terribly displeased with our inborn as well as actual sins, and will punish them in just judgement in time and eternity" (S 310). The Hungarian Confession accordingly distinguishes between the first, corporeal death and the second, eternal death as together composing the punishment for sin imposed on every human being. The first death consists in the fact that the soul leaves the body. This view presupposes the dualistic construction of the human person out of "an immortal soul which, when separated from the body, neither sleeps nor dies, and a mortal body which will nevertheless be raised up from the dead at the last judgment, in order that then the whole man, either in life or in death, abide forever" (C 235; cf. 102; 660, 15ff.). The first, corporeal death is not of everlasting duration, but ends with the resurrection of the dead to judgment. This judgment then has as a consequence the second, eternal death, in which the body, too, is exposed to continual tortures of death (M 379, 32ff.). Eternal death is thus the punishment of everlasting separation from God (M 615, 37ff.), the condemnation "to death itself, and to the pains of hell forever" (S 680).

But it is true not only that every human being is characterized by the fundamental sin as a dispositional sinfulness, and for this reason receives this punishment. Rather the fundamental sin is traced back to Adam's fall. The fact that each particular human individual is a sinner is not the result of his or her free decision. Nor can it be the case that individual human beings first become sinners by the *imitation* of Adam's sin—imitation it would also be possible for them to avoid. The individual is not free either to be a sinner or to be sinless. The individual is in fact always already a sinner. The rejection of the thesis that human beings first become sinners by imitating Adam is directed against a Pelagian understanding of sin. "The error of the Pelagians, who assert that sin proceeds only from imitation" (S 401), is explicitly rejected. With regard to the understanding of sin, the Second Helvetic Confession can declare that "in this whole matter we agree with St. Augustine who derived and defended his view from Holy Scriptures" (C 236).

Indeed, sinfulness is grasped in its radicality only when it is considered as a disposition that is not the result of free actions, and thus is not acquired by the individual. This manner of considering sin finds its expression in the thesis of the Belgic Confession that "infants themselves are infected [with sin] even in their mother's womb" (S 400). Sin is an "innate corruption (*nativa corruptio*) of man" (C 235, S 247), so "that we are all *conceived* and *born* in sin" (S 310; cf. M 268, 16–17). The sinfulness of human beings is not the result of human action, but forms the presupposition of that action. The individual does not *become* a sinner; she already *is* a sinner.

What is the relation between the sin of every individual of the human species and the sin of Adam? Since Augustine the classical answer has been that the sinfulness of individuals is not acquired, but *inherited*. "We believe that all the posterity of Adam is in bondage to original sin, which is an hereditary evil, and not an imitation merely, as was declared by the Pelagians, whom we detest in their errors" (S 365). The French Confession here characterizes sin as original and fundamental sin (*péché originel*), and this in turn as hereditary sin (*vice héréditaire*). The connection between Adam's fall from the original estate of creation and the sinfulness of the human species is such that, "through the disobedience of Adam, original sin (*péché originel*) is extended to all mankind; which is a corruption of the whole nature, and an hereditary disease (*vice héréditaire*), wherewith infants themselves are infected even in their mother's womb" (S 400). Sin is thus an innate corruption of human nature, a corruption that "has been derived or propagated in us all from our first parents" (C 235). That is, sin is a corruption that is always given with the fact of human existence.

This means that all human beings, insofar as they descend from Adam, are sinners. "Original sin standeth not in the imitation of Adam . . . but is the fault and corruption of the nature of every person that naturally is engendered and propagated from Adam: whereby it cometh to pass that man is deprived of original righteousness, and by nature is bent unto sin" (S 530). All human beings except Christ (*solo Christo excepto*) are sinners on the basis of their belonging to the species that descends from Adam (S 640–41). In this context the French Confession explicitly declares it unnecessary to decide between traducianism and creationism: that is, "to inquire *how* sin was conveyed from one man to another"—in other words, how sin is inherited (S 365).

The thesis that on the basis of Adam's sin all human beings are sinners changes in an essential way the understanding of sin advanced by Zwingli. At first it seems that Zwingli's understanding is no different from that encountered in the other confessions. The Zurich Introduction itself says that "we are all sinners from birth, for we are all born of Adam. Before ever giving birth Adam had already fallen into sin, infirmity and death. As a result all who come from Adam inherit from Adam such infirmity. For the fallen, sinful Adam can no more give birth to a sinless human being than a human being can give birth to an angel" (M 8, 2–8). As Adam's progeny, human beings are all infirm (M 8, 21). They are thus incapable of any good and born with the inclination to evil (M 8, 46ff.).

This description of sin certainly matches that of the later confessions. Nevertheless, Zwingli defines the relation of Adam's sin to the sin of the human species in a way that differs from the later confessions. The Account of Faith declares that one can speak of sin in the proper sense (*peccatum proprie captum*) only when a violation of the law occurs (M 82, 30ff.). Zwingli starts from the assumption that sin in the proper sense is a crime (*crimen*) and a misdeed (*facinus*)—that is, an offense (*reatus*). The act of incurring guilt is the transgression of a law, so that sin as guilt presupposes the existence of a law which someone violates. For this reason, while Adam's fall is certainly a sin in the proper sense, "his descendants have not sinned in this manner, for who among us has crushed with his teeth the forbidden apple in Paradise? Hence, willing or unwilling, we are forced to admit that original sin, as it is in the children of Adam, is not properly sin" (Z 40).

Zwingli defines original sin not as sin in the proper sense—that is, as offense (*reatus*), but as sickness (*morbus*) and destiny (*conditio*). For we also fall *as* Adam fell, and we are also born as slaves *as* Adam was made a slave. Original sin is thus understood primarily as the enslavement of the human species. Although on the basis of divine righteousness God could have demanded Adam's annihilation, God did not do so, but made Adam a slave. The one who was free became a slave. Accordingly, all Adam's progeny belong to the estate of slavery. They are in bondage because of their origin, and thus are already in bondage at birth. "A prisoner of war by his perfidy and hostile conduct has deserved to be held as a slave. His descendants become serfs (*oichetai*) or slaves of their master, not by their own fault (*culpa*), crime (*crimen*) or offense (*reatus*), but by their condition which was the result of fault" (Z 41, trans. altered; M 83, 22–25). The innate sinfulness of all human beings is a sickness and a destiny, but unlike Adam's sin it is not their own fault, although Zwingli has nothing against following Pauline usage in designating this sickness and this destiny as sin. Only this presupposition makes comprehensible his agreement with the fourth Marburg Article, which says that "hereditary sin is innate in us, inherited from Adam, and it is a sin that damns all human beings" (BSLK 53, 32–33).

By contrast, the confessions whose lineage does not go back to Zwingli agree with the Augsburg Confession that original sin is not only a sickness and a destiny but a sin in the proper sense. Article 2 of the Augsburg Confession expressly maintains that "this inborn sickness (*morbus*) and hereditary sin is truly sin" (BC 29; BSLK 53, 7–8). The corresponding passage in the French Confession says "that this evil (*vice*) is truly (*vraiment*) sin, sufficient for the condemnation of the whole human race, even of little children in the mother's womb" (S 366). The Belgic Confession puts it as follows: "We believe that, through the disobedience of Adam, original sin is extended to all mankind; which is a corruption of the whole nature, and an hereditary disease (*vice héréditaire*), wherewith infants themselves are infected even in their mother's womb . . . and therefore is so vile and abominable in the sight of God that it is sufficient to condemn all mankind" (S 400).

Original sin must be understood in a double sense. On the one hand, it is an inherited sin that inheres in human beings: that is, a corruption of the whole nature of the human person or an inherited depravity (*haereditarium inhaerens*). On the other hand, original sin is also the sin of Adam imputed to us (*imputatum*). According to the Westminster Confession, God made the covenant of works with Adam not as a private person, but as a public person: namely, as the representative of all humanity. Thus Adam's breaking of that covenant must also be attributed to him as the representative of the human species. "The covenant being made with Adam, not only for himself, but for his posterity, all mankind descending from him by ordinary generation, sinned in him, and fell with him, in his first transgression" (S 679). If Adam sinned not as a private person, but as the representative of humanity, then in Adam all human beings have sinned and in Adam all are guilty. Adam's sin can be directly imputed to them by God. The Westminster Confession thus can say of the first human couple: "They being the root of all mankind, the guilt of this sin was imputed, and the same death in sin and corrupted nature conveyed to all their posterity descending from them by ordinary generation" (S 615).

Because Adam sinned as our head and source (*ut capite et stirpe*), and thus his sin is a crime of all humanity, it is understandable that God punishes us with original sin as inherited depravity (M 864, 36ff.). For this reason the Helvetic Consensus Formula takes a position against Placeus's understanding of sin, which approximates Zwingli's. Placeus is of the opinion that God can consider us guilty only on the basis of inherited depravity that has become our own. Adam sins not as the representative of all humanity, but only as the first in a chain of generations—a chain that is afflicted with the consequences of the first sin. Placeus accordingly asserts that God imputes Adam's sin to us not immediately, but mediately: namely, on the basis of the hereditary depravity proper to us, the depravity that has come down to us from Adam.

But the Helvetic Consensus Formula sees that as a threat to original sin itself. "Therefore everyone is subject to the wrath and curse from the very beginning, before he actually sins, and this in two ways: first, because of the disobedience committed in Adam's loins; second, because of the resulting corruption. Consequently original sin is differentiated into two aspects: imputed sin and hereditary inherent sin. Therefore we do not give assent to those who do not concede that Adam represented us and that his sin is immediately imputed to us, but instead claim that an imputation occurs only mediately and after the fact, on account of the inherited corruption. This position places original sin itself in danger" (M 865, 7–20).

COVENANT OF GRACE
AND RECONCILIATION

THE NEW COVENANT

In adopting covenant theology, the Westminster Confession conceives the relation between God and human beings in the original estate of creation as a covenant that God made with Adam. This covenant was broken by the Fall and thus one-sidedly abrogated. The Westminster Confession then goes on to declare: "Man by his fall having made himself incapable of life by that covenant, the Lord was pleased to make a second, commonly called the covenant of grace" (S 617). God's new covenant with human beings, made after the Fall, differs by its covenant conditions from the old covenant that was canceled by the Fall. The old covenant promises eternal life to Adam, and in Adam to his entire progeny, on condition of his complete obedience. The new covenant no longer poses this condition. The new covenant is not a covenant of works (*foedus operum*) based on the performance of certain works, but a covenant of grace (*foedus gratiae*). The covenant of grace is the expression of the fact that God is not prepared to give up on human beings, despite their apostasy from God. It is also the "no" to the restitution of a covenantal relation, the conditions of which human beings after the Fall are no longer capable of fulfilling. Sinful human beings prove themselves to be totally incapable of performing the works that are required of them in the covenant of works. The covenant of grace is a covenant in which God freely offers life and salvation to sinful human beings. In the covenant of grace God "freely offered unto sinners life and salvation by Jesus Christ, requiring of them faith in him that they may be saved, and promising to give unto all those that are ordained unto life his Holy Spirit, to make them willing and able to believe" (S 617).

Unlike the old covenant, the new covenant relates to Christ, through whom or in whom life and salvation are offered to us. In order to enjoy the promise attached to this covenant, the only condition that must be fulfilled on the side of sinful human beings, incapable of any good work, is to believe in Christ. This covenant of grace can be characterized as a testament. Sinful human beings are heirs who with Christ's death come into their inheritance, which Christ himself as testator has bequeathed upon them. Insofar as sinners are taken up into the covenant of grace only in or through Christ—that is, as Christ's heirs—the role of mediator of the covenant belongs to Christ. Only in Christ are we members of the covenant of grace. As in Adam we were all members of the covenant of works, so in Christ as the second Adam we are members of the covenant of grace (M 615, 47–48). In establishing the covenant of grace, God offers us Christ as mediator and through him life and salvation, not on condition of a required achievement on our part, but on condition of faith alone.

God does not first make this covenant of grace in Christ with sinful humanity at the time of the historical appearance of Jesus of Nazareth. The Heidelberg Catechism poses the question of the source of our knowledge that Christ has been given to us as the mediator for our complete redemption and righteousness. It then gives the following answer: "From the Holy Gospel, which God himself first revealed in Paradise, afterwards proclaimed by the holy Patriarchs and Prophets, and foreshadowed by the sacrifices and other ceremonies of the law, and finally fulfilled by his well-beloved Son" (S 313). The declaration or revelation of the gospel as the message of Christ's reconciling death occurs in Paradise itself: that is, immediately after the Fall. The covenant of grace is made with the fallen Adam, so that potentially all human beings are members of this covenant.

The exegetical basis for this thesis is furnished by the protogospel of Genesis 3:15. As early as the First Confession of Basle we find the promise given directly after the Fall being advanced as a sign for the fact that "God never ceased to care for the human race" (C 92–93; cf. 102–3). And the Scottish Confession says explicitly "that God, after the fearful and horrible departure of man from His obedience, did seek Adam again, call upon him, rebuke and convict him of his sin, and in the end made unto him a most joyful promise, that 'the seed of the woman should bruise the head of the serpent,' that is, that he should destroy the works of the devil" (C 167). God promised Adam that God "would give his Son, who should be made of a woman . . . and would make him happy" (S 402). The covenant of grace in Christ is thus made by God already with fallen Adam, since it is Adam to whom the promise of Christ is first communicated. The Savoy Declaration follows covenant theology's elaboration of the idea of the covenant of grace, grounding the covenant of grace in a pact or covenant made between Father and Son for the redemption of fallen humanity. "It pleased God in his eternal Purpose, to choose and ordain the Lord Jesus his only begotten Son, according to a Covenant made between them both, to be the Mediator between God and Man" (M 560, 27–31).

All of postlapsarian history is to be interpreted in light of the presupposition of the covenant of grace. As a result those who lived before Christ's historical appearance are not excluded from the covenant of grace, but are also addressees of the divine promise of eternal life. This excludes the possibility of interpreting the promises given to the patriarchs merely as promises of temporal goods. This is not to dispute the fact that promises were communicated to the patriarchs, as to us as well, which "were of present or earthly things, such as the promises of the Land of Canaan and of victories, and as the promise today still of daily bread" (C 249). But the decisive point is that both then and now there have been promises not of temporal and earthly things, but "of heavenly and eternal things, namely, divine grace, remission of sins, and eternal life through faith in Jesus Christ" (ibid.). The contents of the promises made to the patriarchs are not merely transitory goods. Instead those promises already relate to Jesus Christ, who is the object of our faith and in whom we participate in life and salvation (S 540–41, 491–92). In this sense the Scottish Confession affirms that the promise that was made to fallen Adam and that grounds the covenant of grace "was embraced with joy, and most constantly received by all the faithful from Adam to Noah, from Noah to Abraham, from Abraham to David, and so onwards to the incarnation of Christ Jesus; all (we mean the believing fathers under the law) did see the joyful day of Christ Jesus, and did rejoice" (C 167).

Because of the substantial identity between the Old Testament and the New Testament, the relation between the two cannot be defined as opposition. In view of this identity it even becomes difficult to speak of two testaments. For if the covenant of grace is characterized as a testament, but applies to both the Old and New Testament, one should actually speak of only one testament. With the exception of the Erlauthal Confession—which, picking up on Melanchthon, explicitly speaks not only of two testaments but also of two covenants: the Old Testament covenant of law and the New Testament covenant of grace (M 273, 44ff.)—the confessions define the relation between the Old and New Testament in such a way that the substantial identity of the covenant of grace comes clearly to expression. Thus we read in the Irish Articles of Religion: "The Old Testament is not contrary to the New. For in both the Old and New Testament everlasting life is offered to mankind by Christ, who is the only mediator between God and man" (S 540).

Given the presupposition that both testaments have to do with the one covenant of grace, the difference between the Old and New Testament can lie only in the diverging administration and economy of this covenant. The Hungarian Confession accordingly declares that since Adam there has always been essentially only a single covenant between God and fallen humanity: namely, the covenant of grace made in Christ. But one can certainly speak of two testaments and even two covenants, in view of the difference in clarity, and above all because of the fact that Christ is an object of each testament in a different way (M 381, 19ff.). "In the Old Testament . . . the promises of Christ (were) more sparingly and darkly propounded, shadowed with a multitude of types and figures, and so much the more generally and obscurely delivered, as the manifesting of them was further off" (S 540). For the Irish Articles the central difference between the Old and New Testament proves to be the fact that Christ is given as the object of faith in a different way in the two cases. While Old Testament faith is directed to the coming mediator, New Testament faith has as its object the mediator who has already come (S 541).

The Westminster Confession and the Helvetic Consensus Formula give conclusive formulation to this view of the difference between the Old and New Testament when they declare that, while there is an identity of substance of the covenant of grace, one must speak of a difference in this covenant's administration. "This covenant was differently administered in the time of the law and in the time of the gospel" (S 617). "There are not, therefore, two covenants of grace differing in substance, but one and the same under various dispensations" (S 618; cf. M 868, 42ff.). The Old and New Testaments do not present two covenants, but two administrations of a single covenant. In the time of the law the covenant's adminstration occurred through promises, prophecies, sacrifice, circumcision, Passover lamb, and so forth, all of which point to Christ as mediator. Under the gospel the covenant's administration is carried out through the proclamation of the word and the distribution of the sacraments of Baptism and the Lord's Supper.

In spite of this differing administration of the one covenant, it can be truly said of the Old Testament covenant institutions, in their exclusive relation to Israel, that they "were for that time sufficient and efficacious, through the operation of the Spirit, to instruct and build up the elect in faith in the promised Messiah, by whom they had full remission of sins and eternal salvation" (S 618). The differing institutions through which the administration of the covenant of grace occurs in the Old and New Testament are thereby means of grace in the strict sense. Through both types of means of grace one and the same substance is offered: namely, the mediator Jesus Christ, whom Old Testament faith has for its object as the one who is coming, and whom New Testament faith has for its object as the one who has come. With their thesis of the double administration of the substantially identical covenant of grace, the Westminster Confession and the Helvetic Consensus Formula oppose the thesis advanced by John Cameron and Moyse Amyraut in the school of Saumur, which holds that there are three substantially different covenants of God with humanity: namely, the covenant of works or of nature, the covenant of grace, and the covenant of law (*foedus legale*) (M 869, 19ff.). The rejection of a particular covenant of law is intended to avoid the impression that persons who lived before Christ's historical appearance are excluded from the covenant of grace and thus are not addressees of the promise of Christ.

RECONCILIATION AND SUBSTITUTION

Christ is the mediator of the covenant of grace, insofar as he appears as reconciler. One would of course be completely misguided if one thought that God's mind first had to be changed, in order for God then to be favorably inclined toward humanity. Instead, God is the subject of the event of reconciliation. God sends the divine Son into the world to take on human nature and thus to be able to be our mediator. Zwingli's Account of Faith understands this to be an expression and revelation of God's goodness (*bonitas*) and mercy (Z 39). "Who can sufficiently marvel at the riches and grace of the divine goodness, whereby He so loved the world, i.e., the human race, as to give up His Son for its life?" (ibid.). If the very sending of the Son is an expression of the loving divine will, this excludes the possibility that it is only by the action and suffering of the Son that God's mind is changed to embrace reconciliation. Such a change of mind does not take place in God, because from eternity God is a loving—that is, a merciful—God.

The French Confession rightly emphasizes "that God, in sending his Son, intended to show his love and inestimable goodness toward us, giving him up to die to accomplish all righteousness, and raising him from the dead to secure for us the heavenly life" (S 369). The French Confession goes on to highlight that Christ's sacrifice does not reconcile God to the world, but the world to God. "We believe that by the perfect sacrifice that the Lord Jesus offered on the cross, we are reconciled to God" (ibid.). Nevertheless, this view is not always strictly maintained, but sometimes is supplemented by the contrary idea that God is reconciled by Christ's sacrifice. Already in Zwingli we read "that our Lord Christ Jesus, true Son of God, has made known to us the will of his heavenly Father, and with his innocence has redeemed us from death, and has reconciled God" (M 2, 21–23). The Latin text of the Scottish Confession declares that Christ is the "fit mediator between God and human beings" (S 445), who "by his death has reconciled the Father to us" (S 447).

Reconciliation is conceived as effected by Christ's substitution. In this context the Heidelberg Catechism, like the Hungarian Confession and the Westminster Confession, takes recourse to Anselm of Canterbury's doctrine of satisfaction, but modifies it at a decisive point. For here Christ's death no longer appears as the achievement of satisfaction that restores God's offended honor, but as the substitutionary suffering of punishment. This view sets God's righteousness in opposition to God's mercy. God's righteousness requires that Adam's sin against God be avenged with the highest penalty—that is, an eternal one—imposed on the body and soul of human beings who, in Adam, are sinful. This raises the question of how we can avoid this penalty and come again to grace. "God wills that his justice be satisfied; therefore must we make full satisfaction to the same, either by ourselves or by another" (S 311). God is merciful not in the sense of simply dropping the penalty. Instead God's righteousness requires that payment be made for our sin. Human sin must be expiated, because otherwise God would not be acting justly. The reconcilation that God wills on the basis of the divine mercy can only occur in such a way that it does not offend God's righteousness.

It is clear that, because of our sinfulness, we are not capable of paying for this sin. We are unable to perform a satisfaction or restitution. As sinners we are not capable of liberating ourselves from the punishment imposed on us because of our sin. Self-redemption is thus excluded. Every attempt to trace redemption back even in part to a human action must shipwreck on the recognition that, as sinners, human beings are not even capable of a good intention. We cannot "ourselves make this satisfaction." Instead "we daily increase our guilt" (ibid.). It is also impossible that any other creature could perform the satisfaction required in order to have the penalty dropped. This excludes the possibility of having another creature substitute for human beings. No creature can pay our debt "for us"—that is, in our place. There are two reasons for this. First, it would be unjust to have another creature atone for the sin of human beings. The punishment for sin can be imposed only upon the sinners themselves. In this sense it is an expression of the divine righteousness that "God will not punish, in any other creature, that of which man has made himself guilty" (S 311–12). Because of the divine righteousness, God does not will to saddle any other species with the penalty that the human species has earned. Yet not only is God, because of the divine righteousness, unable to will that option; it is also the case that "no mere creature can sustain the burden of God's eternal wrath against sin, and redeem others therefrom" (S 312). No creature, regardless of the species to which it belongs, can liberate and unburden human beings by taking away their punishment, because no creature is capable of bearing the punishment imposed by the righteous God on the human species. The guilt of sin and the penalty for sin are proportionate to each other, so that human beings, who by offending God's majesty have brought infinite guilt upon themselves, have earned an infinite penalty (M 382, 22ff.). The highest guilt incurs the highest penalty, which a creature, because of the creature's finitude, is simply incapable of bearing.

The impossibility of human self-redemption and of the redemption of human beings by creaturely substitution demonstrates the necessity of a divine-human mediator who will effect the redemption of the human race. "What manner of mediator and redeemer, then, must we seek? One who is a true and sinless man, and yet more powerful than all creatures; that is, one who is at the same time true God" (S 312). The mediator of the covenant of grace, who alone is capable of redeeming us from our sin by bearing the penalty intended for us, must be both a human being and God. The necessity of the mediator's human nature results from the fact that the divine righteousness requires that humankind, and not some other creaturely species, pay for human sin. The sin of humankind incurs a penalty that must in turn be borne by humankind. For this reason the mediator who bears the penalty for sin must be a member of the human race, a true human being. For "the justice of God requires that the same human nature which has sinned should make satisfaction for sin" (S 312). Such satisfaction or payment cannot be performed by us as members of fallen humanity. For this reason it is necessary that the mediator who pays for our sin be not only a true human being, but also a human being who is free from all sin. The sinlessness of the mediator in no way cancels the mediator's true human nature. As God's creatures, human beings are good according to their essence. They are not created as sinners. They are guilty of sin by their own action. Just as sinfulness does not belong to human nature, human sinlessness does not cancel that nature, with the result that a sinless human being would *eo ipso* not be a true human being. On the contrary, the sinless human being is the human being who corresponds to what he or she was ordained to be in creation, insofar as it is only as sinless that he or she does justice to the image of God.

The mediator who pays for human sin must therefore be a sinless human being, because "no man, being himself a sinner, could satisfy for others" (S 312). A sinful human being could not only not pay for others, he or she could not even pay for him- or herself, because on the basis of his or her sinfulness his or her guilt for sin would daily increase. This means that the mediator must be not only a true human being, but also a righteous one—a human being distinguished by that property of original righteousness that Adam possessed before the Fall and lost by the Fall. But the mediator cannot be merely a true human being and one who corresponds to the image of God: that is, a righteous human being. For no "mere creature" is capable of bearing the penalty for sin that humanity deserves. This penalty is infinite, corresponding to the infinity of guilt. This penalty cannot be borne by a being who is merely creaturely: that is, finite. The mediator must be a human being, but must be one who at the same time is "more powerful than all creatures: that is, one who is at the same time true God" (S 312). As God, the mediator, who is also true human being, is infinite and for this reason possesses the power to bear the penalty imposed on human beings, which as merely human he would be unable to bear. The mediator must be true God, so that "by the power of his God head he might bear, in his manhood, the burden of God's wrath" (ibid.). Only as one who is also God is the human mediator capable of bearing for us—that is, substituting for all of humankind and in its place—the penalty of suffering imposed on sinful humanity and thereby satisfying the divine righteousness. As the reconciliation in general is an expression of God's mercy, the way in which it is carried out is an expression of God's righteousness. It is not a cheap reconciliation, but a costly one (cf. M 381, 39ff.; 616, 40ff.).

It is revealing that the Heidelberg Catechism's doctrine of reconciliation is unfolded in separation from Christ (*remoto Christo*). The necessity of a divine-human mediator is demonstrated completely independently of the fact that Christ is this divine-human mediator. First the question of how we could avoid the just punishment for sin and again attain to grace is answered with reference to the mediator office of a divine-human being who bears the punishment for sin in our place and regains righteousness and life for us. Only then is Christ characterized as "that mediator, who is at the same time true God and a true, sinless man" (S 312). The other confessions take the fact of the revelation in Christ as their *point of departure* and conceive Christ as the divine-human mediator between God and human beings, characterized by his substitutionary suffering of punishment. By contrast, the Heidelberg Catechism abstracts from the revelation in Christ and *constructs*, independently of that revelation, the necessary divine-human nature of the mediator—necessary for the sake of human redemption. This mediator is then finally identified as the Christ attested by the gospel. To be sure, the mediator no longer offers his suffering *in place of* the penalty but bears that suffering *as* the penalty imposed on humanity for sin. Nor does he bear that penalty to satisfy God's *honor*, but rather to satisfy God's *righteousness*. Yet in spite of these differences of content from Anselm's doctrine of satisfaction, the Heidelberg Catechism, like the Hungarian and the Westminster Confession, retains the method of that doctrine: that is, the a priori deduction of the divine-human mediator.

SATISFACTION AND THREEFOLD OFFICE

It is primarily Jesus' death that is understood as making satisfaction. The French Confession declares "that Jesus Christ is our complete and perfect cleansing, and that in his death we have complete satisfaction" (S 369, trans. altered). In the Belgic Confession we read "that God, who is perfectly merciful and also perfectly just, sent his Son to assume that nature in which the disobedience was committed, to make satisfaction (*satisfaceret*) in the same, and to bear the punishment of sin by his most bitter passion and death. . . . [Jesus Christ] hath presented himself in our behalf before the Father, to appease his wrath by his full satisfaction (*plena satisfactione*), by offering himself on the tree of the cross, and pouring out his precious blood to purge away our sins" (S 405–6; M 240, 10, 20). These texts speak of Christ's suffering, culminating in his death, as something that makes satisfaction. That which makes satisfaction is the suffering of punishment that Christ undergoes in our place, and that comes to a conclusion in Jesus' death on the cross. Satisfaction is thus primarily at issue in the interpretation of those statements of the Apostles' Creed that refer to Jesus' suffering and death.

All other events of Jesus' life are placed in functional relation to his death. With regard to the content of Christian preaching the Synodical Declaration of Berne states that "the beginning must be made with Christ's death and resurrection" (M 37, 7). But that raises the question, "If one must begin and end with Christ's death and resurrection, what is the purpose of the evangelists, who describe his birth and his life?" (M 37, 38–40). According to the Geneva Catechism, the Apostles' Creed first talks about the incarnation as the presupposition of the reconciliation that is to occur in human nature. The second article of the Creed immediately proceeds to Christ's suffering, so that the question arises, "Why do you go immediately from His birth to His death, passing over the whole history of His life?" (T 13). The Catechism's answer to this question is revealing: "Because nothing is said here about what belongs properly to the substance of our redemption" (ibid.). The event that constitutes the essence of redemption is Jesus' suffering and death, insofar as they are penalties that Christ takes upon himself for us in a substitutionary way. "He dies to suffer the punishment due to us, and thus to deliver us from it" (T 14). His substitution for us lies not just in the fact that he *died* for us. To highlight the penal character of the death that we have earned as sinners, he was *condemned* to death. "Because we were guilty before the judgement of God as evil-doers, in order to represent us in person He was pleased to appear before the tribunal of an earthly judge, and to be condemned by his mouth, that we might be acquitted before the throne of the celestial Judge" (ibid.).

The Scottish Confession declares that "it behoved the Messiah and Redeemer . . . to present Himself in the presence of His Father's Judgment, as in our stead, to suffer for our transgression and disobedience, and by death to overcome him that was the author of death" (C 169). This substitutionary suffering of punishment presupposes that Christ himself is without sin. "If he had been a sinner He could not have suffered death for others" (T 14). Sinlessness is thus a necessary condition for Christ's substitutionary action. As a sinner he would himself fall under the same judgment whose consequences he takes upon himself in our place. Therefore Christ must indeed be a true human being, but at the same time be sinless. He is like us in all things, with the exception of sin (C 103; M 381, 39ff.; S 496, 531; M 561, 1ff.). He must be sinless in order to be able to *substitute* for us in suffering the punishment for sin. He must be a true human being in order to be able to substitute for *us* in suffering it.

But since sin has corrupted not only our body but also our soul, Christ's becoming human means not merely that he assumed a human body. According to the Belgic Confession, Christ "did not only assume human nature as to the body, but also a true human soul, that he might be a real man. For since the soul was lost as well as the body, it was necessary that he should take both upon him, to save both" (S 403). In becoming human he assumed the *whole* of human nature, because human beings are sinners not only in one part of their nature, but in their entire nature. The subject of sin is the whole human being. For this reason Christ can substitute for *human beings* in suffering the punishment for sin only if he is *wholly* human. Christ is this true—that is, complete—human being, but unlike all other human beings after the Fall he is sinless. As this true but sinless human being Christ takes upon himself the punishment for sin, the death under a curse, intended for us. The substitutionary character of Jesus' death finds its external expression in the fact that Christ is executed despite being found innocent by Pilate. The Geneva Catechism states that "he was justified by the testimony of the judge, to show that He did not suffer for His own unworthiness but for ours, and yet He was solemnly condemned by the sentence of the same judge, to show that He is truly our surety, receiving condemnation for us in order to acquit us from it" (T 14).

The death to which the earthly authorities condemn Jesus is no usual death, but death under a curse. Crucifixion as the chosen manner of death is not something accidental. On the contrary, according to the Heidelberg Catechism, the crucifixion provides the assurance that Christ "took on himself the curse which lay upon me" (S 320). The fact that Christ takes on himself the *curse* that lies upon sinful human beings finds its expression in his dying an *accursed death*. The Geneva Catechism declares that "He hanged on a tree to take our curse upon Himself and acquit us of it (Gal. 3:13). For that kind of death was accursed of God (Deut. 21:23). . . . Since death was the curse on man as a result of sin, Jesus Christ has endured it, and in enduring it overcame it" (T 14–15). The suffering of an accursed death must not be conceived as a merely physical suffering. The one who dies death under the curse experiences God's anger in the soul as well. For death as the punishment imposed on humankind fallen prey to sin affects the soul of human beings as much as the body. It is a punishment that annihilates the whole person, just as it is the whole person, body and soul, and not just a part, who sins. This punishment is eternal death as the removal of any sort of communion with God. In this way the fact that Christ dies for us death under the curse finds its most profound expression in the cry of abandonment by God on the cross. For Christ "suffered, the just for the unjust, as well in his body as in his soul, feeling the terrible punishment which our sins had merited; insomuch that his sweat became like unto drops of blood falling on the ground. He called out, My God, my God, why hast thou forsaken me?" (S 407). "He suffered not only the cruel death of the cross, which was accursed by the sentence of God; . . . also . . . He suffered for a season the wrath of His Father which sinners had deserved" (C 170).

According to most of the confessions, it is this pain of the soul, the pain of the most extreme abandonment by God, to which the Apostles' Creed's statement about Christ's descent into hell refers. The descent into hell is not to be understood as a spatial movement to a particular place. It is not an event that is independent of the crucifixion and temporally posterior to it. The statement about the descent into hell must be grasped as a circumlocution for the "inexpressible anguish, pains, and terrors which he suffered in his soul on the cross and before" (S 321). In Zwingli's Exposition of Faith he gives two meanings for the expression "descent into hell." First, it is used as a circumlocution for the actual death. Second, tying into 1 Peter 3:19, it is used to state that the power of reconciliation reached even down into the underworld, where Christ preaches the gospel to the believers of the old covenant. The interpretation that won out in the confessions picks up on the first meaning and sees the descent into hell as the soul's most profound torment of abandonment by God on the cross. According to the Geneva Catechism, the reference to Christ's descent into hell means Christ "not only suffered natural death, which is the separation of the body from the soul, but also that His soul was pierced with amazing anguish, which St. Peter calls the pains of death (Acts 2:24)" (T 15). The necessity of this death of abandonment by God, this death of the soul, results from the fact that this death, like natural death, belongs to the punishment imposed on fallen humanity, which Christ takes upon himself for our sake. "Because He presented Himself to God in order to make satisfaction in the name of sinners, it was necessary that He should suffer fearful distress of conscience" (ibid.).

This does not mean, though, that God objectively turned away from Christ and made him the object of the divine anger. On the contrary, the Belgic Confession emphasizes that Christ "remained the only, well beloved, and blessed Son of His Father even in the midst of His anguish and torment which he suffered in body and soul to make full atonement for the sins of His people" (C 170). The Geneva Catechism can understand Christ's cry on the cross only as the expression of such torment "*as if* He had been forsaken by God, and even *as if* God had become hostile to Him" (T 15). Jesus' torment is no sign of God's anger being directed against *him*. "But He had to be afflicted in this way in fulfilment of what had been foretold by Isaiah, that 'he was smitten by the hand of God for our sins and wounded for our transgressions'" (ibid.). In addition to natural death, Christ also suffers the death of the soul as the punishment for sin intended for us, although he does so in a way that is quantitatively, though not qualitatively, different. "He was not to remain under it. . . . Thus we see the difference between the torment which He suffered and that which sinners experience when God punishes them in His wrath. For what He suffered for a time in Himself is perpetual in the others" (T 16). In this way it is true that "what was only a needle to sting Him is to them a sword to deliver a mortal wound" (ibid.). Of primary importance, though, is the fact that Jesus' obedience toward God makes his comportment on the cross essentially different from the comportment of sinners. "For Jesus Christ, even in the midst of such distress, did not cease to hope in God. But sinners whom God condemns rush into despair, defy, and even blaspheme Him" (ibid.).

It is primarily Christ's act of taking on the punishment for sin—that is, death under the curse—that is understood as making satisfaction. The act of taking on that punishment is an expression of Christ's obedience toward the Father who sent him into the world as mediator. To be sure, the Father called Christ to the office of mediator. But it is also true "that our Lord Jesus offered Himself a voluntary sacrifice unto His Father for us" (C 169). This means that Christ's death, interpreted as sacrifice, is to be understood as a *self*-sacrifice on Christ's part. "By offering up Himself He made satisfaction to God for our sins and the sins of all believers and reconciled us to God, our heavenly Father" (C 92). Insofar as he voluntarily took death upon himself as the penalty for sin, he demonstrated himself to be the Son who accepts the office proffered him by the Father and thus is obedient to the Father. This obedience is *passive* obedience (*oboedientia passiva*) or obedience in *suffering*.

A series of confessions regard only this obedience in suffering as making satisfaction. For instance, the Canons of the Dordrecht Synod state that "the death of the Son of God is the only and most perfect sacrifice and satisfaction for sin; is of infinite worth and value, abundantly sufficient to expiate the sins of the whole world" (S 586). But even where the penal suffering that Christ bears in our place is not confined to his death—for instance, where the Heidelberg Catechism says of Christ "that all the time he lived on earth, but especially at the end of his life, he bore, in body and soul, the wrath of God against the sin of the whole human race" (S 319)—it is still only Christ's passive obedience that is regarded as making satisfaction. The fact that Christ is a perfectly holy—that is, a sinless—human being (*perfecte sanctus homo*), the fact that Christ completely fulfills God's law and thus is *actively* obedient, is in this case regarded as not itself belonging to the satisfaction that Christ makes. Instead it is regarded as the presupposition and necessary condition of the possibility of that satisfaction (S 586). The power to make satisfaction is a property of Christ's suffering only because Christ himself does not transgress the law, and thus proves that he is holy. The "satisfactory" quality of Christ's suffering obedience requires Christ's perfect fulfillment of the law, even though this fulfillment does not itself make satisfaction. The fulfillment of the law is the indispensable cause (*causa sine qua non*) of the "satisfactory" character of Christ's penal suffering. Nevertheless, we find already in the Second Helvetic Confession the refusal to confine the process of making satisfaction to Christ's suffering. The Confession declares that "by his passion and death and everything which he *did* and endured for our sake by his coming in the flesh, our Lord reconciled all the faithful to the heavenly Father" (C 246; cf. M 185, 8ff.; C 121). This view includes Christ's *active* obedience (*oboedientia activa*) in the process of making satisfaction.

The opposing thesis, advanced by Johannes Piscator and the Saumur school, that as a true human being Christ could fulfill the law only for himself, and had to do so in order to create the precondition for the act of making satisfaction, is finally explicitly rejected by the Helvetic Consensus Formula. According to the latter, Christ's passive obedience forms only the conclusion and point of culmination of a life that includes his active obedience, and bears "satisfactory" character as a whole (M 866, 4ff.). Thus the Irish Articles of Religion can say that "he fulfilled the law *for us* perfectly" (S 531, cf. 620).

In spite of the diversity of interpretive categories familiar to the New Testament, the satisfaction made by Christ is described primarily in priestly categories. Reconciliation is conceived as instituted by a sacrifice: specifically, a self-sacrifice of Christ the High Priest. The Epistle to the Hebrews' doctrine of reconciliation and Christology dominates. We read already in Zwingli's Sixty-seven Articles of 1523 "that Christ is the one, eternal High Priest . . . Who offered Himself up once and for all, [and who] is in eternity a perpetual sacrifice in payment of the sins of all believers" (C 38). "He was crucified, and died to reconcile his Father unto us, and to be a sacrifice not only for original guilt, but also for all our actual transgressions" (S 531; cf. 488; 624). Christ's atoning sacrifice is thus unique and sufficient: that is, valid for all times. It applies not only to the original sin of human beings, but also to all actual sins, "so that there remains no other sacrifice for sin" (C 170). As the one who on the cross offers himself as an atoning sacrifice to the Father, Christ exercises the office of a priest (*munus sacerdotale*). Christ's priesthood "is the office and prerogative of presenting Himself before God to obtain grace and favour, and appease His wrath in offering a sacrifice which is acceptable to Him" (T 11).

The fact that this sacrifice is not only unique, but has occurred once *and for all*, finds expression in the distinction among Christ's priestly activities. Although Christ offers himself as a sacrifice on the cross only once at a particular historical moment in time, he continuously intercedes for us before the Father, pointing to that unique sacrifice. The enduring validity of the sacrifice of the cross entails Christ's everlasting intercession; his act of satisfaction (*satisfactio*), the act of intercession (*intercessio*). In the words of the Heidelberg Catechism, he is the High Priest "who by the one sacrifice of his body has redeemed us, and ever liveth to make intercession for us with the Father" (S 317–18; cf. M 617, 25ff.; S 681). The sufficiency of the sacrifice of the cross would of course be called into question if one understood this intercession in the sense of an action that had to be continually performed anew. According to the Erlauthal Confession, "Christ does not pray on his knees and with outstretched hands [before the Father], in the form of a servant as he was on earth, wailing and in tears" (M 322, 16–18). On the contrary, Christ intercedes for us before the Father in such a way that he makes the power of his unique sacrifice present to the Father. Christ's intercessory office consists in nothing other than the continuous "representation before God of Christ's sacrifice" (*repraesentatio sacrificii coram Deo*). But the Erlauthal Confession declares not only that Christ intercedes for us now before God by pointing to his sacrifice; this intercession is not a task that Christ first took on after his death on the cross, but one that he performed even before he became human (M 322, 19–20). This presupposes that prior to the incarnation there was already a relation to the sacrifice that was still to be performed. Therefore there is ultimately a distinction between, on the one hand, the temporal offering of Christ's sacrifice and, on the other hand, this sacrifice's efficacy and validity, which have been present since the beginning of the world. It is this eternal aspect of the sacrifice of the cross which found expression in the image of the lamb slain from the beginning of the world (Rev. 13:8). Interpreting this image, the Westminster Confession declares: "Although the work of redemption was not actually wrought by Christ till after his incarnation, yet the virtue, efficacy, and benefits thereof were communicated unto the elect, in all ages successively from the beginning of the world, in and by those promises, types, and sacrifices, wherein he was revealed, and signified to be the seed of the woman which should bruise the serpent's head, and the lamb slain from the beginning of the world, being yesterday and to-day the same and for ever" (S 622). This means that, on the basis of the pact made with the Father from eternity, Christ is always already the Son of God who becomes human and who carries out reconciliation by his sacrifice: that is, Christ is always already our High Priest.

But Christ is by no means merely the bearer of the priestly office. Along with this office, all the confessions mention at least his kingly office (C 104; M 160, 1ff.; C 246–47), and most also mention a prophetic office, thereby arriving at a doctrine of three offices. "It pleased God, in his eternal purpose, to choose and ordain the Lord Jesus, his only-begotten Son, to be the Mediator between God and man, the Prophet, Priest, and King" (S 619). This assertion of a threefold office of Christ, here advanced by the Westminster Confession, is found for the first time in Calvin's Geneva Catechism, where it is derived from the title of "Christ." The same derivation is also found in the Heidelberg Catechism and the Westminster Larger Catechism (M 617, 14ff.; S 317–18). The Son of God is "Christ" or "Anointed One" insofar as he is anointed by the Father as king, priest, and prophet. For "according to the Scripture, anointing is used for these three things" (T 10). Christ's anointing to his threefold office is understood not as an anointing with visible oil, but as an anointing with the Holy Spirit's gifts of grace, by which the bearer of the office is equipped with authority and power (*cum authoritate tum potentia*) (M 617, 15ff.).

In what do Christ's prophetic office (*munus propheticum*) and royal office (*munus regis*) consist? Christ is a prophet as "the sovereign messenger and ambassador of God," revealing God's will in a definitive way. At the same time, Jesus' appearance as a prophet signifies the end of prophecy as a whole, because it was Jesus' task to "put an end to all prophecies and revelations" (T 11). As a prophet Christ is "the Master and Teacher of His own." His goal is "to bring us the true knowledge of the Father and of His Truth, so that we may be scholars in the household of God" (T 11–12). The instruments that Christ uses to accomplish this are his word and his Spirit (M 617, 20ff.; S 681). He uses the same means to perform his kingly office, for "it is spiritual, and consists in the Word and Spirit of God, and includes righteousness and life" (T 10). Christ is our eternal king, insofar as his word and Spirit are the means by which he rules us "and defends and preserves us in the redemption obtained for us" (S 318). As a king he calls his people out of the world, and gathers and rules them by means of various institutions (M 617, 30ff.). Christ's kingly dominion consists in the fact that

Christ is the Lord over sin, death, and hell, and liberates us from spiritual bondage for the freedom of God's children (M 662, 27ff.). His kingly office serves to free our conscience from every spiritual coercion so that we can "live in righteousness and holiness" and have the power "to overcome the devil, the flesh, and the world—the enemies of our souls" (T 11). By virtue of his kingly office, Christ rules his people—that is, the church—by word and Spirit. Inasmuch as he does so, he takes them into his dominion so that they may "with free conscience fight against sin and the devil in this life, and hereafter, in eternity, reign with him over all creatures" (S 318).

The Heidelberg Catechism sees participation in Christ's priestly office in the fact expressed when the respondent in the Catechism replies: "I also . . . confess his name . . . [and] present myself a living sacrifice of thankfulness to him" (S 318). The Catechism characterizes prayer as "the chief part of the thankfulness which God requires of us" (S 350). On the basis of the sufficiency of Christ's sacrifice of reconciliation, our prayer can no longer be "a venture in which we do not know whether we will succeed or not" (T 43). For the Geneva Catechism, prayer is an expression of faith—that is, of trust in God, who proves to be gracious and who accepts our prayer. "The ground of our prayers should always be, that they will be received by God, and that we shall obtain what we request as far as it is expedient for us. And therefore St. Paul says that true prayer comes from faith (Rom. 10:14). For if we have no reliance upon the goodness of God, it will be impossible for us to call upon Him in truth" (ibid.). Our prayers are based on God's promise to hear our prayer and to give us that for which we ask. Insofar as faith as trust in God is trust in God's fulfilling that promise, true prayer is incompatible with doubt that the prayer is heard. True prayer is offered to God in the unshakable certainty that it is accepted by God.

In prayer appeal is made to God alone, because all that is good comes from God as our creator and preserver, even when it comes to us through human beings. As an act of thankfulness prayer cannot be directed to creatures, whether they be angels or saints. Because it is idol worship to venerate creatures, a prayer directed toward an angel or a saint would be an act of idolatry. While saints are indeed objects of imitation, they are never objects of veneration. The Second Helvetic Confession acknowledges that "we love them as brothers, and also honor them; yet not with any kind of worship but by an honorable opinion of them and just praises of them. We also imitate them" (C 231–32). On the contrary, the veneration of saints is a violation of the First Commandment, which, according to the Heidelberg Catechism, commands "that, on peril of my soul's salvation, I avoid and flee all idolatry, sorcery, enchantments, invocation of saints or other creatures" (S 342). Nor can we regard the saints as our advocates and mediators before God, for only Christ has an intercessory function. Included in his priestly office is the fact that not only did he sacrifice himself for us once and for all, he also continuously intercedes for us, as this sacrifice, before God. Advocacy cannot be separated from his sacrifice, and just as his sacrifice is sufficient, so is his advocacy, so that the mediation and advocacy of others is forbidden. The French Confession says: "We believe, as Jesus Christ is our only advocate, and as he commands us to ask of the Father in his name . . . that all imaginations of men concerning the intercession of dead saints are an abuse and a device of Satan" (S 373).

In ourselves we are unworthy to appear before God at all. But on the basis of Christ's mediation and advocacy access to God is open to us. For this reason our prayer always occurs in Christ's name. Therefore the Belgic Confession declares that "the meaning is not that we should offer our prayers to God on account of our own worthiness, but only on account of the excellence and worthiness of our Lord Jesus Christ. . . . Therefore, according to the command of Christ, we call upon the heavenly Father through Jesus Christ, our only Mediator, as we are taught in the Lord's Prayer; being assured that whatever we ask of the Father in his name will be granted us" (S 414–16). For through Christ God has become our Father (S 351), so that as God's children we can come to God with our prayers. Since the address "Our Father" is grounded in Christ's office of mediator, one can rightly say of all our prayers that "we pray as it were by His mouth, since He gives us entrance and audience, and intercedes for us (Rom. 8:34)" (T 44).

CHRISTOLOGY AND THE
CALVINIST "EXTRA"
(*EXTRA CALVINISTICUM*)

THE TWO NATURES AND THEIR HYPOSTATIC UNION

The incarnation of God's Son is the indispensable presupposition for the Son of God to carry out the work of reconciliation. Insofar as the divine covenant of grace exists from eternity, God's Son can only be considered as the One who is becoming human or the One who has become human. In this sense divinity and humanity are always bound together. However, the fact that God's Son has become human cannot mean that certain parts of the One who has become human prove to belong to the divine nature, while others belong to the human nature. The Second Helvetic Confession thus insists that Christ "did not have a soul bereft of sense and reason, as Apollinaris thought, nor flesh without a soul, as Eunomius taught"

(C 243). Both cases in effect dispute that Christ became a true human being. According to them the Son of God would only have assumed a part of human nature, while other parts—reason as a part of the soul or the soul itself—would not have been assumed by him. As the presupposition for reconciliation, the incarnation of God's Son can only mean that the second person of the Trinity became *entirely* human.

If the incarnation is concerned with the redemption of that which is lost, and if the whole human being, and not merely a part thereof, must be regarded as lost, and if redemption applies only to that which God's Son actually assumes, then Christ must have assumed human nature in its entirety. Accordingly, Christ "did not only assume human nature as to the body, but also a true human soul, that he might be a real man. For since the soul was lost as well as the body, it was necessary that he should take both upon him, to save both" (S 403). The completeness of Christ's human nature must be maintained for the sake of the redemption of human nature in its entirety. For this reason Apollinaris's view is rejected that "in the human body [of Christ] the Word of God dwelt in place of the rational and intellective human soul; because the very Son and Word of God did not take the place of the rational and intellective soul in his body, but he assumed and preserved a soul like ours (that is, a rational and intellective soul) but without sin" (DS 159, CT 397). Only when the incarnation is not understood in such a way that God's Son takes the place of the principle specific to human beings, the rational soul (*anima rationalis*), can one speak at all of a real incarnation. Otherwise precisely that part which characterizes human beings as human beings would be left out and not assumed by Christ. One would have to say that Christ assumed only that which human beings have in common with other living creatures. The issue in rejecting Apollinaris of Laodicea is the insistence that Christ assumed and thus redeemed not merely that which is not particular to human nature, but that which is particular to human nature.

Because of the incarnation, God's Son is truly human. He has a human body, a human soul, and consequently human reason. At the primary level this is the sole meaning of the story of Christ's birth. According to the Geneva Catechism, the assertion that Christ was "born of the virgin Mary" seeks only to bring to expression that "He was formed in the womb of the Virgin Mary, of her proper substance, to be the seed of David" (T 12–13). Christ is human with regard to his substance. From Mary he received human nature, indeed the whole human being consisting of soul and body (Z 36, C 103). On the basis of this incarnation Christ is no longer merely Son of God, but also Son of humanity (Z 36). He is "the true seed of Abraham and of David" (S 368). The Second Helvetic Confession says that "we also believe and teach that the eternal Son of the eternal God was made the Son of man from the seed of Abraham and David" (C 243). Christ's flesh is no mere appearance, or something that descended from heaven—the position represented by the Valentinians and the Marcionites. The Belgic Confession appeals to the birth from Mary not only in opposition to them, but also in opposition to "the Anabaptists, who deny that Christ assumed human flesh of his mother." On the contrary, the Confession asserts "that Christ is become a partaker of the flesh and blood of the children; that he is a fruit of the loins of David after the flesh; made of the seed of David according to the flesh; a fruit of the womb of the Virgin Mary; made of a woman; a branch of David; a shoot of the root of Jesse; sprung from the tribe of Judah; descended from the Jews according to the flesh: of the seed of Abraham, since he took upon him the seed of Abraham, and became like unto his brethren in all things, sin excepted" (S 403). The fact that the incarnate Christ is born of Mary means that he is a real human being in such a way that, like every other human being, he is a member of a chain of generations and belongs to a particular people. Because Christ, like us, is a human being in this sense, he who is Son of God can also be designated as "Immanuel": "God with us."

But the incarnation cannot be understood in such a way that the Son of God would cease to be true God. The incarnation is not a *kenosis* in the sense that the *Logos* actually *becomes* flesh. The incarnation is not a change of substance whose result would be that the Son of humanity takes the place of the Son of God. As the Son of humanity Christ continues to be the Son of God. Although through Christ we have received the status of children of God, that status is different from Christ's status as God's Son, inasmuch as Christ is God's Son by nature, not by grace. The fact that Christ is God's Son means that Christ is begotten from the essence of the Father, and therefore is of the same essence. Christ is not adopted as God's Son, but is begotten as God's Son (M 121, 4ff.). The essence of the Father and the Son is thus identical. Christ is born "not only when he assumed flesh of the Virgin Mary, and not only before the foundation of the world was laid, but by the Father before all eternity in an inexpressible manner. . . . Therefore, with respect to his divinity the Son is coequal and consubstantial with the Father; true God (Phil. 2:11), not only in name or by adoption or by any merit (*dignatione*), but in substance and nature" (C 242–43). Consubstantiality exists between the Father and the Son (S 488, 531). As the second person of the Trinity, God's Son is "very and eternal God, of one substance, and equal with the Father" (S 619).

Any attempt to call Christ's divinity into question is rejected. This applies to "the impious doctrine of Arius and the Arians against the Son of God, and especially the blasphemies of the Spaniard, Michael Servetus, and all his followers" (C 243). Arius and Servetus are both treated as defenders of one and the same idea, and this means that Servetus falls under the verdict spoken against Arius at Nicaea. Servetus refused to speak of three persons in the one divine substance, because that seemed to him to divide God into three parts. Thus he was also unable to say that the consubstantial Son of God was eternally begotten of the Father. He was willing to speak of divine persons only with regard to the economic forms of God's appearance. In this sense he saw Christ as the visible person of the divinity. By this he meant the *human* Jesus of Nazareth.

Although Servetus vehemently contested Jesus' preexistence, he did present him as the pattern of creation. The French Confession opposes this position as subordinationist and criticizes Servetus for attributing "a fantastical divinity to the Lord Jesus, calling him the idea and pattern of all things, and the personal or figurative Son of God, and, finally . . . a body of three uncreated elements, thus confusing and destroying the two natures" (S 368). While this fantastic divinity of the *human* Jesus is sharply criticized, Christ's actual divinity is asserted by the claim that the *Logos* was preexistent as God's Son, consubstantial with the Father. Only in this way, it was thought, could the thesis of reconciliation in Christ be maintained. Carrying out the work of creation requires that the reconciler be not only true human being, but also true God: that is, consubstantial with God. According to the Heidelberg Catechism, the reconciler must be true God so "that by the power of his Godhead he might bear, in his manhood, the burden of God's wrath, and so obtain for and restore to us righteousness and life" (S 312). For this reason the reconciler cannot be either a mere human being or a god transformed into a human being. Rather it must be that the reconciler "is *and continues* true and eternal God" (S 319, emphasis added).

It thus proves necessary to ascribe two natures, substances, or essences to the incarnate Christ. He is not only human; he is also God. He is thus characterized by both a human and a divine nature. The confessional writings explicitly take their stand on the foundation of the Chalcedonian doctrine of two natures. "We therefore acknowledge two natures or substances, the divine and the human, in one and the same Jesus Christ our Lord" (C 243). Admittedly, the Latin version of the Scottish Confession says that the person of Christ consists "*of* two perfect natures" (*ex duabus perfectis naturis*) (S 444). But this does not mean that in Christ the two natures have fused into one nature. The two natures are indeed inseparably united with each other in the one person, but without surrendering the fact that they are not identical (S 367, 404). To this extent the Chalcedonian formula is less open to misunderstanding: namely, that Christ exists "*in* two natures without any commingling or change or division or separation" (DS 302, CT 414). Furthermore, in Christ the divine and human natures "are bound and united with one another in such a way that they are not absorbed, or confused, or mixed, but are united or joined together in one person—the properties of the natures being unimpaired and permanent" (C 243–44).

The reception of the Chalcedonian formula—as here in the Second Helvetic Confession—entails the rejection of both Nestorianism and Monophysitism. The emphasis on the different natures and their particularities must not dissolve the unity of Christ's person, so that one joins the Nestorians, "who make two of the one Christ" (C 244). Nor must the binding together of the two natures in the one person be understood in such a way as to "destroy the property of the human nature" (ibid.). The unity of the divine and human natures does not entail any surrender of the particularities of each nature in the sense of a fusion of the two natures. That would be the rejected "madness of Eutyches and of the Monothelites or Monophysites" (ibid.). Christ is God's Son and thus true God. But at the same time he is Mary's son and thus true human being, so that he is both divine and human in one person. If he is to be our reconciler, he must be both God and human being really and completely.

On the basis of the "hypostatic" or "personal" union (*unio hypostatica* or *unio personalis*), both natures are bound together in one person, without being fused together into a single nature and without either nature having surrendered its peculiar properties to the other nature. But if this is so, what is the relation between the two natures thus bound together? As early as Zwingli we find the opposition to Nestorius's claim that the human nature has its own hypostasis. If the human nature possessed its own hypostasis, then God's Son, who as such is a hypostasis, would have assumed another hypostasis in becoming human, so we would have to speak not only of two natures, but also of two hypostases in the sense of two persons. Despite the fact that divine and human nature are not identical, Zwingli does not want to separate them in such a way that their connection could be conceived as that of two hypostases or persons. It is exclusively the divine *Logos* who forms the person and assumes the anhypostatic human nature. God's Son assumes human nature in such a way "that the whole man was so assumed into the unity of the hypostasis or person of the Son of God, that the man did not constitute a separate person, but was assumed into the inseparable, indivisible and indissoluble person of the Son of God" (Z 36).

With this assertion of an "anhypostasis" of the human nature and its "enhypostasis" in the hypostasis of the divine *Logos*, the Account of Faith prevents the two natures bound together in Christ from falling apart into two different persons or hypostases. In a similar way we find later assertions, such as the following from the Bremen Consensus, "that this humanity that has been assumed is not a person in its own right. Nor does it have independent being apart from the person of God's Son. On the contrary, it was simultaneously created in Mary's body and assumed by God's Son, and thus began from the first instant of conception to exist in the person of God's Son. It is one person with God's Son, and remains such in eternity" (M 742, 10–16).

The end of the preceding quotation shows that the personal union of the two natures must not be conceived as one that will sooner or later come to an end. To be sure, the hypostatic union begins at a specific point in time: namely, the conception. However, it never ends, but endures eternally. The personal union of the divine and human natures is not merely temporary, but everlasting. Indeed the *possibility* no longer exists of separating the two natures. They are bound together in such a way "that both now and in eternity they neither may nor can be separated from each other" (M 837, 11–12). Christ's humanity is a nature "that he will never set aside" (M 722, 24–25). All the confessions emphasize that the union of the two natures in Christ's person is indissoluble. For the Belgic Confession, divinity and humanity are so closely bound together in Christ "that they were not separated even by his death" (S 404). Even when Christ was on the cross and in the grave "the Godhead did not cease to be in him, any more than it did when he was an infant" (S 405).

Insofar as the union of natures begins with the conception and never ceases, it is fully in accord with the principles of Reformed Christology when Reformed and Lutheran representatives at the Leipzig Colloquy agree on the statement "that at no time and in not a single location, whether in the state of humiliation or in the state of exaltation, did any rupture or separation occur between the natures. Nor did either nature ever depart from the other, not even in death itself" (N 657). What transpires in Christ's death is a separation of the soul from the body, not a separation of the two natures. On the contrary, "after conception the Son of God has neither at any time or in any place been outside of his flesh—that is, without his flesh and separated from it. Nor will he at any time or in any place be without the flesh that he has assumed" (ibid.). God's Son does not exist at any time or in any place without the Son's human nature. It is impossible to encounter the Son other than as God and human being. Were it possible, the two natures would not be inseparably bound together.

THE COMMUNICATION OF PROPERTIES
(*COMMUNICATIO IDIOMATUM*)

In the binding together or union of the two natures, it is presupposed that the two natures are not canceled by being bound together, but instead remain with their peculiar properties (*idiomata*). The personal union (*unio personalis*) is not a fusing or transformation of the natures. We read in the Bremen Consensus: "Thus each nature *an sich* retains forever its essential properties, including its natural will and effects with their specific differences" (M 742, 27–30). The French Confession declares that "each [nature] remains in its proper character (*sa propriété distincte*)" (S 368). Both the divine and the human nature are characterized by specific properties. They cannot lose these specific properties through the personal union that takes place in Christ. Their loss would be tantamount to a cancellation of the natures themselves. One would no longer even be able to say that Christ is God and human being. Instead Christ would be a hybrid.

We have already seen that the confessional writings take a stand against the separation of the two natures, which was advocated by Nestorius. They also take a stand against the position advanced by Eutyches and later the Monothelites: namely, the "mixture, transformation, and destruction of the natures in their essence, properties, will, and effects" (M 742, 37–38). Christology is about the fact that God is human, and specifically that God is human without ceasing to be God. This means that Christology is always concerned with a doctrine of *two* natures. Despite the indissoluble binding together of divinity and humanity in the person of Christ, each of the two natures is preserved unmixed, with its specific properties, "so that in this union the divine nature, retaining its attributes, remained uncreated, infinite, and all-pervading; and the human nature remained finite, having its form, measure, and attributes" (S 368). "As then the divine nature hath always remained uncreated, without beginning of days or end of life, filling heaven and earth, so also hath the human nature not lost its properties, but remained a creature, having beginning of days, being a finite nature, and retaining all the properties of a real body" (S 404).

It is out of soteriological interest in Christ's humanity that Reformed Christology refuses to speak of a communication of the properties of divine majesty to the human nature. Reacting to the Formula of Concord, the Bremen Consensus regards the Lutheran view of the communication of properties, which sees such a communication as a result of the personal union, as a "dangerous innovation" that can only give rise to paradoxes (M 746, 1, 10). In any case, according to Bremen, neither scripture nor the consensus of the ancient church was acquainted with a "pouring out of the divine properties into the humanity of Christ" (M 746, 4–5).

It is not the case that Reformed Christology is totally without a communication of properties. The Second Helvetic Confession expressly declares: "We piously and reverently accept and use the impartation of properties (*communicatio idiomatum*) which is derived from Scripture and which has been used by all antiquity in explaining and reconciling apparently contradictory passages" (C 244). In adopting this position Reformed Christology diverges from Zwingli's specification of the relation of the two natures in Christ. Despite the Account of Faith's emphasis on the unity of the two natures and its sharp rejection of Nestorianism, it does not succeed in showing that both natures participate to an equal degree in Christ's work of reconciliation. On the contrary, Zwingli makes the distinction that all acts that have a soteriological quality are ascribed exclusively to

Christ's divine nature. Thus we read that "the same Christ, according to the character of the human nature, cries in infancy, grows, increases in wisdom, hungers, thirsts, eats, drinks, is warm, is cold, is scourged, sweats, is wounded, is cruelly slain, fears, is sad and endures what else pertains to the penalty and punishment of sin" (Z 36–37). But "according to what is proper to the divine nature, Christ reigns together with the Father over what is highest and what is lowest. He penetrates all things, bears them and watches over them, makes the blind to see, heals the deaf, calls forth the dead, by his word strikes down the enemies, even as a dead person regains life, attains to heaven, and from what is his own sends forth the Holy Spirit" (M 80, 23–27).

For Zwingli, although properties of the one nature are ascribed to the other because of the unity of the two natures, this is only a figurative manner of speaking, an *alloiosis*. For example, forgiveness of sins is proper to the divine nature, while suffering is proper to the human nature. But on the basis of the personal union of the two natures it is possible to make the figurative statements that "the Son of Man forgives sins" and "the Son of God suffered." Rightly understood, these statements mean only that "He who is the Son of God and of man in one person suffered, according to the peculiar quality of His human nature; and He who is the Son of God and of man in one person forgives sins, according to the peculiar quality of the divine nature" (Z 37). The predicates relating to Christ's office or work are thus not ascribed jointly to both natures by Zwingli. He allows Christ's reconciling action to be split into individual parts, each of which is ascribed to one of the two natures.

Precisely on this point, however, Reformed Christology did not follow Zwingli. Instead it emphasized that all statements relating to Christ's office as mediator have as their subject Christ according to both his natures. The Westminster Confession says that "Christ, in the work of mediation, acteth according to *both* Natures" (S 622). Indeed, the personal union of the two natures occurs exclusively for the sake of Christ's office. For this reason the office itself belongs to both natures. According to the Bremen Consensus, "in this assumed human nature, indeed by and with the same, the Son of God carried out the entire work of redeeming the human race. By this human nature God's Son also manifested many visible miracles to confirm his office. God's Son gave this flesh a share in all his victories and triumphs, and continues to do many works by this his humanity" (M 744, 29–34). "Christ's humanity is the means whereby all living power is imparted to us by the eternal Son of God" (M 745, 8–10).

To be sure, there are a plethora of statements from scripture that are to be understood only as figurative ways of speaking, completely in Zwingli's sense, insofar as they take properties of one nature and predicate them of the other nature. Because of the personal union, divine properties are ascribed to the human Christ and human properties are ascribed to the Son of God. Such statements are true when one understands them *in concreto:* that is, when one sees the subject of the statements in the person of Christ, but not in one of the two natures. The truth of such statements is dependent on our placing "such a word or name in the place of the subject in the proposition (*loco subjecti in propositione*), so that the person is indicated: for example, 'Before Abraham was, I am,' and 'The Lord of glory was crucified'" (M 746, 22–25). One must interpret these statements "according to the difference of natures" (M 746, 28). In this case the proposition "The human Christ is creator of the world" means the same as "According to his divine nature, the human Christ is creator of the world." Likewise the statement "The Son of God is dead" can only mean that the Son of God is dead according to his human nature.

These statements are to be understood only as a figurative manner of speaking and are to be interpreted completely in Zwingli's sense. But there are also other statements that concern Christ's office and that apply to both natures. "In this other type of proposition (*genere propositionum*), whereby one grasps both natures together in such a way that each nature effects its work in the common office, it is not only concretely (*in concreto*) that it is rightly said that Christ, God and human, is our mediator, redeemer, sanctifier, king, high priest, head" (M 746, 41–45). Christ is mediator and holds the three offices not merely according to one nature, but according to both. Christ accomplishes the works belonging to his office as mediator (*apotelesmata*—accomplishments) in and according to both natures. In this way he is our mediator and reconciler as a human being and as God. This means that wherever the predicates designate works of the mediator, the statements are true not only when the subject is the concrete person of Christ, but also when one of the two natures is taken as the subject. Christ reconciles not only according to his divine nature, but also according to his human nature. Thus one can also say abstractly (*in abstracto*): "'Christ's flesh is a life-giving food,' 'Christ's suffering is a sanctifying suffering,' 'Christ's blood and death is our righteousness and life,' and so forth, because Christ's humanity has done and still does its part in such works, although the work is not the work of Christ's humanity alone, but the divinity must also do its part" (M 746, 48–M 747, 3; cf. 808, 5ff.).

Both natures participate in Christ's office, insofar as Christ is mediator as God and as human being. Nevertheless—as the Westminster Confession emphasizes—Christ acts according to both natures "by each nature doing that which is proper to itself" (S 622). The fact that the two natures work together in carrying out the office of mediator does not cancel the difference between them. On the contrary, the natures are retained together with their particular properties, even though "by reason of the unity of the person, that which is proper to one nature is sometimes, in Scripture, attributed to the person denominated by the other nature" (S 622). The Second Helvetic Confession is to be understood in this sense when it not only says "that our Lord Jesus Christ truly suffered and died for us *in the flesh*" but goes on to declare "that *the Lord of glory* was crucified for us, according to Paul's words" (C 244). A statement such as "the Lord of glory was crucified and died for us" cannot be interpreted in such a way that the subject is taken abstractly. If that were the case, Christ's suffering and death, which is proper to Christ's human nature, would be predicated of the divine nature. A communication of properties would take place not only concretely but abstractly. The difference of the natures can be maintained only when a communication of properties is disputed. "Therefore, we do not in any way teach that the divine nature in Christ has suffered" (C 244).

However, the fact that the communication of properties takes place only concretely, and not abstractly, does not mean merely that statements such as "the divinity suffered, was crucified, and died" are not permissible. It also means that nothing that is proper to the divine nature can be predicated of the human nature. What is at issue in the conflict between Lutheran and Reformed Christology is not the first case, the "genus of humility" (*genus tapeinoticum*): that is, the question of the communication of human properties to the divinity. What is at issue is exclusively the second case, the "genus of majesty" (*genus maiesticum*): that is, the question of the communication of the properties of divine majesty to the human nature of Christ. This latter communication is decisively denied by Reformed Christology.

This denial is motivated by a soteriological interest in Christ's true humanity, which is not touched in any way by the personal union. The hypostatic union must not be understood in such a way that Christ's human nature would become the subject of properties of the divine nature. Instead it is the case, according to the Bremen Consensus, that Christ "is true God, eternal, infinite, omnipotent, all-knowing, invisible, and inconceivable, not according to his human nature, but according to his divine nature. Christ's human nature . . . nevertheless remained a true human nature and retained in itself the same essential properties. It has not been divinized, nor is it equal to the divine nature with respect either to the infinity of the divine essence or to other essential properties" (M 743, 4–13). This means that Christ is ubiquitous, omnipotent, and all-knowing not according to his humanity, but according to his divinity. One can therefore not use "abstract locutions" to say that "Christ's humanity is omnipotent and all-knowing, and that the body of Christ is ubiquitous" (M 747, 36–38). If one followed that route, "the two different natures and their properties [would be] mixed, or even made equivalent to each other" (M 747, 40–42).

One thing that argues against such a communication of the properties of divine majesty to Christ's human nature is the fact that an actual communion of natural properties would have to be reciprocal. If there were a communication of divine properties to the human nature, there would have to be a communication of human properties to the divine nature (M 806, 15ff.). Such reciprocity is disputed even by the Formula of Concord: "Since there is no variation with God (James 1:17), nothing was added to or detracted from the essence and properties of the divine nature in Christ through the incarnation, nor was the divine nature intrinisically diminished or augmented thereby" (BC 600). The unchangeableness of God is given as the ground of the absence of reciprocity in the communication of properties. But the decisive argument against the communication of the properties of divine majesty to Christ's human nature is not the absence of this primarily formal reciprocity. The key objection is that the communication of the properties of majesty to Christ's humanity makes this humanity, "and that which Christ has done and accomplished according to this humanity, into a mere specter" (M 747, 49–M 748, 1). But this would also annihilate the comfort that we are intended to receive through Christ's incarnation. We could no longer know Christ as the firstborn among many brothers, if his humanity were equipped with properties of divine majesty.

HUMILIATION AND EXALTATION

If the communication of properties, understood in this way, is supposed to be the result of the personal union of the two natures, then it follows logically that Christ's conception is interpreted as an exaltation. Christ's humiliation can then only be conceived in a figurative sense. Specifically, the humiliation consists in the fact that "Christ's humanity . . . in reality (*realiter*) received all divine properties from conception onward, and always had them in first actuality (*actu primo*), but did not always use them in second actuality (*actu secundo*)" (M 748, 6–9). Christ's *kenosis* or emptying is thus Christ's act of not using his divine properties according to his humanity. Over against this view, Reformed Christology takes the preexistent *Logos* as the subject of the humiliation, so that, for Reformed Christology, the humiliation is identical with the incarnation. Christ's humiliation (*humilatio*) is identical with his emptying (*exinanitio*), which consists in the fact that Christ, as the eternal Son of God, consubstantial with the Father, assumes the form of a servant from the moment of his conception until the moment of his resurrection (M 617, 38ff.). "Christ's humiliation consisted in His being born, and that in a low condition, made under the law, undergoing the miseries of this life, the wrath of God, and the cursed death of the cross, in being buried, and continuing under the power of death for a time" (M 645, 19–22). By contrast, Christ's exaltation begins with Christ's rising from the dead, ascending into heaven, and being seated at the right hand of the Father, and ends with Christ's returning to judge the living and the dead (S

682). The humiliation is a humiliation of God's Son and an emptying of God. The exaltation is the exaltation of the Human One and a transfiguration of the human being. "According to the resurrection and ascension, [Christ's human nature] was transfigured and laid aside all the frailties and mortality to which it had previously been subject, and was adorned with a place higher than all angels and human beings" (M 743, 7–9).

Although the personal union cannot be interpreted as a communication of the properties of divine majesty to Christ's human nature, the humanity assumed by this union does not remain untouched in the process. All the confessional writings that go beyond Zwingli agree that, for the sake of the personal union, "Christ's flesh is to be worshiped" (M 744, 8). The humanity assumed in Christ is distinguished from other human beings by specific prerogatives and assets. "The Lord Jesus, in his human Nature thus united to the divine, was sanctified and anointed with the Holy Spirit above Measure; having in him all the Treasures of Wisdom and Knowledge" (M 561, 27–30). Unlike all other human individuals, Christ received the fullness of the Holy Spirit, and not just specific gifts of the Spirit (M 745, 13ff.). Christ's sinlessness is also one of the assets of his humanity that do not cancel the true human nature. Christ's sinlessness is necessary for the sake of reconciliation. The Geneva Catechism uses the virgin birth—that is, the conception by the Holy Spirit—as a construct to explain Christ's sinlessness. Christ was not begotten by a man, according to the course of nature, because "the seed of man is in itself corrupt." Thus "it was necessary that the power of the Holy Spirit should intervene in this conception, in order to preserve our Lord from all corruption, and to fill Him with holiness" (T 13).

But above and beyond the assets of Christ's humanity that were already present, that humanity is "gloriously transfigured" according to the resurrection and ascension. It is "adorned far beyond all creatures with immortality, exalted light and wisdom, with ineffable power, sovereignty, strength, joy, and life that are incomprehensible to us in this life, and with any and all exalted and excellent created gifts, assets, and glories" (M 745, 26–31; cf. 747, 21ff.). It is of decisive importance that the exaltation of Christ that begins with the resurrection is by no means understood as a communication of the properties of divine majesty to Christ's humanity. It is the human being who is exalted, and in the exaltation he remains a human being. This has implications for Christ's corporeality. The French Confession emphasizes that "although Jesus Christ, in rising from the dead, bestowed immortality upon his body, yet he did not take from it the truth of its nature" (S 368–69). If "our salvation and resurrection also depend on the reality of his body" (S 404), even the exalted Christ must also possess a real body. According to the Hungarian Confession, part of the essence of the body is its boundedness and finitude: that is, the fact that it has spatial dimensions and can be assigned a particular location (M 384, 5ff.).

The "local" understanding of the heaven into which Christ ascends proves to be the ultimate consequence of the fact that the one who is exalted is also the reconciler, who not only is God, but also is human, and remains so. The Second Helvetic Confession highlights this identity between the one who is exalted and the one who is humiliated when it declares "that the same Jesus Christ our Lord, in his true flesh in which he was crucified and died, rose again from the dead, and that not another flesh was raised other than the one buried, or that a spirit was taken up instead of the flesh, but that he retained his true body" (C 244–45). It is by showing his wounds to the disciples, and thus revealing to them the identity of his body, that the risen Christ proves that he is the one who was crucified. It is the corporeal human being who rises from the dead and ascends into heaven. Consequently it is true that Christ, "in his same flesh, ascended above all visible heavens into the highest heaven, that is, the dwelling-place of God and the blessed ones, at the right hand of God the Father" (C 245). Although being seated at the right hand of God "signifies an equal participation in glory and majesty," heaven is taken "to be a certain place (*pro loco certo*)" (ibid., S 256). The finitude of human nature and of the corporeality entailed by that nature necessitates a local understanding of the ascension, if Christ ascended into heaven as a true human being, and as such is the firstborn among many siblings (M 163, 15ff.).

Even Zwingli in the Account of Faith understands the ascension as a change of location. Christ's being seated at the right hand of God—which for Zwingli says something about the place of Christ's heavenly residence—implies that Christ, according to his human nature, is no longer on earth, but remains in a particular heavenly location until his return in judgment (Z 51). Scripture permits only the presence of Christ's body in heaven (Z 51–52). With this thesis, Zwingli opposes Luther's assertion, made in the controversy concerning the Lord's Supper, that Christ's body exists in a repletive manner. According to Luther's position, Christ exists not just in a particular location, but in every location, everywhere, and does so according to his human nature as well, not just according to his divine nature. In Zwingli's view, this "would destroy Christ's true humanity. Only the deity can be everywhere" (Z 50). This means that Christ is at a particular place according to his human nature—that is, with his body after his incarnation, and even after his ascension—while according to his divine nature he is present everywhere.

The other confessional writings do not share Zwingli's local understanding of Christ's being seated at the right hand of God. For them, Christ's being seated at the right hand of God is not equivalent to Christ's existence in a heavenly place, as implied in Christ's ascension. The Geneva Catechism differentiates between the statements of the Apostles' Creed, giving the following answer to the question of the meaning of the terms "seated" and "at the right hand": "It is a similitude taken from earthly princes, who are wont to place on their right hand those whom they make their lieutenants to govern in their name" (T 18). Being seated at the right hand of God, or God's right hand itself, is understood here precisely not in a local sense, but as a circumlocution for the act of handing over sovereignty and the power to rule to the risen Christ. The reference to being seated at the right hand of God designates the goal of the ascension. Christ is taken up into heaven "that he might there appear as Head of his Church, by whom the Father governs all things" (S 323). Yet although these texts diverge from Zwingli's in differentiating between the ascension and the act of sitting at the right hand of the Father, they do not abandon the local concept of heaven. The act of sitting at the right hand of God is understood as a similitude and not literally: that is, not locally. But heaven is presented as a specific place. The preservation of a local understanding of heaven is not, however, the preservation of an outdated cosmology. Instead the local nature of heaven is a necessary consequence of Christ's humanity. This means that the local interpretation of the ascension is a consequence of the doctrine of two natures. It is the doctrine of two natures that makes it necessary to understand "the description and history of Christ's ascension into heaven literally" and to believe "that our Lord Jesus Christ with his true body, by . . . journeying from one place to another (*transitionem localem*) . . . was raised on high from the earth, penetrated the visible heavens, and took up heavenly residence, where in glory he retains the essence, property, form and figure of his true body" (M 749, 21–28).

In all this, Reformed Christology is opposing the thesis of the ubiquity of Christ's body, as this thesis follows from the Lutheran understanding of the communication of properties. Insofar as, in the Lutheran understanding, the communication of the properties of divine majesty to Christ's humanity already occurs at conception, a local understanding of the ascension, indeed of heaven at all, is excluded. The actual ascension is identical with the communication of the properties of divine majesty to the human nature of Christ: that is, with his conception. The biblical account of the ascension can then only be interpreted as a disappearance or a process of becoming invisible. On the basis of the ubiquity of Christ's body, Christ "is still on earth today, no less than before, although invisibly" (M 749, 2–3). In opposition to this viewpoint, the Second Helvetic Confession energetically disputes "that Christ according to his human nature is still in this world and thus is everywhere. For neither do we think or teach that the body of Christ ceased to be a true body after his glorification, or was deified" (C 244). And even so, Lutheran theologians present at the Leipzig Colloquy were able to agree with their Reformed counterparts "that the Lord Christ did not ascend into heaven already in the womb, but only on the fortieth day after his resurrection." Moreover,

Christ "ascended into heaven truly, spatially, and visibly, and not, for instance, by disappearance. The heaven into which he ascended and in which the blessed of the heavenly Father are found, is a lovely dwelling and a certain place on high outside of this world and ordained by God, where we are to have our dwelling" (N 659).

If Christ is found, with his body, in a locally conceived heaven, the question arises of how his promise can nevertheless be true that he will be present until the end of the world. The fact that Christ according to his humanity is not on the earth follows from the finitude of his body, and this finitude belongs to his human nature. But this corporeal absence by no means amounts to a general absence. Already in the Account of Faith, Zwingli declares that, despite the local existence of Christ's body in heaven, Christ according to his divine nature is everywhere. Zwingli depicts this by using the example of the sun. Although the sun is found at a particular location, its power extends far and wide (Z 50). Similarly, the Geneva Catechism speaks of Christ's "power, which is spread abroad everywhere" (T 17). Yet it is not enough to speak of the presence of Christ's power. The fact that Christ is present to us with his power means only that he is present according to his divinity and majesty. In addition, Christ's presence is the presence of his grace, and of his Spirit who mediates this grace. Christ "is true Man and true God: according to his human nature, he is now not upon earth; but according to his Godhead, majesty, *grace, and Spirit,* he is at no time absent from us" (S 322). Christ is present not only as almighty God, but also and always as the gracious God: that is, as the reconciler.

Still, the Heidelberg Catechism itself raises the question: "But are not, in this way, the two natures in Christ separated from one another, if the Manhood be not wherever the Godhead is?" (ibid.). When the Catechism answers this question in the negative, it does so because, in spite of the distinction between divinity and humanity, infinity and finitude, the Catechism holds fast to their personal union in Christ. Nor does this distinction mean that there is a divine nature independently of the incarnate Christ. Yet if the divine nature itself is not to be removed, it must retain the infinity and thus also the ubiquity proper to it, just as the human nature must retain the finitude and thus also the limited local presence proper to it. The fact that God is in Christ cannot mean that Christ exists at a particular place according to his divine nature as well as according to his human nature. On the contrary, "since the Godhead is incomprehensible and every where present, it must follow that it is indeed beyond the bounds of the Manhood which it has assumed, but is yet none the less in the same also" (S 322). The Heidelberg Catechism thereby formulated the "extra," which Lutheran Christology made into a reproach under the rubric of the Calvinist "extra" (*extra Calvinisticum*).

However, the Calvinist "extra"—which is by no means specifically Reformed, but instead thoroughly traditional—is not intended to separate

Christ's divinity from his humanity. Christ is God and human being. The two natures are *inseparably* bound together in his person. Yet if the two natures are supposed to be united *without confusion*, ubiquity, which is proper to Christ's divine nature, cannot be predicated of his human nature. Christ is ubiquitous only according to his divinity, and not according to his humanity. It cannot be the case "that Christ according to his humanity, or Christ's human nature and essence, or Christ's body according to its substance and essence, is invisibly present at all places and with all creatures, whether in the condition of humiliation or in the condition of exaltation, whether on account of the personal union or on account of sitting and ruling at the right hand of God" (N 661). Yet it does not follow from this rejection of the ubiquity of Christ's body that Christ could ever be present to us in separation from his human nature. The presence of Christ always means the presence of the divine-human reconciler. For this reason the Calvinist "extra" does not contradict the confession "that the whole Jesus in one undivided person, God and human being, in heaven and on earth, ubiquitously (yet without a corporeal spatiality) rules and governs all things, from one sea to the other" (N 658).

JUSTIFICATION AND FAITH

FORGIVENESS OF SINS AND THE RIGHTEOUSNESS OF CHRIST

In agreement with the Lutheran confessional writings (BC 42, 292), the First Helvetic Confession declares that "in all evangelical teaching the most sublime and the principal article and the one which should be expressly set forth in every sermon and impressed upon the hearts of men should be that we are preserved and saved solely by the one mercy of God and by the merit of Christ" (C 104). Likewise, Zwingli can speak of Christ's sufficient sacrifice of reconciliation, which has redeemed us from death and is our righteousness, as the "sum of the Gospel" (C 36). This places justification at the center of theology. The way in which the confessions understand justification is conditioned by their recognition of the depth of human sinfulness. From the radicality of human sin follows human beings' inability to justify themselves. One can go even further: from the radicality of human sin follows human beings' inability to contribute in any way to their justification. Because every human being is wholly a sinner, and as such is unable to justify herself or to contribute to her justification, that justification must come from outside. This means the collapse of every

doctrine of justification that integrates human beings into the act of justification in such a way that, even if they are not the sole subjects of that act,
they are at least contributing causes.

The inability of every human being to justify himself is a result of his de
facto sinfulness. It is not the case that the sin that defines human beings ex-
hausts itself in individual sinful actions. Rather its radicality lies in the fact
that, as sinners, human beings cannot help but sin. This does not mean that
it is logically impossible for human beings not to sin, as if not sinning con-
tradicted the essence that is now theirs. As human beings they continue to
be God's image and to be created good, even though as sinners they do not
correspond to the destiny intended for them by God. The fact that as sinners human beings cannot not sin means, rather, that they are themselves
incapable of not sinning. This de facto sinfulness shapes their entire existence. There is not, for instance, some part of human beings—that is, one
of their faculties—that is free from sinfulness. This is the meaning of the
statement that our *heart* is bad and perverted. If my heart is perverted, then
it is in fact the case that I am *"prone* to all evil" (S 326). I become aware of
this in my conscience, which is continually bringing charges against me,
not only because of actions I have performed, but also because of this inclination. Human beings always find themselves in the de facto condition
of not only being able to do only what is evil, but also being able to will
only what is evil. The free will has become an enslaved will, the *liberum arbitrium* has become a *servum arbitrium.*

To be sure, the Second Helvetic Confession disputes that the human being has been "changed into a stone or a tree" by his sinfulness. But the Confession emphasizes that "man not yet regenerate has no free will for good,
no strength to perform what is good" (C 237–38). As beings inclined to
evil—that is, inclined to hate God and neighbor—we are incapable of even
willing what is good. As sinners, human beings are the cause only of evil
(*causa malorum*) (M 274, 35ff.). This means that the only works human beings can accomplish are sins (S 495). The Westminster Confession draws
the logical consequence when it denies that human beings even have the
capacity to repent: "Man, by his fall into a state of sin, hath wholly lost all
ability of will to any spiritual good accompanying salvation; so as a natural man, being altogether averse from that good, and dead in sin, is not
able, by his own strength, to convert himself, or to prepare himself thereunto" (S 623). Not only can human beings not perform repentance itself,
they cannot even do the preparation for a repentance effected by God. As
sinners, human beings are totally incapable of working their way out of
their sinfulness. Insofar as human beings' wills are in bondage in such a
way that they can will only what is evil, and thus cannot will to repent, repentance can be understood only as God liberating the wills of sinful human beings so that henceforth they can will not merely what is evil but also

what is good. When the will is freed from the bondage of sin by the repentance effected by God, the will's freedom consists in the repentant sinner being free to will what is good. "When God converts a Sinner, and translates him into the State of Grace, he freeth him from his natural Bondage under Sin; and by his Grace alone enables him freely to will and to do that which is spiritually good" (M 564, 30–36).

If, as sinners, human beings cannot even will what is good, then it is impossible for the actions they perform to be good. For Zwingli's Articles, this means "that our works . . . in so far as they are our works . . . are neither righteous nor good" (C 38). Therefore it cannot be the case "that man's own works are necessary for his justification" (C 57). From the outset—according to the Geneva Catechism—"all that we do of ourselves, by our own nature, is vicious, and therefore cannot please God. He condemns them all" (T 23). Just as a bad tree brings forth bad fruits, so do human beings as sinners bring forth only sins. "Even if our works appear beautiful outwardly, yet they are evil, since the heart . . . is perverted" (ibid.) For this reason we are unable "by our merits [to] anticipate God, and so [to] induce Him to be kind to us" (ibid.). As the sinners that all human beings in fact are, they cannot by their own activity be justified before God. Instead before the judgment seat of God we are convicted of godlessness and found worthy of death. We are never justified before God "on account of our works and merits" (*propter opera et merita nostra*) (S 494). All human activities—that is, "works"—are excluded from being constitutive means of justifying sinners. "As we willingly disclaim any honour and glory for our own creation and redemption, so do we willingly also for our regeneration and sanctification; for by ourselves we are not capable of thinking one good thought, but He who has begun the work in us alone continues us in it, to the praise and glory of His undeserved grace" (C 172). According to the Second Helvetic Confession our justification does not come about by God justifying us on the basis of our own actions. It is "solely by the grace of Christ and not from any merit of ours or consideration for us [that] we are justified, that is, absolved from sin and death by God the Judge" (C 255). Justification occurs "not through any works" (C 256).

Our justification does not occur on the basis of our own actions, since they, because they are in fact sinful, can never provide a reason why God justifies us. Instead our justification springs solely from God's grace. As early as the Zurich Introduction we read about "God's gracious action, called the gospel, which God carries out with us by God's Son" (M 13, 20–21). This gracious action on God's part consists in the fact that "by our works we do not become blessed, but by the pure grace of God, through the Lord Jesus Christ, who pays the price" (M 13, 38–40). Contrary to Scholasticism's understanding of grace as a disposition of character (*habitus*), grace is not viewed here as a specific property or disposition, which is communicated to human beings. Instead, grace is a quality of divine relational behavior toward human beings as sinners. Accordingly, it is possible to replace the concept of grace (*gratia*) with concepts that as synonyms of grace make clear that grace is a manner in which God relates to human beings: concepts such as God's love (M 281, 32), mercy (M 15, 48), or good pleasure (C 57). The fact that God justifies us is the expression of the fact that God is merciful to us. God's grace is the first cause (*causa primaria*)—that is, the sole ground—of justification (M 281, 32).

Admittedly, justification itself is understood in a variety of ways. For the oldest confessions, justification is repeatedly seen as identical with effectively making people just and godly. Thus for the Tetrapolitan Confession, justification consists in the fact that "human beings become godly and just (*fromm und gerecht*)" (M 57, 3), while the First Helvetic Confession explicitly characterizes justification as the "act of making godly (*Frommmachung*)" (M 104, 20). In the Tetrapolitan Confession, the aspect of the forgiveness of sins and the forensic declaration of righteousness recedes completely behind the act of effectively making people just. Justification is understood in this case as a process that embraces the entire life of human beings. To be sure, this does not mean that the exclusive grounding of justification in a divine act of grace is surrendered. "It is evident enough that our works can help us nothing, so that instead of unrighteous, as we are born, we may become righteous. . . . But the beginning of all our righteousness and salvation must proceed from the mercy of the Lord, who from his own favor and the contemplation of the death of his Son first offers the doctrine of truth and his Gospel, those being sent forth who are to preach it" (C 58). Admittedly, along with this effective understanding of justification, we also encounter in the early confessions a forensic understanding of justification. The Synodical Declaration of Berne defines the gospel as a "power of God that lays hold of, changes, and renews the hearts of believers, and takes poor sinners and makes them into children of God and right and heavenly people" (M 37, 2). But this process of renewal is traced back to the primary act of the forgiveness of sins. "In order for one to come to such gifts and graces, the beginning must be with the death and resurrection of Christ. Repentance and forgiveness of sins must be proclaimed in his name" (M 37, 6–8). It is through faith in Christ—that is, by entrusting oneself to the gift of God in Christ—that grace is accepted, "through which all past sin is forgiven us and is no longer reckoned to us for punishment" (M 41, 20–21).

As the process of confessional development continues, though, the forensic aspect of justification assumes the primary position so one-sidedly that in listing the various senses of the word "justify," the Second Helvetic Confession no longer even names the act of effectively making people just. We read there that "according to the apostle in his treatment of justification, to justify means to remit sins, to absolve from guilt and punishment, to receive into favor, and to pronounce a man just" (C 255). Insofar as in the act of justification God as judge stands over against us as the accused and absolves and declares us just, justification is a juridical process, a forensic act (*actus forensis*). In this act God forgives our sins and pardons us for them: that is, God as judge does not reckon them to us, and therefore does not punish us for them. According to the Geneva Catechism, "we on our part could not make any recompence to God, but may only receive pardon for all our misdeeds through the pure generosity of God" (T 21). The forgiveness of sins is thus the absolution, arising out of free grace, from the guilt of sin and the penalty for sin. The sins for which we continually pray to God for forgiveness are "debts . . . making us liable to eternal death" (T 49). In the act of justification we are given amnesty from eternal death (*mors aeterna*) as the just penalty for the guilt that we have incurred by our sinfulness. We are given this amnesty because we are absolved from guilt. By free grace God forgives our sin, absolving us from the guilt of sin and the penalty for sin. On the basis of this forgiveness, we are acceptable to God, "just as if we were righteous and innocent" (T 49–50). When God justifies us, God declares us just. Justification is thereby a declaration of righteousness before the forum of divine judgment.

Justification occurs solely *by* God's grace (*ex gratia Dei*). But at the same time it occurs *on the basis* not of our own works but of Christ's work or merit (*propter meritum Christi*) (M 281, 32ff.). The Erlauthal Confession accordingly differentiates between two causes of justification (*causae iustificationis*): God's grace as first cause (*causa primaria*) and Christ's merit as "cause on account of which" (*causa propter quam*). Christ's merit must be differentiated as follows. On the one hand, there is Christ's merit in Christ himself; on the other hand, there is Christ's merit attributed to us sinners (M 288, 5ff.). In Christ the merit of Christ is present "causally and meritoriously" (*causaliter et meritorie*), while in us it is present "by imputation, by gift and grace" (*imputative, ex donatione et gratia*). Although on the basis of our sinfulness we have merited only eternal death as damnation and exclusion from salvation, God declares us just by grace alone, inasmuch as God attributes Christ's merit to us. That which Christ has merited is "imputed" to us—an expression picked up from the terminology of late medieval Nominalism.

The Belgic Confession therefore also declares that we are justified by Christ Jesus, inasmuch as "Jesus Christ, imputing to us all his merits, and so many holy works, which he hath done for us and in our stead, is our Righteousness" (S 408). Christ's merit consists, however, in his reconciling action, which satisfies God's righteousness. That is, Christ's merit consists in his substitutionary obedience that makes satisfaction for us. By his passive and active obedience, by his suffering of punishment, and by his fulfillment of the law, Christ proves to be the only one who is just. Therefore, for the Second Helvetic Confession the fact that God justifies us on account of Christ's merit means that "God is propitious with respect to our sins and does not impute them to us, but imputes Christ's righteousness to us as our own (2 Cor. 5:19ff.; Rom. 4:25), so that now we are not only cleansed and purged from sins or are holy, but also . . . granted the righteousness of Christ" (C 256). "God alone justifies us, and justifies only on account of Christ, not imputing sins to us but imputing his righteousness to us" (ibid.). Justification occurs by grace on the basis of Christ's merit. Specifically, justification occurs by our sins not being imputed to us, and by Christ's righteousness being imputed to us (M 281, 38–39). It is not the case that our behavior provides the basis for God's justification. Rather, "merely through His goodness, without any regard to our works, He is pleased to accept us freely in Jesus Christ, imputing His righteousness to us, and does not impute our sins to us" (T 23–24).

To the question of how sinful human beings are righteous before God, the Heidelberg Catechism can thus answer that "God, without any merit of mine, of mere grace, grants and imputes to me the perfect satisfaction, righteousness, and holiness of Christ, as if I had never committed nor had any sin, and had myself accomplished all the obedience which Christ has fulfilled for me" (S 326–27).

THE CRITICAL RESPONSE TO THE
TRIDENTINE DECREE ON JUSTIFICATION

By saying that Christ's merit is the "cause on account of which" of the process of justification, and thus that we are justified on account of Christ's merit, the confessional writings set themselves in opposition to all attempts of any sort to ground justification in human merits. Justification rests exclusively on God's action on the basis of Christ's righteousness and merit. In articulating this position, the confessional writings increasingly emphasize the forensic character of justification. They do so primarily in critical response to the Tridentine decree on justification and to the Roman doctrine of justification that received dogmatic form in that decree. The Erlauthal Confession represents an exception when, in spite of the purely forensic doctrine of justification which it advances, it can characterize the Tridentine decree "On Justification, Faith and Works" as a conciliar decree in agreement with the truth of scripture, and can accept (reciimus) it as such (M 327, 9–10).

This is not to dispute that the first three canons of Trent are in thoroughgoing agreement with the Reformers in explicitly excluding a Pelagian doctrine of justification. The Roman side does not dispute the rejection of the claim that "without divine grace through Jesus Christ, man can be justified before God by his own works, whether they were done by his natural powers or by the light of the teaching of the Law" (DS 1551, CT 575). Nor does grace have the function merely of making it easier for human beings to live the righteous life and thereby to merit eternal life. Instead Trent rejects the idea that human beings—with or without the help of grace—can merit (*promereri possit*) eternal life through their free will (DS 1552). The following statement of Trent could seem to be a reception of the Reformation doctrine of justification: "Nothing that precedes justification, neither faith nor works, merits the grace of justification; for 'if out of grace, then not in virtue of works; otherwise (as the same Apostle says) grace is no longer grace'" (DS 1532, CT 565). The justification of sinners can in no way be merited (*promeretur*) by human beings through their own activity.

Does this statement agree with the Reformation position that sinners cannot be justified by their own works? The answer to this question depends primarily on what is excluded by excluding a meriting of justifying grace. Does the Latin term for "merit" (*promereri*) that is employed here instead of the more common *mereri* stand for the achievement only of a "merit of worth" (*meritum de condigno*) or also of a "merit of congruence" (*meritum de congruo*)? It is common opinion (*opinio communis*) that human beings with the works they accomplish prior to justification cannot produce a merit of worth for the reception of justifying grace. By contrast, it is a disputed question whether they are capable of achieving a merit of congruence. If the choice of the expression *promereri* instead of *mereri* in fact means that the Tridentine decree does not want to rule out the ability of sinful human beings to achieve a merit of congruence that would dispose them to receive justifying grace, then the decree contradicts the Reformation's doctrine of justification. The Anglican Articles declare explicitly that all human works accomplished prior to justification are not pleasing (*grata*) to God, and that no grace of congruence (*gratia de congruo*) is merited (*merentur*) by them. Instead, they are exclusively sins (S 495). It is therefore not enough that the concepts of *meritum* and *mereri* are used in the decree on justification. One could speak of agreement between Trent's doctrine of justification and that of the Reformation only if Trent not only did not mention the idea of a merit of congruence preparatory to the reception of justifying grace, but excluded such an idea.

However, one is compelled to say that the way in which the decree concerning justification describes the preparation of human beings to receive justifying grace includes more than excludes the idea of a merit of congruence. This is connected to the fact that the Reformation's rejection of a merit of congruence is grounded in human sinfulness. Because human beings prior to being justified can produce only sins, human beings are incapable of achieving a merit of congruence and thus preparing themselves to be justified. This means that the human will is enslaved and not free. But Trent's statement that nothing that precedes justification merits (*promereri*) the grace of justification not only does not imply such a denial of the freedom of the will, it solemnly rejects such a denial. For the free will, "though weakened and unsteady, was by no means destroyed" in sinners (DS 1521, CT 557). Therefore, "if anyone says that after Adam's sin man's free will was destroyed and lost . . . let him be anathema" (DS 1555, CT 579). It is only against the background of this rejection of the Reformation thesis of the bondage of the will that one can understand the further statement that denies "that all works performed before justification, regardless of how they were performed, are truly sins or merit God's hatred" (DS 1557, CT 581). Disputing the sinfulness of all human actions accomplished prior to justification is of central importance for the Tridentine understanding of justification. Only by disputing that sinfulness is it possible to speak of a positive human preparation for the reception of justifying grace. Such a preparation is regarded as necessary. As a logical consequence, Trent rejects the view "that it is not at all necessary [for 'sinful man'] that he be prepared and disposed by the action of his will" (DS 1559, CT 583).

To be sure, the prevenient grace (*gratia preveniens*) through Christ—that is, "God's call, a call which they [sc. human beings] do not merit" (DS 1525, CT 561)—forms the point of departure for the process of justification. But prevenient grace, which is not merited, functions only to prepare sinners "to turn to their own justification by freely assenting to and cooperating with that grace" (*gratiae libere assentiendo et cooperando*) (ibid.). Indeed the very acceptance of prevenient grace presupposes a free activity of the will on the part of the sinner, so that already at this juncture he is no longer behaving merely passively (*mere passive*) (DS 1554). After the acceptance of prevenient grace, the free will is fully at work in preparing to receive justifying grace. But this means that even faith merely in the sense of acknowledging the truth of the verities of revelation (*fides informis*) is accepted only by the power of the sinner's free will (DS 1526).

The will likewise participates at the other levels of the process of preparing to receive justifying grace: that is, in the fear of divine righteousness, in reflection on God's mercy, in hope for God's grace, at the beginning of love, at the beginning of the hatred of sin, and ultimately in the intention of baptism or penance. According to the Roman view, one must reject the thesis "that the free will of man, moved and awakened by God, in no way coooperates with the awakening call of God by an assent by which man disposes and prepares himself to get the grace of justification" (DS 1554, CT 578). But the importance of such a cooperation of the free human will first becomes fully clear when one considers that, although the Holy Spirit imparts justifying grace to the particular individual, the measure imparted depends by no means exclusively on the Spirit. Instead grace is imparted "according to the disposition and cooperation of each one [sc. of us]" (DS

1529, CT 563). In this way the reception of justifying grace is made dependent on the action accomplished by the free activity of the will of the sinful human being. Reformation theology sets in opposition to such an understanding of justification the thesis that sinners who have not yet been justified behave in a purely receptive manner (*mere passive*) in the act of justification (M 275, 41ff.). Not only do sinful human beings not cooperate in the process of justification in such a way that they prepare to receive justification, but because of their enslaved will they cannot even cooperate in this way. The enslaved will excludes the capacity for such cooperation.

This of course does not delineate the only difference between Trent's doctrine of justification and the Reformation's. The two differ not only with regard to the description of the preparation for justification but also with regard to the description of justification itself. It is no secret that the Tridentine decree opposes the exclusive understanding of justification as a forensic act of not imputing sins and of imputing Christ's righteousness. Trent disputes the view "that men are justified either through the imputation of Christ's justice (*imputatione iustitiae Christi*) alone, or through the remission of sins alone, excluding grace and charity which is poured forth (*diffundatur*) in their hearts by the Holy Spirit and inheres (*inhaereat*) in them, or also that the grace which justifies us is only the good will (*favor*) of God" (DS 1561, CT 585). Trent sees justification not only as forgiveness of sins but also as "sanctification and renovation of the interior man through the voluntary reception of grace and gifts" (DS 1528, CT 563). Through this sanctification and renovation human beings go from being unrighteous to being righteous. The sole formal cause of this sanctification and renovation is that justice of God which God's self does not possess as a property, but "by which he makes us just (*qua nos iustos facit*), namely, the justice which we have as a gift from him and by which we are renewed in the spirit of our mind. And not only are we considered (*reputamur*) just, but we are truly said to be just, and we are (*sumus*) just" (DS 1529, CT 563). Justifying grace is accordingly the infused grace (*gratia infusa*) communicated to us, and which inheres in us on the basis of this communication. The reception of justifying grace effects a qualitative change in us, insofar as we set aside the property of unrighteousness and accept in its stead the property of righteousness.

To be sure, no one is righteous except those to whom Christ's merit is communicated. But this communication occurs by the cardinal virtues of faith, hope, and love being poured into human beings. The "infusion" (*infusio*) of the cardinal virtues is the infusion of the righteousness by which we ourselves are made righteous, and that infusion forms the presupposition of our justification in the sense of our being declared righteous. "The justice that is said to be ours because it inheres in us is likewise God's justice because we have been infused with it through the merit of Christ" (DS 1547, CT 573). Justification accordingly consists in the fact that, on the basis of Christ's merit, we are infused with God's righteousness, which *makes* us righteous so that we not only *are counted* as righteous, but *are* righteous. The act of making just or righteous thus forms the ground and presupposition for the act of declaring just or righteous, so that this act of declaration is not a synthetic judgment, but an analytic one.

Trent gives dogmatic formulation to this understanding of justification: that is, that God makes people just by infusing them with a disposition of character (*habitus*). It is in opposition to this understanding that the Westminster Confession declares that God justifies sinners "not by *infusing* righteousness into them, but by pardoning their sins, and by *accounting and accepting* their persons as righteous (*pro justis reputando atque acceptando*)" (S 626; cf. M 620, 40ff.). It is precisely not the case that justification consists of God infusing sinful human beings with righteousness as a "habitual" gift of grace, and declaring them righteous on the basis of this qualitative change. The judgment that declares the righteousness of human beings is not a true descriptive—that is, analytic—statement about human beings. It is, rather, a synthetic judgment: namely, the judge's word that declares sinners righteous, but does not predicate righteousness of righteous human beings. This judgment is pronounced exclusively on the basis of Christ's obedience and satisfaction: that is, Christ's active and passive obedience.

As a forensic act and as the judgment pronounced by God the judge, justification consists in the fact that our sins are not imputed to us, but alien righteousness—Christ's active and passive obedience—is imputed to us. God declares sinners righteous "by imputing the obedience and satisfaction of Christ unto them, they receiving and resting on him and his righteousness by faith" (S 626). In the words of the Irish Articles, "we are accounted righteous before God only for the merit of our Lord and Saviour Jesus Christ, applied by faith, and not for our own works or merits. And this righteousness, which we so receive of God's mercy and Christ's merits, embraced by faith, is taken, accepted, and allowed of God, for our perfect and full justification" (S 532). God's grace thus does not cancel the divine justice, for Christ alone is just, in our stead. "And thus the justice and mercy of God do embrace each other: the grace of God not shutting out the justice of God in the matter of our justification, but only shutting out the justice of man (that is to say, the justice of our own works) from being any cause of deserving our justification" (S 533).

FAITH AS JUSTIFYING (*FIDES IUSTIFICANS*)

When Christ's active and passive obedience are understood as the only "cause on account of which" of justification, it is impossible to regard faith as that on the basis of which we are justified. But then what does it mean to claim that we are justified only by faith, as opposed to being justified on the

basis of works? In the Zurich Introduction, Zwingli vividly describes justification by faith alone (*iustificatio sola fide*). "This process of becoming just is
nothing other than the human being surrendering himself and placing himself in God's grace. This is true faith" (M 15, 31–33). While the Pharisee trusts
in his works and "builds on earthen soil" (M 16, 5–6), the tax collector "de-
spaired of all his godliness, but did not despair of God" (M 15, 47). The tax
collector is nevertheless declared to be more godly than the Pharisee, not on
the basis of his works, but because he held God to be so merciful and faithful that God would hear him, as God had promised. The righteousness of
faith consists in the fact that this righteousness "condemns nothing other
than itself, takes itself out of the picture, and casts itself solely on God's
mercy and builds on the rock" (M 16, 10–12). The tax collector's righteousness of faith is contrasted with the Pharisee's righteousness of works.

But this contrast is meaningful only if faith itself is not in turn understood as a work. If faith were a work, the righteousness of faith would only
be a particular version of works righteousness. But precisely that is to be
excluded. In the words of the First Confession of Basle, "we confess that
there is forgiveness of sins through faith in Jesus Christ the crucified. . . .
We do not ascribe to works . . . the righteousness and satisfaction for our
sins. On the contrary, we ascribe it solely to a genuine trust and faith in the
shed blood of the Lamb of God. For we freely confess that all things are
granted to us in Christ, Who is our righteousness, holiness, redemption,
the way, the truth, the wisdom and the life" (C 94–95). If in the act of justification human beings behave merely passively, it is impossible for justifying faith itself to be a human work.

Admittedly, the Geneva Catechism says of faith that "it justifies us before God" (T 23). For "in believing the promises of the gospel and in receiving them in true affiance of the heart, we enter into this (sc. Christ's)
righteousness" (T 24). In faith we accept the justice of Christ offered to us
by God in the gospel, so that "we are made partakers of this justice by faith
alone" (S 370, trans. altered). "The good pleasure of God and the merit of
Christ" are thus "to be received by faith alone" (C 57). At the same time the
idea that faith itself is a work that we must perform in order to be justified
by God is vehemently disputed. With reference to Rom. 3:28, the Belgic
Confession declares: "To speak more clearly, we do not mean that faith itself justifies us, for it is only an instrument with which we embrace Christ
our Righteousness. But Jesus Christ, imputing to us all his merits, and so
many holy works, which he hath done for us and in our stead, is our Righteousness" (S 408). We are accordingly justified not on the basis of our faith,
but on the basis of Christ's obedience: that is, Christ's righteousness. It is
Christ's righteousness that is imputed to us, and on the basis of which we
are declared righteous. Our justification does not consist in our faith being
imputed to us as our righteousness. As the Westminster Confession puts

it, God declares human beings righteous not "by imputing faith itself, the act of believing, or any other evangelical obedience to them, as their righteousness" (S 626).

Faith is not another cause on account of which (*causa propter quam*) of justification besides, or even instead of, Christ's merit. On the contrary, faith is solely the instrument for grasping Christ's merit (*meritum Christi*), and thus Christ's righteousness. The First Helvetic Confession states that "we do not obtain such sublime and great benefits of God's grace and the true sanctification of God's Spirit through our merits or powers but through faith" (C 104). As the posture of reception taken up by the human being who is looking to Christ's merit, faith is an instrumental cause (*causa instrumentalis*) of justification (M 281, 34–35). Consequently, the fact that I am righteous by faith alone before God cannot mean, from the perspective of the Heidelberg Catechism, "that I am acceptable to God on account of the worthiness of my faith; but because only the satisfaction, righteousness, and holiness of Christ is my righteousness before God, and I can receive the same and make it my own in no other way than by faith only" (S 327). Faith directed toward Christ's merit is thus "the alone instrument of justification" (S 626). The Irish Articles reject as mistaken the view "that this, our act, to believe in Christ, or this, our faith in Christ, which is within us, doth of itself justify us or deserve our justification unto us (for that were to account ourselves to be justified by the virtue or dignity of something that is within ourselves)" (S 533). Justification by faith alone means that faith is that posture in which human beings receive the righteousness of Christ, by which alone they are justified. For "because faith doth directly send us to Christ for our justification, and that by faith given us of God we embrace the promise of God's mercy and the remission of our sins . . . therefore the Scripture useth to say that *faith without works*—and the ancient fathers of the Church to the same purpose—that *only faith* doth justify us" (ibid.).

Functioning as a medium of reception, an instrument, and an instrumental cause of justification, faith is not a posture or attitude that can be achieved by human beings. Human beings are not summoned so to dispose themselves that they might, as purely receptive, receive justification from God. If human beings behave merely passively in the act of justification, this also means that they cannot themselves produce this purely receptive attitude. As an instrument of justification, faith is not the work of human beings, but the work of God. Human beings are justified by faith alone, "which faith they have not of themselves, it is the gift of God" (S 626). We read in the Second Helvetic Confession: "Because faith receives Christ our righteousness and attributes everything to the grace of God in Christ, on that account justification is attributed to faith, chiefly because of Christ and not therefore because it is our work. For it is the gift of God" (C

256). It is "a pure gift of God" (C 104). This statement can be specified still further. Faith is not a human accomplishment, but a gift of God: more precisely, a gift of the Holy Spirit. In the words of the Scottish Confession, "our faith and its assurance do not proceed from flesh and blood, that is to say, from natural powers within us, but are the inspiration of the Holy Ghost; whom we confess to be God, equal with the Father and with His Son" (C 171). It is the divine Spirit who works faith in us. "We are enlightened in faith by the secret grace of the Holy Spirit" (S 371, trans. altered). The French Confession says of this unmerited gift of grace that God grants it "to whom he will, so that the faithful have no cause to glory" (ibid., trans. altered). Faith is therefore not under our control. In fact it is totally beyond our reach. Only in this way is its character as a gift preserved. Otherwise it would be made into a posture or attitude that we could produce. The fact that faith is a gift communicated to us by God through the Holy Spirit means that God gives us faith "according to his measure when, to whom and to the degree he wills" (C 257).

The early confessions identify faith with "heartfelt trust in such inconceivable grace of God" (M 41, 11–12; cf. C 95). By contrast, in the development of Reformed Orthodoxy the cognitive and intellectual aspect of faith increasingly comes to the fore. But this does not lead to Christian faith being confused with a merely human opinion. "Christian faith is not an opinion (*opinio*) or human conviction (*humana persuasio*), but a most firm trust (*firmissima fiducia*) and a clear and steadfast assent of the mind (*evidens ac constans animi assensus*), and then a most certain apprehension of the truth of God (*certissima comprehensio veritatis Dei*) presented in the Scriptures and in the Apostles' Creed, and thus also of God himself, the greatest good, and especially of God's promise and of Christ who is the fulfillment of all promises" (C 257, S 268). According to the preceding quotation from the Second Helvetic Confession, the faith worked by God is thus threefold. Given the Orthodox identification of revelation with scripture, faith is a certain knowledge of God's truth as revealed in scripture and confessed in the Creed. In this sense faith is a cognitive act. If we believe, that also means that we hold that revealed truth of God to be true. "By this faith a Christian believeth to be true whatsoever is revealed in the Word, for the authority of God himself speaking therein" (S 630). As a cognitive act, faith is thus "a certain knowledge whereby I hold for truth all that God has revealed to us in his Word" (S 313). Faith has to do with the "Articles of Christian Religion." The Heidelberg Catechism answers the question about the content of faith by saying that everything must be believed "that is promised us in the Gospel, which the articles of our catholic, undoubted Christian faith teach us in sum" (S 314). On this view faith is a cognitive comprehension of formulated faith-ideas, which is supplemented by the volitional act of the heart's assent.

Nevertheless, Christian faith is not exhausted by historical faith (*fides historica*), supported by assent (*assensus*) (M 282, 30–31). According to the Erlauthal Confession, a merely historical faith is not a justifying faith, because the former faith is also the property of demons and unbelievers. The definition of faith (*fides*) as trust (*fiducia*) remains determinative even where, under the influence of the Orthodox identification of revelation with scripture, the cognitive aspect of faith is pushed into the foreground. Justifying faith is fiduciary faith, directed toward the promise of the forgiveness of sin. In this sense, according to the Heidelberg Catechism, justifying faith is "a hearty trust . . . that not only to others, but to me also, forgiveness of sins, everlasting righteousness and salvation, are freely given by God, merely of grace, only for the sake of Christ's merits" (S 313). It is only in this act of trusting in personal forgiveness of sins and justification that faith attains its goal. In the words of the Westminster Confession, "the principal acts of saving faith are accepting, receiving, and resting upon Christ alone for justification, sanctification, and eternal life, by virtue of the covenant of grace" (S 630–31). Through this faith, seen as trust, we are incorporated into Christ in such a way that we gain a share in all of his good deeds. As we read in the Belgic Confession, faith "embraces Jesus Christ with all his merits, appropriates him, and seeks nothing more besides him. For it must needs follow, either that all which are requisite to our salvation are not in Jesus Christ, or if all things are in him that then those who possess Jesus Christ through faith have complete salvation in Him" (S 408). Defined as trust, faith in the forgiveness of sins consists of entrusting ourselves to Christ. In the act of entrusting ourselves we are incorporated into Christ, so that in faith that union with Christ (*unio cum Christo*) arises in which we gain a share in his righteousness.

SANCTIFICATION AND PENANCE

FAITH AND LOVE

In Reformation theology justification occurs not on the basis of works but on the basis of Christ's righteousness. Nevertheless, faith and works are placed in close relation to each other. This is especially clear where justification is understood not only as a forensic declaration of righteousness and forgiveness of sins but as the process of effectively making human beings just. The Tetrapolitan Confession, in particular, conceives justification as a "making godly": that is, as the process of becoming "godly and just" (*fromm und gerecht*) (M 57, 31). Faith here is not to be understood "as though we placed salvation and godliness (*Frömmigkeit*) in slothful thoughts of the mind, or in faith destitute of love, which [people] call faith without form" (C 58; M 58, 3–5). On the contrary, the Tetrapolitan Confession means "evangelical" faith—"to wit, that which is efficacious through love" (C 59). This love is the fulfillment of the law. Through this faith we are born anew and "reformed to the perfect image of God" (ibid.). The Tetrapolitan Confession can even declare that we could not be saved at all without good works: that is, without being made just. This could give the impression that the Confession was approximating the Roman doctrine of justification. Yet this is not the case, because the recourse here to love does not mean that human work is granted a constitutive place in the process of justification. On the contrary, justification as a whole, understood as the process of making human beings just, is traced back to God. God pronounces the sinner righteous not merely to leave her as she is, but to recreate her as a righteous person, the image of Christ. "This renewal and restoration of human beings, described above, comes by faith and exists by faith, and through love shows itself and becomes whole—all of which in such a way that this renewal and restoration must not be ascribed to any other power than the Spirit of Christ Jesus" (M 59, 3–6). We become godly and just not by our own works, but by the grace of God, who makes us just. Accordingly, we read in the First Helvetic Confession: "And although godly believers constantly exercise themselves in such fruits of faith, yet we do not ascribe the piety and the salvation obtained to such works, but only to the grace of God" (C 104).

This rooting of justification solely in the grace of God is naturally in full force where justification is no longer regarded as the process of effectively making human beings just, but as a forensic declaration of justice. Although in this latter case faith is also intimately tied to works, works are not an integral part of justification, but its result. Works are the fruits of faith and as such cannot be the ground of justification. The First Confession of Basle thus declares: "Although this faith is continually exercised, signalized, and thus confirmed by works of love, yet do we not ascribe to works, which are the fruit of faith, the righteousness and satisfaction for our sins. On the contrary, we ascribe it solely to a genuine trust and faith in the shed blood of the Lamb of God" (C 94–95). Similarly, the French Confession says "that the good works which we do proceed from his [sc. God's] Spirit, and cannot be accounted to us for justification" (S 372). In the final analysis "we should always be doubting and restless in our hearts, if we did not rest upon the atonement by which Jesus Christ hath acquitted us" (ibid.). Our good works thus cannot be candidates for the role of ground of our justification. "For it is by faith in Christ that we are justified, even before we do good works, otherwise they could not be good works any more than the fruit of a tree can be good before the tree itself is good"

(S 411; cf. 494 and M 398, 34ff.). The purpose of good works cannot be that we "earn eternal life by them for, as the apostle says, eternal life is the gift of God" (C 259).

In all this the confessions decisively distance themselves from the Tridentine doctrine of justification. According to Trent's decree on justification, justification is a temporally extended process of becoming just, with faith being regarded as only the beginning of this process (DS 1532, CT 565). Justification does not consist exclusively of the forgiveness of sins on the basis of the imputation of Christ's righteousness (DS 1561, CT 585). The remission of sins (*remissio peccatorum*) represents only one aspect of the process of justification. This aspect is supplemented by the aspects of sanctification (*sanctificatio*) and renewal (*renovatio*) (DS 1528, CT 563). Admittedly, on this basis it can be said that we are justified by faith and not by our own merit. But here being justified by faith means only that "'faith is the beginning of man's salvation,' the foundation and source of all justification" (DS 1532, CT 565). Faith is comprehended here not as the continual and exclusive medium by means of which Christ's alien righteousness is appropriated to us, but as the point of departure for a process of justification. For this reason Trent can speak of a growth in justification. Justifying grace is an infused quality that inheres in us and that permits an increase. "When faith works along with their works (see James 2:22), the justified increase in the very justice which they have received through the grace of Christ and are justified the more, as it is written: 'He who is just, let him be just still'" (Apoc. 22:11) (DS 1535, CT 537). The infused righteousness by which we are justified can be increased by the good works which that righteousness enables us to perform. This means though—and this is the decisive difference—that good works (*bona opera*) can be considered as a cause of growth in justification, and thus of justification itself (DS 1574, CT 598). They are merits (*merita*) of those who are justified (DS 1582, CT 606). To be sure, righteousness in the sense of justifying grace is *infused* into us, and in that sense is *God's* righteousness. We ourselves are not its source. But at the same time it is *our* righteousness, because it *inheres* in us (DS 1574, CT 598). Only for this reason is it possible to put forward good works as *merits* of justified human beings, for which the *reward*, according to God's promise, is eternal life (DS 1545, CT 573). This is the reason for rejecting the thesis that, "by the good works he performs through the grace of God and the merits of Jesus Christ (of whom he is a living member), the justified man does not truly merit an increase of grace, life everlasting, and, provided that he dies in the state of grace, the attainment of that life everlasting" (DS 1582, CT 606).

According to the Roman view, good works as merits of the justified are a constitutive part of the process of justification. They are the reason for the growth in justification, and thus for justification itself, since it is conceived as an ongoing process. This view goes hand in hand with the rejection of the Evangelical connection between justification and good works: "If anyone says that justice which has been received is not preserved and even increased before God through good works, but that such works are merely the outgrowth and the signs of the reception of justification, not the cause of its increase as well: let him be anathema" (DS 1574, CT 598). To be sure, Reformation theology also asserts that there is a necessary connection between the justification of the sinner and the good works of the justified. Yet the manner of this necessary connection is fundamentally different from the one that obtains in the Roman understanding. For the Tridentine decree on justification, good works are merits, and thus the *ground* of the increase in justification. According to the Reformation's understanding, good works are seen in two ways. Where justification is understood as the process of making human beings just, as in the Tetrapolitan Confession, good works are the work of the God who recreates sinners. Where justification is conceived as the mere declaration of righteousness, as in the majority of the Reformed confessions, good works fall under the concept of sanctification, and are the consequence of justification, which is understood as their ground.

In this last case, the relation between ground and consequence is depicted by means of the example of the tree and its fruits. This example is intended to emphasize not only that faith and love belong together, but that they do so of necessity. As the Westminster Larger Catechism puts it, sanctification is inseparably (*inseparabiliter*) connected with justification (M 621, 45ff.). Faith "is continually exercised, signalized, and thus confirmed by works of love" (C 94–95). Therefore one cannot say that we are justified *without* good works, although we are not justified *on the basis* of good works. There is a difference between the two, insofar as the statement that we are not justified without works by no means implies that works are the ground of our justification. The point is to exclude this latter position without separating faith from works and rendering the connection between faith and works merely contingent. Therefore it is impossible to say that we are justified without doing good works.

The Geneva Catechism emphasizes that "to believe in Jesus Christ is to receive Him as He has given Himself to us. He promises not only to deliver us from death and to restore us to favour with God His Father, through the merit of His innocence, but also to regenerate us by His Spirit, that we may be enabled to live in holiness" (T 25). For the Belgic Confession "it is impossible that this holy faith can be unfruitful in man: for we do not speak of a vain faith, but of such a faith as is called in Scripture 'a faith that worketh by love,' which excites man to the practice of those works which God has commanded in his Word" (S 411). The Second Helvetic Confession declares that "works necessarily proceed from faith"

(C 260). If the connection between faith and works is necessary in such a way that not only is faith the necessary condition of works, but works are the necessary consequence of faith, then it is in fact impossible for us to be justified *without* works: that is, without faith having good works as its consequence, and thereby being formed faith, or faith active through love. The Irish Articles accordingly state: "When we say that we are justified by faith only, we do not mean that the said justifying faith is alone in man without true repentance, hope, charity, and the fear of God (for such a faith is dead, and can not justify)" (S 533). Faith, hope, and love are certainly proper to us as justified persons, but "because faith doth directly send us to Christ for our justification, and that by faith given us of God we embrace the promise of God's mercy and the remission of our sins . . . therefore the Scripture useth to say that 'faith without works'—and the ancient fathers of the Church to the same purpose—that 'only faith' doth justify us" (ibid.).

In advancing the thesis of justification by faith alone, the Irish Articles differentiate themselves from the Tridentine decree on justification, which assigns to faith only a subordinate role in the process of justification. The reason for the latter is that faith is comprehended here in a completely different way. In the Tridentine view, faith is precisely not "confidence that divine Mercy remits sins for Christ's sake" (DS 1562, CT 586). Faith as "faith by hearing" (*fides ex auditu*) is by no means trust, effected by the Holy Spirit through the word, in the divine promise. Instead it is the act of holding the truths of revelation to be true—an act that disposes one to receive justifying grace. This reception in turn is mediated exclusively sacramentally: namely, through the sacraments of baptism and penance (DS 1526, CT 562). By contrast, in justification, besides sins being forgiven, that faith is infused into human beings which "'gives eternal life.' But faith, without hope and charity, cannot give eternal life" (DS 1531, CT 564). Justifying faith is precisely not that trust in the forgiveness of sins, but faith formed by love. Because the faith that arises "by hearing" is understood here only as the act of accepting the truth of the articles of faith, it can be understood merely as preparation for infused righteousness: that is, for hope and love. "For faith without hope and charity neither perfectly unites a man with Christ nor makes him a living member of his body" (ibid.).

By contrast, the Irish Articles—and the Westminster Confession, which follows them—declare that justification happens only by faith. However, this by no means signifies the exclusion of hope and love, which in the Tridentine view are what, unlike faith, produce complete unity with Christ. The decisive difference is that the Irish Articles and the Westminster Confession define justifying faith not as a mere—even implicit—act of accepting the truth of articles of faith, with this act then requiring a secondary supplementation by the cardinal virtues of hope and love. Justifying faith, defined as trust (*fiducia*), is *eo ipso* living faith, not dead. Admittedly, the Westminster Confession states that "faith thus receiving and resting on Christ and his Righteousness, is the *alone* Instrument of Justification." Yet this faith is never "alone in the person justified, but is *ever* accompanied with all other saving graces, and is no dead faith, but worketh by love" (S 626).

The thesis of justification by faith alone aims to exclude not the necessary connection between faith and love, but the inclusion of love, as a human work, in the constitutive conditions of justification. For this reason the Second Helvetic Confession says that "we do not share in the benefit of justification partly because of the grace of God or Christ, and partly because of ourselves, our love, works or merit, but we attribute it wholly to the grace of God in Christ through faith" (C 256–57). Nevertheless, this justifying faith is identified with "living, quickening faith," which "is called a living faith because it apprehends Christ who is life and makes alive, and shows that it is alive by living works" (C 257). Although justifying faith is necessarily living faith and in this way is connected with love, the works of love cannot be regarded as necessary for salvation in such a way that they would be part of the foundational condition for justification. "Nevertheless . . . we do not think that we are saved by good works, and that they are so necessary for salvation that no one was ever saved without them. For we are saved by grace and the favor of Christ alone. Works necessarily proceed from faith. And salvation is improperly attributed to them, but is most properly ascribed to grace" (C 259–60).

PRACTICAL SYLLOGISM (*SYLLOGISMUS PRACTICUS*), WORKS AND REWARD

Insofar as the connection between faith and good works—that is, the connection between justification and sanctification—is treated as necessary, one can also say something about the relation between the knowledge of our sanctification and the knowledge of our justification. If works are those fruits which are the necessary and exclusive consequence of faith, then good works permit one to move in the reverse direction and draw a conclusion about faith. As necessary fruits of faith alone, works are also an indicator of faith. Just as good fruits permit one to draw a conclusion about the good tree, so do good works permit one to draw a conclusion about faith as their ground. What is at work in drawing this conclusion is the practical syllogism. The Synodical Declaration of Berne appeals to the community "to examine itself and to learn whether or not this . . . gracious will of God through Christ has been established and has gone to work in them: that is, that everyone know what he has truly received from Christ and what he lacks in the understanding and knowledge of Christ, which is nothing other than renewal of the heart and the internally spiritual, heavenly human being, who is without sin" (M 43, 17–23).

The Heidelberg Catechism's answer to the question of why we should do good works at all is in part a reference to certainty of faith. The performance of good works accordingly serves the purpose "that we ourselves may be assured of our faith by the fruits thereof" (S 338). The practical syllogism from works to justifying faith, which is *eo ipso* living faith—that is, faith active in love—declares works to be not the ontological ground of faith and justification, but their epistemological ground (M 391, 24ff.). Works are not only the fruits of faith; in addition, they make faith manifest. The Erlauthal Confession thus characterizes works as "seals of justifying grace" (*sigilla iustificationis gratiae*) (M 285, 35–36). The Westminster Confession says that "these good Works, done in Obedience to God's Commandments, are the Fruits and Evidences of a true and lively Faith" (M 574, 23–26). Indeed, if faith and love belong together like sun and light, fire and warmth (M 393, 6ff.), then it is possible to reason from works, as effects of faith, back to faith, as the effective cause of works (M 391, 37ff.).

The works at issue here are exclusively those of the justified. One must distinguish sharply between works of the justified and works of the unjustified. Works produced by unjustified sinners—that is, by unbelievers—can never be good works in the required sense. It is of course possible for the unjustified, also, to perform works that are good in the sense that they materially correspond to the actions commanded by God. Speaking of "works done by unregenerate Men," the Westminster Confession explicitly says that "*for the matter of them* they may be things which God commands, and of good use both to themselves and others" (S 635). Yet in spite of the usefulness of these deeds that materially correspond to the actions commanded by God, they are not good works in the strict sense. According to the Heidelberg Catechism, the only things that count as good works in the strict sense are those "which are done from true faith, according to the law of God, for his glory" (S 339–40). Their being good presupposes that they flow out of or emanate from faith. In this sense they always require faith and justification. Good works are necessarily works of the justified. They are works whose content is oriented toward God's law, "and not such as rest on our own opinion or the commandments of men" (S 340). "The law of God, which is his will, prescribes for us the pattern of good works. . . . And indeed works and worship which we choose arbitrarily are not pleasing to God. These Paul calls . . . 'self-devised worship'. . . . Therefore, we disapprove of such works, and approve and urge those that are of God's will and commission" (C 258–59). Just as the Second Helvetic Confession rejects special "spiritual" works, it also rejects supposed "philosophical" virtues. Instead "we diligently teach true, not false and philosophical virtues, truly good works, and the genuine service of a Christian" (C 260).

Although it is the case that good works *necessarily* emanate from the faith of the justified sinner, it is out of the question to ascribe any meritorious value to them. "We can not, by our best works, merit pardon of sin, or eternal life at the hand of God, by reason of the great disproportion that is between them and the glory to come, and the infinite distance that is between us and God, whom by them we can neither profit nor satisfy for the debt of our former sins" (S 634–35). According to the Heidelberg Catechism, "even our best works in this life are all imperfect and defiled with sin" (S 327). For this reason they can in no case be meritorious. For "the righteousness which can stand before the judgment-seat of God must be perfect throughout, and wholly conformable to the divine law" (ibid.). Since the law requires from us a perfect righteousness that we are unable to achieve, even as justified persons, because of the imperfection of even our best works, we cannot fulfill God's law even as justified persons. For this reason it is completely misguided for people to think "that by their own satisfactions they make amends for sins committed. For we teach that Christ alone by his death or passion is the satisfaction, propitiation or expiation of all sins" (C 255).

The fact that justification happens by grace alone removes our focus from the law's requirement, which we must fulfill in order to be just. When, as justified persons, we nevertheless do good works, albeit imperfect and always stained with sin, the reason for this cannot in any case lie in the meritoriousness of those works. In the words of the Irish Articles, "the regenerate can not fulfill the law of God perfectly in this life. For in many things we offend all; and if we say we have no sin, we deceive ourselves, and the truth is not in us" (S 534). The good works that we do as justified persons and that, because of their imperfection, cannot have any meritorious character, are performed by us exclusively out of gratitude for the justification that has occurred. The Second Helvetic Confession therefore asserts that the performance of good works "is not to be proudly obtruded upon God as a satisfaction for sins, but is to be performed humbly, in keeping with the nature of the children of God, as a new obedience out of gratitude for the deliverance and full satisfaction obtained by the death and satisfaction of the Son of God" (C 255).

Along the same line, the Heidelberg Catechism treats the theme of the Christian life in general under the heading "Of Thankfulness." As life in new obedience to God's law, the Christian life is nothing other than a grateful response to God's prevenient grace. "Since, then, we are redeemed from our misery by grace through Christ, without any merit of ours, why must we do good works? Because Christ, having redeemed us by his blood, renews us also by his holy Spirit after his own image, that with our whole life we may show ourselves thankful to God for his blessing, and that he may be glorified through us" (S 338). The only sacrifices that we can still make for Christ's sacrifice of atonement, performed once and for all, are sacrifices of praise and thanksgiving for this sacrifice of atonement, which is the ground of our justification. Good works contribute nothing to the satisfaction for our sins, because such satisfaction has occurred exclusively through Christ. In the view of the Basle Confession, the sole function of good works is to show "in some degree our gratitude to the Lord God for the great kindness He has shown in Christ" (C 95).

One wonders whether the Roman idea—that the good works of the justified are merits—might not be justified by the fact that the New Testament certainly does talk about *reward*. The concept of reward seems to require the concept of merit and achievement. If that were the case, then one would have to concede that it is in fact not enough to regard good works exclusively as fruits and signs of justification. On the contrary, one would have to ascribe to them a meritorious character, with the result that one could certainly speak of justified sinners meriting eternal life. As early as the Tetrapolitan Confession, though, we find opposition to this view. Appealing to Augustine, the Confession declares that "God rewards *his own* works in us" (C 60). Likewise, the Second Helvetic Confession says "that God does not crown in us our merits by *his* gifts" (C 261). In no way does this totally dispense with the idea of reward, but it does totally break the proportionality that obtains in the human realm between achievement and reward. To the question, "How is it that our good works merit nothing, while yet it is God's will to reward them in this life and in that which is to come?" the Heidelberg Catechism, appealing to Luke 17:10, responds by pointing out that "the reward comes not of merit, but of grace" (S 327).

The reward that God promises to us as those who accomplish good works is not a reward for merit. It is not a reward to which we could rightfully lay claim. On the contrary, it is a reward of grace. Any sort of immanent worthiness can no more be attested for the works of the justified than for our person. Just as our person is accepted by grace, so also our works. In the words of the Geneva Catechism, such works are pleasing to God "in that He generously accepts them, not however in virtue of their own worthiness" (T 24). For even though these works proceed from the Holy Spirit, a weakness of our flesh still adheres to them and defiles them. According to the Belgic Confession, "we can do no work but what is polluted by our flesh, and also punishable; and although we could perform such works, still the remembrance of one sin is sufficient to make God reject them" (S 412). Nevertheless, God accepts our good works as good, even though they are characterized by unworthiness: that is, God accepts as perfect the totally imperfect obedience of the justified in the not-yet-completed process of sanctification. God "covers our works, which are defiled with many stains, with the righteousness of His Son" (C 174).

To be sure, "in the works even of the saints there is much that is unworthy of God and very much that is imperfect. But because God receives into favor and embraces those who do works for Christ's sake, he grants to them the promised reward" (C 260–61). Therefore the works of justified sinners are pleasing to God only when they are done in faith. According to the Geneva Catechism, this faith means "that a person is assured in his conscience that God will not examine him harshly, but covering his defects and impurities by the purity of Jesus Christ, He will regard him as perfect" (C 24). Just as there is a justification of the person of the sinner, so there is also a justification of the works of the justified sinner, which consists in God accepting the good works insofar as God covers their unworthiness with Christ's righteousness. For, as the Westminster Confession puts it, "the persons of believers being accepted through Christ, their good works also are accepted in him, not as though they were in this life wholly unblamable and unreprovable in God's sight; but that he, looking upon them in his Son, is pleased to accept and reward that which is sincere, although accompanied with many weaknesses and imperfections" (S 635).

If the idea of merit is detached from the idea of good works, how much more is this true of the idea of a *superfluous* merit, which is supposed to be grounded by works of supererogation. "Therefore, whoever boasts of the merits of his own works or puts his trust in works of supererogation, boasts of what does not exist" (C 174–75). For the Scottish Confession, the doctrine of supererogatory merit reveals only the false starting point of the consideration of good works in general. The doctrine of supererogatory merit presupposes that the justified sinner is capable not only of perfectly fulfilling God's law, but also of carrying out particular works that are not contained in God's law, but which generate merit for the justified sinner. Over against a teaching of this type the Irish Articles advance the view that "voluntary works, besides over and above God's commandments, which they call works of supererogation, can not be taught without arrogancy and impiety; for by them men do declare that they do not only render unto God as much as they are bound to do, but that they do more for his sake than of bounden duty is required" (S 534). In no case do good works provide a ground for merit, and since the only work that counts as good is one enjoined by God's law, it is all the more clear that there can be no such thing as a supererogatory work. The reward that we receive always remains a reward of grace. In the words of the Second Helvetic Confession, "we do not ascribe this reward, which the Lord gives, to the merit of the man who receives it, but to the goodness, generosity and truthfulness of God who promises and gives it, and who, although he owes nothing to anyone, nevertheless promises that he will give a reward to his faithful worshippers" (C 260).

PENANCE AS REPENTANCE

Justification and sanctification are necessarily bound together. Sanctification is the result of justification. Sanctification is this result not as a meritorious achievement but as a divine gift of grace. Sanctification is that process by which Christ, through the Spirit, renews the justified sinner into Christ's image (S 338). Accordingly, we read in the Westminster Shorter Catechism that "sanctification is the work of God's free grace, whereby we are renewed in the whole man after the image of God, and are enabled more and more to die unto sin, and live unto righteousness" (S 683). From this perspective, sanctification consists in human beings' repentance: that is, their conversion. Since sanctification is the necessary result of justification, the Heidelberg Catechism must give a negative answer to the question, "Can they, then, not be saved who do not turn to God from their unthankful, impenitent life?" (S 339). Repentance is the conversion (*conversio*) of the whole human being, and consequently also the conversion of her way of living. Repentance is conversion from an ungrateful and impenitent manner of living to a grateful and penitent one. In this sense conversion is identical to penance, for penance is nothing other than the repentance or turning of a human being to God for the entire duration of the person's life. For this reason the Heidelberg Catechism speaks of human beings' "penance *or conversion*" (S 339, trans. altered; cf. M 707, 13–14). This conversion is not a one-time act, but an enduring process that can be described as "the dying of the old man, and the quickening of the new" (S 339).

Repentance is the result of justification. For this reason repentance presupposes faith. Accordingly the Erlauthal Confession, using Aristotelian terminology, can describe penance with regard to its various causes. The effective cause is God's grace; the formal cause, the Holy Spirit; the instrumental cause, faith with the word; the final cause, the new obedience (M 289, 6ff.). It is not the case that faith only comes after penance. On the contrary, penance is possible only on the presupposition of faith. Penance without faith is false penance. In this sense the Geneva Catechism sums up faith and penance together: "Faith, then, not only does not make us careless of good works, but is the root from which they are produced. . . . For this reason the doctrine of the Gospel is comprehended in these two points, faith and penance" (T 25, trans. altered; cf. J 30). In this understanding penance is defined as "dissatisfaction with and a hatred of evil and a love of good proceeding from the fear of God, and inducing us to mortify our flesh, so that we may be governed and led by the Holy Spirit, in the service of God" (T 25). According to the Second Helvetic Confession, the penitent ought to be vigilant and diligent "in striving for newness of life and in mortifying the old man and quickening the new" (C 254). But what is the meaning of the expression "the dying of the old human being"? The Heidelberg Catechism's answer is: "Heartfelt sorrow for sin; causing us to hate and run from it always more and more" (S 339). The "quickening of the new man" is accordingly described as "heartfelt joy in God; causing us to delight in living according to the will of God in all good works" (ibid.). As repentance, penance always has two sides. Seen negatively, it is putting the old human being to death (*mortificatio*); seen positively, it is making the new human being alive (*vivificatio*) (M 289, 8ff.; 392, 10ff.).

The Reformed view of penance must be understood against the background of the Roman doctrine of the sacrament of penance. According to this doctrine, penance is not an act that permeates the entire life of the believer, but an act that stands in relation to individual trespasses. This difference, in turn, is related to the different conceptions of the doctrine of justification. In the Evangelical view, the justified sinner is both sinner and justified. The Roman side, insofar as it conceives justification primarily as a qualitative change in human beings, disputes the Reformation slogan "at once both just and a sinner" (*simul iustus et peccator*). In this view penance cannot be understood as an act that permeates the entire life of the justified sinner. Instead it must be an action that stands in relation to the loss of justifiying grace as an inherent quality. Insofar as Baptism is regarded as the instrumental cause of justification (DS 1529, CT 563), effecting not only the forgiveness of all guilt but also the complete remission of punishment (DS 1316, CT 686), and insofar as a loss of justifying grace is possible, the sacrament of penance takes over the function of "the second plank after the ship has been wrecked and grace has been lost" (DS 1542, CT 571). Therefore "if anyone, failing to distinguish between the sacraments, says that the sacrament of Baptism as such is the sacrament of penance, as though they were not two distinct sacraments," that person is declared "anathema" (DS 1702, CT 801). The difference between baptism and penance lies primarily in the juridical character of penance. In penance the priest functions as a judge whose power of jurisdiction extends to all persons who, through baptism, have become members of the church. The baptized are to "stand accused before this tribunal of penance in order that the judgment of the priests might set them free, and not once only, but as often as they turn from the sins they have committed to the tribunal in true repentance" (DS 1671, CT 789). Absolution is thus a judicial act (DS 1673, CT 790; cf. DS 1685, CT 795; DS 1709, CT 808), the result of which is reconciliation with God (DS 1674, CT 790; cf. DS 1701, CT 800). The sacrament of penance is instituted as the administration of the power of the keys— that is, the power to bind and to loose (John 20:22–23)—in which "the power of remitting and of retaining sins, and of reconciling the faithful who have fallen after baptism was communicated to the apostles and to their legitimate successors" (DS 1670, CT 788; cf. DS 1703, CT 802).

If the words of absolution constitute the form of the sacrament of penance, the works of the penitent—namely, contrition, confession, and satisfaction—constitute the sacrament's quasi-material, which is necessary for the complete remission of sins (DS 1673, CT 790; DS 1323, CT 776; DS 1704, CT 803). Contrition is here understood as comprising two parts. First, there is pain of the soul and detestation of the sin that has been committed, which serve as preparation for receiving the sacrament. Second, this pain and detestation are coupled with the intention to do better (DS 1676, CT 791). The term *contritio* actually signifies contrition that is made *perfect* by love (DS 1677, CT 791). But the term is used here to mean, at the initial level, *imperfect* contrition, or *attritio* (DS 1678, CT 791). Attrition is that fear-based contrition that "is engendered by the examination, consideration, and detestation of sins, as a person reviews all his years with a bitter heart, meditating on the seriousness of his sins, their number and heinousness, the loss of eternal happiness and the eternal damnation incurred, and so proposes to lead a better life" (DS 1705, CT 804). Even this fear-based contrition is regarded as a gift of God and a necessary step in the penitent's self-preparation to receive the grace of the sacrament of penance (DS 1678, CT 791).

But in order to receive this grace it is also necessary to make a *complete* (*integra*) confession in private before the priest, at least of all *mortal* sins (DS 1706–7; CT 805–6). "If priests did not know the case, they could not exercise this judgment, nor could they observe equity in imposing penances if the penitents declared their sins in a general way only, instead of specifically and particularly" (DS 1679, CT 793). After all, unlike baptism, priestly absolution does not deal with the guilt of sin and with all penalties for sin. On the contrary, this doctrine of penance explicitly disputes the view "that our Lord never remits guilt without forgiving all punishment" (DS 1689, CT 797, trans. altered; cf. DS 1712, CT 811). Absolution applies exclusively to the guilt of sin and the *eternal* penalties for sin, so that the temporal penalty for sin still remains to be paid when the eternal penalty has been removed by the power of absolution (DS 1715, CT 814; DS 1692–93, CT 798–99).

But this means that "it is in accord with divine mercy that sins should not be forgiven us without any satisfaction" (DS 1690, CT 797). To be sure, the works of the penitent to make satisfaction are made possible in the first place by Christ's satisfaction. But the latter does not remove from the penitent the duty of doing things to make satisfaction. Instead, "satisfaction for the temporal punishment due to sins . . . [is] made to God through the merits of Christ either by the penances sent from God and patiently endured or by those imposed by the priest . . . [or] by penances voluntarily undertaken, such as fasts, prayers, almsgiving, or other works of piety" (DS 1713, CT 812; cf. DS 1543, CT 571). Finally, instead of oneself performing deeds to make satisfaction and thereby wipe out the temporal penalties for sin, indulgences can be substituted for such deeds. Indulgences represent a remission of temporal penalties for sin. Specifically, they are a remission that the church is authorized to impart on the basis of the treasure of Christ's merits, which is administered by the church. This remission can in turn be attained by believers through good works and demonstrations of piety (DS 1025–26, CT 817–18; DS 1835, CT 828).

The confessional writings' criticism of this Roman understanding of penance is directed primarily against the judicial regulation of penance. For the confessions, penance is nothing other than true repentance and conversion to God. The confessions regard as offensive in the Roman treatments of penance "auricular confessions, his [i.e., the pope's] desperate and uncertain repentance . . . his satisfaction of men for their sins . . . works of supererogation, merits, pardons, peregrinations, and stations" (S 482–83). The Second Helvetic Confession states: "We especially condemn the lucrative doctrine of the Pope concerning penance," as this doctrine finds expression in the practice of granting indulgences (C 254–55). For—in the words of Zwingli's Articles—"whoever remits sin solely for the sake of money is the partner of Simon and Balaam and is really a messenger of the devil" (C 42). "We also disapprove of those who think that by their own satisfactions they make amends for sins committed" (C 255).

The immediate target of the confessional writings' criticism are: (1) the penitential deeds done to make satisfaction, and which according to Roman teaching are necessary for absolution; (2) the allied practice of granting indulgences. Of course, the priestly absolution is pronounced *before* penitential deeds are performed. But these deeds are nevertheless supposed to be the *necessary condition* for the complete remission of sin. Zwingli's Articles see this position as disputing the sufficiency of Christ's satisfaction. "Christ has borne all our pain and misery. Whoever now attributes to works of penance what belongs to Christ alone, errs and blasphemes God" (C 42). Satisfactory character belongs only to the work of Christ, not to human works. The Second Helvetic Confession thus understands the Roman doctrine of the sacrament of penance as a denial of the sole sufficiency of Christ's work of satisfaction—even if that doctrine explains that penitential deeds have satisfactory character only on the basis of Christ's merit and apply exclusively to the temporal penalties for sin. "For we teach that Christ alone by his death or passion is the satisfaction, propitiation, or expiation of all sins" (and according to Evangelical understanding it is impossible to separate sin from the punishment for sin) (C 255).

However, the confessional writings not only reject the human activity of making satisfaction, which calls into question the sufficiency of Christ's work of satisfaction, but also reject the required second penitential deed, the complete private confession (*integra confessio privata*) before a priest, who functions as judge. In rejecting such confession, they call attention to the impossibility of a complete listing of all sins, and renounce a juridical understanding of penance. According to the Irish Articles, it is not "God's pleasure that his people should be tied to make a *particular* confession of all their known sins unto any *mortal man*" (S 539). It is here denied that the bearer of the office has any direct power of absolution. Such power belongs exclusively to God, while the bearer of the office has the responsibility "in his name to *declare and pronounce* unto such as truly repent and unfeignedly believe his holy Gospel the absolution and forgiveness of sins" (ibid.).

This by no means hinders the Westminster Confession from emphasizing that a "general Repentance" is not enough, but that the individual has the duty "to endeavor to repent of his particular sins particularly" (S 632). The decisive point here is that absolution and the forgiveness of sins are no longer understood as a juridical act, but are understood as a declaration of the gospel to those who are truly penitent and believing: that is, they are understood as response to the confession of sins. In the words of the Second Helvetic Confession, "neither do we think that this absolution becomes more effectual by being murmured in the ear of someone or by being murmured singly over someone's head. We are nevertheless of the opinion that the remission of sins in the blood of Christ is to be diligently proclaimed, and that each one is to be admonished that the forgiveness of sins pertains to him" (C 253–54).

In this act of proclaiming forgiveness of sins, the power of the keys is exercised. Christ handed over the keys to the apostles "when he sent out his disciples and commanded them to preach the Gospel in all the world, and to remit sins" (C 253). It is, after all, claimed that "an access to God is open to all sinners, and that he forgives all sinners of all sins except the one against the Holy Spirit" (C 254; cf. S 534). The Second Helvetic Confession is here thinking not of the individual's private confession of sins before God, but of a public and general act in worship. To be sure, it is the duty of every human being to confess his sins privately to God and to trust the promise of forgiveness (M 573, 38ff.). But besides this private confession "between God and the sinner," the Second Helvetic Confession also recognizes open guilt: that is, the "general and public confession of sin which is usually said in Church and in meetings for worship" (C 252–53).

When, over and above these two types of confession of sins, private auricular confession is rejected, it is clear already with Zwingli that this is not meant to dispute the legitimacy of freely and without compulsion "seeking counsel from one's pastor or neighbor" (BSLK 66, 26; cf. C 42, 78). In the formulation of the Second Helvetic Confession, if "anyone is overwhelmed by the burden of his sins and by perplexing temptations, and will seek counsel, instruction and comfort privately, either from a minister of the Church, or from any other brother who is instructed in God's law, we do not disapprove" (C 252–53). Private confession is thus totally stripped of its juridical character and is considered exclusively from the perspective of the care of souls.

The confession of sins is itself an expression of the penance and repentance of the sinful human being who—as the Second Helvetic Confession says—"immediately acknowledges his innate corruption and all his sins accused by the Word of God; and . . . grieves for them from his heart, and not only bewails and frankly confesses them before God with a feeling of shame, but also . . . with indignation abominates them; and . . . now zealously considers the amendment of his ways" (C 251). The contrition referred to here is not imperfect contrition in the sense of *attritio*, which is only contrition on the basis of the fear of punishment. Instead the Irish Articles characterize the contrition that is here at issue as *"godly sorrow . . . for offending God, their merciful Father, by their former transgressions"* (S 534). For this reason contrition is always connected with the intention to amend one's life. As an integral component of penance, contrition is already a fruit of faith, and is possible only in faith.

Speaking of penance defined as the complete recoverery of one's senses (*resipiscentia*), the Westminster Confession declares that in this penance "a sinner, out of the Sight and Sense, not only of the Danger, but also of the Filthiness and Odiousness of his Sins, as contrary to the holy Nature and righteous Law of God; and *upon the Apprehension of his Mercy in Christ* to such as are penitent, so grieves for and hates his Sin, as to turn from them all unto God, purposing and endeavouring to walk with him in all the Ways of his Commandments" (M 572, 17–M 573, 9). The Second Helvetic Confession likewise presents penance as grounded by faith when the Confession understands penance as "the recovery of a right mind in sinful man awakened by the Word of the Gospel and the Holy Spirit, and received by true faith" (C 251). Penance is thus "a sheer gift of God . . . and not a work of our strength" (ibid.). As such the Westminster Confession characterizes it as "an evangelical grace" (S 631).

Penance consists of putting the old human being to death and making the new alive. But this process of making alive is the will to do good works, and as persons converted to God, we do not possess the ability completely to observe God's commandments. Penance is thus a process that stretches throughout the entire life of believers. "Even the holiest men, while in this life, have only a small beginning of this obedience, yet so that with earnest purpose they begin to live, not only according to some, but according to all the commandments of God" (S 349). Therefore the proclamation of these commandments also has the purpose, "first, that all our life long we may learn more and more to know our sinful nature, and so the more earnestly seek forgiveness of sins and righteousness in Christ; secondly, that we may continually strive and beg from God the grace of the Holy Ghost, so as to become more and more changed into the image of God, till we attain finally to full perfection after this life" (ibid.). For this reason the Heidelberg Catechism can characterize prayer as "the chief part of the thankfulness which God requires of us" (S 350). Prayer brings to expression the fact that sinners are continually dependent on God's grace. It is not the case that justified human beings are able of their own accord to fulfill God's commandment. On the contrary, they must continually pray to God anew for this ability. Prayer is necessary for the Christian because "God will give his grace and Holy Spirit only to such as earnestly and without ceasing beg them from him and render thanks unto him for them" (ibid.).

JUDGMENT AND COMPLETION

The renewal of the human being in the image of Christ does not come to conclusion in this life. The goal of our earthly existence is not a condition within this world, but eternal life. The Geneva Catechism states "that our happiness is not situated on the earth." Therefore "we are to learn to pass through this world as though it were a foreign country, treating lightly all things and declining to set our hearts on them. Secondly, we are not to lose courage, no matter how much we fail to perceive as yet the fruit of the grace which the Lord has wrought for us in Jesus Christ, but wait patiently until the time of revelation" (T 22). Our earthly life has a super-earthly goal, and finds its fulfillment in this goal. The metaphor of the world as a foreign land through which we are to wander thus presents itself. The chiliastic conception of an intramundane fulfillment of human life is accordingly rejected. In the view of the Second Helvetic Confession, such conceptions are only "Jewish dreams that there will be a golden age on earth before the Day of Judgment, and that the pious, having subdued all their godless enemies, will possess all the kingdoms of the earth" (C 245–46).

The conception of purgatory as an intermediate condition between earthly and superearthly life is also rejected. The Account of Faith declares that "the figment of purgatorial fire is as much an affront to the redemption of Christ freely granted to us as it has been a lucrative business to its authors. For if it be necessary by punishments and tortures to expiate the guilt of our crimes, Christ will have died in vain and grace will have lost its meaning" (Z 58). The Second Helvetic Confession likewise states: "But what some teach concerning the fire of purgatory is opposed to the Christian faith, namely, 'I believe in the forgiveness of sins, and the life everlasting,' and to the perfect purgation through Christ, and to these words of Christ our Lord: 'Truly, truly, I say to you, he who hears my word and believes him who sent me, has eternal life; he shall not come into judgment, but has passed from death to life' (John 5:24)" (C 295).

The idea of purgatory as an intermediate condition in which the temporal penalties for sin are to be paid calls into question the sufficiency of Christ's sacrifice. For this reason it is asserted "that the faithful, after bodily death, go directly to Christ, and, therefore, do not need the eulogies and prayers of the living for the dead and their services" (ibid.). Likewise, "unbelievers are immediately cast into hell from which no exit is opened for the wicked by any services of the living" (ibid.). Death is thus understood as a corporeal death. While the bodies of human beings pass away after death, their souls are immortal. There can be no talk of a death or sleep of souls. On the contrary, after corporeal death the immortal souls go directly to God or into hell.

The Westminster Confession declares that "the souls of the righteous, being then made perfect in holiness, are received into the highest heavens, where they behold the face of God in light and glory, waiting for the full redemption of their bodies: and the souls of the wicked are cast into hell, where they remain in torments and utter darkness, reserved to the judgment of the great day" (S 670–71). At the Last Day all the dead will arise and the identical bodies, although equipped with new qualities and properties, will be reunited with the immortal souls. "The bodies of the unjust shall, by the power of Christ, be raised to dishonor; the bodies of the just, by his Spirit, unto honor, and be made conformable to his own glorious body" (S 671). In the words of the Geneva Catechism, "those who were formerly dead will resume their bodies, but with another quality; that is, they will no longer be subject to death or corruption, even although their substance will remain the same" (T 22). "Those who then survive will suddenly be changed so that their corruption will be abolished, and their bodies will put on incorruption" (T 18).

The resurrection of the flesh—that is, of bodies—and their reunification with the immortal souls occurs at the time of the judgment according to works. The Basle Confession accordingly states "that there will be a Day of Judgment on which the resurrection of the flesh will take place, when every man will receive from Christ the Judge, according as he has lived in this life: eternal life, if out of true faith and with unfeigned love he has brought works of righteousness which are the fruit of faith; or everlasting fire if he has done either good or evil without faith or with a feigned faith without love" (C 95). Resurrection occurs either for salvation or for damnation. Christ, who has ascended to heaven and is reigning at the right hand of God, comes in a bodily and visible manner—that is, in human form—to judge the living and the dead. The Belgic Confession declares that "then the books (that is to say, the consciences) shall be opened, and the dead judged according to what they shall have done in this world, whether it be good or evil" (S 434).

According to the Geneva Confession, the Apostles' Creed is right to speak of eternal life, but not of hell. This is because the idea of the Last Day and of judgment is not conceived as an idea that is supposed to terrify the consciences of believers. The Apostles' Creed mentions only those things which "tend to the consolation of faithful consciences. It relates to us only the benefits which God performs for His servants" (T 22). The idea of judgment is comforting for believers because they can be sure that Christ will appear only for their salvation. We do not need to be afraid of the Last Judgment, "since we are not to come before any other Judge than He who is our Advocate, and who has taken our cause in hand to defend us" (T 19). The judge is identical with the one who was judged for us. For this reason Christ's return in judgment can comfort me in such a way—according to the Heidelberg Catechism—"that in all my sorrows and persecutions, with uplifted head, I look for the self-same One who has before offered himself for me to the judgment of God, and removed from me all curse, to come again as Judge from heaven; who shall cast all his enemies into everlasting condemnation, but shall take me, with all his chosen ones, to himself, into heavenly joy and glory" (S 324). The Scottish Confession looks to "life everlasting with Christ Jesus, to whose glorified body all His chosen shall be made like when He shall appear again in judgment and shall render up the Kingdom to God His Father, who then shall be and ever shall remain, all in all things, God blessed forever. To whom, with the Son and the Holy Ghost, be all honour and glory, now and ever" (C 184).

ELECTION AND REJECTION

INFRALAPSARIANISM AND SUPRALAPSARIANISM

Pushed to its logical extreme, the thesis of the justification of sinners and of their sanctification by grace alone results in the doctrine of God's gracious election. The fact that sinful human beings are declared righteous cannot in any way be traced back to human beings themselves and their action, but instead is an expression of God's free grace. By diverting human beings from fixing their attention on themselves, the idea of election enables them to seek their salvation from God alone. The fact that sinners are declared righteous is grounded in God's eternal decree. Zwingli's Account of Faith derives election from the providence that is to be ascribed to God as the highest good (*summum bonum*). Unlike human wisdom,

God's decree is not defined by a preceding consideration that relates to future events. Instead God, "who from eternity to eternity surveys the universe with a single, simple look (*unico et simplici intuitu*), has no need of any reasoning process or waiting for events; but being equally wise, prudent, good, etc., He freely determines and disposes all things, for whatever is, is His" (Z 38; M 81, 14). In this case Christ's sacrifice takes on the function of the temporal revelation of God's essential goodness. Insofar as Christ is the only mediator between God and human beings, election also applies to Christ. "Those whom [God] elected before the foundation of the world He elected in such a manner as to make them His own through His Son" (Z 39–40).

Zwingli can characterize as the sum of the Letters to the Romans and to the Galatians the claim that election, with its exclusively christological anchoring, occurs not on the basis of our works, but already prior to creation. It is, moreover, fallen, sinful human beings who are the object of God's election and of the manifestation of God's goodness. We read in the First Helvetic Confession: "Although man through . . . his guilt and transgression is worthy of eternal damnation and has come under the righteous wrath of God, yet God, the gracious Father, has never ceased to be concerned about him. We can perceive and understand this sufficiently, clearly and plainly from the first promise and from the whole law . . . and from Christ the Lord who was appointed and given for that purpose" (C 102–3). Thus it is true that "God has saved man by his eternal counsel" (C 102). The fact that sinners are justified is not the result of their works, but has its ground exclusively in God's eternal counsel or resolve. The goal of the election of sinners is their salvation: that is, eternal life. In order to realize this goal, God decides from eternity on the justification of sinners by grace alone. As the French Confession puts it: "We believe that from this corruption and general condemnation in which all men are plunged, God, according to his eternal and immutable counsel, calleth those whom he hath chosen by his goodness and mercy alone in our Lord Jesus Christ, without consideration of their works" (S 366–67). The only ground for their salvation is God's goodness and mercy: that is, God's grace, the freedom of which is expressed by the idea of election.

The gracious *deed* of the justification of the sinner rests upon God's gracious *election*. The Scottish Confession says that God "by grace alone chose us in His Son Christ Jesus before the foundation of the world was laid" (C 169). In the view of the Belgic Confession, God manifests God's self as a merciful and gracious God by delivering and liberating all "whom he, in his eternal and unchangeable council [sic], of mere goodness hath elected in Christ Jesus our Lord, without any respect to their works" (S 401). Finally, the Second Helvetic Confession declares that "from eternity God has freely, and of his mere grace, without any respect to men, predestinated or elected the saints whom he wills to save in Christ, according to the saying of the apostle, 'God chose us in him before the foundation of the world' (Eph. 1:4)" (C 240). Insofar as the subject of the article on God's eternal gracious election is the fact that fallen and sinful human beings are not abandoned to their eternal damnation, but rather God has decided from eternity to liberate them through Christ from that damnation, the Sigismund Confession is definitely on the mark when it characterizes this article as "one of the most comforting . . . on which not only all the others, but most especially our salvation is grounded." For it is the sum of Christian faith that God, "by pure grace and mercy, without any regard for human worthiness, apart from any merits or works, before the foundation of the world was laid (Eph. 1:4), elected and ordained to eternal life all who endure in faith in Christ (Matt. 10:22; 24:13; Rom. 8:29–30)" (M 841, 21–28).

The doctrine of God's gracious election is clearly a conclusion a posteriori. The contingent act of the justification of the sinner occurs because from eternity God has elected the sinner. And because the sinner is justified on the basis of the imputation of Christ's alien righteousness, election can only be in or on account of Christ: that is, mediated by Christ. "Therefore, although not on account of any merit of ours, God has elected us, not directly, but in Christ, and on account of Christ," declares the Second Helvetic Confession (C 240). God's gracious election is thus the election of the sinner in and on account of Christ. Accordingly the Canons of Dordrecht describe election as God's immutable decision prior to creation to elect sinners from the fallen race, in Christ as mediator, in order to reveal God's mercy (S 582). God's gracious election is the condition and presupposition of the justification of sinners. In view of the act of justification one inquires after its preconditions, which lie in God's election. God justifies fallen human beings because God has elected them. The justification of sinners is the result, occurring in time, of eternal election. Election is ontically prior (*prius*); justification, ontically subsequent (*posterius*). But election is noetically subsequent; justification, noetically prior.

The noetic point of departure suggests treating election within the framework of soteriology: that is, a posteriori. Insofar as God's gracious action toward sinful human beings is grounded in God's gracious eternal election, election can be treated as the ground of justification and sanctification, and examined at the conclusion of soteriology. In some confessions—for example, the French and Belgic Confessions—the article on election thus follows the articles on justification and sanctification. But alongside of these there are other confessions that do not treat election as the conclusion of soteriology, but import it into the doctrine of God. Where this happens the point of departure is no longer God's saving historical action in the process of justification and sanctification, but God's pretemporal decree. In this case the doctrine of election is no longer constructed a posteriori, but a priori, and thus is integrated into a general divine decree. The doctrine of election thus becomes a special part of the general doctrine of divine decrees.

A doctrine of election anchored in the doctrine of decrees is worked out to its most logical conclusion where election is conceived in a supralapsarian manner. In this case the object of God's action of election is not fallen human beings and sinners. The object of election is instead human beings before the Fall, indeed even before creation, so that supralapsarianism is identical with supercreationism. The Account of Faith, on the basis of its doctrine of God as the almighty good, can integrate even the Fall into the divine decree, stating that, "although having knowledge and wisdom, [God] in the beginning formed man who should fall . . . at the same time [God] determined to clothe in human nature His Son, who should restore him when fallen" (Z 38). With Zwingli, supercreationism is wrapped up in a total conception whose fundamental idea is the revelation of God's essential goodness. In Calvinism, by contrast, supercreationism serves to emphasize the sovereignty of the just and merciful God who glorifies God's self.

According to the Hungarian Confession, God decided from eternity to manifest God's glory. All God's actions are subordinate to this goal, so that their only purpose is to attain this goal, and so that they are all means to its realization. God wills to reveal God's glory, though, by electing some human beings (M 379, 1ff.). The particularity of God's gracious election results from the fact that God does not will to elect all human beings. The fact that God does not elect some human beings, but rejects them, serves for its part only to demonstrate God's glory. Some are elected by God on the basis of the divine mercy, while others are rejected on the basis of the divine justice (M 379, 3ff.). Everything else that occurs—the creation of the world, the Fall, the work of Christ—serves solely to realize this one divine purpose. God creates human beings and permits them to sin, gives faith to some of them and not to others, because God wills to reveal the divine glory in the election of some human beings and the rejection of others. Everything happens for the sake of the execution of an absolute divine decree.

If God creates human beings, permits them to sin, and elects some but rejects others in order to reveal the divine glory, this seems to suggest that we are also to consider the Fall as a God-intended means for realizing this purpose. The Fall ultimately forms the necessary condition for there being *sinners* at all, of whom God can elect some and condemn others. If God's primary goal is the revelation of the divine glory, but this goal can be realized only if some sinners are elected while others are damned, God must ultimately also have foreordained the Fall (M 379, 13ff.). Accordingly the Geneva Consensus, authored by Calvin, also declares: "Human beings will find the cause of their corruption nowhere but in themselves. Yet behind this proximate cause one can give honor to God's decree, which foreordains the fall" (N 252). Nevertheless, even the supralapsarian confessions shy away from joining Zwingli in drawing the logical conclusion from the deterministic approach and ultimately declaring God to be the author of sin as well (M 377, 9ff.). The Westminster Confession sets a limit when it declares: "God from all eternity did, by the most wise and holy counsel of his own will, freely and unchangeably ordain whatsoever comes to pass; yet so as thereby neither is God the author of sin, nor is violence offered to the will of the creatures, nor is the liberty or contingency of second causes taken away, but rather established" (S 608, cf. 613). It is not God who is the author of sin, but exclusively human beings, who as God's good creatures were equipped with the freedom either to sin or not to sin. The Fall is thus an expression of the mutability possessed by the human will in the original estate.

But even if God is not the *author* of the Fall, God must at least have *permitted* the Fall. Accordingly the Westminster Confession, speaking with regard to the sin of the first human couple, says: "This their sin God was pleased, according to his wise and holy counsel, to *permit*, having purposed to order it to his own glory" (S 615).

Supralapsarianism or supercreationism is certainly the most logically developed form of an a priori construction of the doctrine of predestination. Yet aside from the Geneva Consensus and the Hungarian Confession, one finds in the confessions not supralapsarian doctrine, but infralapsarian. In this case the object of God's decrees is not the still uncreated human being, but the fallen one. Here one should note that no confession teaches a double *predestination* (*gemina praedestinatio*). On the contrary, predestination is always a predestination to life and thus identical with eternal election. The concept that designates the opposite counterpart of election is that of reprobation or rejection. Election and rejection are never subsumed under predestination as two species of the same. Instead the common concept encompassing them is that of decree. The Irish Articles, the Westminster Confession, and the Canons of the Dordrecht Synod speak not of a double predestination, but of a double decree. "By the same eternal counsel God has predestinated some unto life, and reprobated some unto death" (S 528; cf. 523).

Of course, when the doctrine of decrees is developed in a supralapsarian manner, it gives the impression that election and rejection, predestination and reprobation are acts of the will that are in principle of equal status. Predestination seems simply to stand side by side with reprobation, since both are means for realizing one and the same purpose—the revelation of God's glory. At first the infralapsarian version also seems to imply that predestination and reprobation enjoy equal status. At any rate both the Lambeth Articles and the Irish Articles make no distinction in speaking of election and rejection as two forms of the divine decree. Nevertheless, the

Westminster Confession, the Canons of the Dordrecht Synod, and the Helvetic Consensus Formula all make clear that there is a fundamental difference between predestination and reprobation. Unlike predestination, reprobation can in no way be considered a positive act of God's will, so that election and rejection also cannot be understood as two parallel acts of the divine will. On the contrary, rejection or reprobation is only nonelection. With regard to those sinners whom God does not elect, the Westminster Confession does not say that God rejects them. Instead it says that "the rest of mankind God was pleased . . . *to pass by*" (S 610). Rejection is identical with the fact that God *passes over* (*praeteriit*) some sinners in the process of election (M 613, 48). Even the Canons of Dordrecht and the Helvetic Consensus Formula characterize rejection and reprobation as a passing over.

To be sure, the Canons of Dordrecht speak explicitly of a "decree of election and reprobation" (*decretum electionis et reprobationis*), through which a merciful and also just separation of fallen humanity is carried out (S 552–53, 582). But even here reprobation is defined only such that God "leaves the non-elect in his just judgment to their own wickedness and obduracy" (S 582). Not all are elected, for some sinners are not elected: that is, passed over (*praeteritos*). Specifically, those who are passed over are those "whom God, out of his sovereign, most just, irreprehensible and unchangeable good pleasure, hath decreed to leave in the common misery into which they have willfully plunged themselves" (S 584). This is presented as the decree of reprobation, which makes God not the author of sin, but its avenger. It is thus not the case that God wills and foreordains sin as one of the means of God's own glorification. On the contrary, God created human beings pure and whole (*integer*), but admittedly in such a way that they could sin. God thereby at least permitted (*permittere*) the Fall.

God's eternal decree consists in having mercy on some members of fallen humanity, while leaving the others in the "corrupt mass" (*corrupta massa*) and punishing them on account of their sin (M 863, 26ff.). According to the Bremen Consensus, God "passed over some persons in the gracious divine election, decided to permit them to remain in their corruption (wherein they are born in Adam, and into which they plunge deeper and deeper), and ordained them to eternal damnation and death" (M 761, 5–8). God foresaw that all human beings would be under damnation, but delivered only some of them from damnation, and in that deliverance passed over—that is, rejected—the rest of them. As the Sigismund Confession puts it, God has "from eternity *overlooked*" the latter (M 841, 37). It is not the case "that God is a cause of human corruption, nor that God enjoys the death of sinners, nor that God is a source and promoter of sin . . . but that the cause of sin and of corruption is to be sought only in Satan and the godless, whom God consigned to damnation because of their unbelief and disobedience" (M 841, 42–49).

Even where the confessions that teach infralapsarianism talk about a divine decree of reprobation and rejection, reprobation is understood not as a postive act of the divine will, but exclusively as a passing over or overlooking of some sinners in the act of election, which is the sole positive act of the divine will. Rejection is identical with the nonelection of some sinners. It is an expression of the particularity of God's gracious election. The fact that God does not elect some sinners, but passes over them or overlooks them in the act of election, has the result that they remain consigned to the eternal damnation from which the elect are delivered. The ground of their damnation—that is, of eternal death—is not the abstract will of God, but human sin, which God does not effect, but only permits.

The Sigismund Confession thus renounces the view that God "does not wish blessedness for the majority, which God condemns simply and absolutely, without any cause, including that of sin. The just God has not decreed damnation for anyone except because of sin, and for this reason the decree of rejection unto damnation is not to be esteemed an absolute decree (absolutum decretum), as the Apostle attests concerning the rejected Jews: They, the branches, are broken on account of their unbelief (Rom. 11:20)" (M 842, 13–19). From this moderate German Reformed perspective, one cannot speak of an absolute divine decree, according to which God would create some human beings only in order to condemn them for the sake of demonstrating the divine glory. Instead the ground of condemnation is sin, which God has admittedly permitted, but to which human beings have fallen prey by their own free will. It is likewise the sin of human beings that provides the ground for their eternal rejection, insofar as rejection, like election, applies exclusively to fallen human beings.

Rejection occurs—as the Reformed at the Leipzig Colloquy concede in relation to the Lutherans—"not on the basis of an absolute decree, or sheer will and decree, as if the major part of the world or some human beings were either ordained from eternity or created in time by God unto eternal damnation, without regard for their sins and unbelief. Instead both rejection and damnation occurred on the basis of God's righteous judgment, the cause of which is in human beings themselves: namely, their sin, impenitence and unbelief, so that the entire blame for and cause of the rejection and damnation of unbelievers is in themselves" (N 665).

ELECTION AND FAITH

Human sin would be a sufficient ground for the rejection and damnation of all human beings. For all human beings have fallen prey to sin, the punishment of which is eternal damnation. Insofar as, according to infralapsarian teaching, election and rejection apply to sinners, a rejection of all would certainly correspond to divine justice. If God did not elect a single sinner, God would by no means be acting unjustly. The fact that God elects some sinners, and thus delivers them from eternal damnation, is an expression of God's mercy. The election is an election of grace: that is, a selection. While nonelection or rejection has its ground in the human beings themselves who are rejected, or not elected, the same cannot be said of election. Human beings are rejected or not elected on the basis of their sin. But it is not on the basis of any property or attitude that could be ascribed to them that they are elected, or not rejected. On the contrary, the ground of election is exclusively God's free grace. One cannot name a ground in human beings for election. The French Confession declares: "For the ones are no better than the others, until God discerns them according to his immutable purpose which he has determined in Jesus Christ before the creation of the wold. Neither can any man gain such a reward by his own virtue, as by nature we can not have a single good feeling, affection, or thought, except God has first put it into our hearts" (S 367). The ground of election is solely God's good pleasure and grace.

This excludes the view that the faith of the justified sinner is the ground of election. For one could indeed think that, just as the sin of human beings is the ground of their rejection, the faith of human beings, as this faith is foreseen by God, provides the ground of their election. In both cases there would be a human property or attitude that conditioned God's decree. But in this regard the Irish Articles state, "The cause moving God to predestinate unto life is not the foreseeing of faith, or perseverance, or good works, or of any thing which is in the person predestinated, but only the good pleasure of his glory, and his glory being to appear both in the works of his mercy and of his justice, it seemed good to his heavenly wisdom to choose out a certain number toward whom he would extend his undeserved mercy, leaving the rest to be spectacles of his justice" (S 529, cf. 523). According to the Westminster Confession, the reason for the election of some sinners is God's "free grace and love, without any foresight of faith or good works, or perseverance in either of them, or any other thing in the creature, as conditions, or causes moving him thereunto" (S 609). For the Bremen Consensus, "the election that occurred in Christ before the foundation of the world was laid, stands not on foreseen faith or on a good work in us, but solely on the gracious good pleasure and purpose of God, who in God's time works in the elect both faith in Christ and good works" (M 757, 15–19).

The confessions reject as a Pelagian or Semi-Pelagian error the thesis that God elected some human beings because God foresaw their faith in Christ. The Staffort Book rejects "a number of New Pelagians, who posit foreseen faith as the cause of election (*praescitam fidem tanquam causam*). Nothing that is an effect of election (*quod praedestinationis effectus est*) can be posited as the cause of election (*ut causa praedestinationis*) (M 803, 42–47; cf. 842, 11–12). God does indeed reject *because* of sins. But God elects not *because* of faith, but because of the divine mercy, although election does not occur except *through* faith in Christ. This means that the foreseen faith of human beings is not the ground of God's election, but its result. Faith is itself a gift of grace, so that election provides the ground of faith, and thus occurs not *on the basis* of faith, but *unto* faith (S 583). The Canons of the Dordrecht Synod therefore reject the thesis that the "election of specific persons is not yet finalized, or occurs in light of foreseen faith" (S 557). Faith can never be the necessary condition for God electing sinners. To accept that position would be to confuse ground and result, for faith is the gift that God gives, by free grace, to God's elect (S 582).

On this point the Leipzig Colloquy did not reach an agreement between Lutherans and the Reformed. The Reformed theologians declared that "no cause or occasion or preparatory means or condition of such election was found or seen beforehand in the elect themselves, neither their good works nor their faith nor the first salutary inclination, movement or assent to faith. Instead all good that is in them flows originally solely from God's pure, voluntary grace, which in Jesus Christ was from eternity ordained for them and given to them ahead of others" (N 665). To be sure, the Lutheran theologians also assert that "in election God did not find any cause or occasion of such election in the elect themselves." Nevertheless they maintain that God elected only those "of whom God saw that, through the power and action of God's word and Spirit, they would in time believe in Christ and persevere in him to the end" (N 666). In this view election occurs with regard to foreseen faith (*ex praevisa fide*), although it is emphasized that foreseen faith is not the ground of election.

The Lutheran theologians base their statements on the doctrine of the Formula of Concord (BC 625). They consider as right and in accordance with scripture everything that "is taught in the Book of Concord concerning this article of God's gracious election. Specifically, God has indeed elected us by grace in Christ, but in such a way that God foresaw who would persevere in true faith in Christ. These God ordained and elected to be saved and glorified" (N 667). The thesis that God elects only those whose faith God foresees is not an object of controversy at all if it is only supposed to say that God elects those to whom God also gives faith. But the relation between election and faith must then be conceived in such a way that faith is not the ground or condition of election, but its result, and thus has to do not with the grounding of election but with election's realization. This is indeed the view of the Augsburg Confession when, picking up on the Marburg Articles, it declares that through the gospel and sacraments, "as through means, [God] gives the Holy Spirit, who works faith, *when and where he pleases* (*ubi et quando visum est*), in those who hear the Gospel" (BC

31). Faith is accordingly a gift of God of which it is rightly said: "*Where the Holy Spirit pleases*, the Spirit gives and creates the same in our hearts when we hear the gospel or word of Christ" (BSLK 59, 27–29). Faith is given to the elect: that is, to those to whom God wills to give it. It is therefore impossible for faith to be the ground or condition of election itself.

It is difficult to harmonize the thesis that God elects on condition of foreseen faith with the statement that God gives faith to God's elect. *Taken for itself*, the former thesis can more readily be understood as the Arminian position rejected at Dordrecht: namely, that faith is something that human beings are to accomplish, and that provides the necessary presupposition for election. This is precisely not the Lutheran view, according to which faith is not a human work, but the work of God in human beings. To be sure, the Arminian doctrine applies election only to those "who would believe and would persist in faith and in the obedience of faith" (S 556). But the Arminian doctrine regards faith as an achievement required of human beings. The Arminian view distinguished between a general and indefinite election and a singular and definite one. The latter, in turn, is supposed to be in part incomplete, revocable, and not final (that is, conditioned) and in part complete, irrevocable, and final (that is, absolute) (S 557). In the Arminian view, election consists in the fact that "out of all possible conditions (among which are also the works of the law) or out of the order of all things, God elected the act of faith, which in itself is without nobility, and the imperfect obedience of faith, to serve as the condition of salvation. And God graciously willed to count this imperfect obedience as perfect, and to esteem it worthy of the prize of eternal life" (ibid.).

The election that is not final, and thus is conditional, supposedly happens by virtue of God's foreseeing faith, repentance, holiness, and piety, either incipient or continued for a while. By contrast, the final and thus absolute election happens by virtue of perseverance in the foreseen faith. For this reason "faith, the obedience of faith, holiness, piety and perseverance are not in this view fruits or effects of the immutable election to glory, but necessary conditions and causes that are required of those who are to be completely elected, and the accomplishment of which must be foreseen" (ibid.). In this case faith is no longer understood as a gift that God works where and when God pleases in those who hear the gospel. Instead faith itself becomes a human action and accomplishment. It is thus only logical when free will is named along with grace as a partial cause of the beginning of conversion, and is even given precedence over grace in the causal order (S 570). "Faith, through which we are first converted and according to which we are called the faithful, is not a quality or a gift infused by God, but solely an act of human beings" (S 569–70). The Canons of Dordrecht reject the Arminian position that "in the rebirth of human beings God does not bring to bear those of his omnipotent powers whereby God would powerfully and infallibly bend the human will to faith and conversion. Instead, when all the effects of grace which God uses in the conversion of human beings have been brought into play, human beings can still resist God and the Spirit who intends their rebirth and wills to birth them anew. Indeed they often do resist, so that they totally block their rebirth, and it remains in their own power whether they will be reborn or not" (S 570).

Over against this Semi-Pelagian doctrine of election, the confessions apply effective vocation (*vocatio effectiva*), justification (*iustificatio*), and sanctification (*sanctificatio*) exclusively to those sinners who are elected by God. Election is not the result of faith, but its ground (S 497). In the words of the Irish Articles, "such as are predestinated unto life, be called according unto God's purpose (his spirit working in due season), and through grace they obey the calling, they be justified freely; they be made sons of God by adoption; they be made like the image of his only-begotten Son Jesus Christ; they walk religiously in good works; and at length, by God's mercy, they attain to everlasting felicity" (S 529). Only the elect are effectively called to faith, justified, and sanctified. According to the Canons of Dordrecht, effective vocation to faith, justification, and sanctification are the means by which God realizes the election of sinners to eternal life. It is by God's eternal decree that in time God gives some sinners the gift of faith and softens their hearts (S 582). God gives Christ to the elect and effectively calls them by the divine word and Spirit to communion with God: that is, God gives them true faith and justifies, sanctifies, and glorifies them (ibid.). The effective vocation effected by God through word and Spirit stands at the beginning of the temporal realization of the decree of election. The fact that human beings convert is not to be ascribed to human free will, but "to God, who, as he hath chosen his own from eternity in Christ, so he calls them effectively (*efficaciter vocat*) in time, confers upon them faith and repentance, rescues them from the power of darkness, and translates them into the kingdom of his own Son" (S 589–90).

Effective vocation is thus identical with conversion. The fact that God effectively calls the elect not only means that God causes the gospel to be preached externally and so illumines them by the Holy Spirit that they understand it; the vocation is effective because God causes the Spirit to penetrate into the innermost reaches of the human being. The Spirit "opens the closed and softens the hardened heart, and circumcises that which was uncircumcised; infuses new qualities into the will, which, though heretofore dead, he quickens; from being evil, disobedient, and refractory, he renders it good, obedient, and pliable; actuates and strengthens it, that, like a good tree, it may bring forth the fruits of good actions" (S 590). The effective vocation cannot be understood as if God were offering us faith as a gift that we could then grasp with our free will. On the contrary, God works in us the will to believe as well as faith itself (S 591). For as sinners human beings are totally incapable either of effecting their conversion or even of participating in its preparation (S 623). They are completely passive with regard to the effective vocation until the Holy Spirit renews and enables them to react to the vocation itself (S 624, 623). "The will thus renewed is not only actuated and influenced by God, but, in consequence of this influence, becomes itself active. Wherefore, also, man is himself rightly said to believe and repent, by virtue of that grace received" (S 590).

Before effective vocation and conversion the human will is enslaved, so that sinful human beings by their own powers cannot even will their conversion. Nevertheless, as the creaturely image of God, they are not totally deprived of their will and transformed into a stone or a block of wood. Even sinners remain human beings who act voluntarily. But before they are reborn they have no free will in the sense of being able to will what is good. Thus the Second Helvetic Confession states that "in regeneration the understanding is illumined by the Holy Spirit in order that it may understand both the mysteries and the will of God. And the will itself is not only changed by the Spirit, but it is also equipped with faculties so that it wills and is able to do the good of its own accord (Rom. 8:1ff.). Unless we grant this, we will deny Christian liberty and introduce a legal bondage" (C 238).

In regeneration God liberates our will from the bondage which consists of the fact that by our own powers we cannot will the good, and therefore cannot do the good. By means of regeneration we are given freedom of the will, so that we can now also will the good. "The regenerate, in choosing and doing good, work not only passively but actively. For they are moved by God that they may do themselves what they do. . . . The Manichaeans robbed man of all activity and made him like a stone or a block of wood" (C 239). The Westminster Confession accordingly declares that "when God converts a sinner . . . he freeth him from his natural bondage under sin, and by his grace alone enables him freely to will and to do that which is spiritually good" (S 623). "This effectual call is of God's free and special grace alone, not from anything at all foreseen in man; who is altogether passive therein, until, being quickened and renewed by the Holy Spirit, he is thereby enabled to answer this call, and to embrace the grace offered and conveyed in it" (S 624–25). God effectively calls God's elect, "renewing their wills, and by his almighty power determining them to that which is good, and effectually drawing them to Jesus Christ; yet so as they come most freely, being made willing by his grace" (S 624).

The fact of regeneration does not mean, though, that we become completely free of sin already in this life. The Second Helvetic Confession declares that "in the regenerate a weakness remains. For since sin dwells in us, and in the regenerate the flesh struggles against the Spirit till the end of our lives, they do not easily accomplish in all things what they had planned. Therefore that free will is weak in us on account of the remnants of the old Adam and of innate human corruption remaining in us until the end of our lives" (C 239). Nevertheless, believers are free because the effect of the remnants of the old Adam is not so strong that they would be in a position to completely choke out the effectiveness of the Holy Spirit. Due to the enduring corruption of human beings, regeneration does not have the immediate result that the converted will and do only that which is good. According to the Canons of Dordrecht, the converted are indeed free from the "slavery of sin in this life . . . though not altogether from the body of sin and from the infirmities of the flesh" (S 592). It is only in the state of glory (*status gloriae*) that human beings attain that perfect and immutable freedom of the will which is free to will only the good (S 624). Since because of the remnants of sin the free will of converted human beings is always weak, they fall daily into sin, so that left to their own powers, they would never be able to persevere in grace. "But God is faithful, who having conferred grace, mercifully confirms and powerfully preserves them therein, even to the end" (S 593).

God effectively calls God's elect, and justifies and sanctifies them in such a way that they can no longer fall definitively from grace. To be sure, the elect and effectively called continually sin anew. But this does not mean that they are abandoned by God. The effective vocation is definitive, because it is the beginning of the temporal realization of election. Together with faith God gives perseverance in faith. The Canons of Dordrecht consequently reject the Arminian thesis that perseverance is a condition of the new covenant—a condition that human beings must fulfill by their own free will prior to their definitive election (S 574). Perseverance in faith, like faith itself, is not an act that human beings can by their own power decide to carry out, but rather a gift that God communicates to the elect along with faith, so that the actual sins of the elect and effectively called cannot present a basis for annulling their election. Such a basis would be the sin against the Holy Spirit. It is thus impossible for those who are effectively called to commit such a sin. The "lamentable fall of David, Peter, and other saints" proves that "converts are not always so influenced and actuated by the Spirit of God as not in some particular instances sinfully to deviate from the guidance of divine grace, so as to be seduced by, and to comply with, the lusts of the flesh" (S 593). But although by these sins they offend God, incur mortal guilt, wound their conscience, and for a time lose the consciousness of grace, it is no less true that "God, who is rich in mercy, according to his unchangeable purpose of election, does not wholly withdraw the Holy Spirit from his own people, even in their melancholy falls; nor suffer them to proceed so far as to lose the grace of adoption and forfeit the state of justification, or to commit the sin unto death; nor does he permit them to be totally deserted, and to plunge themselves into everlasting destruction" (S 593; cf. M 577, 4ff.).

In an attempt to clarify the perseverance of the effectively called, as this perseverance is grounded in God's eternal election, the Bremen Consensus uses the following example: When the elect sin, they do indeed temporarily lose God's grace, "just as disobedient children lose their parents' favor when they arouse their parents' anger . . . although the parents neither totally lay aside their parental heart nor kick their children out of house nor disinherit them" (M 764, 25–31). The elect sin "as children, not as enemies" (M 765, 10). But children sin not "out of envy or hatred for the father. . . . Instead filial love remains in them" (M 765, 15–17). The Bremen Consensus thus rejects the view that "one who today is a faithful, chosen sheep of Christ can tomorrow become a rejected goat of Satan" (M 765, 35–36). Otherwise the comfort provided by the idea of perseverance as this idea is grounded in the doctrine of election would be removed, and perseverance in faith would be made to depend on human beings' own decisions, rather than on God's gracious election.

PARTICULARISM AND UNIVERSALISM

The Reformed Orthodox doctrine of predestination is strikingly successful at elaborating the unconditionality of election. At the same time, the particularity of election seems to call into question the universality of grace. If only some sinners are elected, while others, if not rejected, are at least passed over, is it still possible to maintain the thesis that Christ died for *all*, or must one say that he died only for those who have been *elected* from eternity? Does not the particularity of God's gracious election entail the particularity of the effective power and the sphere of validity of Christ's sacrifice?

The Canons of the Dordrecht Synod oppose the Arminian teaching that, "insofar as the matter depends on God, God willed to confer equally on all human beings those benefits that are acquired by Christ's death. The fact that some participate before others in the forgiveness of sins and in eternal life is a difference that depends on their free will as it conforms to the indiscriminately offered grace. The difference does not depend on a particular gift of mercy that would effectively work in them in such a way that they would appropriate that grace to themselves before others" (S 563–64). According to this view God's saving intention is universal insofar as it extends to all sinners, so that Christ's death is valid for all sinners. Admittedly, the Canons of Dordrecht themselves assert that Christ's sacrifice is as such "of infinite worth and value, abundantly sufficient to expiate the sins of the whole world" (S 586). The effective power of Christ's sacrifice is definitely sufficient to deliver the entire world: that is, all sinners. But, according to the Canons of Dordrecht, this does not mean that Christ's sacrifice is also used as the means of saving the entire world. In the view of the Canons, as the means of salvation Christ's sacrifice is applied only with regard to the elect: that is, with regard to *some* sinners. "For this was the sovereign counsel and most gracious will and purpose of God the Father, that the quickening and saving efficacy of the most precious death of his Son should extend to all the elect, for bestowing upon them alone the gift of justifying faith, thereby to bring them infallibly to salvation: that is, it was the will of God, that Christ by the blood of the cross . . . should effectually redeem out of every people, tribe, nation, and language, all those, and those only, who were from eternity chosen to salvation, and given to him by the Father" (S 587). God's saving intention is thus not universal, but particular, so that Christ's sacrifice, although in itself it is sufficient to save *all* sinners, is only the means to save *some* sinners.

The Bremen Consensus makes both points when it declares "that Christ's death is in its perfection a universal sufficient sacrifice for the sin of the whole world" and "that without the application of faith Christ's death benefits no one, so that the fruit and effect of Christ's death belongs only to the faithful" (M 750, 24–28). Christ did not die for many in the sense of dying even for those who are not to be reborn. For this reason one must say, according to the Bremen Consensus, "that Christ died both for all and not for all" (M 750, 38–39). He died for all in the sense that the perfection of his sacrifice suffices to expiate all sins. And he died not for all, but only for all elect, because the effect of his sacrifice shows itself exclusively in the faithful.

Suppose one understood literally the statement of scripture that Christ's sacrifice occurred for the whole world. According to the Bremen Consensus, one would then have to apply Christ's sacrifice not only to humanity, but also to all other creatures, including "Satan together with his angels" (M 751, 9–10). This interpretation would lead to accepting a restoration of all things: that is, it would lead to accepting the *apokatastasis*. "Thus Origen and his follower tried to force from the aforementioned sayings the conclusion that even the devil and the damned spirits would be redeemed by Christ and, in his time, would enter into blessedness and glory" (M 751, 10–13). The Consensus rejects not only the idea of a restoration that entails the election of all *creatures* but also the more narrow thesis of a redemption of all *human beings*. The fact that Christ died for all cannot mean that Christ also died for "all Epicureans, unconverted heathen, Turks, and anti-Christians" (M 751, 24–25). Along with Origen's restoration of all things, the Bremen Consensus rejects Samuel Huber's universalism of redemption, according to which "all godless, accursed, and eternally condemned Turks, heathen, and Epicureans both within and outside the church of Christ would really be reconciled, purified, sanctified, and made blessed along with all chosen, faithful Christians and blessed children of God" (M 752, 25–28). Instead the universalistic statements of the Bible are understood in such a way that the expressions "world," "all," and "many" apply exclusively to God's church in the sense of the communion of those who have been elected from eternity (M 751, 32ff.). The effect of Christ's sacrifice is imparted not to all human beings, but only to those who believe: that is, to those who are effectively called and converted. In this way "all" in the universalistic statements always means "all who believe in Christ." Even in those places where, unlike 1 Tim. 2:6 and Rom. 3:22, the universal quantifier is not supplemented by the predicate "believe," this predicate must be tacitly (*tacite*) understood (M 752, 30ff.). "God wills that all human beings be saved: namely, on the condition that they believe" (M 753, 4–6).

Granted, even the universalistic statement read in this way still admits of several interpretations. The same is true for the thesis propounded by the Canons of Dordrecht that God sent God's Son into the world "that whosoever believeth on him should not perish, but have everlasting life" (S 581). Such statements seem at least to adhere to the universality of God's saving intention. God ultimately wills that *all* who believe be saved. From this perspective one can understand Moyse Amyraut's attempt to assert the universalism of God's saving intention alongside the particularism of God's gracious election. Amyraut teaches "that God, moved by a love for the entire fallen human race, by means of a universal decree that is prior to God's election itself . . . intended the salvation of each and every human being who believes in Christ, and ordained Christ as the mediator for each and every fallen human being" (M 863, 42–47). Amyraut does not wish to abandon the particularity of election, but at the same time he wants to assert the universality of God's saving intention, which precedes God's gracious election. The universalism that he propounds is exclusively a hypothetical universalism. God wills that all be saved insofar, and only insofar, as they believe in God. Presupposing the particularity of election, this condition is fulfilled exclusively in the case of the elect. It is only to the elect that God gives faith. It is by no means the case that this hypothetical universalism links God's universal saving intention with an acceptance located in free human decision. If one wishes to avoid this Arminian conception, one must regard the acceptance of the offer of salvation as solely the effect of God's action.

With regard to God's universal saving intention, this means, according to the Helvetic Consensus Formula, that it is only "with conditioned will, powerless wish . . . and inefficacious desire" that God "intended the salvation of each and every human being who believes in Christ, and ordained Christ as the mediator for each and every fallen human being" (M 863, 44–47). God's universal will for salvation must indeed be powerless if God wills to save all who believe, but at the same time wills that only some believe, since God gives faith only to some. In opposition to this view, the

Consensus Formula emphasizes that scripture "knows no powerless wishes in God, but only an immutably firm will that succeeds in that which it purposes" (M 864, 6–8). The Consensus Formula consequently also rejects the thesis that Christ "died for all according to the Father's plan and own intention, although on the impossible condition that all believe in him" (M 866, 21–24). According to the Father's intention and the Father's own plan, Christ died only for the elect and reconciled only them with God. Only the elect have died in Christ and through him have been declared righteous and sanctified. Only to them has Christ given the Spirit of regeneration and the gift of faith.

The Canons of Dordrecht declare that God has chosen "a certain number of persons to redemption in Christ, whom he from eternity appointed the Mediator and head of the elect, and the foundation of salvation" (S 582). Election is defined here as election in Christ. However, this is not to be understood as if God must be moved by Christ to the election of sinners. Christ's reconciling death is not the ground or foundation of election, although that death represents the foundation of the actual order of salvation. God did not need first to be reconciled by Christ's death, in order then to decree the divine election. On the contrary, because God has from eternity decided to elect by grace, God allows the Son to die the death of redemption. Christ is not the ground of God's gracious election, but the means of carrying out this election. The Helvetic Consensus Formula thus declares: "Christ himself is included in this gracious decree of divine election, not as its meritorious cause, nor as the prior foundation for the election itself. Instead Christ himself was also elected, foreknown before the foundation of the world was laid, and had to be the preeminent means of executing the election of grace, our chosen mediator and firstborn brother, whose precious merit God the heavenly Father willed to use in order to confer salvation on us while preserving the divine righteousness" (M 863, 31–37).

If it is the case that God's gracious election is particular, so that Christ died only for the elect and only the elect are effectively called, reborn, justified, sanctified, and preserved in faith, then it does not seem to be a big step for human beings to assure themselves by self-examination that they are among the elect. The Westminster Confession holds that it is nothing less than a duty to assure oneself thus. "And therefore it is the duty of every one to give all diligence to make his calling and election sure" (S 639). From this perspective, it is even definitely possible to have a certainty of election in this life. All who truly believe, "may in this life be certainly assured that they are in a state of grace" (S 638). This certainty is not a mere "conjectural and probable persuasion, grounded upon a fallible hope." It is instead "an infallible assurance of faith" (ibid.). What is decisive in the process of coming to assurance concerning one's election is, however, the fact that the question of being elected cannot be decided a priori. We cannot explore the hidden will of God and in this sense "start from the top down" (M 804, 13). Picking up on Luther, the Staffort Book says that we are compelled "to look primarily at the certain and actual fruits of eternal election, and the gifts proper to the elect, and to see them as first fruits of God's powerful calling. . . . In addition to this powerful calling there then follows faith in Christ, which Paul also establishes as a sign. . . . Such faith assures us of peace with God" (M 804, 16–21). From this perspective we are certain of our election on the basis of the faith effected by the Holy Spirit and on the basis of the fruits of that faith. According to the Bremen Consensus, one must not explore election "without the word in the abyss of God's secret counsel." One must explore it only in "its effects or revelation, in the calling through the word and subsequent conversion to God and true faith, which proves itself by the proper fruits of good works, and which remains steadfast and perseveres to the end" (M 757, 31–35). The perception of the infallible fruits of election forms in itself the a posteriori basis of one's own certainty of election. This perception takes the place of an inquisitive and futile exploration of the mysteries and profundities of God (S 583–84, 594).

Nevertheless, the following question arises with regard to assuring oneself of election: How can persons stand up to the experience of tribulation who "according to their impressions and feelings find no stirring or movement of the holy Spirit in themselves" (M 758, 14–15)? It is not the case, though, that the individual is left exclusively to her own devices in the case of such an attack that would cause her to doubt her election. What is decisive here is not self-perception, but the divine offer of grace. "At the time of such high spiritual assault one should not look to that which we feel in ourselves, but rather to the certain and infallible promises of the divine word. One should bring these same promises to mind, consider them, and reflect upon them, holding fast to them against all doubt, and thereby striving and fighting against our own feelings, heart, and mind until we again find the comfort of the holy Spirit. The Spirit is assuredly powerful through the contemplation of the word, and helps our great weakness, and calls out in us with ineffable sighs: Abba, Father" (M 758, 20–28).

This also makes clear that the relation between experience and faith in natural things differs from that in spiritual things. In natural things experience comes first and provides the ground for belief or for holding something to be true. In spiritual things the order is precisely the opposite. Here faith comes first, believing God's word of promise in the face of all doubt and timidity. Then the internal experience of the Holy Spirit follows faith. Those who suffer spiritual attack are thus directed "to the comfort of the gospel against their own feelings": that is, to word and sacrament as means of grace (M 760, 37–38). According to the Sigismund Confession, those who do not yet detect the fruits of election in themselves, but who "persist in the use of the means which God hath appointed for working these graces in us, ought not to be alarmed at the mention of reprobation, nor to rank themselves among the reprobate, but diligently to persevere in the use of means" (S 585). Therefore "no one's salvation should be doubted as long as the means of salvation are used, because God orders everything according to the divine good pleasure, and is bound by no time. Thus all human beings are ignorant both of the time when God calls God's own in power, and of who will or will not come to believe" (M 841, 49–M 842, 2).

Spiritual assaults concerning election cannot be countered with internal experience, but only with the external consolation of the gospel: that is, by focusing not on the person under attack, but on Christ as the elected mediator. Even if the number of the elect be small, "we must hope well of all, and not rashly judge any man to be a reprobate" (C 240–41). According to the Second Helvetic Confession we must instead regard Christ as the "looking glass, in whom we may contemplate our predestination. We shall have a sufficiently clear and sure testimony that we are inscribed in the Book of Life if we have fellowship with Christ, and he is ours and we are his in true faith" (C 242). In the face of spiritual attack concerning election we are to hear and believe the gospel with its promise directed to all believers, and to remember "that by baptism we are ingrafted into the body of Christ, and [that] we are often fed in his Church with his flesh and blood unto life eternal" (ibid.). "The preaching of the Gospel is to be heard, and it is to be believed; and it is to be held as beyond doubt that if you believe and are in Christ, you are elected" (C 241).

THE CHURCH AND ITS
CHARACTERISTIC MARKS

INVISIBLE AND VISIBLE CHURCH

For the Reformed confessional writings, the doctrine of the church is intimately connected with the doctrine of election. The Heidelberg Catechism, which touches upon the doctrine of election only in this context, answers the question, "What dost thou believe concerning the Holy Catholic Church?" by saying "that out of the whole human race, from the beginning to the end of the world, the Son of God, by his Spirit and word, gathers, defends, and preserves for himself unto everlasing life, a chosen communion in the unity of the true faith" (S 324–25). The church, which following the Apostles' Creed is characterized as the holy, catholic, and Christian church, is the community elected by Christ from all of humanity to eternal life. The church named as an object of faith in the Apostles' Creed is not identical with some sort of ecclesiastical and sociological entity that is confusingly also called a church. Instead, as an elect communion, the church stands in relation to the whole of humanity. It is universal in a double sense: temporally and spatially. The church as an elect communion existed in all times and places and will exist in all times and places. Christ gathers, defends, and preserves the church "out of the *whole* human race, from the *beginning* to the *end* of the world."

How is the temporal universality of the church grounded? The Second Helvetic Confession answers the question by pointing to God's will for salvation. "Because God from the beginning would have men to be saved, and to come to the knowledge of the truth (1 Tim. 2:4), it is altogether necessary that there always should have been, and should be now, and to the end of the world, a Church" (C 261). This means that the church did not arise at some point in human history, but that there has been a church as long as there have been human beings. In accordance with this view the Scottish Confession says "that God preserved, instructed, multiplied, honoured, adorned, and called from death to life His Kirk in all ages since Adam until the coming of Christ Jesus in the flesh" (C 167). The church is thus the "Church of all faithful and elect from Adam, the first human being, until the end of the world" (M 663, 26–27). While the Heidelberg Catechism, following Melanchthon, applies election to the *church* as a whole, and thus speaks of a chosen communion, the accent has now been shifted, insofar as it is *individuals* who are called elect. For the Account of Faith, the church is composed of the "elect, who have been predestined by God's will to eternal life" (Z 43). The church is no longer defined as a *community* elected by Christ, to which individuals belong, but as a communion of elect *individuals*. This understanding picks up on the Augustinian definition of the church as the "convocation of the predestined" (*convocatio praedestinatorum*)—a definition that had been put forward earlier by Wycliffe and Hus, and then had been rejected at the Council of Constance (DS 1206). The church is not an elect community but a communion of the elect. Accordingly we read in the Westminster Confession that "the catholic or universal Church, which is invisible, consists of the whole number of the elect, that have been, are, or shall be gathered into one, under Christ the head thereof" (S 657; cf. T 19).

Not only the temporal universality of the church as the communion of the elect is asserted, but also its spatial universality. After declaring "that from the beginning there has been, now is, and to the end of the world shall be, one Kirk, that is to say, one company and multitude of men chosen by God," the Scottish Confession describes the church as "Catholic, that is, universal, because it contains the chosen of all ages, of all realms, nations, and tongues, be they of the Jews or be they of the Gentiles" (C 175). This means that Israel also belongs to the church as the communion of the elect. As proof that God has preserved the church since the time of Adam, the data in Israel's history of salvation are recounted from the time of the ancestors until the return from exile. To be sure, the old and the new people of God are distinguished from each other. In the view of the Second Helvetic Confession, there are in fact "two peoples . . . namely, the Israelites and Gentiles, or those who have been gathered from among Jews and Gentiles into the Church" (C 262). Yet the new people of God does not stand in opposition to the old, but forms with it a united entity, the one universal church as the communion of the elect. Both peoples are "*one* fellowship, *one* salvation in the one Messiah; in whom, as members of *one* body under *one* Head, all [are] united together in the same faith" (ibid.). The unity of the church in all times and places follows from the fact that there is only one God and one mediator, namely Christ, who is the head of his body. For the Belgic Confession the church "hath been from the beginning of the world, and will be to the end thereof; which is evident from this, that Christ is an eternal king, which, without subjects, he can not be" (S 417).

In spite of the fundamental unity, though, there are differences between the Israelite-Jewish community and the Christian church that cannot be overlooked. The former is an *ethnic* community confined to Israel and Judaism, while the community composed of Jews and Gentiles fundamentally encompasses *all* peoples. In the words of the Westminster Confession, this community is "not confined to one nation as before under the law" (S 657). The unity of the universal church thus does not entail the immutability of its administration. On the contrary, according to the Second Helvetic Confession the church "was set up differently before the Law among the patriarchs; otherwise under Moses by the Law; and differently by Christ through the Gospel" (C 262). What is decisive is not only that after the canceling of the Old Testament ceremonial law "the light shines unto us more clearly, and blessings are given to us more abundantly, and a fuller liberty" (C 262–63), but also that the church now is no longer confined to one people. Only since Christ is spatial universality a property of the church. Only since Christ is the church "spread and dispersed over the whole world," as the Belgic Confession emphasizes (S 417). The assertion of the spatial and temporal universality of the church also contests the right of individual ecclesiastical entities to identify themselves with the one universal church. No particular ecclesiastical entity is identical with the universal church. The Second Helvetic Confession places the Donatists, "who confined the Church to I know not what corners of Africa," on the same level as the Roman clergy "who have recently passed off only the Roman Church as catholic" (C 262). Both make the same mistake of equating their own ecclesiastical entity with the universal church.

Instead of being characterized as the communion of the *elect*, the one universal church can be designated as the "universal company of all the *saints* that ever were, are, or shall be" (S 538). The communion of the elect is the "communion of saints" (*communio sanctorum*). However, the concept of the *communio sanctorum*, which is taken from the Apostles' Creed, is not univocal. Originally personal, the genitive *sanctorum* was soon taken as neuter, so that the meaning became equivalent to "communion *in* that which is holy." The concept still occurs with this meaning in the Frankfurt Confession, which conceives participation in the benefits of salvation acquired through Christ's death—forgiveness of sins and resurrection of the flesh—as falling under the *communio sanctorum* (M 663, 36ff.). Along this same line, the question of what is meant by the *communio sanctorum* receives in the Heidelberg Catechism the answer "that believers, all and every one, as members of Christ, have part in him and in all his treasures and gifts" (S 325). Primarily, though, the concept of the *communio sanctorum* is taken not as neuter, but in the sense of the "communion *of* saints." Luther's confession and under its sway the Augsburg Confession reduce the concept to this meaning. Luther writes "that there is one holy Christian church on earth, which is the communion and number or assembly of all Christians in all the world" (BSLK 61, n. 1). The Augsburg Confession characterizes the church as the "assembly of all believers" (*congregatio sanctorum*) (BC 32; BSLK 61, 4), and as the "assembly of all believers and saints" (*congregatio sanctorum et vere credentium*) (BC 33; BSLK 62, 1–2).

When the Reformed confessional writings designate the church as the *communio sanctorum*, they mean primarily the universal assembly *of* the saints and believers spoken of by the Augsburg Confession. According to Zwingli's Articles, the church catholic (*ecclesia catholica*) is the "fellowship of the saints." That is, "all who live in the Head are His members and children of God" (C 37). In the view of the Tetrapolitan Confession, the church is composed of those "who have truly obtained a place among the children of God because they firmly believe in Christ" (C 73). "The Holy Ghost rules" this communion, and from it "Christ is never absent" (ibid.). The church is the "assembly of believers . . . in which all are citizens who truly confess that Jesus is the Christ . . . and who also confirm such faith by works of love" (C 92). The Second Helvetic Confession answers in a corresponding way the question, "What is the church?" The church is "an assembly of the faithful (*coetus fidelium*) called or gathered out of the world; a communion, I say, of all saints (*communio sanctorum*), namely, of those who truly know and rightly worship and serve the true God in Christ the Savior, by the Word and Holy Spirit, and who by faith are partakers of all benefits which are freely offered through Christ" (C 261, S 272). The faithful are saints insofar as they are sanctified by Christ's blood. As such they are citizens of a single communion under Christ as their Lord (cf. T 19; S 325, 375, 416–17; C 175; M 426, 35ff.; 599, 20ff.).

According to the First Helvetic Confession, the church as the universal communion of the elect and faithful saints "is open and known to God's eyes alone" (C 105; cf. Z 43). The one, holy, and catholic Christian church spoken of by the Apostles' Creed is an invisible church (*ecclesia invisibilis*) (S 657; M 619, 43ff.). As such it is differentiated into the church that is still militant and the church that is already triumphant. If the invisible church encompasses *all* the elect, then it "includes both the chosen who are departed, the Kirk triumphant, those who yet live and fight against sin and Satan, and those who shall live hereafter" (C 175). Admittedly this gives rise to the question whether the invisibility of the church believed in the confession does not turn the church into that *civitas Platonica* or fanciful church that the Roman critics of the Augsburg Confession claimed to see in the Confession's "assembly of believers" (*congregatio sanctorum*) (BC 171, BSLK 238). The Augsburg Confession does not apply the designation *congregatio sanctorum* to the church in general, but only to the church (*proprie dicta*): that is, the church in the proper sense (BC 33; BSLK 62, 1ff.). The same is true for the Tetrapolitan Confession. Only those who truly believe, "with the exclusion of the false Christians who are lumped together with them, are properly called this Church and the communion—i.e. society— of saints, as the term 'Church' is explained in the Apostles' Creed" (C 73; M 70, 27–30).

This means that both the confessions presented at Augsburg distinguish between the church in the proper sense and the church in the improper sense, *proprie et large dicta*. Zwingli's Account of Faith places on the one side the church as a communion of all elect known only to God, and on the other side the equally universal visible church (*universalis et sensibilis ecclesia*) (M 85, 1ff.). To the latter belong not only the truly faithful and elect saints, but all those who outwardly confess the name of Christ. Even Judas is a member of this sole universal, visible church. It also includes the ancestors of the old covenant. It is the communion of those "who have enlisted under Christ and committed themselves entirely to his faith; with whom, nevertheless, until the end of the world, those are mingled who feign faith in Christ, but do not truly have it" (C 72–73). The universal and visible church is a mixed body (*corpus mixtum*). This trait distinguishes it from the universal and invisible church (*ecclesia universalis et invisibilis*). The Westminster Confession sets in opposition these two meanings of the word *church*. On the one side is the "catholic or universal Church, which is *invisible*," and which encompasses "the whole number of the elect." On the other side is the "*visible* Church, which is also catholic or universal under the gospel (not confined to one nation as before under the law)" and which numbers among its members "all those, throughout the world, that profess the true religion, together with their Children" (S 657; cf. M 619, 43ff.). The visible church is distinguished from the invisible church not because the former lacks the mark of catholicity, but because, as a mixed body, everyone belongs to it who externally confesses Christ.

The invisible church is not some "Platonic republic": that is, an ideal existing outside of empirical reality. Rather the invisible church exists as the communion of the elect only *within* the visible church as the communion of those who externally confess Christ. In regard to the invisible church, the Scottish Confession is right on target when it says that "out of this Kirk there is neither life nor eternal felicity" (C 175), "no salvation" (S 418; cf. 538). "For since there is neither life nor salvation without Christ Jesus; so shall none have part therein but those whom the Father has given unto His Son Christ Jesus, and those who in time come to Him, avow His doctrine, and believe in Him" (C 175). Since the invisible church is the communion of *all* those elected to salvation, it is an analytic proposition to say that there is no salvation outside of the *invisible* church.

Of course, on the basis of the fact that the invisible church exists not outside but inside the visible church, one cannot let that proposition stand as is. The Westminster Confession also applies the thesis that "there is no salvation outside of the church" (*extra ecclesiam nulla salus est*) to the universal *visible* church, "out of which there is no ordinary possibility of salvation" (S 657). Yet there is still a difference here. Outside of the invisible church there is no salvation because it is logically impossible: the invisible church is by definition the communion of all who are elected to salvation. By contrast, outside of the visible church there is only "no *ordinary* Possibility of Salvation." Although it is extraordinary, it is not impossible that some persons become partakers of salvation outside of the visible church. This presupposes, however, that the fact that there is no salvation outside of the visible church is not necessary, but contingent. God has in fact tied the mediation of salvation to the visible church, so that *normally* no one can be saved who does not belong to it. If someone who did not belong to the visible church were nevertheless to be saved, this would rest on God's *extraordinary* decision. It is in this way that Zwingli is able to arrive at this thesis that pious pagans are also accepted into eternal life. Zwingli himself names Hercules, Theseus, Socrates, Aristides, Numa, Camillus, Cato, and Scipio. Along the same line, the Zurich Confession says that along with members of the Old and New Covenants, scripture "indicates all sorts of pagans for whose salvation and blessedness we can indeed hope. . . . Should there not also have been some friends of God from among the Romans and Greeks?" (M 153, 20–23).

However, opposition to this idea of a deliverance of the pious pagans is already to be found in the Geneva Catechism when it answers affirmatively the question of whether "outside the Church there is nothing but damnation and death." "For all those who separate themselves from the community of the faithful to form a sect on its own, have no hope of salvation so long as they are in schism" (T 21). And in this case what is meant by the church is not the communion of all the elect, but the visible church, in which alone there can be elect. Admittedly, the Westminster Confession does explain with reference to elected children who die shortly after birth that they are immediately saved "by Christ through the Spirit, who worketh when, and where, and how he pleaseth. So also are all other elect persons, who are uncapable of being outwardly called by the ministry of the Word" (S 625). But with regard to people "not professing the Christian religion," they cannot be saved "in any other way whatsoever, be they never so diligent to frame their lives according to the light of nature and the law of that religion they do profess; and to assert and maintain that they may is very pernicious, and to be detested" (S 625–26). According to the Helvetic Consensus Formula, the particularity of the effective calling to grace and thus of salvation follows from the particularity of election. The calling does not happen in an unconditionally universal manner, "so that there are still many who hear nothing of Christ. Of course, even to these others he has not left himself unattested, since he reveals himself to them through the works of nature. But this is not a sufficient revelation to replace the external call of grace in making known the secret of mercy. It only leaves human beings without excuse. . . . For this reason not a few err who think that the external call of grace can also be implemented through the mere works of nature and providence, and thus is a thoroughgoing and universal call, so that there is no one in the world who is not at least objectively called" (M 867, 47–M 868, 4). If election is particular, then the effective calling must also be particular, and thus cannot encompass all. This means that not all can be saved, and the restoration of all things must be denied. "We . . . condemn those who thought that the devil and all the ungodly would at some time be saved, and that there would be an end to punishments" (C 245).

As a third use of the word *church*, besides meaning the visible and the universal invisible churches, the Account of Faith names the use of this word for that which Zwingli customarily designates as *Kilchhöre:* that is, "for every particular congregation (*particularis coetus*) of this universal and visible Church . . . as the Church of Rome, of Augsburg, of Lyons" (Z 44–45; M 85, 24). According to the Irish Articles, these individual congregations or particular churches consist "of those who make profession of the faith of Christ, and live under the outward means of salvation" (S 538). Of course, Presbyterianism and Congregationalism go their separate ways in defining the relation between the particular church and the universal visible church. The Westminster Confession regards the particular churches as members of the "catholic visible Church," which encompasses all human beings who outwardly confess Christ. To this universal visible church Christ has given "the ministry, oracles, and ordinances of God, for the gathering and perfecting of the saints, in this life, to the end of the world" (S 658). Here the *universal* visible church forms the ecclesiological starting point.

By contrast, the Savoy Declaration's congregational emendation of the Westminster Confession begins with the *particular* church, by which is meant the specific *local* congregation (*particularis coetus*). Each local congregation is autonomous and subject to Christ alone as its head, from whom the congregation *directly* receives all authority. "Besides these particular Churches, there is not instituted by Christ any Church more extensive or Catholic intrusted with power for the administration of his Ordinances or the execution of any authority in his Name" (S 724). The church is thus defined as the visible local congregation. This congregation is a "*true* visible Church" (M 540, 4): namely, the community of those who are called by Christ himself out of the world "in particular Societies or Churches" (S 724). The church as the "congregation of the saints" or "of the faithful" (*congregatio sanctorum* or *fidelium*) is in this case an empirical entity, the particular local congregation as "a company of people called and separated from the world by the word of God, and [joined] together by voluntarie profession of the faith of Christ, in the fellowship of the Gospell" (M 540, 4–7). The members of such congregations are therefore "Saints by Calling, visibly manifesting and evidencing (in and by their profession and walking) their Obedience unto that Call of Christ" (S 725). This means that the definition of the universal visible church given by the Westminster Confession cannot be accepted for two reasons, even if one is prepared to adopt the concept of the "visible catholic Church of Christ." First, the congregational understanding of the church excludes the possibility that this visible universal church "*as such* . . . is . . . intrusted with the administration of any ordinances, or hath any officers to rule or govern in or over the whole Body" (S 721–22). Second, it is insufficient to designate as the members of this universal visible church all those who "profess the true religion, together with their children" (S 657). According to the congregational interpretation of the concept of the *communio sanctorum*, the universal church can only be "the whole body of men throughout the world, professing the faith of the gospel, and obedience unto God by Christ according unto it, not destroying their own profession by any errors everting the foundation, or unholiness of conversation" (S 721).

Unlike the Congregationalist ecclesiology, the Westminster Confession understands the church precisely not as the particular church. The particular churches exist rather as members of the visible universal church, which has sometimes been more visible, and sometimes less. Along the same line the Second Helvetic Confession can declare: "Yes, and it sometimes happens that God in his just judgment allows the truth of his Word, and the catholic faith, and the proper worship of God to be so obscured and overthrown that the Church seems almost extinct" (C 266). Nevertheless—in the words of the Belgic Confession—God preserves God's church, "though she sometimes (for a while) appear very small, and, in the eyes of men, to be reduced to nothing" (S 417). There is also an additional difficulty. Many visible communities do indeed lay claim to the designation "church." But the mere fact that they lay claim to the concept "church" does not say anything about whether they are entitled to do so. Whether their claim is legitimate or illegitimate can only be decided if there are specific recognizable conditions that a community must fulfill in order to belong to the visible universal church. These conditions are "clear and perfect notes" that serve to distinguish the true church of God from communities that illegitimately designate themselves as the church (C 176). But what are these indices (*indicia*), signs (*signa*), or marks of the church (*notae ecclesiae*) (M 244, 20; 256, 43; 428, 9–10)?

THE MARKS OF THE CHURCH (*NOTAE ECCLESIAE*)

Faith arises from the hearing of God's word, and the church as the communion of the faithful is itself a creature of the word (*creatura verbi*). The church is not autonomous, but lives from the word of God, which stands over against it and ever grounds it anew. The first of the Theses of Berne puts the relation this way: "The holy, Christian Church, whose only Head is Christ, is born of the Word of God, abides in the same, and does not listen to the voice of a stranger" (C 49). As the communion of the faithful the church is always a gathering around God's word, which includes both forms of that word: the audible and the visible. The Augsburg Confession accordingly states that the church is "the assembly of all believers among whom the Gospel is preached in its purity and the holy sacraments are administered according to the Gospel" (BC 32).

The two signs of the true visible church are the pure teaching of the gospel (*pura doctrina evangelii*) and the right administration of the sacraments (*recta administratio sacramentorum*): pure preaching of the gospel and administration of the sacraments in accord with their institution. In the view of the Tetrapolitan Confession, the church exists only "where the holy gospel and the sacraments have primacy" (M 70, 42; cf. C 92–93). This naming of the marks of the church is directed against the assumption that other marks are necessary, either in place of them or in addition to them. The Scottish Confession has the Roman church in mind when it declares that the marks of the true church can be "neither antiquity, usurped title, lineal succession, appointed place, nor the numbers of men approving an error" (C 176). Neither age nor episcopal succession nor connection to Rome nor even consensus are marks of the church. The Second Helvetic Confession states that the unity of the church rests not "in outward rites and ceremonies," but exclusively "in the true and harmonious preaching of the Gospel of Christ, and in rites that have been expressly delivered by the Lord" (C 267–68). This confession acknowledges as necessary or sufficient marks of the true church only the "lawful and sincere preaching of the Word of God as it was delivered to us in the books of the prophets and apostles, which all lead us unto Christ," and the use of the "sacraments instituted by Christ, and delivered unto us by his apostles," in accord with their institution (C 265). Finally, the Bremen Consensus, which rejects the Roman papal church as Donatist, explicitly harkens back in its original version to the Augsburg Confession when it declares that, while the universal church does indeed exist in all times and places, it is recognized in the particular churches by means of "the pure teaching of the gospel and the right use of the sacraments" (M 740, 16–17). The universal Christian church exists wherever "the doctrine of the holy Gospels is purely preached and the holy sacraments are administered according to Christ's institution of them" (M 740, 22–24).

A number of the confessional writings name these two marks and leave it at that. The Anglican Articles adhere completely to the Augsburg Confession when they define the visible church as a "congregation of the faithful, in which the pure word of God is preached and the sacraments . . . are rightly administered in close observance of Christ's institution" (*coetus fidelium, in quo verbum Dei purum praedicatur, et sacramenta . . . iuxta Christi institutum recte administrantur*) (S 499). The same is true of a number of Calvinist confessions. The Lausanne Articles emphasize that the members of the true church, although of course known only to God, can be outwardly recognized by means of the ceremonies instituted by Christ: preaching and sacrament (C 115). The Geneva Confession says that the differentiating characteristic of the true church is that in it the gospel is "purely and faithfully preached, proclaimed, heard, and kept" (*purement et fidèlement presché, annoncé, escouté et gardé*), and the sacraments are rightly administered (*droitement administréz*) (C 125; M 115, 24–27). The French Confession follows this line when it declares that "properly speaking, there can be no Church where the Word of God is not received, nor profession made of subjection to it, nor use of the sacraments" (S 375).

These last confessions, however, exhibit an initially insignificant seeming supplement to the Augsburg Confession. They speak not only of the proclamation of the gospel but also of its being *heard* and *kept*. Attention is thus directed to the behavior of the addressee of the proclamation. On this basis, though, one can understand the broadening of the marks of the church. Alongside word and sacrament as that which grounds the communion of the faithful, discipline takes its place as the third mark of the true church. This is already the case in the First Helvetic Confession, which says that the universal "Church and congregation of Christ is open and known to God's eyes alone, yet it is not only known but also gathered and built up by visible signs, rites and ordinances, which Christ Himself has instituted and appointed by the Word of God as a universal, public and orderly discipline. Without these marks no one is numbered with this Church" (C 105). Similarly, the Scottish Confession explicitly names as the third mark of the church, besides the pure preaching of God's word and the right administration of the sacraments of Jesus Christ in their confirmation of that word, "ecclesiastical discipline uprightly ministered, as God's Word prescribes, whereby vice is repressed and virtue nourished" (C 177). For the Belgic Confession the true church is present only where "church discipline is exercised in punishing of sin" (S 419). Besides the pure teaching of the word of God (*pura doctrina verbi Dei*) and the right administration of the sacraments (*recta administratio sacramentorum*), the third mark of the true church is ecclesiastical discipline (*disciplina Ecclesiastica*) in accordance with God's word (M 428, 1ff.; 740, 14ff.).

Yet despite the fact that there are these cases in which community discipline is presented as the third mark of the true church, most of the confessions limit the marks of the church in the sense of the necessary and sufficient conditions of the existence of the true church to the word being rightly preached and the sacraments rightly administered. The reason for this is that discipline is aligned with the administration of the sacraments, insofar as discipline has the function of preserving the purity of the community gathered for the Lord's Supper.

The Westminster Confession declares that the particular churches are "more or less pure, according as the doctrine of the gospel is taught and embraced, ordinances administered, and public worship performed more or less purely in them," although "the purest churches under heaven are subject both to mixture and error" (S 658, cf. 538). The degree of purity of the individual particular churches is measured by the extent to which their proclamation of the word and administration of the sacraments corresponds to scripture, and there are gradations of difference in this correspondence. In this context the question that most presents itself is whether the Roman church can still be regarded as a true church. The Westminster Confession observes that some particular churches have degenerated to the point that they have changed from being churches of Christ to being synagogues of Satan (cf. C 176; S 481). The primary reason for the seeming impossibility of still characterizing the Roman church as a true church is the designation of the pope—not on the basis of the personal qualification of the officeholder, but on the basis of the claim bound up with the office— as "that Antichrist, that man of sin and son of perdition, that exalteth himself in the Church against Christ, and all that is called God" (S 659, cf. 540). But this reasoning forgets that the Antichrist, whom the pope is said to be, "exalts himself *in* the church against Christ." On the one hand, therefore, the French Confession accordingly condemns the "papal assemblies, as the pure Word of God is banished from them, their sacraments are corrupted, or falsified, or destroyed, and all superstitions and idolatries are in them" (S 376). It is thus forbidden to take part in them. On the other hand, it is not disputed that "some trace of the Church" is still present in the Roman church. In particular, "the virtue and substance of baptism" have remained there, so that a second baptism is not necessary. The validity of Baptism, like that of every sacrament, does not depend on those administering it, but only on its being carried out in accordance with the manner in which it was instituted. In the Roman church the sacrament of Baptism is administered "rightly" (*rite*): that is, in accordance with the manner in which it was instituted. But this is true only of Baptism, not of the sacrament of the Lord's Supper understood as a sacrifice.

WORD AND SACRAMENT

WORD AND SPIRIT

God effects faith in us, not in an unmediated manner but with the help of the "preaching office." Indeed the purpose of instituting the office of preaching is to effect faith in us. The office of preaching is the "ministry of teaching the gospel and extending the sacraments" (*ministerium docendi evangelii et porrigendi sacramenta*). God "provided the Gospel and the sacraments," and "through these, as through means (*tamquam per instrumenta*), he gives the Holy Spirit, who works faith, when and where he pleases (*ubi et quando visum est*), in those who hear the Gospel" (BC 31; BSLK 58, 5–7). The reference here in the Augsburg Confession to the sacraments had not yet been added in the Schwabach Articles. Instead it is the "office of preaching or the oral word—namely, the gospel—through which . . . as through a means, [God gives] faith and God's Holy Spirit, where and as God wills" (BSLK 59, 1–10). This position rejects the Enthusiasts' thesis of the immediacy of the Spirit: namely, that "the Holy Spirit comes to us . . . without the bodily word of the Gospel" (BC 31, trans. altered).

The oral word of proclamation and preaching (Schwabach Articles) or the oral word *and* the sacraments (Augsburg Confession) are the only means of grace: that is, the only media and instruments by which God grants faith. There is no way of obtaining faith other than through hearing the preached word and receiving the sacraments. It is revealing that the reference to the sacraments is missing from the Marburg Articles. Luther and Zwingli reach an understanding only so far as to say "that the Holy

Spirit, in the Spirit's regular operation, gives no one such faith or the gift of the Spirit without being preceded by the preached or oral word or gospel of Christ, but through and with that oral word the Spirit effects and creates faith where and in whom the Spirit wills." The Spirit effects faith in us "when we hear the gospel or word of Christ" (BSLK 59, 22–29). Here *only* the proclamation of the word or gospel—that is, preaching—is mentioned as a means of grace. The sacraments are absent. But preaching is a *means* of grace, insofar as the Spirit effects faith "through and with" it. The Spirit does not effect faith in everyone who hears preaching. Since the Spirit's actions are *free,* the Spirit effects faith only "where and in whom the Spirit wills."

The difference between Luther and Zwingli is illustrated not only by the fact that the Marburg Articles contain no reference to the sacraments as a means of grace; it is also illustrated by the qualification, which appears only here, that the Holy Spirit, "in the Spirit's regular operation," effects faith only through preaching. For Zwingli the Spirit is not bound to preaching as a means of grace in such a way that the Spirit could not and does not also effect faith without mediation. The working of the Spirit by the means of grace is only the regular working of the Spirit. There can also be, and there is, an irregular working of the Spirit. This admittedly makes it difficult to demarcate this view over against the Enthusiasts' position that is rejected in the Augsburg Confession: namely, "that the Holy Spirit comes to us . . . without the bodily word of the Gospel" (BC 31). It goes without saying that Zwingli is not advancing the thesis criticized here— the thesis that faith or the Holy Spirit "comes to us *through our own preparations,* thoughts, and works" (ibid.). Zwingli makes room for an irregular or extraordinary genesis of faith in order to protect *God's* freedom over against the means of grace by which God effects faith "in the Spirit's regular operation."

This gives rise to the question of how the working of the Spirit relates to preaching. Speaking with regard to the canonical scriptures characterized as God's word, Bullinger declares in the Second Helvetic Confession: "When this Word of God is now preached in the church by preachers lawfully called, we believe that the very Word of God is proclaimed, and received by the faithful; and that neither any other Word of God is to be invented nor is to be expected from heaven" (C 225). On the basis of Luke 10:16: "Whoever listens to you listens to me," Bullinger can even dare to propound the thesis that "the preaching of the Word of God is the Word of God" (ibid.). However, this identification, carried out from the standpoint of faith, is not to be understood in such a way that preaching would be simply identical with the word of God. Instead, the purpose of making this identification as an interpretation of Luke 10:16 is to assert, in opposition to a Donatistic understanding of the office of ministry, that the validity of the proclamation of the word is independent of the subjective character of the person occupying the ministerial office. The validity of the proclamation of the word depends solely on its content: that is, it depends on whether or not the sermon does in fact give expression to God's word. Therefore "the Word itself which is preached is to be regarded, not the minister that preaches; for even if he be evil and a sinner, nevertheless the Word of God remains still true and good" (ibid.).

Preaching is God's word independently of the ethical qualifications of the preacher, in the sense that the preacher speaks in Christ's place. However, the Second Helvetic Confession regards preaching only as an *external* word, distinguished from the *internal* illumination of the Spirit. It is not that external preaching is rendered useless by the fact that instruction in the true faith depends on the internal illumination of the Holy Spirit. God wills that God's word be publicly preached, and confirms this in the Great Commission. But there is a fundamental difference between preaching as an external process and the illumination of the Spirit as an internal one. The two processes actually run parallel, so that one cannot say that the Spirit illumines us through or with the sermon. In this case preaching is in the strict sense not a *means* of grace at all. There is merely a parallelism of the external and internal processes. Thus "in Philippi, Paul preached the Word outwardly to Lydia, a seller of purple goods; but the Lord inwardly opened the woman's heart" (ibid.). Since preaching is not actually a means of grace at all, it is easy to take the further step of assuming an internal activity of the Spirit without an external proclamation of the word to accompany it. "God could indeed, by his Holy Spirit, or by the ministry of an angel, without the ministry of St. Peter, have taught Cornelius in the Acts." It is accordingly the case "that God can illuminate whom and when he will, even without the external ministry, for that is in his power" (ibid.). The illumination of the Spirit accompanied by the external proclamation of the word is only the *"usual"* way of instructing men, delivered unto us from God, both by commandment and examples" (ibid.).

By contrast, the Hungarian Confession conceives preaching as an actual *means* of grace, and not merely a process that unfolds *parallel* to the activity of the Spirit. It is the Holy Spirit who works faith in us, but to this end the Spirit makes use of word and sacraments as instruments. In this context "word" refers not to God's Son as the living Word of God, nor to the canon as the written word of God (M 405, 1ff.), but to the external preaching of the gospel (*exterior praedicatio Evangelii*) (M 411, 22ff.). This clears away at the outset the misunderstanding that could be suggested by the assertion that the preaching of God's word is God's word. It is explicitly emphasized that designating the external proclamation of the word as an instrument of the Holy Spirit is not meant to ascribe any salvific power to either the preaching minister or the actual words of the sermon. Preaching is an instrument of the Holy Spirit insofar as the Spirit uses preaching as a canal or vehicle to communicate grace. The sermon as the preached word of God is thus an external and ordinary means by which God communicates divine grace to us. It is the Spirit who causes the sermon itself to have a saving effect (M 635, 36ff.). In the words of the Westminster Shorter Catechism, "the Spirit of God maketh the reading, but especially the preaching of the word, an effectual means of convincing and converting sinners" (S 695–96). Preaching itself is one of the "outward and ordinary means whereby Christ communicateth to us the benefits of redemption" (S 695). But the external and ordinary means of grace becomes an effective means of grace only by being used by the Holy Spirit.

According to the Bremen Consensus, there are thus two extremes that must be avoided. The one extreme is the view advanced by Schwenkfeld and the Spiritualists that "God gives rebirth and blessedness apart from any external element," and that "the preached word is a dead letter or a creaturely word of the letter" (M 766, 20–22). This view presupposes the distinction between the internal and the external person, and regards preaching exclusively as an action affecting the external person. This action gives rise only to an "external, historical faith." By contrast, the gospel alone, characterized as the power of God (Rom. 1:16), is seen as "the spiritual word, Christ." Accordingly, the hearing from which faith comes (Rom. 10:17) is solely "the internal hearing of the living Word of God, which is Christ." The Bremen Consensus thus rejects, on the one extreme, the immediacy of the Spirit asserted by Spiritualism. It rejects the associated denigration of preaching—that is, of the external word—which is no longer understood as a means of grace. But the Consensus also rejects the other extreme, ascribed to the Lutheran "Ubiquitists," who teach "as if God's power to make blessed were in and under the external voice of the preacher . . . to such an extent, and thus in a hidden way, that the entire action of the preaching office . . . both externally and internally, was that of the minister: that is, that the minister . . . gave the Holy Spirit in and under his voice" (M 768, 35–41). The first extreme disputes that God's gracious action is tied to the external word of preaching. The second extreme disputes that the God who binds God's self to the external word of preaching nevertheless remains subject of the action of grace.

Over against both extremes, the Consensus calls for taking a "middle path." With regard to the Spiritualist thesis of the immediacy of the Spirit, the point must be emphasized that the God who renews us by the divine Spirit "could also carry out God's work of grace *without means* and establish it in all the elect in an instant. But it has pleased God to awaken faith in us *through the ministry of the church* (that is, through the oral preaching of the word . . .), and thereby to give us new birth by the power of God's Spirit" (M 767, 13–18). Although God certainly *could* communicate divine grace to us *without* the oral preaching of God's word, God ties the communication of divine grace to the oral word in such a way that God communicates divine grace *not without* that word, but *through* it. Yet despite this characteristic of preaching as a means of grace, one must distinguish between "internal and external action of the Holy Spirit and of ministers, in opposition to all superstitious misunderstanding that ascribes God's power to the ministers or means, and thus diminishes God's glory" (M 768, 2ff.). God's power must not be contained within preaching in such a way "that it would rest in the mouth and hands of the ministers." Instead God's sole effectuality must be preserved in the sense "that Godself, in and through that which has been divinely ordered, according to God's good pleasure, how, when and where God wills, works in such a way that God alone, in and through that which has been divinely ordered, by the divine power penetrates, moves and establishes hearts, which happens internally and spiritually in the whole ministry of the church" (M 768, 9–14). This emphasis on God's sovereignty in the action of grace is not meant to separate God's internal power from the word of preaching. But each is to receive its due. Thus despite the distinction between Spirit and preaching, "on account of the promised internal power of God's will, the entire ministry of the church is a powerful means and instrument of God, in and through which God with the Holy Spirit moves and changes hearts, and without which God does not ordinarily will to give faith and blessedness" (M 768, 31–35).

SACRAMENT AS MEANS OF GRACE

For the majority of the confessional writings, not just the preached word but also the sacraments are means of grace in this sense. Admittedly Zwingli contests this emphatically. According to the Account of Faith, it is the Spirit alone who works grace without mediation. The sacraments are so far from conferring (*conferant*) grace that they also cannot adduce (*adferant*) it or dispense (*dispensant*) it (M 86, 8–10). The Spirit needs no "vehicle" (*vehiculum*)—that is, no mediation—to work grace. It is exclusively the Spirit's own self who is the power (*virtus*) that works grace. This thesis of the Spirit's immediacy and of the associated rejection of the sacraments as means of grace is intimately connected to Zwingli's understanding of the Holy Spirit within the framework of the fundamental opposition between flesh and spirit, visible and invisible. For Zwingli, God's gracious action is in no way tied to the sacraments as means. He must accordingly understand the sacraments otherwise than as means of grace.

This is indeed the case. The Account of Faith does in fact take up Augustine's definition of a sacrament, by which a sacrament is a sacred ceremony (*sacra ceremonia*), with the sacrament being constituted by the accession of the word to the element (*accedit verbum ad elementum, et fit sacramentum*) (M 87, 24–25). There is no question that sacraments can also be seen as visible forms of invisible grace (*invisibilis gratiae visibilis forma*) (M 87, 15–16). But the decisive point is that sacraments are understood only as visible signs of grace that has already *been imparted*. This disputes the view that grace is initially *mediated* by sacraments. The sacrament is not a *means* of grace, but a publicly offered *testimony* to the grace that has already been privately imparted (*testimonium publicum gratiae*) (M 86, 47–48). Through the sacrament as a public testimony and confession of the grace that has been attained we visibly bind ourselves to the church, into which we have already been invisibly accepted through the Spirit's gracious communicable action. The sacrament is understood as an oath. By taking the place of an oath, the sacrament is a sign of confession and obligation on the part of those in whom God or the Spirit has worked grace privately and immediately. Although the sacraments are instituted by God, they are instituted solely as confessing actions of the visible church, and not as means to which God would tie God's self in such a way as to work grace through them.

Even the early Swiss confessions do not follow Zwingli in this view of the sacraments. Already the First Helvetic Confession explicitly refuses to conceive the sacraments only as "outward signs of Christian fellowship" (C 107). If they are understood not as means of grace, but merely as signs of confession and obligation, they are "mere, empty signs" (ibid.). In its terminology the First Helvetic Confession does not distinguish itself from the Account of Faith when it defines sacraments as "significant, holy signs of sublime, secret things" (ibid.). Yet there is an essential difference in the two confessions' views of the sacraments. For the Account of Faith, the sacraments are signs of confession of the *faithful*, in whom the Spirit has already worked grace without mediation. For the First Helvetic Confession, the sacraments are "signs of *divine grace*" (ibid.). They are not public and visible *reactions* to a grace that has been received privately and invisibly, but public and visible signs of the *communication* of grace. One must accordingly distinguish between two parts of the sacraments, for they "consist of the sign and substance" (ibid.). This admittedly makes it impossible to understand the sacraments as mere confessing actions, but it remains unclear how the signs and the signified substance or "essential things" (*wesentliche Dinge*) relate to each other (M 106, 28). The First Helvetic Confession defines this relation in the sense of a parallelism of two different processes. "*As* the signs are bodily received, *so* these substantial, invisible and spiritual things are received in faith" (C 107). As the signs of the sacraments are received externally, so the signified spiritual things are received internally.

The same sacramental parallelism is still being taught in the Second Helvetic Confession. To be sure, Bullinger does mention Zwingli's view of the sacraments: through them, God "distinguishes us from all other people and religions, and consecrates and *binds* us wholly to himself, and signifies what he requires of us" (C 277). But at the same time Bullinger holds that God "outwardly represents (*exterius repraesentat*), and, as it were, offers unto our sight those things which inwardly he *performs* (*interius praestat*) for us, and so strengthens and increases our faith through the working of God's Spirit in our hearts" (ibid., S 285). This passage presupposes the distinction between an *external* process, which involves only signs (*symbola*), and an *internal* process, which involves only the signified spiritual substance (*res*). The minister gives the sign, but only God gives the signified substance (C 278). To be sure, "the signs and the things signified are sacramentally joined together" (C 280). But the external reception of the sign and the internal reception of the signified substance are processes that are clearly distinguished from each other. When they both take place, they still run parallel. This means that the internal reception of the signified substance, when it takes place with the external reception of the sign, takes place with it in the sense that the two processes are simultaneous.

This view of the sacraments goes beyond the understanding of the sacraments as mere signs of confession and obligation. But the confessions directly influenced by Calvin go still further. For them a sacrament is not only an external sign of the grace that is internally effected at the same time as the sign. They conceive the sacraments, like the proclaimed word, as *means* of grace in the strict sense. Sacraments can only be *means* of grace, though, if the communication of grace takes place not only *at the same time* as the communication of the sign, but also *through* the communication of the sign. This is the view of the Geneva Catechism. The Spirit is of course the subject of the action of grace, but "the Lord Himself makes use of the Sacraments as inferior instruments (*tamquam secundis organis*) according as it seems good to Him" (T 54; M 146, 45). "They are outward signs *through* which (*par eux*) God operates by his Spirit" (S 379). Or, as the Belgic Confession puts it, "they are visible signs and seals of an inward and invisible thing (*Symbola et sigilla visibilia rei internae et invisibilis*), by means whereof (*per quae, seu media*) God worketh in us by the power of the Holy Ghost" (S 424; M 245, 42–43). Thus a mere sacramental parallelism of external and internal process is abandoned in favor of the view that the sacraments are full *means* of grace: that is, signs *through* which the Spirit works grace. It is only this understanding of the sacraments that corresponds to the conception of the sacraments presented in the Augsburg Confession, "that the sacraments were instituted not only to be signs by which people might be identified outwardly as Christians, but that they are signs and testimonies of God's will toward us to awaken and strengthen our faith *through* them" (BC 35, trans. altered).

The sacraments, like preaching, are *means* of grace. But one must not negate their instrumental character by making them the *subject* of the communication of grace. *God* works grace, *by means* of the sacraments. "To be sure, it is God alone who by God's Spirit renews, sanctifies and saves us in Christ Jesus. God could certainly also carry out the divine work of grace without means. . . . But it pleased God to awaken faith in us *through* the ministry of the church (that is, through the oral preaching of the word and administration of the holy sacraments), and thereby to birth us anew by the power of God's Spirit" (M 767, 12–18). The Bremen Consensus characterizes the sacraments as "powerful signs and seals of God's grace, through which God not only visibly informs us of the divine will, but also assures us in the most certain way, strengthens and increases our faith, offers and gives Christ with all his benefits to the faithful" (M 767, 44–47). In doing so the Bremen Consensus characterizes the sacraments as means of grace in the strict sense of the word. But it holds fast the distinction between the Spirit as subject of the communication of grace and the sacraments as the Spirit's instrument. The Spirit of course is not to be *separated* from the sacraments as external signs. On the contrary, the Consensus emphasizes that the Spirit works *through* the sacraments. But "to each shall be given and ascribed that which is theirs" (M 768, 30–31). "The means and servants for themselves can not with their service give internal conversion where Godself with the power of God's Spirit does not internally preach, baptize and feed" (M 768, 14–15). What is envisioned here is not a mere parallelism of external and internal process, but rather that it is God's self who, although working "through God's order"—that is, through the sacraments—does so "how, when and where God wills" (M 768, 10–11).

The Zurich Consensus, which seals the union between, on the one hand, Bullinger's view of the sacraments as influenced by Zwingli and, on the other hand, Calvin's view, at first seems to lack the explicit thesis that God works grace *through* the sacraments, and that the sacraments are thus *means* of grace in the proper sense. Zwingli's understanding of the sacraments as "marks and tokens of the Christian profession and society" (*notae ac tessarae christianae professionis et societatis*) is certainly mentioned (M 160, 30). But the Consensus says that the essential purpose of the sacraments is that "through them God attests (*testare*), represents (*repraesentare*), and seals (*obsignare*) divine grace" (M 160, 33–34). Evidently it is not *through* the sacraments that God *works* divine grace. Instead the sacraments represent (*figurare* or *repraesentare*) grace *externally:* that is, for the senses. But God works or gives (*praestare*) grace *internally* (*intus*) by God's Spirit (M 160, 40ff.). Admittedly, this does not separate sign and signified substance. But their connection consists only in the parallelism of external and internal process, with the former replicating and exhibiting the latter. But the goal here is only to reject the view that the sacraments themselves by their own power (*propria virtute*) communicate grace. The goal is to safeguard God's position as the sole subject of the activity of grace: "the entire faculty of acting remains with God alone" (*tota agendi facultas maneat apud ipsum solum*) (M 161, 20ff.).

This is not to dispute the fact that God, although the sole subject of the communication of grace, does indeed use the sacraments as instruments and means of that communication. At the time of the Zurich Consensus Bullinger's thesis of a sacramental parallelism was indeed dominant. But the Consensus does not rest content with that thesis, but moves on to embrace the view that the sacraments are real means of grace. To be sure, Zwingli's proposition that "sacraments do not confer grace" (*Sacramenta non conferunt gratiam*) (M 161, 49) finds a reception in the claim that the sacraments do not by their own power work grace. But they are instruments through which God effectively acts where and when God wills: "*Organa quidem sunt, quibus efficaciter, ubi visum est, agit Deus*" (M 161, 31). Here the distinction between an external symbolic action and the internal communication of grace does not mean a mere parallelism or a mere simultaneity of the two processes. Rather the external symbolic action definitely has an instrumental character insofar as through this action God works grace internally, where and when God wills. It is this view of the sacraments that is dominant in the Reformed confessions. Thus the Anglican Articles define the sacraments as "certain testimonies and efficient signs of grace" (*certa testimonia et efficentia signa gratiae*), *through which* (*per quae*) God invisibly works in us and not only awakens our faith, but strengthens it (S 502). A sacrament is "an outward and visible sign of an inward and spiritual grace given unto us . . . *as a means whereby* we receive the same, and a pledge to assure us thereof" (S 521). Building on this definition the Irish Articles characterize sacraments as "effectual or powerful signs of grace and God's good will toward us, by which he doth work invisibly in us, and not only quicken, but also strengthen and confirm our faith in him" (S 541). The sacraments thus have exhibitive character. "The grace . . . is *exhibited in or by* the sacraments, rightly used" (S 661). They are "effectual means of salvation" (*media salutis efficacia*) (S 696; M 636, 33).

SACRAMENT, WORD, FAITH

The understanding of the sacraments as *means* of grace actually already implies that they themselves are not the subject of the action of grace. By naming God or the Holy Spirit as that subject, the confessional writings stand in opposition to the conception that grace is "contained" or "enclosed" within the sacraments. That which is proper to the Spirit alone can not be transferred to the sacraments themselves without making an idol of created reality (M 161, 15ff.; 294, 31). They are indeed instruments that the Spirit uses to effect grace. But the Spirit uses them in such a way as not to transfer the Spirit's effectual power to them (M 415, 3ff.). For this reason one must not understand the explicitly emphasized exhibitive character of the sacraments in such a way that grace would be effected by a power intrinsic to them (*vis intrinseca*) (M 636, 33–34; S 696). The Geneva Catechism is convinced "that we are not to be taken up with the earthly sign so as to seek our salvation in it, nor are we to imagine that it has a peculiar power enclosed within it" (T 55). The Westminster Catechism insists that "the grace which is exhibited in or by the sacraments, rightly used, is not conferred by any power in them" (S 661). According to the Second Helvetic Confession, if grace were effected directly by the distribution of the sacraments, one must logically come to the conclusion that "grace and the things signified are so bound to and included in the signs that whoever participate outwardly in the signs, no matter what sort of persons they be, also inwardly participate in the grace and things signified" (C 281). The scope of the rejection of the assumption that grace is worked directly through the sacraments includes the thesis that the sacraments confer (*conferre*) grace to all those who do not erect the barrier of a mortal sin (*non ponentibus ovicem peccati mortalis*) (M 161, 49ff.). The claim that the sacraments work grace "by virtue of the work having been performed" (*ex opere operato*) is rejected (M 514, 41ff.).

The doctrine rejected here is obviously the Roman view of the sacraments, implied in the Tridentine Canons on the Sacraments in General. In this view, the sacraments "contain (*continere*) the grace that they signify" (DS 1606, CT 670). This grace is conferred (*conferre*) on all who do not place a barrier (*non ponentibus obicem*) to it. But if the conferring of this grace is tied only to this condition, that conferring happens *ex opere operato* (DS 1608, CT 672): that is, solely by virtue of the performed rite. When the confessional writings reject the view that the sacraments work grace by virtue of the performed rite, their rejection is aimed at a particular understanding of the sacramentally mediated effectuation of grace. In this understanding, the necessary condition of the salvific reception of the sacrament is not fiduciary faith directed toward Christ, but only the absence of conscious unbelief or some other mortal sin.

Introducing faith as such a condition does not in any way mean that the validity of the sacrament is at all dependent on the subjective disposition of its receiver. Making the sacrament's validity dependent on either its receiver or its dispenser calls into question the objectivity of the sacrament as a means of grace. But such dependence is indeed introduced when "the person of the minister effecting the sacrament with the intention of doing what the Church does" (DS 1312, CT 663) is named as a constitutive element in carrying out the sacrament. In the Roman view, the sacrament has not even been accomplished when the one dispensing it does not have the "intention of doing what the church does" (*intentio faciendi, quod facit Ecclesia*). To be sure, the Roman church shares with the churches of the Reformation an anti-Donatistic understanding of the office of ministry, so that the validity of the sacrament's effectuation is not conditioned by the ethical quality of the one dispensing the sacrament (DS 1612; cf. S 538). But the Roman church rejects the thesis that "the intention, at least of doing what the Church does, is not required in the ministers when they are effecting and conferring the sacraments" (DS 1611, CT 675). But this is precisely what the Westminster Confession asserts when it says that the "efficacy of a sacrament" is not conditioned by the "intention of him that doth administer it" (S 661; cf. M 636, 34ff.).

Just as the validity of the sacrament's effectuation is not dependent on the right intention of its dispenser, it is also not dependent on the receiver's faith: that is, the receiver's subjective disposition. In the words of the Second Helvetic Confession, "as we do not estimate the value of the sacraments by the worthiness or unworthiness of the ministers, so we do not estimate it by the condition of those who receive them" (C 281). Just as in the case of the proclamation of the word, those who dispense or receive the sacraments do not constitute their validity. "For as the Word of God remains the true Word of God, in which, when it is preached, not only bare words are repeated, but at the same time the things signified or announced in words are offered by God . . . so the sacraments, which by the Word consists of signs and things signified, remain true and inviolate sacraments" (C 281). Every sacrament consists of signs and things signified, and by God's action (*ex parte Dei*) the two are always bound together. As through the proclamation of the word, Christ together with his benefits is offered to *all*: that is, to good and bad human beings (*offertur omnibus bonis, et malis*) (M 294, 36ff.). By its nature the gospel is the word of life and salvation, even when unbelievers pervert it into the odor of death. In this way the sacraments do not cease being true sacraments even when they are received by the unworthy or unbelieving. Unbelief cannot destroy what God has appointed (M 415, 23ff.; cf. 420, 1ff.).

Conversely, the validity of the sacraments can also not be conditioned by faith. Their validity depends exclusively on God. For the Westminster Confession, their becoming *effective* means of grace rests "upon the work of the Spirit, and the word of institution, which contains, together with a precept authorizing the use thereof, a promise of benefit to worthy receivers" (S 661; cf. M 636, 35–36). "The sacraments become *effectual* means of salvation . . . only by the blessing of Christ, and the working of his Spirit in them that by faith receive them" (S 696; cf. M 162, 6ff.). The fact that they are *effective* means of grace means that God in fact effects grace through them. But on the side of the recipient, faith is the necessary condition for the reception of grace. Only believers receive grace. By contrast—as the Geneva Catechism puts it—"although the unbelievers and the wicked make of none effect the grace offered to them through the Sacraments, yet it does not follow that the proper nature of the Sacraments is also made of none effect" (T 55; cf. M 514, 41–42). The belief of the recipients does not play a role in constituting the character of the sacraments as means of grace. But the salvific effect of the sacraments' reception presupposes the fiduciary faith of the recipient as a necessary condition.

Faith is directed toward the word, and insofar as both the sacraments and the proclamation of the word are means of grace, the question arises concerning the relation between the two means of grace. The sacraments are unequivocally *sub*ordinate to the word insofar as it is not the word that is understood as the seal of the sacrament, but the sacrament that is understood as the seal of the word. The Zurich Consensus characterizes the sacraments as "appendices to the gospel" (*evangelii appendices*) (M 159, 28; cf. 415, 41). They are seals (*sigilla*) of the gospel (M 414, 31), and as such are *appended* to the gospel and its promises as a testimony to God's grace—a testimony that makes a stronger impression on the senses, and thus accommodates human weakness (M 413, 42ff.). For the Geneva Catechism, the sacrament is "an outward attestation of the grace of God which, by a visible sign, represents spiritual things to imprint the promises of God more firmly in our hearts, and to make us more sure of them" (T 54). The sacrament's corroborating, assuring, and sealing the word occurs for the sake of our weakness: that is, our corporeality. "If we were spiritual by nature, like the angels, we could behold God and His graces" (T 55, S 378–79). The sacraments are thus the readily accessible corroboration of the divine promise of grace. The Second Helvetic Confession says that "the Word of God is like papers or letters, and the sacraments are like seals which only God appends to the letters" (C 278). In total accord with this statement of the Second Helvetic Confession, the Heidelberg Catechism gives the following answer to the question of what the sacraments are: "The Sacraments are visible, holy signs and seals, appointed of God for this end, that by the use thereof he may the more fully declare and seal to us the promise of the Gospel" (S 328; cf. M 160, 29ff.; 294, 5ff.).

This makes it clear that the sacraments are subordinate to the word. Both are indeed means of grace (*instrumenta gratiae*), of which God or the Spirit makes use (M 415, 9ff.). But they differ from each other in several respects, and not just by virtue of the fact that the sacraments, unlike the word, are not limited to the sense of hearing (M 416, 36ff.). Since the sacraments are a sealing of the word (M 415, 41ff.), it is clear that the sacraments are impossible without the preceding word. By contrast, the word is very much possible without sacraments. The sacrament as seal does not lend validity to the word, but only corroborates it. The sacrament is thus dependent on the word, while the word does not necessarily need the seal (M 416, 5ff.). For this reason the Hungarian Confession can deny that reception of the sacraments is necessary for salvation, without this damaging the sacraments' character as means of grace. Only faith, *effected* by the Spirit through the word, is necessary for salvation. Worthy reception of the sacraments, which *presupposes* faith, is not necessary (M 416, 12ff.). In this sense the Heidelberg Catechism is perfectly logical in clearly differentiating the two means of grace, word and sacrament, with regard to faith, by which alone "we are made partakers of Christ and all his benefits": "The Holy Ghost *works* it in our hearts by the preaching of the holy Gospel, and *confirms* it by the use of the holy Sacraments" (S 328). The appropriate reception of the sacraments presupposes the faith worked by the Spririt through the word. But as beings tied to our senses, God offers us the reception of the sacraments for the strengthening of our faith. Thus one reads in the Geneva Catechism: "It is not sufficient for faith once to be generated in us. It must be nourished and sustained, that it may grow day by day and be increased within us. To nourish, strengthen, and increase it, God gives us the Sacraments" (T 56; cf. C 123; M 162, 12ff.).

TYPE AND NUMBER OF SACRAMENTS

According to most of the confessions, the sacraments and the proclamation of the word are means of grace. The specific difference between them consists in the fact that the sacraments are externally visible signs (*signa*), so that they are directed toward an object (*res sacramenti*) that they signify. The concept of a sign is to be conceived here in such a way that it applies not only to particular empirical objects, such as water, bread, or wine, but also to an action (*ceremonia* or *ritus*) (M 417, 22ff.). For the Second Helvetic Confession, sacraments are "mystical symbols, or holy rites (*ritus sancti*), or sacred actions (*sacrae actiones*), instituted by God himself, consisting of his Word, of signs and of things signified" (C 277, S 285). That is, they are symbolic actions instituted by God. "The author of all sacraments is not any man, but God alone. Men cannot institute sacraments" (C 277–78).

The object signified by the sacraments, and offered through them as means of grace, is identical with the object offered to all through the proclamation of the word: namely, "Christ the Savior—that only sacrifice, and that Lamb of God slain from the foundation of the world" (ibid.; cf. M 419, 5ff.). Generally speaking, Christ together with his benefits is the *res sacramenti:* that is, the substance or matter of the sacraments (S 286). This statement, however, can be rendered more specific with regard to the individual sacraments, insofar as there is an analogy between the individual sacraments as symbolic actions and the signified object (M 417, 43ff.).

For example, in baptism the sign is the visible washing carried out with water, and this washing signifies the remission of sins (*remissio peccatorum*) (S 287). The connection between the sacramental sign and the thing signified by it is characterized as the "sacramental union" (*unio sacramentalis*). The Westminster Confession declares that "there is in every sacrament a spiritual relation or sacramental union, between the sign and the thing signified; whence it comes to pass that the names and the effects of the one are attributed to the other" (S 660–61). The sacramental union of sign and thing signified exists exclusively on the basis of God's will in instituting the sacraments. In the words of the Second Helvetic Confession, God "who instituted water in baptism did not institute it with the will and intention that the faithful should only be sprinkled by the water of baptism . . . but that they should spiritually partake of the things signified, and by faith be truly cleansed from their sins, and partake of Christ" (C 280).

A result of this sacramental union is that, in the effectuation of the sacrament, the signs (*Zeichen*) assume the *names* of the things signified (*bezeichnet*) by them. Pouring baptismal water on the neophyte is itself characterized (*bezeichnet*) as washing away sins. The sacramental union is most definitely a change and to that extent a transformation (*mutatio*) of the empirical objects and actions employed as signs. Yet this transformation is not a change of the substance of the things that function as signs into the signified object. "Not that the symbols are changed into the things signified, or cease to be what they are in their own nature. For otherwise they would not be sacraments. If they were only the thing signified, they would not be signs" (C 280). According to the Second Helvetic Confession, the change is not in the substance and the natural constitution of the empirical objects used in the sacramental symbolic action. Instead it is only those objects' function, use, and purpose that change. The change is a *mutatio* of *finis*, not of *substantia* or *essentia:* that is, the change is a "trans-purpose-iation" (M 295, 33ff.; 418, 6ff.). This is not effected by the recitation of certain words, which are then designated as the form of the sacrament. "Therefore, we do not at all approve of those who attribute the sanctification of the sacraments to I know not what properties and formula or to the power of words pronounced by one who is consecrated and who has the intention of consecrating" (C 280–81; cf. M 418, 25ff.).

To be sure, the Second Helvetic Confession speaks explicitly of a consecration of the sacraments. By this consecration specific objects are removed from their customary use and are ordained for holy use. But this consecration does not occur through the recitation of words designated as the form of the sacrament. Instead, "when the Word of God is added to them, together with invocation of the divine name, and the renewing of their first institution and sanctification, then these signs are consecrated, and shown to be sanctified by Christ" (C 280). The consecration occurs not by the recitation of words (*recitatio verborum*) performed by a consecrated priest with the right intention. Instead "Christ's first institution and consecration of the sacraments remains always effectual in the Church of God, so that those who do not celebrate the sacraments in any other way than the Lord himself instituted from the beginning still today enjoy that first and all-surpassing consecration. And hence in the celebration of the sacraments the very words of Christ are repeated" (ibid.). The "trans-purposeiation" of the sacramental signs occurs on the basis of their consecration, which in turn is a participation in the first consecration on account of the sacrament being celebrated in accordance with its institution. Christ's words of institution are the "soul of the signs" (M 418, 29). Only through those words does it become clear that the individual objects are removed from their customary use and for the duration of the sacrament's effectuation function as sacramental signs.

As far as the number of sacraments is concerned, the first step that must be taken is to separate the sacraments of the old covenant from those of the new. "Some sacraments are of the old, others of the new, people. The sacraments of the ancient people were circumcision, and the Paschal Lamb, which was offered up" (C 277, cf. 179). Besides the various sacrifices, the Old Testament knows two particular sacraments, which, like the sacrifices, are instituted by God's self as means of grace (cf. M 413, 21ff.). Thus the sacraments of the old covenant are not at all different from those of the new with regard to their content. "In respect of that which is the principal thing and the matter itself in the sacraments, the sacraments of both peoples are equal. For Christ, the only Mediator and Savior of the faithful, is the chief thing and very substance of the sacraments in both" (C 278; cf. M 294, 21ff.; 414, 25ff.). Or, as the Westminster Confession says in agreement with the Second Helvetic Confession, "the sacraments of the Old Testament, in regard of the spiritual things thereby signified and exhibited, were, for substance, the same with those of the New" (S 661). Generally speaking, then, the sacraments are "seal[s] of the covenant of *grace*" (S 662).

If Old Testament and New Testament sacraments do not differ with respect to their substance, the question of course arises concerning what their difference is. That such a difference exists at all is not disputed. The sacraments of the new covenant have taken the place of the sacraments of the old covenant. The former have abrogated (*abrogare*) the latter (S 287). For the former ultimately attest to the fact that "both the substance and the promise have been fulfilled or perfected in Christ; the former signified what was to be fulfilled" (C 279). The central difference between the sacraments of the old covenant and those of the new is that, although both designate the same object—namely, Christ with all his benefits—they do so in different ways. The Old Testament sacraments designate Christ as the one who *is coming* (*exhibiturum*), while those of the New Testament designate him as the one who *has come* (*exhibitum*) (M 294, 21ff.; 414, 13ff.). The difference between the two kinds of sacraments thus does not lie exclusively in the signs and external rite (DS 1603; cf. M 414, 17–18). Yet because the substance is identical in both cases and both are in fact means of grace, the difference is not as great as maintained by the Decree for the Arminians, according to which the Old Testament sacraments "did not cause grace but were only a figure of the grace that was to be given through the Passion of Christ; but our sacraments both contain grace and confer it on those who receive the sacraments worthily" (DS 1310, CT 663).

The Decree refers here to the sacraments of the new covenant, whose number it fixes at seven. The first of Trent's Canons on the Sacraments in General accordingly excludes whoever says that "the sacraments of the New Law were not instituted by Jesus Christ our Lord; or that there are more than seven or fewer than seven—that is, baptism, confirmation, the Eucharist, penance, extreme unction, holy orders, and matrimony; or that any one of these is not truly and properly a sacrament" (DS 1601, CT 665). By contrast Melanchthon, who in the Apology of the Augsburg Confession still presents penance or absolution as a sacrament and shows himself disposed to regard ordination as a sacrament, in the Saxon Confession names only Baptism and the Lord's Supper as sacraments of the new covenant, instituted by God's own self (cf. BC 211–12). The number of sacraments is ultimately reduced to these two symbolic actions. Thus the Anglican Articles explicitly emphasize that penance lacks a sign instituted by God, which is necessary in order to be a sacrament (S 502–3). With regard to the five other ceremonies regarded as sacraments on the Roman side, the Irish Articles declare: "Those five . . . are not to be accounted Sacraments of the Gospel; being such as have partly grown from corrupt imitation of the Apostles, partly are states of life allowed in the Scriptures, but yet have not like nature of Sacraments with Baptism and the Lord's Supper, for that they have not any visible sign or ceremony ordained of God, together with a promise of saving grace annexed thereto" (S 541).

Confirmation, penance, extreme unction, ordination, and marriage are not regarded as sacraments because they do not fulfill the general definition of a sacrament: that is, they are not visible signs or ceremonies instituted by God or Christ, to which a general promise of grace is connected. But this does not mean that they are all rejected. Instead a distinction is drawn between penance, ordination, and marriage, on the one hand, and confirmation and extreme unction, on the other. The Second Helvetic Confession recognizes "repentance, the ordination of ministers (not indeed the papal but apostolic ordination), and matrimony as profitable ordinances of God, but not as sacraments. Confirmation and extreme unction are human inventions which the Church can dispense with without any loss" (C 277). One must distinguish between (1) confirmation and extreme unction as human inventions, (2) penance, ordination, and marriage as useful ordinances of God, and (3) Baptism and the Lord's Supper as sacraments. Like the proclamation of the word, both sacraments are distinguished by the fact that they are means of grace, "which the Lord Jesus has instituted *for the whole company of the faithful*" (T 56). They are given not merely for specific persons for a specific purpose, but in general for all believers. Yet there is the following difference between Baptism and the Lord's Supper: "Baptism is for us a kind of entrance into the Church of God, for it testifies that instead of our being strangers to Him, God receives us as members of His family. The Supper testifies that God as a good Father carefully feeds and refreshes the members of His household" (ibid.).

THE DOUBLE FORM
OF GOD'S WORD

LAW AND GOSPEL

Faith is the work not of human beings, but of the Holy Spirit. The Spirit works faith in our hearts not in an unmediated way, but uses the word as an instrument. The word does not address us as a simple word, but as a double one: namely, as law and gospel. According to the Hungarian Confession, the word of God (*verbum Dei*) is law (*lex*) and gospel (*evangelium*) (M 405, 1ff.). This gives rise to the question of what function is to be conceded to the law as a form of the word of God.

We encounter what is both the earliest and the most extensive treatment of the theme "law and gospel" in the Zurich Introduction. Here Zwingli defines the function of the law in the context of the question of the knowledge of sin. "Since our sense does not on its own recognize what is just and divine, God has revealed the law to us, in which we see what is just and what is unjust" (M 10, 9–11). The law is defined as an "opening of God's will": that is, as revelation (M 10, 14). As a revelation of the divine will, the law is eternal, like that will itself. The law means only that which "serves the piety of the inner person" (M 10, 18–19). It says how the human person ought to be: namely, shaped by piety. This law, directed to the inner person, is familiar from the outset to every human being. But it does not follow from the law's universality that the law is itself a creature of reason. "And even though the heathen recognize the law, it does not come from human reason" (M 10, 24ff.). For example, the "law" of love for neighbor is the universal "law of nature," the Golden Rule (M 10, 21). This law of nature, known to all human beings, stems from God because human beings are so self-absorbed that human reason "regards only itself, and does not consider that it should be for others, but rather that others should be for it and serve it" (M 10, 26–28). The universal law cannot be regarded as a work of human reason. Instead it is universally revealed to reason by God.

The law itself does not possess the power to make fallen human beings righteous. The law merely indicates how human beings ought to live in accordance with God's will. We do not become righteous by hearing the law. Becoming righteous requires action. The function of the law is first of all to uncover our sin, insofar as we continually transgress the law. This transgression occurs not just by the execution of a particular intention, but already with the intention itself. "Our God is not blind, but sees the hearts of human beings. If God finds desires or machinations therein, the person is already fallen before God. It is impossible for us to be without temptations and desires, because we carry the beam of Adam, for the flesh continues to beget its fruits" (M 11, 4–8). With regard to Rom. 7:8ff., the Zurich Introduction says that one knows of sin only through the law. At the same time one learns that one is oneself incapable of fulfilling the law, and thus is liable to death. The law leads us to knowledge of sin in such a way "that we must despair of our ability to come to God on our own" (M 11, 44–45). "Here God's grace through Christ will present and demonstrate itself to us" (M 11, 45–46). The gracious message of the gospel delivers us from the despair into which the law drives us. Through the gospel we know that Christ has fulfilled the law for us. Thus the gospel "can not be understood without the law" (M 23, 18–19).

On the basis of the universality of the revelation of the law one must say that the law also has a particular function in relation to unbelievers. It indeed serves to uncover sins in relation to unbelievers as well. For only if they know how they ought to be does God have a right to punish them. The law makes it impossible for them to make an excuse before God for their actions. "In regard to unbelievers it seems but to convict and make them inexcusable before God," declares the Geneva Catechism (CT 39). The task of the law in relation to believers is different. The law makes clear to them "that they cannot justify themselves by their works, it humbles them and disposes them to seek their salvation in Jesus Christ" (ibid.). One finds corresponding words in the Second Helvetic Confession: "We teach that this law was not given to men that they might be justified by keeping it, but that rather from what it teaches we may know (our) weakness, sin and condemnation, and, despairing of our strength, might be converted to Christ in faith" (C 248). In this sense that law is a taskmaster (*paedagogus*) who leads us to Christ (M 270, 13ff.). By charging us with our sins, the law drives us to Christ (M 273, 18ff.). Therein lies the first use of the law (*primus usus praedicationis legis*) (M 408, 31–32). And this use is a spiritual use (*usus spiritualis*) (N 627).

Indeed the law's use as taskmaster (*usus paedagogicus*) consists in the law's uncovering our spiritual misery and holding it before our eyes. "Whence knowest thou thy misery? Out of the Law of God," declares the Heidelberg Catechism (S 308). The preaching of the law serves the purpose "that all our life long we may learn more and more to know our sinful nature, and so the more earnestly seek forgiveness of sins and righteousness in Christ" (S 349). The law is unable to serve human beings as a means of attaining salvation. The Canons of the Dordrecht Synod thus say of the Decalogue that "though it discovers the greatness of sin, and more and more convinces man thereof, yet as it neither points out a remedy nor imparts strength to extricate him from misery, and thus being weak through the flesh, leaves the transgressor under the curse, man can not by this law obtain saving grace." For what "neither the light of nature nor the law could do, that God performs by the operation of his Holy Spirit through the word or ministry of reconciliation: which is the glad tidings concerning the Messiah" (S 588). While the law makes human sin manifest, and on that basis God's wrath, by virtue of the gospel we are freed from God's wrath. The Second Helvetic Confession emphasizes that "the Gospel is, indeed, opposed to the law. For the law works wrath and announces a curse, whereas the Gospel preaches grace and blessing" (C 249; cf. M 624, 42ff.). Through the law we know that we do not receive eternal life as a reward for doing the law, because sin has made us incapable of good works. Instead we know through the law that we are delivered over to damnation. But the gospel declares us free from our sins and righteous through the imputation of Christ's righteousness, because we are unable to justify ourselves (M 270, 42ff.).

Although both law and gospel are God's word, there are profound differences between them. The law is innate in us. As a creature of God, every human being knows about the law. By contrast, the gospel is not given with creation. The gospel is a contingent intervention in fallen creation. It is not immanent in creation, but transcendent to it. It is not a universal revelation of God, but a particular one. Moreover, the difference between law and gospel is not identical with the difference between the Old and the New Testament. Instead, according to the Second Helvetic Confession, it is certain "that the ancients were not entirely destitute of the whole Gospel" (C 249). "For they had extraordinary evangelical promises such as these are: 'The seed of the woman shall bruise the serpent's head' (Gen. 3:15) . . . " (ibid.). The protogospel and the so-called messianic prophecies serve as proofs that the gospel is already contained in the Old Testament. This is not to dispute, though, that "the Gospel is properly called that glad and joyous news, in which, first by John the Baptist, then by Christ the Lord himself, and afterwards by the apostles and their successors, is preached to us in the world that God has now performed what he promised from the beginning of the world" (C 250, trans. altered). The gospel is primarily the story of Christ's suffering and dying for us, reported as history by the Gospel writers. The preaching of the apostles, and contemporary preaching that takes its orientation from the apostles' preaching, is likewise evangelical teaching. The promise that found its fulfillment in Christ's life and death can only be secondarily designated as gospel.

The immanence of the law and the transcendence of the gospel are not the only difference between law and gospel (M 406, 14ff.). Although both are manifestations of God's righteousness, the way in which righteousness is manifest in them is different. While the law shows God's righteousness as a righteousness that terrifies and kills, the gospel refers us to Christ's righteousness, which God imputes to us by grace. The law enjoins the fulfillment of the commandments, and in this way places death before our eyes. The gospel indicates where we find our redemption, and in so doing frees us from the curse of the law. In the gospel we are justified not on the basis of fulfilling the law, which is impossible for us, but on the basis of that which Christ has done for us and which we are to accept in faith. This acceptance, though, is an effect of the Holy Spirit, and in that sense is not a work that lies within our power. Therein lies another difference between law and gospel. The law does not operate mediately on the basis of the Holy Spirit, but immediately and in itself. In this sense law and gospel are related to each other like letter and spirit. "That same preaching of the Gospel is also called by the apostle 'the spirit' and 'the ministry of the spirit' because by faith it becomes effectual and living in the ears, nay more, in the hearts of believers through the illumination of the Holy Spirit (2 Cor. 3:6). For the letter, which is opposed to the Spirit, signifies everything external, but especially the doctrine of the law which, without the Spirit and faith, works wrath and provokes sin in the minds of those who do not have a living faith. For this reason the apostle calls it 'the ministry of death'" (C 250). The gospel is falsified when it is viewed as a dead doctrine about particular objects of faith. In that case it becomes a law and thus a letter, while according to its essence it is spirit: that is, the effectual organ and instrument of the Holy Spirit, by which the Spirit endows us with justifying faith (M 407, 10ff.).

The relation between law and gospel has been defined until now in such a way that the gospel presupposes the law in the latter's use as taskmaster. There is a clear and asymmetrical relationship between the two. According to the First Helvetic Confession, it is undisputed that "the most sublime and the principal article and the one which should be expressly set forth in every sermon and impressed upon the hearts of men should be that we are preserved and saved solely by the one mercy of God and by the merit of Christ" (C 104). By contrast, as in the doctrine of revelation so also here the Synodical Declaration of Berne represents an exception, insofar as it characterizes the knowledge of sin mediated by the law as the specifically Jewish form of the knowledge of sin, and says that we are freed from this form of the knowledge of sin. "In Christ's death the apostles adroitly taught us to recognize our condemned nature, as the Jews recognized their sin, with great effort and difficulty, in the law of Moses. Thus they informed the Gentiles of their sin and the reconciliation through Christ simply and without the law, and did not refer anyone back to Moses" (M 38, 36–40). By dispensing with the preaching of the law as a presupposition for the preaching of the gospel, the Synodical Declaration of Berne takes the position of antinomianism. In contrast to the Jews, the Gentiles do not need the law in order to recognize sin. The knowledge of sin occurs in them in Christ without the law. For as those who believe in Christ as the forgiveness of sins, they do not need the law as schoolmaster to bring them to a knowledge of sin and thus into despair. "Accordingly, Moses' office is at an end" (M 39, 24–25). "We who come from Gentiles, and who deal with Gentiles and not with Jews, should proclaim grace in Christ without the law" (M 40, 13–15). Preaching is thus never the preaching of the law, because the law is a thing of the past. Preaching is exclusively like the apostles' preaching to the Gentiles, inasmuch as "in Christ without the law [they] indicated sin, and proclaimed grace and forgiveness from him and through him" (M 40, 36–38).

CHRIST AS END OF THE LAW

As early as Zwingli's Zurich Introduction we find a distinction among several ways in which Christ can be thought to have abrogated the law. The Introduction presupposes as a given that we are free from the Jewish ceremonial law. With regard to the ceremonial law Christ is the end of the law insofar as he supersedes its content. The ordinances of this law no longer have binding force for Christians, for with the coming of Christ the ceremonies of the Old Testament have fulfilled their function. They are exclusively types that point to Christ. "The ceremonies of the Old Testament—that is, external sacrifices, washings, censing, burning—have been abrogated, with clothing, utensils, form of the temple, etc. Those things were only a pointer toward Christ" (M 18, 28–31). But what is decisive is not this liberation of Christians from the Jewish ceremonial law. Rather the question arises of the sense in which one can say that the law having to do with the inner human being has been abrogated. The commandment to love God and neighbor touches the inner person. As the essence of the law it is finally the good and holy will of God, which in its content cannot be superseded. This good and holy will of God does not kill us in itself, to be sure. But the law kills us insofar as by the law we recognize that we are liable to death on the basis of the fact that we cannot fulfill the law. The curse of the law consists in the fact that by the law we recognize that we are damned. But since Christ fulfills God's righteousness and thus fulfills the law, "we are redeemed from the law: that is, we are pardoned, so that the law can not kill us" (M 19, 1–3). Therefore Christ says: "After John announced that I am the Savior, it [sc. the law] has not been able to put to death those who have put their faith in me, for I am the payment and redemption" (M 19, 10–12). Christ is the end of the law, insofar as he takes away the law's curse: namely, that we are damned because of our inability to fulfill the law. There are thus two redemptions and liberations from the law. "One is from ceremonies: that is, from flickering works or ecclesiastical phantasms. The other is from the penalty for our wrongdoing" (M 20, 27–29).

Regarded in itself the law is good. The Scottish Confession says that the law "is most just, equal, holy, and perfect, commanding those things which, when perfectly done, can give life and bring man to eternal felicity; but our nature is so corrupt, weak, and imperfect, that we are never able perfectly to fulfil the works of the law" (C 174). But because of our sin we are unable to fulfill the law. We would necessarily fall prey to God's curse were it not for Christ, who is the only human being to have obeyed the law as is required of human beings in general. "It is therefore essential for us to lay hold on Christ Jesus, in His righteousness and His atonement, since He is the end and consummation of the Law and since it is by Him that we are set at liberty so that the curse of God may not fall upon us" (ibid.). Since the law is God's law, and thus a form of God's word, there is no disputing that the law in itself is good and holy.

The Second Helvetic Confession puts it thus: "We teach that the will of God is explained for us in the law of God, what he wills or does not will us to do, what is good and just, or what is evil and unjust. Therefore, we confess that the law is good and holy" (C 247). But because no human being can satisfy the law, according to the gospel "Christ is the perfecting of the law and our fulfilment of it (Rom. 10:4), who, in order to take away the curse of the law, was made a curse for us (Gal. 3:13). Thus he imparts to us through faith his fulfilment of the law, and his righteousness and obedience are imputed to us" (C 248). Because Christ alone was capable of fulfilling the law, and at the same time is the end of the law, God's law has been abrogated and superseded in a very specific sense. This cannot mean that the law is superseded and abrogated in its content: that is, as God's good and holy will. God's law can be abrogated only because it loses its condemning and death-dealing character by virtue of Christ's fulfillment of the law. "The law of God is therefore abrogated to the extent that it no longer condemns us, nor works wrath in us. For we are under grace and not under the law" (ibid.). The decisive sense of the gospel's supersession of the law lies in the supersession of the latter's death-dealing character. Through the gospel we are certain that we are no longer delivered over to the condemnation with which the law threatens us. In this sense we are free from the law: namely, the law's curse, God's wrath.

The gospel shows itself as liberation from the wrath of God, to which we are delivered over by the law. "The liberty which Christ hath purchased for believers under the gospel consists in their freedom from the guilt of sin, the condemning wrath of God, the curse of the moral law." For the Westminster Confession this also means that we receive "free access to God" (S 643). In addition, though, as for the Zurich Introduction, Christian freedom also lies in the fact that Christians are no longer subject to the Jewish ceremonial law. "Under the New Testament the liberty of Christians is further enlarged in their freedom from the yoke of the ceremonial law, to which the Jewish church was subjected; and in greater boldness of access to the throne of grace, and in fuller communications of the free Spirit of God, than believers under the law did ordinarily partake of" (S 643–44). Through Christ we are freed not only from the curse of the law, but also from specific forms and parts of the law: namely, from the Jewish ceremonial law. For this reason the French Confession can declare "that the figures of the law came to an end at the advent of Jesus Christ; but, although the ceremonies are no more in use, yet their substance and truth remain in the person of him in whom they are fulfilled" (S 372, trans. altered). According to the Second Helvetic Confession, "Christ has fulfilled all the figures of the law. Hence, with the coming of the body, the shadows ceased, so that in Christ we now have the truth and all fulness" (C 248).

The same thing that is true of the Jewish ceremonial law also applies to the Jewish positive law that relates to the past state of Israel. The end of that state brings with it the end of the positive law that was valid in it, as codified in the Old Testament. The Irish Articles declare that "the Law given from God by Moses as touching ceremonies and rites . . . [is] abolished, and the civil precepts thereof . . . [are] not of necessity to be received in any commonwealth" (S 541, cf. 491–92). And the Westminster Confession concludes: "God was pleased to give to the people of Israel, as a Church under age, ceremonial laws, containing several typical ordinances, partly of worship, prefiguring Christ, his graces, actions, sufferings, and benefits; and partly holding forth divers instructions of moral duties. All which ceremonial laws are now abrogated under the New Testament. To them also, as a body politic, he gave sundry judicial laws, which expired together with the state of that people, not obliging any other, now, further than the general equity thereof may require" (S 640–41).

Christ supersedes not only the curse of the universal law but also the entire particular ceremonial and civil laws of the past state of Israel. In this sense Christ is the end of the law. The attainment of this freedom of Christians from the law declares God to be the sole Lord of the conscience. This means that a Christian is free from all civil or ecclesiastical laws that make absolute claims. Such laws can never bind the conscience. "God alone is Lord of the conscience, and hath left it free from the doctrines and commandments of men which are in any thing contrary to his Word, or beside it in matters of faith or worship" (S 644). According to the Westminster Confession, faith in human ordinances that contradict God's word proves to be a betrayal of the true freedom of the conscience. Likewise, requiring a *fides implicita,* a blind faith, or an absolute and blind obedience destroys a Christian's freedom of conscience. This proclamation of freedom of conscience acknowledges God alone as Lord of the conscience and thus of ethical decisions, and is directed against the transformation of faith into legalism. Such a transformation is present where specific human or ecclesiastical doctrines and ordinances are declared to be absolutely binding.

As early as the Zurich Introduction we find the insistence that as Christians we are also "free from all the laws that have been placed upon us as if through them we would become good and holy. Such are all the papal laws that are not grounded in God's word: prohibitions of foods, commandments of purification, of oaths, of auricular confession, of sacrifices, of monetary compensations, of indulgences . . . we are also free from the doctrine invented by human beings: the intercession of the saints, purgatory, images, temple adornments, Mass exhibitions, and other things, for they are not grounded in God's word" (M 21, 23–31). The Roman church falls away from Christian freedom when it reactivates Jewish ceremonial laws and ceremonies, and through them binds the conscience. It cannot use God's word to support this practice, but places the word of human beings in its place (M 325, 20ff.). In this way the Roman church takes Christians, whose conscience is subject to God alone, and makes them slaves of human beings. In this way it perverts Christian freedom.

THE THIRD USE OF THE LAW

It is clear from the above that Christian freedom is by no means freedom from God's law, period. The conscience is free only when God is the sole Lord of the conscience, and this means that the law as God's unsuperseded goodwill is also valid for Christians who have been redeemed and set free from the law's curse. There is not only the law's use as taskmaster but also a "third use pertaining to those who have been reborn" (*tertius usus ad renatos pertinens*) (N 627; M 412, 3ff.). Although Christ has redeemed us from the curse of the law affecting the inner human being, "every law, insofar as it concerns the inner human being, remains unabrogated for eternity" (M 19, 13–14). The Zurich Introduction clarifies this by means of the following example. "'Thou shalt not steal' is an eternal commandment. If someone has stolen something and you go before the judge and redeem that person from the gallows, he is redeemed from the law: that is, from the law's penalty. But he is not redeemed for the purpose of thinking it right to steal in the future. Although one redeems him from the gallows, he is never made free in the sense that he is no longer under the obligation to observe the law" (M 19, 14–20). Christ redeems us from the curse of the law, but this redemption in no way negates the content of the law. Instead, according to the French Confession, "we must seek aid from the law and the prophets for the ruling of our lives, as well as for our confirmation in the promises of the gospel" (S 372–73). In the corresponding formulation of the Second Helvetic Confession, we "know that in the law is delivered to us the patterns of virtues and vices," so that "its [sc. the law's] reading is not to be banished from the church" (C 249). The law thus also applies to the justified, serving as a standard of orientation for sanctification. For this reason the Westminster Confession declares that "the moral law doth forever bind all, as well justified persons as others, to the obedience thereof; and that not only in regard of the matter contained in it, but also in respect of the authority of God the Creator who gave it. Neither doth Christ in the gospel any way dissolve, but much strengthen, this obligation" (S 641).

Nevertheless the question arises here concerning the extent to which one can speak at all of the *law* being valid for the justified: that is, to what extent can one speak of a *third* use of the law? After all, it is not just that the antinomian Synodical Declaration of Berne speaks of "Paul's paranetic instructions and exhortations" rather than of the law (M 43, 14–15). Zwingli, who explicitly declares that the content of the law is in no way abrogated, observes that one cannot actually say that the justified person continues to be subject to God's law as law. For "as we are serenely abandoned to God, so we no longer need any law, since it is now Godself who leads us. And as God needs no law, neither do those in whom God dwells need any law, for God leads them. For where God's Spirit is, there is freedom. . . . Therefore those who are serenely abandoned to God are also free from the laws concerning the inner human being. They do freely and joyfully all things proper to a Christian. Those who are free in this way are seen by their fruits" (M 20, 29–36). As justified sinners we no longer stand under the law, but rather under the grace of God, which makes us free to act well. But if we are free from the law in the sense that we no longer stand under the law, this does not mean that those actions which a free Christian does joyfully differ in content from those actions which the law commands. The actions are materially the same. In this sense the law remains valid even for those who have been born again, since it is the standard for judging good and evil.

By contrast, things are different with regard to the original meaning of the law. The Westminster Confession clarifies this state of affairs within the framework of the Confession's covenant theology. "God gave to Adam a law, as a covenant of works" (S 640). The law originally belongs to the covenant of works. Through the law Adam is obligated to obey, and in him as a collective person, so is all of humankind. The promise of eternal life is bound up with the fulfillment of this obligation. In the covenant of works eternal life and eternal death thus depend upon the fulfillment or non-fulfillment of the law, given as a means of salvation. In the covenant of works justification is justification through the good works of human beings. Justification is tied to their meritorious accomplishments. In the covenant of grace the law has lost this function as the summation of the good works to be accomplished for the sake of justification. In the covenant of grace justification by the imputation of Christ's alien righteousness replaces justification by one's own achievements. For this reason the law cannot have the same function for the justified as it has in the covenant of works, even though the content of the law remains valid. "True believers . . . [are] not under the law as a covenant of works, to be thereby justified or condemned" (S 641). As persons freed from the covenant of works, Christians are at the same time freed from the law as a means of justification. Thus the Helvetic Consensus Formula declares that "human beings are declared righteous in two ways: either through their works in accordance with the law or through Christ's imputed obedience, which is given by grace in the gospel to those who believe. In the former way human beings in the condition of innocence should be declared righteous; in the latter way, by contrast, the sinner. There are accordingly only two covenants: that of works and that of grace. The former was made with Adam, and in him with all his descendants, but became powerless by virtue of sin. The latter was made with the elect in Christ, and for eternity" (M 868, 32–40).

In the covenant of grace the law has lost the original function that it had in the covenant of works. It no longer serves as a means of justification. It nevertheless remains a standard for justified sinners in shaping their lives, since God's good and holy will has not changed materially (*materialiter*), but remains the same. Materially the law remains in force even in the covenant of grace, although the law has completely changed its function. It is no longer a means of justification, but rather a standard of sanctification. But sanctification is nothing other than thanksgiving for the justification that has occurred, which consists of the imputation of Christ's alien righteousness. The third use of the law (*tertius usus legis*) consists of justified sinners showing their gratitude in the form of obedience to the law for the justification that has occurred. The good works that the grateful Christian carries out are—according to the Heidelberg Catechism—only those "which are done from true faith, according to the law of God, for his glory;

and not such as rest on our opinion or the commandments of men" (S 339–40). To this extent for the Westminster Confession the law remains in the covenant of grace, which according to its substance is in both the Old and the New Testament, and is "a rule of life, informing them of the will of God and their duty" (S 641–42).

Yet although the law serves the justified as a rule for the shaping of their lives, and although those who have been born again show their gratitude by following the law, this does not mean that they are now in the position of being able to fulfill the law. "But there is some infirmity in us, so that no man acquits himself perfectly in it," says the Geneva Catechism (T 38). Yet "provided we take care to conform our life to what we are told here, although we are very far from reaching perfection, the Lord does not impute our faults to us" (ibid.). No one is able to observe God's commandments completely, "but even the holiest men, while in this life, have only a small beginning of this obedience, yet so that with earnest purpose they begin to live, not only according to some, but according to all the commandments of God" (S 349). For the Heidelberg Catechism the preaching of the law thus not only has the function of driving us to Christ so that we will seek our deliverance there, but also serves the goal "that we may continually strive and beg from God the grace of the Holy Ghost, so as to become more and more changed into the image of God, till we attain finally to full perfection after this life" (ibid.). According to the Geneva Catechism, the law shows the justified sinner, who is continually in renewed need of justification, "the mark at which we ought to aim, that each of us, according to the grace God has bestowed on him, may strive continually to press toward it, and to advance day by day" (T 39). The Christian's conscience is freed from all human ordinances that carry with them claims of absoluteness, and freed from the law as a means of justification. The goal of the Christian's actions is progress in the fulfillment of the law.

The law in its validity not only declares sinners guilty and drives them to the gospel, but also serves as a standard of sanctification for the justified sinner. If one asks about the content of this law, the confessional writings point to the Decalogue, or to the double commandment of love that summarizes the Decalogue. For the essence of the two tables of the Decalogue, the first of which concerns our service to God and the second of which concerns our service to human beings, issues in the commandment to love God and neighbor. As the Geneva Catechism puts it, the double commandment of love is "a short summary of the whole law" (T 37). To love God means "to have and hold Him as Lord, Saviour and Father, and this requires reverence, honour, faith, and obedience along with love" (ibid.). The commandment to love one's neighbor is directed against our inclination to self-love, with our neighbor in this case being not only parents, friends, and acquaintances, "but also those who are unknown to us, and even enemies" (T 38). We are bound together with them by that connection "which God has placed among all men on the earth, and is so inviolable, that it cannot be abolished by the malice of any man" (ibid.). The fact that a human being hates us does not stop that person from being our neighbor. Instead we must regard every human being as our neighbor, since God has bound us together with all human beings.

When the object of discussion is the Decalogue, or the double commandment of love that summarizes the Decalogue, this does not necessarily mean the fixed written form of the Decalogue. Instead what is meant is the law given in the covenant of works. This means that it was given to Adam, and in Adam to all humanity. It applies not only to the Old Testament people of the covenant but to all peoples. Unlike the fixed form of the Decalogue, it must be a universal law. For this reason the Second Helvetic Confession declares that it was "written in the hearts of men by the finger of God (Rom. 2:15), and is called the law of nature" (C 247). It is the moral law (*lex moralis*), which is binding on all human beings and which God has revealed to all human beings (M 624, 16ff.). In the words of the Savoy Declaration, "this Law so written in the heart, continued to be a perfect Rule of righteousness after the fall of man, and (as such) was delivered by God upon Mount Sinai in Ten Commandments, and written in Two Tables" (M 581, 26–31). In this context the relation between the Decalogue and the universal law is such that the Decalogue is nothing other than the fixed written form of the universal moral law that is revealed to human conscience. It is the "moral law which is contained in the Decalogue or two Tables and expounded in the books of Moses" (C 247). The law is to be understood as that moral law which was familiar by nature (*naturaliter*) to all human beings and later, for the sake of greater clarity, received written form in the Decalogue (M 405, 17ff.). By comparison, all exhortations, admonitions, commands, and remonstrances of the prophets and apostles, including the New Testament paranetic instruction, are for the Geneva Catechism only "clarifications of the Law, leading us into obedience to it rather than turning us away from it" (T 40, trans. altered).

Of course, in this context a question arises about how one is to understand the identification of the Decalogue with the universal moral law. Here one can take two paths. Either one interprets the Decalogue on the basis of the universal moral law, or one takes the opposite tack and interprets the universal law on the basis of the Decalogue. The latter case presents a biblicistic reduction of the moral law.

In the confessions the different interpretive approaches are seen primarily within the framework of integrating the first table, and in particular in the treatment of the commandment concerning a day of rest. Already in the Irish Articles we read: "The first day of the week, which is the Lord's day, is wholly to be dedicated unto the service of God; and therefore we are bound therein to rest from our common and daily business, and to bestow that leisure upon holy exercises, both public and private" (S 536). The Westminster Confession, which is dependent upon the Irish Articles, sharpens this commandment to hallow the Lord's day insofar as it presents the Lord's day as the Christian Sabbath. All that was true of the Sabbath is now to be true of the Lord's day. The commandment to hallow the Lord's day is presented as the commandment to hallow the Sabbath. It is thus biblicistically identified with the fourth commandment, using the supposedly Hebrew numbering that was adopted by the Reformed confessions. On the basis of the natural law it is only the case that an appropriate time should be preserved to worship God. But according to the Westminster Confession, in the Decalogue God specifies this universal law of worship in a universally binding way. "In his Word, by a positive, moral, and perpetual commandment, binding all men in all ages, he hath particularly appointed one day in seven for a Sabbath, to be kept holy unto him" (S 648). Of course, the particular time of the special day of rest has changed insofar as, from the beginning of the world until Christ's resurrection, it was the last day of the week, while from the resurrection until the end of the world it is the first day of the week. But this does nothing to change the fact that in both cases it is one and the same day of rest that is at issue: namely, the Sabbath. In one case it is the Jewish Sabbath; in the other, the Christian. The Lord's day is accordingly interpreted as a strict day of rest in the Jewish sense, so that the Old Testament Sabbath laws are applicable to it. "This Sabbath is then kept holy unto the Lord, when men . . . do not only observe an holy rest all the day from their own works, words, and thoughts, about their worldly employments and recreations; but also are taken up the whole time in the public and private exercises of his worship, and in the duties of necessity and mercy" (S 649). The Lord's day thus becomes a day of rest in the sense of the Jewish Sabbath, on which "such worldly employments and recreations as are lawful on other days" (M 689) are forbidden.

Admittedly, outside of Puritanism this sort of biblicistic interpretation of the commandment to observe a day of rest as part of the universal moral law is completely foreign to the other confessions. They do not use the fourth commandment, literally understood, to interpret the commandment to observe a day of rest—a commandment that stood firm for them on the basis of the moral law. Instead they follow the reverse order and interpret the fourth commandment on the basis of the universal moral law. In this way they never even arrive at the point of identifying the Lord's day with the Sabbath. On the contrary, for them the fourth commandment, as the commandment to observe the Sabbath, is a part of Jewish ceremonial law, and thus is abrogated. To the question of whether any form of work is forbidden on a weekday by the fourth commandment, the Geneva Catechism replies that "this commandment must be carefully considered, for the observance of rest is part of the ceremonies of the ancient Law, which was abolished at the coming of Jesus Christ" (T 31, trans. altered). Insofar as it is a ceremonial law, the fourth commandment was given only for the Jewish worshiping community. For this reason a question arises concerning why the fourth commandment was issued at all. The Catechism answers: "To represent rest, in aid of ecclesiastical polity, and for the relief of servants" (ibid.).

What remains of the fourth commandment after its abrogation as a ceremonial law is the following: "That we observe the order constituted in the Church, to hear the Word of God, to engage in public prayers and in the Sacraments, and that we do not contravene the spiritual order among the faithful" (T 33). In this case the fourth commandment is interpreted metaphorically, and not as a commandment to observe the Sabbath in the Jewish sense. We read in the Heidelberg Catechism: "What does God require in the fourth commandment? In the first place, that the ministry of the Gospel and schools be maintained; and that I, especially on the day of rest, diligently attend church, to learn the Word of God, to use the holy Sacraments, to call publicly upon the Lord, and to give Christian alms. In the second place, that all the days of my life I rest from my evil works, allow the Lord to work in me by his Spirit, and thus begin in this life the everlasting Sabbath" (S 345). The fourth commandment is not understood along Jewish lines as a commandment to observe a strict day of rest, but rather as a commandment to worship, applying not only to public worship but to sanctification in general (M 371, 12ff.). The Second Helvetic Confession accordingly observes: "In this connection we do not yield to the Jewish observance and to superstitions. For we do not believe that one day is any holier than another, or think that rest in itself is acceptable to God. Moreover, we celebrate the Lord's Day and not the Sabbath as a free observance" (C 291).

BAPTISM

ESSENCE AND ADMINISTRATION OF BAPTISM

Of the two sacramental means of grace besides the proclamation of the word, Baptism represents in a sense access to the church. Every conception of sacraments that goes beyond that of Zwingli implies that Baptism cannot be treated merely as a sign of confession (*professionis signum*) and as a mark for distinguishing between Christians and non-Christians (*discriminis nota*) (S 504–5, 542). Baptism is primarily a sign not of human action toward God, but of God's actions toward humans, and thus of divine grace. The Anglican Articles understand Baptism as a sign of regeneration (*signum Regenerationis*), by which as by an instrument (*per instrumentum*) the person baptized is incorporated into the church, the promise of the forgiveness of sins and of adoption as God's children by the Holy Spirit is made visible, faith is strengthened, and grace is increased (S 504–5). In the corresponding formulation of the Irish Articles, "Baptism is . . . a Sacrament of our admission into the Church, sealing unto us our new birth (and consequently our justification, adoption, and sanctification) by the communion which we have with Jesus Christ" (S 542). Baptism is an external symbolic action (*signe extérieur*) through which God attests to us that God wants to accept us as God's children (M 114, 23ff.). Baptism is a sign of adoption into God's covenant—an adoption effected by God alone. The Tetrapolitan Confession accordingly defines Baptism as "the sacrament of the covenant that God makes with those who are his, promising to be their God and Protector, as well as of their seed, and to have them as his people" (C 74). The Westminster Confession can likewise define Baptism as "a sign and seal of the covenant of grace, of his ingrafting into Christ, of regeneration, of remission of sins, and of his giving up unto God, through Jesus Christ, to walk in newness of life" (S 662).

Like every sacrament, Baptism consists of two different parts: namely, the sacramental sign (*signum*) and the thing signified (*res*) (M 420, 33ff.). The external sign is not only the empirical element of water, a "matter," but also a particular action (*ceremonia*): that is, washing—immersion in or sprinkling with water. The sign of Baptism is "water; wherein the person is baptized in the name of the Father, and of the Son, and of the Holy Ghost" (S 521, cf. 662). In opposition to the Baptist view, immersion (*immersio*) of the person being baptized is not regarded as necessary for the right administration of the sacrament, "but baptism is rightly administered by pouring (*superfusio*) or sprinkling (*inspersio*) water upon the person" (S 662).

As far as the person administering Baptism is concerned, the Westminster Confession allows only a lawfully called minister of the word to impart Baptism (ibid.). As a sacrament Baptism is administered by persons who have been rightfully called to and rightfully occupy the office of proclaiming the word and administering the sacraments. This statement is primarily directed against the Roman thesis that although the person administering Baptism ought by office to be the priest, "in the case of necessity not only a priest or a deacon but even a layman, or a woman, or even a pagan and a heretic can baptize provided that they keep the form of the Church and intend to do what the Church does" (DS 1315, CT 686). Over against this thesis, formulated in the interest of extending the authority of ecclesiastical dominion, the Second Helvetic Confession teaches "that baptism should not be administered in the Church by women or midwives. For Paul deprived women of eccesiastical duties, and baptism has to do with these" (C 283). In this case the rejection of baptism by women results from tying the administration of the sacrament to the particular office of the pastor. The reason why the Bremen Consensus rejects the idea that women—that is, midwives—can perform an emergency baptism when the child's life is in danger is that administering the sacraments "pertains to the office of the lawful ministers of the church, and the Apostle does not permit either private persons nor the female sex to occupy that office" (M 782, 13–15). This reasoning prohibits a fortiori baptism by pagans or heretics. The general rejection of baptism by women follows from baptism being tied to the particular office only when one introduces the additional premise that women cannot occupy this particular office. The right and the duty to perform baptisms belong only to those who hold the office, not to private persons. Nevertheless, the validity of Baptism does not depend upon the one who administers it.

Admittedly, the Scottish Confession counts it as part of the "right administration" of the sacraments "that they should be administered by lawful ministers, and we declare that these are men appointed to preach the Word, unto whom God has given the power to preach the Gospel, and who are lawfully called by some Kirk" (C 180–81). This condition would not be fulfilled if—as is possible according to the Roman understanding—baptisms were performed by women, "whom the Holy Ghost will not permit to preach in the congregation" (C 181). But if it actually happened that a baptism was performed by someone who did not hold the particular office, so that the right administration was not preserved, one would be logically compelled to dispute that the baptism, not administered by an officeholder, was actually a Baptism. The Scottish Confession does not back down from asserting the thesis that only those sacraments which are administered by a lawfully called officeholder are true sacraments. "Otherwise they cease to be the sacraments of Christ Jesus. This is why we abandon the teaching of the Roman Church and withdraw from its sacraments" (C 181). Although the other confessional writings regard only the lawfully called officeholder as the rightful administrator of the sacrament of Baptism, they do not go so far as to call into question the validity of baptisms that were not administered by the officeholder. Baptisms by private persons are a misuse of the sacrament and are to be halted, but that misuse does not call into question the sacrament's validity.

The same holds true of what the Scottish Confession calls adulterations of Baptism by means of ceremonies. This adulteration is such "that no part of Christ's original act remains in its original simplicity. The addition of oil, salt, spittle, and such like in baptism, are merely human additions" (C 181). In the Roman church baptism is not performed "in the elements and manner which God has appointed" (ibid.). It thus loses its basis for claiming to be a real sacrament. The Roman baptismal action is indeed supplemented by a number of ceremonies. The confessional writings reject these ceremonies, for they are not in agreement with that form of the sacrament which accords with Baptism's origin: namely, that form "by which Christ was baptized, and by which the apostles baptized" (C 283). In both cases we see the carrying out of the baptismal office instituted by God, the simple rite of baptism by water (C 282). The Second Helvetic Confession thus rejects all things "which by man's device were added afterwards and used in the Church. . . . Of this kind is exorcism, the use of burning lights, oil, salt, spittle, and such things as that baptism is to be celebrated twice every year with a multitude of ceremonies" (C 283; cf. S 542; M 778, 1ff.).

But these ceremonies do not in any way impugn the validity of Baptism. They are merely overgrowth that needs to be cleared away from the action of baptism itself. For in the words of the Irish Articles, "without them the Sacrament is fully and perfectly administered, to all intents and purposes, agreeable to the institution of our Saviour Christ" (S 542). This means, though, that in the Roman church Baptism has not been destroyed, but has been preserved beneath the ceremonies piled up around it. Baptism performed in the Roman church is thus definitely a real and true sacrament. Its Baptism is not to be repeated—that is what must be asserted. Thus the Hungarian Confession says that in the Roman church true Baptism (*verus Baptismus*) has been maintained (M 422, 44ff.). The French Confession puts it in the following way: Since "in the papacy . . . the virtue and substance of baptism remain, and as the efficacy of baptism does not depend upon the person who administers it, we confess that those baptized in it do not need a second baptism. But, on account of its corruptions, we can not present children to be baptized in it without incurring pollution" (S 376).

Baptism is a sacrament administered by someone who holds the office of publicly proclaiming the word and administering the sacraments. Baptism's sign is sprinkling or washing with water in the name of the triune God. There is a correspondence between the sign and the thing signified by it. In the symbolic action of baptism God places the forgiveness of sins and regeneration before our eyes (M 420, 37ff.). The Geneva Catechism clarifies this analogy between, on the one hand, washing with water and, on the other hand, forgiveness of sins and regeneration. "The forgiveness of sins is a kind of washing, by which our souls are cleansed from their defilements, *just as* the stains of the body are washed away by water. . . . The beginning of our regeneration and its end is our becoming new creatures, through the Spirit of God. Therefore the water is poured on the head as a *sign* of death, but in such a way that our resurrection is also *represented,* for instead of being drowned in water, what happens to us is only for a moment" (T 57). Baptism is not only a *sign,* but also a tangible *representation* of that which is signified: that is, of the forgiveness of sins and of regeneration. "*As* water washeth away the filth of the body, when poured upon it, and is seen on the body of the baptized, when sprinkled upon him, *so* doth the blood of Christ, by the power of the Holy Ghost, internally sprinkle the soul, cleanse it from its sins, and regenerate us from children of wrath unto children of God" (S 426). According to the Heidelberg Catechism, baptism as an "outward washing of water" makes clear "that, *like as* the filthiness of the body is taken away by water, *so* our sins also are taken away by the blood and Spirit of Christ" (S 330–31).

If the washing with water that is performed in baptism symbolically represents washing with Christ's blood and Spirit, then one can join the Bremen Consensus in distinguishing between two washings: namely, "an external washing, attested by the eyes and other senses, and an internal washing, of which the word of promise speaks" (M 769, 7–8; S 426). The holder of the ministerial office performs the external washing with water, but God performs the internal washing with Christ's blood and Spirit. Unlike the Erlauthal Confession, though, the Bremen Consensus does not draw the conclusion that there are two baptisms, an external (*externus*) and an internal baptism (*internus baptismus*) (M 296, 11ff.), baptism with water and baptism with the Spirit. Instead, in baptism the external and the internal washings are bound together in a single overall action, so that "it does not follow that there should be two baptisms, and not one" (M 769, 18–19).

This raises the question of the relation between the two actions that are bound together in baptism to form one overall action. In accord with the difference in the general doctrine of sacraments, the confessional writings do not put forward one unanimous position. For the Account of Faith, Baptism, like the other sacrament, is an act of confession. Baptism is bestowed in the presence of the community on the person "who before receiving it either confessed the religion of Christ or has the word of promise, whereby he is known to belong to the Church" (Z 47). Baptism is a public testimony (*testimonium publicum*), and in this sense a sign of the grace that *has already been imparted* (*factae gratiae signum*) (M 87, 13). Yet apart from the confessions that have Zwingli as their author, Baptism is understood precisely not merely as a sign of confession of grace that *has already been imparted* but as a visible sign of the invisible grace that *is being imparted*.

Within this overall understanding, though, the relation between sign and that which is signified continues to permit differing interpretations. The fact that external and internal washing are bound together in baptism can mean, as in the Synodical Declaration of Berne, that both processes occur "simultaneously" (M 45, 26–27). The external washing can also be viewed as the pledge and seal of the internal washing. According to the Second Helvetic Confession, "inwardly we are regenerated, purified, and renewed by God through the Holy Spirit; and outwardly we receive the *assurance* of the greatest gifts in the water" (C 282). Baptism is not only a symbolic representation but also a divine pledge and token of the forgiveness of sins and of regeneration. It is not merely the case that the blood and Spirit of Christ cleanses us from our sins *just as* water cleanses our bodies. In addition, we are cleansed from our sins *just as certainly and truly* as our bodies are cleansed with water (M 148, 18ff.; S 329, 331).

Yet precisely the Heidelberg Catechism's correlation of external and internal washing can give the impression that the external washing, while not the *confessional* sign of a grace that *has already been imparted,* is indeed the pledge of such a grace. After all, Christ instituted baptism to assure us "that we are as really washed from our sins spiritually as our bodies are washed with water" (S 701). Finally, the external washing can also be understood as a *means* of grace in the strict sense: that is, neither merely as a confessional sign of a grace that has already been imparted, nor as a mere pledge of the communication of grace, but as the instrument of that communication. According to the Geneva Catechism, although the internal washing is not ascribed to the water, internal and external washing are bound together in such a way "that *in* Baptism the forgiveness of sins is offered to us and we receive it" (T 57). The Bremen Consensus is still clearer in saying that internal and external washing are bound together in a single baptismal action and "will never be parted or separated. *With and through* the external washing God most surely *gives and increases* the internal washing for the converted and faithful" (M 769, 21–23). Baptism is a "divine means, in the right use of which the Holy Spirit makes us participants in such grace" (M 769, 36–37). God uses the external washing to perform the internal washing. Since God is the subject of the action as a whole, the hidden power of the forgiveness of sins and of regeneration does not belong to water or to the act of sprinkling with water (M 771, 45ff.). But as a means of grace, Baptism is not to be treated "as a mere water, but as a water caught up in God's word and thereby sanctified" (M 769, 1–2; cf. BSLK 63, 12ff.).

FAITH AND INFANT BAPTISM

Faith, though, is the condition for the appropriate and therefore salvific reception of Baptism. The faith of the recipient is the necessary condition for the salvific reception of Baptism: that is, for the salvific reception of the communication of grace accomplished by God through the external washing. The fact that God makes use of the external washing as a means of grace does not mean that God communicates the grace of the forgiveness of sins and of regeneration to everyone who undergoes the external washing. To be sure, in its essence as a means of grace Baptism is independent of the disposition of both the one administering and the one receiving it. But unbelievers "make it [sc. the grace offered through baptism] of no effect by their perversity," so that according to the Geneva Catechism "none but believers feel its (sc. baptism's) efficacy" (T 57). Baptism is only received on condition of faith (*fides*) and penitence (*poenitentia*) (M 148, 44ff.). The Second Helvetic Confession puts it thus: "We, therefore, confess our faith when we are baptized, and obligate ourselves to God for obedience, mortification of the flesh, and newness of life" (C 283). The Anglican Catechism accordingly gives this answer to the question of what is required of persons being baptized: "Repentance, whereby they forsake sin; and Faith, whereby they steadfastly believe the promises of God made to them in that Sacrament" (S 521). And the Sigismund Confession explicitly cites Luther for its thesis that Baptism "benefits and sanctifies only the faithful . . . but not unbelievers. This sign of grace no more helps unbelievers than does circumcision" (M 838, 23–26).

The central biblical statement for this position is Mark 16:16: "The one who believes and is baptized will be saved; but the one who does not believe will be condemned." If in accordance with this statement the communication of grace through Baptism is tied to the faith of the recipient, the question arises concerning whether it is right to baptize children: that is, infants. All the confessions, however, are united in defending infant baptism. Even Zwingli, whose concept of the sacraments would most readily provide a comprehensible basis for rejecting infant baptism, declares in the Marburg Articles "that the baptism of infants is right, and that through it they are taken to God's grace and into Christendom" (BSLK 63, 30–31). But how can the legitimacy of *infant* baptism be asserted if Baptism is defined as a sign of *confession?* The Account of Faith in fact seems to back away from an exclusive understanding of the sacrament as a sign of confession when it maintains that Baptism requires only one of the following two things: "either confession (*confessio*), i.e., a declaration of allegiance or a covenant (*foedus*), i.e., a promise (*promissio*)" (Z 46; M 86, 5–6). In the case of grown persons being baptized, their own confession of faith precedes the action of baptism. Matters are different when those being baptized are children. In this case baptism occurs only in response to the express wish of the parents. In the former case faith precedes baptism; in the latter case, God's promise precedes it. "For when members of the Church offer it, the infant is baptized under the law that, since it has been born of Christians, it is regarded by the divine promise among the members of the Church" (Z 47).

However, with this justification of infant baptism the Account of Faith by no means abandons its definition of the sacrament as a confessional sign. To be sure, in infant baptism the person being baptized does not herself make a confession. Nor is a child's faith assumed on the part of the person being baptized (Z 45–46). But the divine promise provides the confession for the person being baptized. The element common to both the baptism of adults and the baptism of children is that by baptism the church publicly adopts those who have already *been adopted* by grace. Precisely because the Account of Faith conceives the sacrament as a confessional sign in the sense of a sign of the *grace that has already occurred*, infant baptism causes the Account of Faith no problem, even though in this case, because of its rejection of a faith on the part of the child, it assumes not faith, but rather the divine promise as the presupposition for administering the sacrament.

Of course, this does not answer the question concerning the relation between baptism and *faith*. Instead, in the case of infant baptism the *promise* has taken the place that faith occupies in the baptism of adults. The Synodical Declaration of Berne, which strictly distinguishes between baptism by water and baptism by the Spirit, establishes for the case where a child is being baptized the order of first baptism by water, then baptism by the Spirit. "We baptize our children in such a way that by baptism we accept them *externally* into God's community, with the strong hope that the Lord will subsequently, in accordance with the eternal divine goodness, also execute the Lord's office in them and *truly* baptize them with the Holy Spirit" (M 45, 28–31). Here the relation between baptism and faith is defined with regard to infant baptism in such a way that Spirit baptism is distinguished from water baptism, with the Spirit baptism being accomplished only on condition of faith. Infant baptism is performed as an external action oriented toward baptism with the Spirit. This approach loosens the unity of baptism. If one wants to hold fast to that unity, there are still various possibilities for defining the relation between baptism and faith.

Over against the Anabaptists, the Scottish Confession declares "that children should be baptized before they have faith and understanding" (C 182). The connection between faith (*fides*) and reason (*ratio*) shows that here faith is also understood as a cognitive act, for which children are claimed not to possess the capacity. Children are baptized even though they are not yet *able* to believe. If despite this presupposition one wishes to hold fast to the connection between baptism and faith, this is possible only if one joins the Geneva Catechism in disputing "that faith and repentance should always *precede* the reception of the Sacrament. . . . They are only required from those who are capable of them" (T 58). Instead it is sufficient "if infants produce and manifest the fruit of their Baptism *after* they come to the age of discretion" (ibid.).

There is indeed a connection between baptism, on the one hand, and faith and repentance, on the other. But this connection is not such that faith and repentance as cognitive acts must *precede* baptism. Instead it is sufficient if faith and repentance on the part of the person baptized follow baptism. Admittedly, this does not give a final definition of the relation between baptism and faith. The fact that it does not is shown by the Anglican Catechism in its answer to the question of why children who, because of their age, are incapable of faith and repentance, are nevertheless baptized: "Because they promise them both by their Sureties; which promise, when they come to age, themselves are bound to perform" (S 521). The basis for infant baptism is the baptismal promise offered by the sponsors who represent the children or, alternatively, offered *by* the childen *through* the sponsors. That is, the basis for infant baptism is the promise of faith and repentance—a promise that indeed is to be kept at the appropriate age. While here faith is still regarded as something that cannot be presupposed in the person being baptized, because it does not lie within her capacity, the Hungarian Confession speaks of a "seed of faith" (*semen fidei*) in children (M 422, 3ff.). The Bremen Consensus likewise says that the children of Christian parents are not "to be regarded as unbelieving like the children of Jews and Turks, but as believing. For they believe according to their measure: that is, they have a seed of faith through the secret working of the Holy Spirit before, in and after baptism. Holy baptism seals and increases this seed of faith" (M 770, 16–20). With the seed of faith, faith is assumed on the part of the child, so that faith does not merely follow baptism, but instead faith and baptism are simultaneous.

In the context of the question of infant baptism one must not lose sight of the fact that it is always and exclusively a question about the baptism of children of believers: that is, of Christian parents. It is about the baptism of those children who, in the formulation of the First Helvetic Confession, "have been born of us who are a people of God" (C 109, trans. altered). According to the Westminster Confession, "not only those that do actually profess faith in and obedience unto Christ, but also the infants of one or both *believing* parents are to be baptized" (S 662–63). Moreover, a congregational understanding of the church requires insisting that infant baptism, if it is retained at all, be limited to the children of believing parents. In accordance with this the Savoy Declaration supplements the Westminster Confession by adding that besides believing adults "the infants of one or both believing parents are to be baptized, *and those onely*" (S 662–63; M 603, 41). For when on the congregational side the church is understood as a community of the saints that is constituted through voluntary confession of faith (M 540, 4ff.), the question arises of the extent to which children, who are unable to make a voluntary confession of faith, can be numbered among the members of the church at all. From this the Savoy Declaration in its original form draws the logical conclusion and rejects the statement made in the Westminster Confession that the universal visible church consists of all those "that profess the true religion, *and of their children*" (S 657). The later version, though, no longer limits the church to all those "professing the faith of the Gospel and obedience unto God by Christ according unto it" (M 597, 39–40), but again expands the circle of the church's members to include those named immediately above *"and their children with them"* (M 598, 42). Only in this way can the distribution of a sacrament to children be justified. For as a seal of the divine covenant of grace the sacraments ought to be administered "only to the faithfull" (M 541, 16). But since the children of the faithful already belong to this covenant, the statement that the sacraments should be administered only to the faithful can be supplemented by adding the words "and Baptisme *to their seed or those under their governement*" (M 541, 16–17).

These reflections make clear, however, that neither a faith that is already present in the children, nor a faith promised by them through their sponsors, nor a faith expected when they reach maturity is the decisive basis for infant baptism. Rather what is decisive is—as is already true for Zwingli's Account of Faith—the fact that the children of believing parents belong to God's covenant of grace. If one *also* regards faith as a cognitive act, accepting infant baptism is out of the question. The faith that is not yet present in the young child, but will develop only later, can also not be promised by the sponsors in the child's place. For this reason, as far as the relation between baptism and faith is concerned the Geneva Catechism confines itself to assuming that baptism does not presuppose faith, but that it is sufficient "if infants produce and manifest the fruit of their Baptism after they come to the age of discretion" (T 58). The Catechism grounds the claim that this is not absurd by pointing to the sacrament in the Old Testament that corresponds to Baptism: namely, circumcision. "Circumcision was also a Sacrament of repentance, as Moses and the prophets declare (Deut. 10:16; 30:6; Jer. 4:4); and was a Sacrament of faith, as St. Paul says (Rom. 4:11, 12). And yet God has not excluded little children from it" (T 58). For Zwingli's Account of Faith the children of believers belong to the church and, because of this belonging grounded in God's promise, receive the sacrament of circumcision as a sign of the church. "I believe that to this Church belong Isaac, Jacob, Judah and all who were of the seed of Abraham, and also those infants whose parents in the first beginnings of the Christian Church, through the preaching of the apostles, were won to the cause of Christ. For if Isaac and the rest of the ancients had not belonged to the Church, they would not have received the Church's token, circumcision. Since these, then, were members of the Church, infants and children belonged to the primitive Church. Therefore I believe and know that they were sealed by the sacrament of baptism" (Z 45). The correspondence between circumcision and Baptism requires infant baptism. Otherwise one would be withholding from the children of the New Covenant something that the children of the Old Covenant received: namely, "the sign of the bounty and mercy of God," which is given to us for our "consolation, and to confirm the promise given since the beginning" (T 59, trans. altered). As the "Circumcision of Christ" (Col. 2:11), Baptism is administered to children just as circumcision, which mediated the same grace, was administered to the children of Israel (S 427–28).

Like circumcision, Baptism is a sign of the covenant (*signum foederis Dei*) (S 291, 662). The Heidelberg Catechism also grounds infant baptism in the fact that children of Christian parents belong to God's covenant. "For since they, as well as their parents, belong to the covenant and people of God, and both redemption from sin and the Holy Ghost, who works faith, are through the blood of Christ promised to them no less than to their parents, they are also by Baptism, as a sign of the covenant, to be ingrafted into the Christian Church, and distinguished from the children of unbelievers, as was done in the Old Testament by Circumcision, in place of which in the New Testament Baptism is appointed" (S 331). The fact that the children of believing parents, like the parents themselves, belong to the divine covenant of grace is grounded with God's promise to Abraham, valid in both the New and the Old Covenant: "I will be thy God and the God of thy seed" (C 75). Children are baptized as "heirs of God's blessing promised to the seed of the faithful" (T 59; cf. S 379–80). Infant baptism is thus grounded in covenant theology. On the basis of the promise given to Abraham as the father of faith (Gal. 3:7) and to his offspring, the children of believing parents belong in God's covenant of grace "from the womb onward" (M 771, 10). The Bremen Consensus compares the status of belonging to the divine covenant of grace with citizenship. For ultimately the children of believers are subject to the "spiritual citizenship of the Christian churches, which are the city of God," just as all children of citizens are subject to the "external citizenship of worldly police" (M 771, 13–15).

NECESSITY AND SUFFICIENCY OF BAPTISM

If the children of believing parents already belong to the covenant of grace "from the womb onward" and thus enjoy the spiritual citizenship of the Christian church, a question arises concerning the relation between, on the one hand, belonging to the covenant of grace and, on the other hand, baptism as a means of grace. If on the basis of the divine promise the children of believers are already members of the covenant of grace before their birth, that relation can at least not be such that baptism is *necessary for salvation*. In interpreting the German version of the Augsburg Confession's statement that Baptism "is necessary" with the phrase "that it is necessary for salvation" (*quod sit necessarius ad salutem*) (BC 33; BSLK 63, 2–3), the Latin version of the Augsburg Confession corresponds to the Roman view, to be sure (DS 1618), but can give rise to misunderstanding. The Synodical Declaration of Berne at any rate rejects the emergency baptism that is derived from the necessity of baptism for salvation. It is a false belief "when one pretends that if the little child is not externally baptized, he or she must be eternally lost" (M 46, 17–18). But precisely this would have to be asserted if baptism were necessary for *salvation*. The requirement of emergency baptism is indeed ineluctably entailed by the assumption that baptism is necessary for salvation. In opposition to such a view of baptism the Westminster Confession explicitly declares that "grace and salvation are not so inseparably annexed unto it [sc. baptism], as that no person can be regenerated or saved without it" (S 663). The Confession disputes that baptism is necessary for *salvation*, and thus that unbaptized children are excluded from salvation. But if original sin extends to children, the absence of original sin cannot serve as the basis on which salvation includes unbaptized children. Instead the only possible basis is that the children of believing parents already belong to the covenant of grace on the basis of the divine promise, and thus before baptism. In the words of the Bremen Consensus, "the fact that the children of Christians participate in the gift of the Holy Spirit and in God's covenant does not by any means deny original sin. For nature and grace are different. By nature the children of believing parents are children of wrath like the rest (Eph. 2:3). But grace is promised to them from the womb onward" (M 770, 24–28). Since the unborn children of Christian parents already belong to the covenant of grace, it is false to assume that prior to baptism there is no difference between children of Christians and children of non-Christians, and that baptism is the ground and commencement of children's salvation. "From the womb onward the children of Christians are not Turks, Jews or pagans, but Christians" (M 770, 46–47).

The Bremen Consensus does not in any way dispute that Baptism, as a sacrament instituted by Christ, is necessary in the church. The fact that baptism is not necessary for salvation does not mean that it can be omitted in all circumstances. The necessity of baptism is certainly recognized, but it is limited by specific conditions. In any case grace is not tied to baptism in such a way that everyone who is not baptized is necessarily excluded from salvation. Under certain circumstances unbaptized persons also participate in salvation. Such circumstances are present when, "due to a lack of water, the absence of a minister, or other occasion, one would have to do without baptism (as with the thief on the cross, the young Caesar Valentinianus, many thousands of unbaptized martyrs, and many Christians' children who died prior to baptism)" (M 769, 47–M 770, 1). Baptism is thus necessary in all cases except those where it is impossible to administer baptism in accordance with its institution. For "Christ does not automatically condemn those who are not baptized (namely, without contempt for baptism)" (M 770, 2–3) and who do not have the possibility of receiving baptism in accordance with its institution: that is, as a sacrament of acceptance into the church and thus "not without the church being present" (M 46, 12).

Only with this caveat is it possible to receive the statement that Baptism is necessary.

Like circumcision, baptism is a rite of initiation, a *signum initiale* (S 290). For the Second Helvetic Confession baptism is the "sign of initiation for God's people" (C 282). As a rite of initiation, however, it cannot be repeated and thus is administered only once. "The sacrament of baptism is but once to be administered to any person" (S 663, cf. 379). Baptism, like the regeneration of which it is a sign, is a unique and unrepeatable event (S 426–427). Baptism is never to be repeated, "since we can not be born twice" (S 427). This does not mean that baptism is a rite whose benefit only applies to a specific period of our life. Baptism is not merely "the *door* of the spiritual life" (DS 1314, CT 686). "The efficacy of baptism is not tied to that moment of time wherein it is administered" (S 663). Its meaning and benefit extend to the entire course of our life (*ad totum vitae nostrae curriculum*) (M 246, 34–35), indeed to life and death (S 379). In this sense the French Confession is thoroughly accurate when it characterizes baptism as a "*permanent* signature" (*signature permanente*) of the forgivenenss of our sins and of our regeneration (S 379, trans. altered). The Second Helvetic Confession observes that "baptism once received continues for all of life, and is a *perpetual* sealing (*perpetua obsignatio*) of our adoption" (C 282).

Precisely the notion of a permanent signature could give rise to the suspicion that the position presented here is merely taking up the Roman thesis that baptism impresses on the soul a mark (*character*): that is, an indestructible spiritual sign (*spirituale signum indelebile*) (DS 1313). Yet this is by no means the case. According to the Roman view baptism is not the permanent signature of the *forgiveness of sins* and of *regeneration*, but needs to be supplemented by further sacraments: namely, confirmation, penance, and extreme unction. To be sure, baptism imparts an indestructible mark. But the effect of baptism is supplemented by the effect of confirmation, in which the Holy Spirit is imparted for the strengthening of the confirmand (DS 1319), and in which an indestructible mark is also imparted to the confirmand (DS 1313). The Tridentine Canons on the Sacrament of Confirmation reject the claim that confirmation was originally nothing more "than a certain catechesis by which those nearing adolescence explained the basis of their faith before the church" (DS 1628, CT 710). On the Reformation side, confirmation was rejected as a particular sacrament that supplements and completes Baptism. It is this rejection that the Canons are attacking. For the Second Helvetic Confession, confirmation and extreme unction are merely "human inventions which the Church can dispense with without any loss" (C 277). But the Confession explicitly requires ecclesiastical instruction in the sense of a catechetical instruction. The "practice . . . to examine children in the churches on articles of faith common to all Christians" (T 5) is also welcomed. But the view that confirmation is more than this—namely, a sacrament that supplements the value of Baptism—is decisively rejected.

Baptism communicates and attests the grace of the forgiveness of sins and of regeneration—a grace whose effectiveness extends to the *whole* of life. It must be seen as a grievous insult to this grace—still more grievous than that of the Tridentine doctrine of confirmation—when Trent declares that Baptism works only the remission of all sins committed *prior* to the reception of Baptism, and that the sacrament of Baptism, on the basis of its limited effectuation of grace, requires supplementation by the sacrament of penance as the "*second* plank after the ship has been wrecked and grace has been lost" (DS 1542, CT 571; cf. DS 1668, CT 788; DS 1702, CT 801). Where the effect of Baptism is limited in such a way that it does not extend at all to those sins committed *after* it has been received, the fundamental difference between Baptism and penance must be asserted, and the latter must be raised to the level of a means of grace in its own right (DS 1702). Baptism becomes a *mere* rite of initiation, the benefit of which does not extend to the *whole* of life. Baptism does indeed impart an indestructible mark to the person baptized, according to the Roman view. But this mark is not a permanent signature that assures us "that although we are baptized only once, yet the gain that it symbolizes to us reaches over our whole lives and to our death" (S 379). The forgiveness of sins and regeneration promised in Baptism then no longer apply to the entire course of our life (S 427). But this explicitly disputes that which, according to the confessional writings, constitutes the essence of Baptism: namely, that its effectiveness is not limited to the point in time at which it is received, along with the past (S 663), but rather that it is the "*perpetual* sealing of our adoption" (C 282).

THE LORD'S SUPPER

THE CRITIQUE OF THE SACRIFICE OF THE MASS

As the sacramental act of acceptance into the church, Baptism is only performed once. By contrast, the Lord's Supper is a sacramental action that we are specifically exhorted to repeat frequently. The Reformation is united not only in this way of defining the relation between Baptism and the Supper. It is also united in the view that the sacrament of the Lord's Supper is fundamentally different from the Roman Mass. An extensive critique of the Mass is to be found only in the early confessions, for an understandable reason. After the Mass was completely done away with in the Reformed church, its treatment no longer had an object. "We are not now discussing what kind of mass once existed among the fathers, whether it is to be tolerated or not. But this we say freely that the mass which is now used throughout the Roman Church has been abolished in our churches for many and very good reasons which, for brevity's sake, we do not now enumerate in detail" (C 288).

The point of departure for the critique of the Mass is a very specific understanding of the Mass. The Mass is attacked not merely as an empty spectacle and as presenting the possibility of merit. What is essential, rather, is that "the priest is said to effect the very body of the Lord, and really to offer it for the remission of the sins of the living and the dead" (ibid.). According to the words of the Mass, the priests appear as ones who, "as mediators between Christ and His Kirk . . . should offer to God the Father a sacrifice in propitiation for the sins of the living and the dead" (C 182). To be sure, the fact that the forgiveness of sins occurs through Christ's sacrifice on the cross is not called into question. But according to the Heidelberg Catechism, the claim is made "that the living and the dead have not forgiveness of sins through the sufferings of Christ unless Christ is still daily sacrificed for them by the priests" (S 335, trans. altered). This means that the forgiveness of sins through the sacrifice of the cross occurs only on the condition that Christ is sacrificed in the daily Mass. The sacrifice of the Mass activates the sacrifice of the cross insofar as the former applies the forgiveness of sins inherent in the latter. At this point there is no further specification of the relation of the sacrifice of the cross to the sacrifice of the Mass. The Reformed critics do not use the concept of repetition. They only observe—correctly—that the canon of the Mass says that the priest offers and sacrifices Christ to God, so that the Mass involves an actual sacrifice. The Roman theory of the sacrifice of the Mass receives its magisterial form in the Tridentine decree "On the Sacrifice of the Mass." This decree says explicitly that in the Mass an actual and proper sacrifice (*verum et proprium sacrificium*) is offered to God (DS 1751). The subjects who carry out the sacrifice are the priests, to whom Christ's commandment of repetition at his last meal turned over the task of sacrificing his body and his blood (DS 1752). The sacrifice of the Mass, performed for the living and the dead, for sins and penalties, to perform satisfaction and for other afflictions, is a propitiatory sacrifice (*sacrificium propitiatorium*) whose benefit is independent of sacramental Communion (DS 1753). In this sense the Reformation critique is right on the mark in taking as its basis the understanding of the sacrifice of the Mass as an actual sacrifice of propitiation.

This understanding of the sacrifice of the Mass manifestly threatens the sufficiency of Christ's sacrifice on the cross. In Zwingli's Theses this objection constitutes the center of the critique of the Roman Mass: "That Christ, Who offered Himself up once and for all, is in eternity a perpetual sacrifice in payment of the sins of all believers, from which it follows that the Mass is not a sacrifice but a recollection of the sacrifice and an assurance of the redemption which Christ has manifested to us" (C 38). In the background of the reproach that the sacrifice of the Mass contests the sufficiency of Christ's sacrifice on the cross is the Letter to the Hebrews' doctrine of atonement. Christ "sacrifices himself, because on the cross he suffers death for us and with his one death purifies and pays the sin of the whole world for eternity" (M 26, 38–40). The uniqueness of Christ's sacrifice is a necessary consequence of the Zurich Introduction's identification of Christ's sacrifice and Christ's death. Like Christ's death, Christ's sacrifice is also a one-time, unrepeatable, historical event. For "his dying is a sacrificing for us, and his sacrificing is his dying" (M 26, 43–44). "If he once died, he was also once sacrificed" (M 27, 7–8). The one-time nature and the sufficiency of Christ's sacrifice on the cross make every sacrifice of the Mass superfluous. More than that, "the mass as now in use, in which Christ is offered up to God the Father for the sins of the living and the dead, is contrary to Scripture, a blasphemy against the most holy sacrifice, passion and death of Christ" (C 49). In the formulation of the Heidelberg Catechism, the Mass understood in this way proves to be a "denial of the one sacrifice and passion of Jesus Christ" (S 336, cf. 76–77). Over against such a Mass we are to hold fast to the fact that Christ's sacrifice on the cross is the complete redemption (*redemptio*), propitiation (*propitiatio*), and satisfaction (*satisfactio*) for all the sins of the entire world. As the Anglican Articles put it, the sacrifices of the Mass are "blasphemous fancies" (*blasphema figmenta*) (S 507). According to the Irish Articles, they are "most ungodly and most injurious to that all-sufficient sacrifice of our Saviour Christ, offered once forever upon the cross, which is the only propitiation and satisfaction for all our sins" (S 543, cf. 664). Christ's one sacrifice of propitiation on the cross is sufficient in such a way that it makes all other sacrifices of propitiation superfluous, and one must regard the latter as calling the former into question.

Admittedly, one must concede that the decided focus of the Tridentine decree on the sacrifice of the Mass is the preservation of the sufficiency of Christ's sacrifice on the cross. The decree unfolds the doctrine of the sacrifice of the Mass against the background of the Reformation's critique, and takes this critique into account as far as it is possible for the decree to do so. Ultimately it emphatically disputes "that the Sacrifice of the Mass constitutes a blasphemy to the sacred sacrifice that Christ offered on the cross, or that the Mass detracts from that sacrifice" (DS 1754, CT 759). It thus calls into question the Reformation's critique. The decree thinks that it can do this because it explicitly holds fast to the claim that in the sacrifice of the Mass "the same Christ who offered himself once in a bloody manner on the altar of the cross is present and is offered in an unbloody manner" (DS 1743, CT 749). "For it is one and the same victim: he who now makes the offering through the ministry of priests and he who then offered himself on the cross; the only difference is in the manner of the offering" (ibid.). The relation between the bloody sacrifice of the cross and the bloodless sacrifice of the Mass is defined with the help of the concept of representation (*repraesentatio*). The sacrifice of the Mass "was to re-present (*repraesentaretur*) the bloody sacrfice which he accomplished on the cross once and for all. It was to perpetuate his memory until the end of the world (see 1 Cor. 11:23 ff.). Its salutary strength was to be applied (*applicaretur*) for the remission of the sins that we daily commit" (DS 1740, CT 747). In this way Trent's decree on the sacrifice of the Mass certainly attempts to elude the Reformation's objection that the sacrifice of the Mass vitiates the one-time sacrifice of the cross. At the same time, though, the question arises of the extent to which, given the presupposition that such a vitiation does not occur, one can nevertheless speak of an actual sacrifice of propitiation offered to God by the priest.

Moreover, there is the question of why the application of the forgiveness of sins given with the sacrifice of the cross needs itself to occur through a sacrifice of propitiation. The opinion that the sacrifice of the cross and its fruit are in turn applied by the sacrifice of the Mass suggests itself only if one understands Christ's commandment of repetition as an institution of the priesthood of the Mass. But according to the Reformation's view, this interpretation rests upon a misunderstanding. The action commanded by Jesus at his last meal is indeed an action in which the sacrifice of the cross with its fruit is applied. But this action itself is not a sacrifice of propitiation, but the celebration of a meal. For this reason the Sendomir Consensus can cite the Saxon Confession, which rejects the interpretation of the sacrifice of the Mass as an applicatory sacrifice of propitiation, and can declare that the application of Christ's sacrifice on the cross occurs through word and sacrament, instead of through the sacrifice of the Mass (N 558). The Lord's Supper is not instituted in order for us to sacrifice to God the body of Christ for the forgiveness of sins. But—as the Geneva Catechism puts it—Christ "commands us only to receive His body, not to sacrifice it" (C 61, trans. altered). The commandment of repetition is a charge not to sacrifice Christ's body and blood, but to receive them. We are not summoned to give something, but we are summoned to receive something. For on the cross "the unique and perpetual sacrifice was offered for our redemption. Therefore there remains for us nought but to enjoy it" (ibid.).

Yet although the receiving, "katabatic" aspect of the understanding of the Supper stands unequivocally in the foreground, the giving, "anabatic" aspect is by no means entirely excised. The fact that the Supper is also a sacrifice is not called into question. According to the Erlauthal Confession, the difference between sacrifice and sacrament lies in the fact that a sacrifice is something that is offered to God, while in a sacrament God gives us something. Here it is clear that the Supper in its substance is not a sacrifice, but a sacrament (M 309, 7ff.). The Supper is called a sacrifice only on the basis of the activities of those who participate in the meal. Naturally God's gift to us in the Supper cannot be received without our offering God a sacrifice of praise and thanksgiving. The Supper can therefore be characterized *pars pro toto* as a sacrifice, albeit not a sacrifice of propitiation, but a sacrifice of thanksgiving as the human response to Christ's one-time sacrifice of propitiation, which is applied to us in the Supper. The Supper is not a propitiatory sacrifice, but a eucharistic sacrifice (N 681–82; M 308, 5ff.). In the Old Covenant the various cultic sacrifices point to Christ and find their fulfillment in him. But Christ himself offered the sole and sufficient sacrifice of propitiation for the sins of the whole world. What remains for us is the spiritual sacrifice of thanksgiving, which we as a royal priesthood are enabled to offer to God. In this sense the Supper cannot be a sacrifice of propitiation that we offer to God. Instead the Westminster Confession declares that "in this sacrament Christ is not offered up to his Father, nor any real sacrifice made at all for remission of sins of the quick or dead, but only a commemoration of that one offering up of himself, by himself, upon the cross, once for all, and a spiritual oblation of all possible praise unto God for the same" (S 664).

ESSENCE AND ADMINISTRATION
OF THE LORD'S SUPPER

As a sacrament the Supper is a symbolic action: that is, according to the Bremen Consensus, "a ceremony or external sign or a work, through which God offers us that which is attached to the same ceremony— namely, the divine promise" (M 813, 29–31). The Supper consists of two parts: namely, the external sign of grace and Christ's word connected to that sign. This word of Christ's is composed of the commandment of repetition and the promise of the words concerning the bread and the cup (M 772, 15ff.). The Hungarian Confession names as signs of the sacrament of the Meal not only bread and wine, but the entire act of the meal in its essential components, which includes the clear explication of the words of institution by the person presiding at the meal, the invocation of God's name, the breaking of the bread, the distribution of the bread and wine, as well as the actions of eating and drinking (M 423, 18ff.). The sacrament is the entire action of the meal.

With regard to the elements, "just as we should take and use a natural, true wine, well-pressed from the vine, so should we take and use natural and true bread" (M 840, 10ff.). Yet over against this instruction from the Sigismund Confession, the Church Order of Julich and Berg observes that "those who by nature are put off by wine, so that they can tolerate neither the smell nor the taste, ought to receive from the hand of the church's minister, along with the bread, the kind of drink to which they are accustomed" (Ni 322, 17–20). It is evidently decisive in choosing the elements that they be basic means of nourishment. The symbolic character of the meal lies in the fact that, just as we are externally nourished and fed by basic means of nourishment as gifts of creation, so we are internally and spiritually nourished and fed by Christ as the gift of grace. According to the Geneva Catechism, "as it is the particular virtue of bread to nourish our bodies, to refresh and sustain us in this mortal life, so it pertains to His body to act toward our souls, i.e. in nourishing and quickening them spiritually. Likewise as wine strengthens, refreshes, and rejoices a man physically, so His blood is our joy, our refreshing and our spiritual strength" (T 60).

The sacramental meal is not just a memorial meal and an act of confession. The majority of Reformed confessional writings emphatically reject Zwingli's understanding of the Supper. The Supper is certainly *also* a memorial meal and an act of confession, as it is *also* a sacrifice of thanksgiving and an expression of thanksgiving. Whoever celebrates the meal "gives thanks with a joyful mind for his redemption and that of all mankind . . . makes a faithful memorial to the Lord's death, and testifies before the Church that he is a member of that body," declares the Second Helvetic Confession (C 286, trans. altered). The Zwinglian understanding of the Supper as a remembrance or act of remembering finds particularly clear expression in the Zurich Confession, which says "that the remembrance of the body that was offered up and of the blood that was shed for the forgiveness of our sins is the true keystone and the goal toward which the entire action of the Supper ultimately moves" (M 156, 14–17). In this view the Supper is much more than a subjective remembrance of a past event. The Supper is not a *"mere* commemoration" (*nuda commemoratio*) (DS 1753). The concept of remembrance here is a full one. It means the act of remembering "that Christ gave his body up to death for us and shed his blood to wash away our sins. But without true faith such a memory can not occur rightly and as the Lord commanded. Therefore the remembrance in the Supper is not an empty fantasy" (M 156, 22–26).

To be sure, the past salvific events are not really (*realiter*) present. But the "faithful imagination" renews the salvific events in such a way that it makes them present "to the faithful mind and heart" (M 156, 27ff.). In Zwingli's Account of Faith, the presence of Christ's body means nothing other than a true presence in faith's contemplation (*fidei contemplatione*). That is, in faithful contemplation the participants in the Eucharist render the whole history of salvation present (Z 49). According to the Second Helvetic Confession, through the Supper God wills "to keep in fresh remembrance that greatest benefit which he showed to mortal men, namely, that by having given his body and shed his blood he has pardoned all our sins, and redeemed us from eternal death and the power of the devil" (C 284).

Yet this still does not adequately grasp what happens in the Supper. Not only do we remember the events of salvation in faithful contemplation. Not only does God call our remembrance to these events. Rather, in the Supper we receive Christ's body and blood. The assertion that the sacraments are by no means empty signs is directed against the Zwinglian understanding of the Supper. The Scottish Confession accuses of "vanity . . . those who affirm the sacraments to be nothing else than naked and bare signs" (C 179). The sign of the Supper refers to a thing signified, a *res*. This signified object, which is offered in the Supper, is Christ's body and blood. We read in the Geneva Catechism: "The body of the Lord Jesus which was once offered to reconcile us to God, is now given to us, to certify to us that we have part in this reconciliation. . . . The Lord Jesus, who once shed His blood in payment and satisfaction for our offences, gives it to us to drink, that we may have no doubt at all of receiving its fruit" (T 61). Here "body" and "blood" do not actually stand for two different materials—that is, parts of Christ. Instead they designate the whole person of the Christ sacrificed for us, the person along with his work (M 423, 26ff.). In the words of the First Helvetic Confession, "in the Lord's Supper the Lord truly offers His body and His blood, *that is, Himself,* to His own . . . to enjoy" (C 108). The Supper is not participation in the separate substances of Christ's body and blood, but participation in Christ's person and work.

According to the Geneva Catechism, we must really participate in Christ's body and blood, for "since the whole affiance of our salvation rests in the obedience which He has rendered to God, His Father, in order that it may be imputed to us as if it were ours, we must possess Him: for His blessings are not ours, unless He gives Himself to us first" (T 60). We are to "receive Him, in order that we may feel in ourselves the fruit and the efficacy of His death and passion" (ibid.). The reference to Christ's body and blood thus serves to highlight the relation between the person and the sacrifice of atonement. In the Supper we do not receive a share in Christ's person as such, but in Christ's person as sacrificed for us. What is at issue is "the body and blood of Christ Jesus, once broken and shed for us" (C 179). If in the Supper we participate in Christ together with his work, a union with Christ (*unio cum Christo*) occurs in this sacrament. By no means should we only believe "that He died and rose again, in order to deliver us from eternal death, and acquire life for us, but also that He dwells in us, and is conjoined with us in a union as the Head with the members, that by virtue of this conjunction He may make us partakers of all His grace" (C 60). This union with Christ is the center of the Supper. It forms the basis for all statements about participation in the fruits of Christ's work of reconciliation. We participate in the fruits of this work because we participate in Christ himself.

According to the French Confession, in the Supper we experience that Christ "not only died and rose again for us once, but also feeds and nourishes us truly with his flesh and blood, so that we may be one in him, and that our life may be in common" (S 380). "Christ Jesus is so joined with us that He becomes the very nourishment and food of our souls" (C 179). To this statement from the Scottish Confession one needs immediately to add that by no means is union with Christ carried out solely in the Supper. Incorporation into Christ does not yet name what is specific to the Supper. According to the Geneva Catechism, we also receive this communion "through the preaching of the Gospel, as St Paul declares (1 Cor. 1:9): in that the Lord Jesus Christ promises us in it, that we are flesh of His flesh and bone of His bone (Eph. 5:30), that He is that living bread which came down from heaven to nourish our souls (John 6:51), and that we are one with Him, as He is one with the Father (John 17:21)" (T 60–61, trans. altered; cf. M 423, 26ff.). Indeed, with regard to the gift of grace, there is no difference between the Supper, on the one hand, and Baptism and preaching, on the other. God communicates the same thing in word and sacrament, but does so in differing ways. The difference between the Supper and Baptism or preaching lies not in what is communicated, but only in the manner of communication. The specific property (*proprium*) of the Supper understood as a means of grace is its character as a meal.

This raises the question of how the external elements of the symbolic action relate to the gift of grace communicated in the meal itself. First one must recognize that there are two different things here, although they are in a particular relationship to each other. The sign is not identical to that which is signified. The Scottish Confession says that "we make a distinction between Christ Jesus in His eternal substance and the elements of the sacramental signs" (C 180). Along the same lines, for the Geneva Catechism the Supper contains two different things: "material bread and wine, which we see by the eye, handle by the hands, and perceive by the taste, and Jesus Christ by whom our souls are inwardly nourished" (T 62). Admittedly, this does not yet say how receiving or eating of the elements is related to receiving or eating the body of Christ. The confessional writings by no means provide a univocal answer to this question. On the one hand we encounter a sacramental parallelism. The Belgic Confession says that Christ instituted the Supper "to testify . . . unto us, that, as certainly as we receive and hold this Sacrament in our hands, and eat and drink the same with our mouths, by which our life is afterwards nourished, we also do as certainly receive by faith (which is the hand and mouth of our soul) the true body and blood of Christ our only Saviour in our souls, for the support of our spiritual life" (S 429).

In the Heidelberg Catechism, the action of the Supper serves in a similar way as an assurance. Bread and wine are the "visible sign and pledge"

(S 335) by which we are assured that, just as we receive and eat or drink the tokens of bread and wine, so are we truly made participants in Christ's body and blood. For the Catechism, too, the Supper is a meal of remembrance, by which the participants are reminded that Christ's body "was offered and broken on the cross for me, and his blood shed for me, as certainly as I see with my eyes the bread of the Lord broken for me, and the cup communicated to me" (S 332). The event of reconciliation on the cross is depicted by the symbolic action itself. This aspect is also emphasized in the Zwinglian tradition when, as in the Zurich Confession, the following distinction is made between sign and thing signified: "The sign is the entire visible, external action, in which the bread is broken and eaten, and in which the drink is poured out and drunk. That which is signified is the Lord Jesus, true God and human being, his flesh and blood, his agony, crucifixion and dying" (M 158, 11–15). The action of the meal serves as a commemorative sign and has symbolic character. In this context the Hungarian Confession connects the remembrance of Christ's suffering above all with the act of the breaking of the bread. The breaking of the bread (*fractio panis*) makes present Christ's being broken under the pains of death (M 424, 17ff.).

Yet for the Heidelberg Catechism, unlike the Zwinglian confessions, the Supper's function as a commemorative sign is not exhaustive. Not only does the Supper remind me of Christ's sacrifice, it also assures me "that with his crucified body and shed blood he himself feeds and nourishes my soul to everlasting life, as certainly as I receive from the hand of the minister, and taste with my mouth, the bread and cup of the Lord, which are given me as certain tokens of the body and blood of Christ" (S 332). The sacrament of the meal assures me that I am fed by Christ with his sacrifice of propitiation. Christ instituted the Supper "to assure us that by the communication of His body and blood, our souls are nourished, in the hope of eternal life" (T 59).

If the Supper is viewed in this sense as assurance, that does not necessarily imply that it is also understood as a means of grace in a strict sense. This is only the case where it is said, as in the French Confession, that *in* the Supper "God *gives* us really and in fact that which he there sets forth to us; and that consequently with thse signs is given the true possession and enjoyment of that which they present to us" (S 380–81). Already in the First Confession of Basle we find the emphasis that "the true body and blood of Christ is . . . offered to us *with* the bread and wine of the Lord, together with the words of institution" (C 93). In this case the sacrament is not the means of assurance, but of the grace that Christ shows to us (C 108). For the Bremen Consensus Christ is present in the Supper such that "*in* the right and saving use of this holy bread and wine as such means as he himself ordained, he truly *gives* to us, *appropriates* to us, and seals for us the communion of his body and blood as well as of his merit and power"

(M 773, 12–15). The Supper is not only a sealing and an assuring, but also has exhibitive character (N 682). In the expression of the Leipzig Colloquy, "the true, essential body, broken for us, and the true, essential blood of Jesus Christ himself, shed for us, are truly and presently offered, distributed and enjoyed *by means* of the blessed bread and wine" (N 662–63). The relation between the distribution of the earthly elements and Christ's body and blood cannot be grasped merely as signification or sealing. Instead we are dealing with an "inseparable distribution of the earthly elements and of the true body and blood of Jesus Christ" (N 663). The distribution of Christ's body and blood occurs by means of or through the distribution of bread and wine. Indeed, one could go so far as to say that the former action is performed in, with, and under the latter.

For this reason it is definitely possible for the Reformed side to accept the altered Augsburg Confession's article on the Supper. This article says that Christ's body and blood are distributed *with* the bread and wine (*cum pane et vino*) (BSLK 65, 45–46). By contrast, there are two views that the Reformed side rejects. One is the Roman doctrine of transubstantiation. According to this doctrine, through the consecration of the bread and wine the entire substance of the bread is changed into the substance of Christ's body, and the entire substance of the wine is changed into the substance of Christ's blood (DS 1642). By virtue of the words of consecration the body of Christ supposedly exists under the form (*species*) of the bread, and the blood of Christ exists under the form of the wine, while on the basis of the "concomitance" (*concomitantia*) that binds all parts of Christ together, the body is present under the form of the wine, the blood is present under the form of the bread, and the soul is present under the form of the wine and bread (DS 1640). The decisive point, which grounds the Eucharist's primacy in relation to the other sacraments, is that, on the basis of the consecration at each Eucharist and on the basis of the transubstantiation wrought by that consecration, saving power inheres in the sacrament even before its use. The result of transubstantiation is the substantial presence of Christ's body and blood under the forms of bread and wine. This presence is completely independent of communion as the use of the sacrament, and consequently exists *extra usum* (DS 1654).

The Reformed side rejects the doctrine of transubstantiation precisely because it does not tie the presence of Christ's body and blood to the use— that is, to the eating and drinking—but asserts that presence independently of the sacramental use. If the sacraments are means of grace, and thus instruments with whose help God communicates grace, it is impossible to accept a presence of the saving power in the sacrament independently of the sacrament's use. Such an acceptance would disregard the instrumental character of the sacrament of the meal. Christ promises us his presence in the meal, not outside of it. For this reason the Westminster Confession can rightly declare: "That doctrine which maintains a change of the substance of bread and wine, into the substance of Christ's body and blood (commonly called transubstantiation) by consecration of a priest, or by any other way, is repugnant, not to Scripture alone, but even to common-sense and reason; overthroweth the nature of the sacrament; and hath been and is the cause of manifold superstitions, yea, of gross idolatries" (S 666, cf. 505–6, 542). The reproach of idolatry refers to the adoration of the consecrated host: that is, Christ under the form of the bread (DS 1643, 1656–57). For the Heidelberg Catechism the Mass is an "accursed idolatry" because it teaches "that Christ is bodily under the form of bread and wine, and is therefore to be worshiped in them" (S 335–36). The adoration, the necessity of which can be derived from the doctrine of transubstantiation, negates the purely instrumental character of the sacrament of the meal. If the adoration is an implication of the doctrine of transubstantiation, then the latter must be rejected just as the former is (cf. M 163, 9ff., 22ff.). The Scottish Confession accordingly declares: "To adore or venerate the sacrament, to carry it through streets and towns in procession, or to reserve it in a special case, is not the proper use of Christ's sacrament but an abuse of it. Christ Jesus said, 'Take ye, eat ye,' and 'Do this in remembrance of Me.' By these words and commands He sanctified bread and wine to be the sacrament of His holy body and blood, so that the one should be eaten and that all should drink of the other, and not that they should be reserved for worship or honoured as God" (C 181).

CHRIST'S PRESENCE IN THE SUPPER

The confessional writings do not stop with the rejection of the Roman dogma of transubstantiation. Zwingli's Account of Faith objects to every type of substantial or real presence of Christ's body in the Supper. The Account of Faith rejects the opinion of the Papists and of certain theologians who long for the fleshpots of Egypt: namely, that Christ's natural body is really and essentially (*per essentiam et realiter*) present (*adsit*) in the sacrament (M 87, 48ff.). According to Zwingli, Christ's body is present only in faith's contemplation (*fidei contemplatione*). But even where in the Calvinist tradition one definitely speaks of being fed in the Supper with Christ's body and blood, and thus presupposes some sort of presence of the body, a *local* presence under the elements is rejected. The Zurich Consensus holds the thesis that Christ's body is present under the bread or is connected to the bread to be just as absurd as the doctrine of transubstantiation (M 163, 13–14). In the words of the Synodical Declaration of Berne, "the corporeal body is not in the bread, nor is the corporeal blood in the wine, as the old error pretended" (M 46, 9–10). It is not the case "that the body and blood of the Lord is naturally united with the bread and wine, or that they are spatially enclosed within them, or that a bodily, fleshly presence is posited here" (C 108, trans. altered; S 225). The Bremen Consensus rejects just as sharply as it rejects the Roman doctrine of transubstantiation the notion "that Christ's body and blood are included under the bread and wine, and must be essentially and bodily in and at the place where the bread and wine are" (M 773, 4–8). It is thus impossible to speak of a "flesh-bread" or "blood-wine," as one might do on the basis of such a union of the bread and wine with Christ's body and blood in the sacrament (M 774, 35ff.).

The question of why an essential and real presence of Christ's body in the sense of a local presence of Christ's natural body in the Supper is not possible can be answered by turning back to Christology. Whatever the departure from Zwingli in the docrine of the sacraments, one remains faithful to him in what is here the decisive point of Christology. Christ is indeed ubiquitous according to his divine nature. But ubiquity cannot be a predicate of his human nature. The property of bodiliness and corporeality is constitutive of the human nature. But this property implies extension and dimensionality. The statement that a body is extended is not a synthetic statement, but an analytical one, whose negation is necessarily false (Z 49–50). As extended, a body can only be located at one particular place at a particular time, not at several places. If Christ is not only truly human, but also true God, this can only mean that he is now located at a particular place. After the ascension this place is a heavenly place, not an earthly one (Z 51).

The Basle Confession says that "consequently we do not adore Christ in these signs of bread and wine which we commonly call sacraments of the body and blood of Christ, but in heaven at the right hand of God the Father" (C 94; cf. M 154, 15ff.). The Zurich Confession also concludes that a local presence of Christ as a human being under the elements of the Supper is excluded (M 162, 36ff.). As a finite body, Christ's body is located only in heaven, as at one place (M 163, 15ff.). To be sure, Christ as a person, and thus the God-human, is present everywhere. But this does not mean that Christ as a human being—that is, according to his human nature—is present everywhere (M 300, 12ff.) The Anglican Articles of 1552 emphasize that having the body of a human being be at many places simultaneously is a contradiction of human nature. Consequently Christ's body must be located at only one place at any particular time. Since after the ascension that place is heaven, a real and bodily presence of Christ in the Supper does not enter into consideration (M 516, 8ff.).

The rejection of the thesis of Christ's local presence in, with, and under the bread and wine entails a particular understanding of the Supper's words of institutition. Here, too, Zwingli's interpretation carried the day. According to the Account of Faith, the statement "This is my body" cannot be understood naturally (*naturaliter*), but only figuratively (*significative*) (M 87, 46ff.). The same rule applies to it as to the statement "This is the Passover" (Ex. 12:11). The latter must also be interpreted figuratively. The lamb that is consumed every year together with the feast is not itself the passing over, but only a sign of God's sparing the people and of God having once passed over. The statement "This is my body" can only mean "This is the sacrament of my body." The Zurich Consensus retains this Zwinglian view when it declares that one must not interpret the words of institution in accord with their precise literal sense (*praecise literalem sensum*). Instead they are to be taken figuratively (*figurate*). Bread and wine are called "Christ's body" and "blood" because they signify Christ's body and blood. On the basis of the rhetorical figure of metonomy, the concept of the signified object is applied and transferred to the objects that signify it (M 162, 42ff.). What is employed here is a rhetorical trope (M 423, 40ff.).

The Westminster Confession declares: "The outward elements in this sacrament, duly set apart to the uses ordained by Christ, have such relation to him crucified, as that truly, yet sacramentally only, they are sometimes called by the name of the things they represent, to wit, the body and blood of Christ; albeit, in substance and nature, they still remain truly, and only, bread and wine, as they were before" (S 665–66). According to the Heidelberg Catechism the "sacred bread" in the Supper is not itself the body of Christ, but is only called the "body of Christ" "agreeable to the nature and usage of sacraments" (S 334). In this context one can certainly also speak of a transmutation (*transmutatio*). This is not a bodily change of the elements of bread and wine into Christ's body and blood: that is, a transubstantiation in the sense of a change of material and form, which leaves only the accidents, under which Christ's body and blood are present. Instead the substance of the bread and wine are preserved. What changes are the use and purpose, the "use, function and condition" (*usus, officium et conditio*) of the bread and wine (M 302, N 681).

But if one rejects a local presence of Christ in, with, and under bread and wine, how can one still speak at all of Christ's substantial and real presence? For unlike the Zwinglian confessions,the Calvinist confessions assert that Christ's body is really (*realiter*) present to the person enjoying the sacrament. This presupposes that there is a real and substantial presence of the body of Christ that is not *eo ipso* a local presence. Since one departs from Zwingli in the question of the real and substantial presence in order to elaborate the character of the Supper as a real gift, an agreement is possible with the Lutherans on this point. The Sendomir Consensus concludes that in the Supper Christ's body and blood is distributed to those who are eating, and that one can thus speak of "Christ's substantial presence" (*substantialis praesentia Christi*) (N 554). The Consensus appeals to the Saxon Confession's statement on the Supper, which says that in the use (*usus*) of the sacrament Christ is truly and substantially (*vere et substantialiter*) present, and that Christ's body and blood are given to those enjoying the sacrament (N 556).

It is primarily the French Confession that explicitly retains the concept of substance and defends it over against the Ramistic critique of this Aristotelian category. According to this Confession, in the Supper we are nourished with the substance of Christ's body and blood (*la substance de son corps et de son sang*) (S 380). The National Synod of La Rochelle reconfirmed this statement in 1571 and declared that it did not mean any coarse, fleshly mixture, connection, change, or transformation. Nor does the Synod permit one to say that some third thing arises out of the connection of Christ's substance or person with our person, although this connection is indeed supposed to be a union with Christ, the intensity of which surpasses that of all other natural or artificial connections. In the Supper we not only gain a share in Christ's merit and gifts, but also participate in Christ's body given for us and Christ's blood shed for us. The union with Christ is a union with Christ as the mediator (M 230–31). For this reason the Scottish Confession declares "that the faithful, in the right use of the Lord's Table, do so eat the body and drink the blood of the Lord Jesus that He remains in them and they in Him; they are so made flesh of His flesh and bone of His bone that as the eternal Godhood has given to the flesh of Christ Jesus, which by nature was corruptible and mortal, life and immortality, so the eating and drinking of the flesh and blood of Christ Jesus does the like for us" (C 180).

On the basis of such statements is it possible to agree with the Lutheran side at the Leipzig Colloquy that "not only power, benefit and effect, but also the essence and substance of the body and blood of Jesus Christ himself are enjoyed in the use of the Holy Supper as it occurs right here on earth" (N 663)? Only because we have a share in the substance of Christ's body do we also participate in the fruits of his sacrfice. Insofar as Christ is mediator not only as God, but as God and as human being, in the Supper we must participate in him both as God and as human being. This means, though, that we must also be fed with the substance of his body, which belongs constitutively to his human nature (N 682).

If Christ's body is not bodily and locally present either under the form of bread or in, with, and under the bread, then the question is: How can we still talk about a real and substantial presence of Christ's body? The Geneva Catechism answers this question by referring to the role of the Holy Spirit in the Supper. "The incomprehensible power of His Spirit . . . conjoins things that are separated spatially" (T 62, trans. altered). Since Christ's body is not in the bread in the sense of being located in it (*localiter*), "we must lift up our hearts on high to heaven, where Jesus Christ is in the glory of His Father, from whence we expect Him in our redemption, and do not seek Him in these corruptible elements" (ibid.). The charge to "lift up our hearts" (*sursum corda*) is not to be understood as an exhortation to elevate ourselves, by our own strength, to Christ's body not present in the Supper. Instead it is an expression of the fact that we are to expect the gift of Christ's body not from the bread but from the Holy Spirit descending upon us. It is the Spirit who, in the Supper, gives up Christ's body and blood with bread and wine. Christ nourishes us with the substance of body and blood "by the secret and incomprehensible power of his Spirit" (S 380).

In the words of the Scottish Confession, union with Christ's body in the Supper "is wrought by means of the Holy Ghost, who by true faith carries us above all things that are visible, carnal, and earthly, and makes us feed upon the body and blood of Christ Jesus, once broken and shed for us" (C 179). The Supper involves a table fellowship in which, through the Holy Spirit, Christ feeds us with his body and blood. We are gathered around a spiritual table "at which Christ communicates himself with all his benefits to us, and gives us there to enjoy both himself and the merits of his sufferings and death, nourishing, strengthening, and comforting our poor comfortless souls, by the eating of his flesh" (S 430). For this reason, although according to his human nature Christ dwells in heaven, this in no way obviates his real and substantial presence in the Supper. Even after his ascension into heaven, Christ is not distant from his community. "The sun, which is absent from us in the heavens, is notwithstanding effectually present among us. How much more is the Sun of Righteousness, Christ, although in his body he is absent from us in heaven, present with us, not corporally, but spiritually" (C 287).

However, this spiritual presence emphasized by the Second Helvetic Confession must not be falsely spiritualized and understood merely as the presence either of Christ's divine nature or—as the image of the sun and its rays could suggest—of the power of his body. Instead the Holy Spirit is that instrument which Christ uses in order to give his body and his blood in the Supper to the partakers of the meal. In this way that union with Christ arises concerning which the Heidelberg Catechism says that we are "so united more and more to his [i.e., Christ's] sacred body by the Holy Ghost, who dwells both in Christ and in us, that although he is in heaven, and we on the earth, we are nevertheless flesh of his flesh and bone of his bones, and live and are governed forever by one Spirit, as members of the same body are by one soul" (S 333). We thus become "partakers of his true body and blood, through the working of the Holy Ghost" (S 335).

EATING (*MANDUCATIO*) AND FAITH

It is through the Holy Spirit that Christ feeds us with his body and blood: that is, with himself as our mediator, and therefore as God and as human being. But one must still ask what the relation is between the eating of Christ's body mediated by the Spirit and the eating of the bread. The former is a spiritual eating, while the latter is an oral eating. But given the presupposition that the Supper is a means of grace, the spiritual eating occurs by means of or through the corporeal eating. The two are not separated from each other, nor do they run parallel as two simultaneous processes. Instead they are instrumentally bound together on the basis of the sacramental union. This sacramental union must not be understood, though, as if the body of Christ were eaten *corporeally* with the bread and like the bread. It is not just the Second Helvetic Confession that rejects as "Capernaitic" a corporeal—that is, oral—eating of Christ's body in the sense that "food is taken into the mouth, is chewed with the teeth, and swallowed into the stomach. In times past the Capernaites thought that the flesh of the Lord should be eaten in this way, but they are refuted by him in John, ch. 6. For as the flesh of Christ cannot be eaten corporeally without infamy and savagery, so it is not food for the stomach" (C 284–85). For this reason the Confession decisively rejects the confession of faith to which the Roman side compelled Berengarius of Tours: namely, "that the body of Christ is to be eaten corporeally or essentially with a bodily mouth" (C 285; cf. DS 690), indeed, is to be bitten into pieces by the teeth (Z 49). It is this corporeal eating of Christ's body—that is, the *manducatio oralis*—which the Zurich Consensus rejects when it declares that one must not conceive the eating of Christ's flesh (*manducatio carnis Christi*) as a mixing up (*commixtio*) or pouring out (*transfusio*) of substance (M 163, 3ff.).

The eating (*manducatio*) of Christ's body is never an oral eating (*manducatio oralis*), which is identified with Capernaitic eating, but a spiritual eating (*manducatio spiritualis*). This spiritual eating must not be understood as if the food itself—namely, the body of Christ—were transformed into spirit. According to the Second Helvetic Confession, "the body and blood of the Lord, while remaining in their own essence and property, are spiritually communicated to us, so that we are nourished . . . in a spiritual way by the Holy Spirit, who applies and bestows upon these things which have been prepared for us by the sacrifice of the Lord's body and blood for us" (C 285, trans. altered). The Holy Spirit preserves our life through Christ's body and blood, which are given to us for food. This is by no means "illusory food," but in fact the spiritual food of Christ's body and blood, received in a real and substantial way. Since this food alone preserves our life, the spiritual eating of Christ's body is necessary for salvation. Without the spiritual eating we are lost and abandoned to eternal death. "This eating of the flesh and drinking of the blood of the Lord is so necessary for salvation that without it no man can be saved" (C 286). Of course, this eating and drinking also occurs outside of the Supper: namely, "as often and wherever a man believes in Christ" (ibid.). Spiritual eating is identical to faith.

This could give rise to the impression that the Supper is superfluous, since spiritual eating also occurs outside of the sacrament of the meal. Appealing to John 6, can one join the Zurich Confession with its Zwinglian influence and say "that whoever has truly eaten Christ's flesh and truly drunk his blood believes in Christ as true God and true human being, crucified for us? For believing is eating and eating is believing" (M 156, 45–48). In this case the ready objection is that the guest at the Supper receives nothing more at all in the Supper itself, since she already brings faith with her (M 157, 5ff.). If spiritual eating is identical to faith, and Christ's body is only eaten spiritually in the Supper, then we indeed seem to receive nothing more than bread and wine in the meal itself. The possibility seems excluded of receiving a spiritual gift that would go beyond the spiritual food that has already been received. Participation in the Supper could still be understood as the external manifestation of a faith that was already present. The Supper would be a confessional sign in Zwingli's sense. The confessional writings do not generally dispute that it is *also* this. As the Geneva Catechism puts it, Baptism and the Supper "are also signs and marks of our profession. That is to say, by them we declare that we are of the people of God, and make confession of our Christianity" (T 63). But what is essential about the Supper is not our action, but the fact that in the Supper we receive something from God's hand: namely, Christ's body and blood. This gift-character of the sacrament of the meal is manifestly endangered when spiritual eating is identified with faith in the sense outlined above.

It is precisely the sacrament's character as a gift that confessions influenced by Calvin emphasize over against the Zwinglian confessions. The Bremen Consensus explicitly rejects the thesis that the "spiritual enjoyment of Christ's flesh and blood is nothing other than faith that Christ suffered for us and shed his blood for us, and that we do not have communion with Christ's flesh and blood themselves, nor are truly drawn into or incorporated into the whole Christ" (M 774, 26–30). Insofar as it is the Holy Spirit who nourishes us with Christ's body and blood, it is certainly impossible to predicate the spiritual eating of unbelievers and the godless. This always refers to unbelieving and godless *Christians,* since only baptized Christians are admitted to the meal. Faith forms a necessary condition not only for the *salvific* reception of Christ's body, but for *any* reception of Christ's body. Insofar as the eating of Christ's body signifies a union with Christ, which cannot be conceived except as salvific, an eating of the impious (*manducatio impiorum*) is impossible. If Christ's body were eaten by unbelievers, then it would have to be "a strict internal judge and tormentor" (M 775, 11–12). Therefore the unfaithful and the godless do not receive the body of Christ. In the Supper Christ certainly gives and offers his body as food. But according to the French Confession only those "who bring a pure faith, like a vessel, to the sacred table of Christ, receive truly that of which it is a sign" (S 381). It is only "with and through faith that we grasp and accept" the body of Christ as spiritual food offered to us by the Holy Spirit, "just as Christ's merit and power are known and accepted only through faith" (M 773, 27–29). Faith is, as it were, the mouth with which Christ's crucified body is received. According to the Sigismund Confession, the Supper does not benefit unbelievers. Indeed, they do not even receive Christ's body, because Christ, "where he speaks of the blessed use of this Supper in John 6:54, clearly says: 'Whoever eats my flesh and drinks my blood has eternal life,' and earlier in v. 47: 'Truly, truly I say to you, whoever believes in me has eternal life,' makes it clearly understood that the salvific enjoyment of his holy flesh and blood requires faith" (M 839, 37–42).

One must not think of the sacramental union in such a way that everyone who takes the bread and wine thereby also takes Christ's body and blood. Since the union with Christ that is carried out in the eating of Christ's body and the drinking of Christ's blood can only be conceived as salvific, the Holy Spirit does indeed give us Christ's body and blood by means of bread and wine. But Christ's body and blood are received and enjoyed with the bread and wine if and only if faith is present on the side of the recipient. In the words of the Second Helvetic Confession, whoever "comes to this sacred Table of the Lord without faith, communicates only in the sacrament and does not receive the substance of the sacrament whence comes life and salvation; and such men unworthily eat of the Lord's Table. Whoever eats the bread or drinks the cup of the Lord in an unworthy manner will be guilty of the body and blood of the Lord, and eats and drinks judgment upon himself" (C 286–87). Judas indeed participated in the sacramental meal and took bread and wine, but he did not eat of Christ's body or drink of Christ's blood. Speaking of Judas and Simon the Magician, the Belgic Confession says that "both, indeed, received the Sacrament, but not Christ, who was signified by it, of whom believers only are made partakers" (S 431). Faith is the medium and instrument with which Christ's body is received and consumed (S 506). As the Irish Articles put it, the body of Christ "is really and substantially presented unto all those who have grace to receive the Son of God, even to all those that believe in his name. And unto such as in this manner do worthily and with faith repair unto the Lord's table, the body and blood of Christ is not only signified and offered, but also truly exhibited and communicated" (S 542–43, cf. 666). If worthiness is put forward as a necessary condition for receiving Christ's body and blood, and if participants in the Supper are accordingly exhorted to examine themselves (1 Cor. 11:28), the Geneva Catechism understands this to mean that the participant in the Supper must examine whether "he has a true faith and repentance, if he loves his neighbour in true charity, and is not tainted by hatred or rancour or discord" (T 63). Yet there is no requirement here of a perfection "from which nothing is wanting" (ibid.), since the Supper is instituted precisely to support us in our weakness. According to the Heidelberg Catechism, the ones who are worthy in the sense of possessing true faith and true repentance are those who "are displeased with themselves for their sins, yet trust that these are forgiven them, and that their remaining infirmity is covered by the passion and death of Christ" (S 336). What is decisive is trust in the promise of the forgiveness of sins that is given in the Supper. For this reason the Sigismund Confession says, as "Herr Luther testifies in the Children's Catechism, that the ones who are right worthy and well prepared are those who believe in the words 'given for you, shed for you,' since the word 'for you' simply requires believing hearts" (M 839, 42–45; cf. 833, 8ff.). Those who take part in the meal with this trust in the promise—that is, with the admission of their own unworthiness—can be certain that they receive Christ's body and blood really (*realiter*) and substantially (*substantialiter*). In this way "faith is kindled and grows more and more, and is refreshed by spiritual food. For while we live, faith is continually increased" (C 286). Participation in the Supper admittedly presupposes faith as a necessary condition for receiving the body of Christ. The eating of Christ's body in the Supper, though, is not just this faith that is brought to the meal, but instead occurs for the support and strengthening of that faith.

MINISTRY:
THE OFFICE AND THE OFFICES

UNIVERSAL PRIESTHOOD AND PARTICULAR OFFICE

In the Reformed view there is no special priesthood besides the priesthood of all who are baptized and believe. The title "priest" cannot serve to designate a particular office within the communion of believers, which is the universal priesthood. Thus the Second Helvetic Confession observes: "To be sure, Christ's apostles call all who believe in Christ 'priests,' but not on account of an office, but because, all the faithful having been made kings and priests, we are able to offer up spiritual sacrifices to God through

Christ" (C 271). The priesthood that is called *universal* because *all* believers participate in it is grounded in the relation of the individual believer to Christ the High Priest. Christ is the fulfillment and the annulment of the Old Testament priesthood, "which had an external anointing, holy garments, and very many ceremonies." "He himself remains the only priest forever" (C 272). Yet every believer is a Christian only insofar as she is a member of Christ and thus participates in his anointing to the threefold office of prophet, priest, and king. All Christians participate in Christ's priestly office, and this participation finds its expression in the fact that— in the formulation of the Heidelberg Catechism—they "present [themselves] a living sacrifice" (S 318). Priesthood and sacrifice reciprocally condition each other. On the basis of the universal priesthood, all Christians are enabled to offer themselves as a sacrifice of *thanksgiving*. By contrast, the offering of a sacrifice of *propitiation* is excluded by the sufficiency of Christ's one-time sacrifice of propitiation on the cross. In the church there can be no special priestly office whose prerogative it was to offer a sacrifice of propitiation. For it to be otherwise would dispute the sufficiency of Christ's sacrifice. "Lest we derogate anything from him, we do not impart the name of priest to any minister. For the Lord himself did not appoint any priests in the Church of the New Testament who, having received authority from the suffragan, may daily offer up the sacrifice, that is, the very flesh and blood of the Lord, for the living and the dead" (C 272). Just as pointing to the sufficiency of Christ's sacrifice of propitiation disputes a particular priesthood of the Mass, pointing to that same sufficiency grounds the universal priesthood of believers (cf. C 181).

The thesis of the universal priesthood is directed against the special priesthood asserted by the Roman church and required by the understanding of the Lord's Supper as an actual sacrifice of propitiation. The Tridentine decree on the sacrament of ordination declares: "In conformity with God's decree, sacrifice and priesthood are so related that both exist in every law. Therefore, in the New Testament, since the Catholic Church has received the holy and visible sacrifice of the Eucharist according to the institution of the Lord, it is likewise necessary to acknowledge that there is in the Church a new, visible, and external priesthood" (DS 1764, CT 840). The institution of this priesthood coincides with the institution of the sacrifice of the Mass. At his last meal Christ offered his body and blood to the Father under the forms of bread and wine, and "gave his body and blood under the same species to the apostles to receive, making them priests of the New Testament at that time. . . . He ordered the apostles and their successors in the priesthood to offer this sacrifice" (DS 1740, CT 747; cf. DS 1752). The episcopal administration of the sacrament of ordination confers the authority to transform Christ's body and blood and to offer them to God as an actual sacrifice of propitiation. This position disputes the claim "that all Christians without exception are priests of the New Testament or are endowed with equal spiritual power" (DS 1767, CT 843). By contrast, the thesis of the universal priesthood directly entails the annulment of the difference in status between clergy and laity, and applies the term *clergy* to the whole church (M 433, 39ff.).

However, dispensing with a special priestly office does not in any way amount to dispensing with the particular office of ministry in the church or with particular offices of ministry. Priesthood and the office of ministry differ from each other. We read in the Second Helvetic Confession that "the priesthood . . . is common to all Christians; not so is the ministry. Nor have we abolished the ministry of the Church because we have repudiated the papal priesthood from the Church of Christ" (C 271–72). Indeed Zwingli declares that the office of prophecy or preaching (*munus prophetiae sive praedicationis*) is *necessary* (M 92, 1–2). But he disputes that this necessary office of ministry is the office of the priest of the Mass, who is equipped with an indelible character (*character indelebilis*), conferred by ordination (C 43; cf. DS 1767). Instead "the Scriptures do not recognize any priests except those who proclaim God's Word" (C 43). The particular office of ministry in the church is defined by the function of proclaiming the word. It is ministry to God's word, office of ministry (*ministerium*), just as a bearer of that office is a minister of God's word (*minister verbi Dei*) (cf. 116, 5ff.). The ministers of the word are responsible for leading the community by the word of God, so that, *insofar as they rightly carry out their ministry*, they are to be regarded as God's messengers and ambassadors (*messagiers et ambassadeurs de Dieu*), to whom one must listen as to God's self (M 116, 16–17).

Their office, though, is the proclamation of the word not only in interpreting scripture but also in administering Baptism and the Supper (N 327). This is the "office of publicly preaching or administering the sacraments in the church" (*munus publice praedicandi, aut administrandi Sacramenta in Ecclesia*) (S 501), the office of proclaiming the word and administering the sacraments (cf. C 116). Proclamation of the word means here the *public* proclamation of the word, just as the particular office of ministry in the church is in any case a *public* office of ministry (*publicum docendi munus*) that stands in relation to the ecclesiastical community (M 152, 23; 433, 36; 636, 1ff.). Right preaching and administration of the sacrament are tied to this public office. Its status as the fundamental particular office of ministry in the church results from the fact that right preaching and administration of the sacraments are the necessary and sufficient conditions as well as the marks of the true church. The French Confession accordingly says that "the Church can not exist without pastors for instruction." At the same time the Confession rejects all "visionaries who would like . . . to destroy the ministry and preaching of the Word and sacraments" (S 374; cf.

180–81, 272; M 767, 15ff.). With regard to this ministry of proclamation of the word and administration of the sacraments (S 281), the Second Helvetic Confession declares that "God has always used ministers for the gathering or establishing of a Church for himself, and for the governing and preservation of the same; and still he does, and always will, use them so long as the Church remains on earth. Therefore, the first beginning, institution, and office of ministers is a most ancient arrangement of God himself, and not a new one of men" (C 268). God wills to deal with human beings through the ministry of human beings, and for this reason instituted the particular office of preaching and of administration of the sacraments.

The non-Calvinist confessions recognize only the one particular ecclesiastical office of ministry, existing by divine arrangement and law (*iure divino*), and responsible for the right proclamation of the word and administration of the sacraments. For example, although the Second Helvetic Confession is familiar with the New Testament diversity of ministerial offices, it speaks exclusively of this office, which however unites within itself the remaining functions of various New Testament ministerial offices and thus can assume their names. "Therefore, the ministers of the churches may now be called bishops, elders, pastors, and teachers" (C 270). The functions of the one particular ministerial office are accordingly diverse (cf. C 275). Nor do those confessions which, under Calvin's influence, divide the various functions into various offices differently than in Zurich, doubt that the office of proclaiming the word and administering the sacraments is the decisive ministerial office. After all, right proclamation of the word and administration of the sacraments are the necessary and sufficient conditions as well as the marks of the true church.

Yet besides these two constitutive functions and tasks, the church of course recognizes many others, which on the basis of divine arrangement it should likewise carry out. A number of confessions assign several of these tasks to particular ministerial offices besides the pastoral office, which is alone responsible for proclamation of the word and administration of the sacraments. The same Calvin who in the Geneva Catechism speaks only of the office of preaching and administration of the sacraments introduces in the Ecclesiastical Ordinances of Geneva four offices (*offices*) "that our Lord established for the administration of his church: namely, Pastors (*Pasteurs*), then Teachers (*Docteurs*) (of Holy Scripture), then Elders (*Anciens*), and fourthly Deacons (*Diacres*)" (Ni 43, 18–20; cf. Ni 292, 40–41). The preservation of these four offices is the condition not only for the church persisting at all but also for it remaining well ordered (*bien ordonnée*) (Ni 43, 21). However, the fact that the French Confession, also drafted by Calvin, recognizes only three orders shows that here one is to think not of the offices as such, but of the functions assigned to them. "As to the true church, we believe that it should be governed according to the order established by our

Lord Jesus Christ. That there should be pastors (*pasteurs*), overseers (*surveillants*), and deacons (*diacres*)" (S 376). The Belgic Confession likewise speaks only of three ministerial offices: pastors (*Ministri seu Pastores*), who proclaim the word of God and administer the sacraments, elders (*Seniores*), and deacons (*Diaconi*) (M 244, 45–47).

Which functions are connected to the three ministerial offices correlated with the office of pastor? The answer is most detailed in Beza's Hungarian Confession and in the Ecclesiastical Ordinances of Geneva. The Hungarian Confession first speaks of the offices of apostles, evangelists, and prophets—offices that were necessary for founding church communities and that are limited to the early church. Along with them are the perpetual offices (*Munera perpetua*) of pastors, teachers, elders (*Presbyteri*), and deacons (M 434, 9). In this arrangement the teachers have the task of scriptural explanation and instruction. In the words of the Ecclesiastical Ordinances of Geneva, teachers are "to instruct the faithful in sound doctrine, so that the purity of the gospel not be corrupted either by ignorance or by bad opinions" (Ni 48, 27–29). Yet the office of teacher is not limited to this. Instead it includes "the aids and instruments for conserving seed for the future, and insuring that the church not be desolated for lack of pastors and ministers" (Ni 48, 30–32). Although the office of teacher applies primarily to theology as the exposition of scripture, it also serves to procure the necessary presuppositions for the study of theology: that is, to inculcate those areas of study that are auxiliary to theology.

As the difference between pastors and teachers, the Hungarian Confession names the fact that the latter are entrusted with research and teaching, exegesis, and catachesis—as an example the Confession mentions Origen as the leader of the Alexandrian school of catechists—while pastors are responsible for applying scripture for use in the church (M 434, 20ff.). However, the French Confession with its reduction of the ministerial offices to those of pastor, elder, and deacon is already proof that the tasks of the ecclesiastical teaching office, primarily the instruction of the young, need not be connected to a particular office in every community, but in a given case can be taken over by the pastor. In this case the pastor is identical with the teacher; the two offices are fused.

The offices of elder and deacon are placed alongside the office of pastor—or the offices of pastor and teacher—as two further perpetual offices. The office of deacon is sufficiently distinguished from the office of pastor by its function (M 437, 40ff.). The office of pastor is that of public proclamation of the word and administration of the sacraments, while the office of deacon is that of support for the poor and sick (S 376–77, 421–22). In the ancient church there were always two types of deacons: "The one group was assigned to receive, dispense and conserve the goods of the poor, both daily alms and possessions, taxes and pensions. The other group was assigned to attend and care for the sick and to feed the poor" (Ni 49, 36–40). According to the Ecclesiastical Ordinances of Geneva, diaconal work includes both the administration of the account for the poor by an account administrator as well as care for the poor and the sick by a hospital director. In the view of the French Confession, the task of diaconal work is precisely not "to preach the word or to administer the sacraments, although they can assist in doing so" (Ni 77, 32–33).

OFFICE OF ELDERS AND CHURCH DISCIPLINE

When what is at stake is not merely the existence and being (*esse*) of the true church, but its being well-ordered and its well-being (*bene esse*), reference to the right preaching of the word and administration of the sacraments is not enough. Alongside this fundamental function, which is constitutive of the church, other functions, tasks, or ministries appear. Among these are not only the ministry or office of teacher and deacon, but also that of elder. Part of the well-being of the church is that it continually examines itself. According to the Ecclesiastical Ordinances of Geneva, this ecclesiastical self-examination and self-discipline (*disciplina ecclesiastica*) is to occur "without hate or partiality" (Ni 49, 25), in the form of "fraternal corrections" (*corrections fraternelles*) (Ni 43, 27; 49, 2) of those who make themselves guilty of "idolatries, blasphemies, dissolutions and other things contrary to God's honor and to the reformation of the gospel" (Ni 49, 20–21). Only to this extent is it the task of the elders "to attend to the life of each person and lovingly admonish those whom they see stumble and lead a disordered life" (Ni 48, 48–Ni 49, 1).

Of course, this task needs to be defined more precisely. The Hungarian Confession speaks of a spiritual *jurisdiction* (*spiritualis jurisdictio*) practiced by the elders. At the same time it sharply demarcates this jurisdiction as *spiritual* over against *secular, civil* jurisdiction (*civilis jurisdictio*) (M 439, 41ff.). The two must not be mixed together. Spiritual jurisdiction is independent of secular jurisdiction. According to the Westminster Confession, church government lies in the hands of "Church officers, distinct from the civil magistrate" (S 667). While Zwingli regards church discipline as a task of the secular authority, Calvin follows Oecolampadius and Bucer in arguing for a strict separation between ecclesiastical and civil jurisdiction. Calvin ultimately attained autonomy for the ecclesiastical jurisdiction, which was tied to the office of elders. This autonomy is the result of that hotly contested struggle with the Geneva Council which is reflected in the Ecclesiastical Ordinances of Geneva. In Geneva the board of elders was composed of members of the city council (Ni 49, 4ff.), so that there was a ready danger that spiritual and civil jurisdiction would be confused. For

this reason the Ecclesiastical Ordinances emphatically oppose the custom
"that one of the four mayors presides in the Consistory with his staff
(which has the appearance of civil jurisdiction [*iurisdiction civile*] rather
than of spiritual government [*regime spirituel*]) (Ni 63, 20–22). There must
be a sharp distinction between the magistrate's authority and power of the
sword (*le glaive et authorité du Magistrat*) and the church's office of oversight (*la superintendence*) (Ni 63, 24–25). Only the latter is to "direct all
Christians to obedience and to true service of God, and to stop and correct
scandals" (Ni 63, 25–56). Political officeholders of the state are not members of the consistory as holders of state offices, but exclusively in their
function as elders.

In carrying out their spiritual jurisdiction, the elders' concern is for the
order of the church, the *disciplina ecclesiastica*. However, where the constitutive marks of the true church are involved—right proclamation of the
word and administration of the sacraments—the danger is not only to the
church's order but to its existence. The definition of the true church as the
communion of saints in which the word is rightly (*recte*) proclaimed and
the sacraments properly (*rite*) administered already implies that there
must be an office whose primary concern is to be that the proclamation of
the word and the administration of the sacraments are done in accordance
with scripture and with the institution of the sacraments. This same office
has the task not only of seeing to it that this ministry, constitutive of the
church, is not carried out in a way contrary to scripture, but also of stop-
ping a pastor from exercising this ministry on the grounds of unworthiness—that is, of ethical disqualification—because the unworthiness of the
pastor also harms the reputation of this ministry that is foundational for
the church. This is the only way, in the opinion of the Ecclesiastical Ordinances of Geneva, "to preserve the ministry in reverence, and for the word
of God not to be dishonored or scorned through bad rumors concerning
the ministers" (Ni 46, 2–4).

There is, however, a fundamental difference between, on the one hand,
unscriptural proclamation of the word and administration of the sacraments, and, on the other hand, unworthy living. All the confessional writings are united in rejecting a Donatistic understanding of the office of
ministry, which would make the validity of the execution of the pastoral
office dependent on the worthiness—that is, the ethical qualifications—of
the officeholder. The Second Helvetic Confession appeals to Augustine in
rejecting the "error of the Donatists who esteem the doctrine and administration of the sacraments to be either effectual or not effectual, according
to the good or evil life of the ministers. For we know that the voice of Christ
is to be heard, though it be out of the mouths of evil ministers . . . [and] that
the sacraments are sanctified by the institution and the word of Christ, and
that they are effectual to the godly, although they be administered by

unworthy ministers" (C 276). In rightly proclaiming the word and in administering the sacraments in accordance with their institution, the pastor
acts not in his name, but in Christ's (*non suo sed Christi nomine*) (S 503). The
validity of the performance of the office depends not on the ethical quality
of the officeholder, but on the institution of that performance of the office
by Christ, by whose mandate the pastor acts (cf. S 538; M 436, 3ff.).

Nevertheless, it is the duty of the office to which ecclesiastical discipline
(*disciplina ecclesiastica*) is assigned to see to it that no unworthy persons
take on or practice the office of the public proclamation of the word and
administration of the sacraments. The Irish Articles state that "it apper-
taineth to the discipline of the Church that inquiry be made of evil ministers, and that they be accused by those that have knowledge of their
offenses, and finally, being found guilty, by just judgment be deposed" (S
538–39). This case, that of the *unworthy* holder of the office of ministry, is
fundamentally different from the case of the *heretical* officeholder. Ethical
disqualification does not touch the validity of the ministries instituted by
Christ. But practicing these ministries contrary to scripture and to their institution—that is, practicing them heretically—does affect their validity (M
436, 11ff.). In the words of the Second Helvetic Confession, heretical officeholders "are to be deposed, and like wolves driven away from the flock
of the Lord by the true shepherds. For, if they be false teachers (*pseudodoc-
tores*), they are not to be tolerated at all" (C 276, S 285).

Since the pastors are to carry out the ministry of the right proclamation
of the word and administration of the sacraments, and since this ministry
is the foundational one for the church, ecclesiastical discipline is to be directed primarily to the teaching and life of the pastors. But it is also directed
to the church community in general (cf. T 64–65, C 177, S 421–22). However,
the rule is to be observed "that everything is to be done for edification, de-
cently and honorably, without oppression and strife" (C 276). The visible
church is a mixed body insofar as not all who nominally belong to the
church are "saints, and living and true members of the Church" (C 267).
"Although while they simulate piety they are not of the Church, yet they
are considered to be in the Church, just as traitors in a state are numbered
among its citizens before they are discovered; and as the tares or darnel and
chaff are found among the wheat," so that even the true church is like "a
field, in which both wheat and tares are found" (ibid.). Precisely for this reason we are forbidden to reach a hasty judgment that would result in exclusion, "because there would be danger lest the wheat also be plucked up" (C
276): that is, there would be the danger of injury to the church itself.

It goes without saying that the visible church is not, cannot be, and must
not claim to be the communion of saints in the sense of there no longer being any who are unworthy among its members. The function and possibility of church discipline is limited from the outset by the fact that, as is

shown by the application to the church of the parable of the weed among the wheat, the church as the communion of saints is fundamentally a mixed body. The purpose of church discipline cannot be to free the church of hypocrites—after all, Judas himself was admitted to the Last Supper, because his wickedness was not yet known publicly. Likewise, one "cannot exclude [hypocrites] as unworthy, but must wait until God has revealed their iniquity" (T 64). The purpose of church discipline can only be to avoid the situation where "while the pious snore the wicked gain ground and do harm to the church" (C 267). The Westminster Confession declares: "Church censures are necessary for the reclaiming and gaining of offending brethren; for deterring of others from the like offenses; for purging out of that leaven which might infect the whole lump; for vindicating the honor of Christ, and the holy profession of the gospel; and for preventing the wrath of God, which might justly fall upon the Church, if they should suffer his covenant, and the seals thereof, to be profaned by notorious and obstinate offenders" (S 668).

The discipline necessary to maintain church order (*censurae ecclesiasticae* or *correctio ecclesiastica*) (S 668; M 443, 11)—the Hungarian Confession explicitly warns against using it in a Pharisaic and monkish manner (M 443, 6ff.)—has a tiered ordering of penalties (cf. Ni 60ff.). Beginning with personal admonition (*admonitio*) and proceeding to temporary suspension from the Supper (*suspensio*), the penalties reach their apex in exclusion from the church community (*excommunicatio*) (cf. S 668). For the Emden Church Order, church discipline configured in this way observes "the rule that Christ clearly prescribes in Matt. 18" (Ni 281, 28; cf. 78). Appealing to Matt. 18:15ff., the Savoy Declaration states: "The Censures so appointed by Christ are Admonition and Excommunication; and whereas some offenses are or may be known only to some, it is appointed by Christ that those to whom they are so known do first admonish the offender in private (in public offenses where any sin, before all), and in case of non-amendment upon private admonition, the offense being related to the Church, and the offender not manifesting his repentance, he is to be duly admonished in the Name of Christ by the whole Church . . . and if this Censure prevail not for his repentance, then he is to be cast out by Excommunication, with the consent of the Church" (S 727). The person thus excluded from the community of the faithful is to be treated as a "heathen and publican" (S 539, cf. 508).

However, the purpose of excommunication is exclusively that of repentance and amendment of life. This means that exclusion from the church community is never final, but always directed toward welcoming back the repentant. Thus we read in the First Confession of Basle that "the Christian Church excommunicates solely for the sake of the reclamation of offenders, and consequently it gladly receives them again after they have put away their scandalous life and have improved" (C 94, cf. 125, S 424).

Excommunication serves exclusively to keep the community gathered at the Supper pure of such members "who show themselves to be, by their confession and life, unbelieving and ungodly" (S 336). For this reason both the Heidelberg and the Emden Catechisms treat church discipline in the context of the Supper: specifically, as a part of the power of the keys. In part this power consists of the preaching of the gospel, which proclaims forgiveness of sins for the sake of Christ to believers and thus opens the reign of heaven to them, but which proclaims eternal damnation to unbelievers and hypocrites, and thus closes the reign of heaven to them. However, the office of the keys as the power to bind and to loose is executed not only by the preaching of the gospel, but also by the Christian discipline for repentance. This discipline prescribes the following treatment for members of the church who "show themselves unsound either in doctrine or life." If after repeated warnings they show no sign of improvement, they are reported to the church itself. Insofar as they do not pay heed to the church's warning, they are "excluded from the holy Sacraments and the Christian communion, and by God himself from the kingdom of Christ; and if they promise and show real amendment, they are again received as members of Christ and his Church" (S 338; cf. M 678, 23ff.).

The authority to practice excommunication is not the privilege of a specific group bearing a certain status within the church, but belongs to the entire church community. In his Sixty-Seven Articles Zwingli opposes placing the power of jurisdiction (*potestas iurisdictionis*) in episcopal hands, declaring "that no single individual may impose a bann of excommunication upon anyone. Only the Church may do it, which is the fellowship of those among whom the one worthy of excommunication dwells, together with the minister, who is their watchman" (C 40). Yet although Zwingli treats the authority to excommunicate as belonging to the entire church community, he confers the power of spiritual jurisdiction on the state authority: "The so-called ecclesiastical estate pretends that the administration of justice rightfully belongs to it. But all this pertains to temporal rulers if they want to be Christians" (ibid.).

By contrast, in the Calvinist constitution of the church, it is precisely the sense of the office of elder strictly to separate spiritual jurisdiction as a part of church discipline from the state's jurisdiction. Like the Heidelberg Catechism, the Bremen Consensus distinguishes between two parts of the power of the keys. Following Melanchthon's reappropriation of the Roman terminology, the Consensus calls these two parts the "power of order" (*potestas ordinis*) and the "power of jurisdiction" (*potestas iurisdictionis*). Both powers belong to the office of preaching, but the power of order consists of the power to bind and to loose by proclaiming the gospel, while the power of jurisdiction consists of the power to bind and to loose by carrying out Christian discipline aimed at repentance. The latter power is the "spiritual coercion of judgment" (M 794, 23), the right of banning. Here the Bremen Consensus follows church tradition in differentiating two degrees of bans. The minor ban (*excommunicatio minor*) is the *separatio vel suspensio ab usu Sacramentorum*, a "separation from the use of the holy sacraments and from other communion in Christian offices" (M 794, 28–32). The great ban (*excommunicatio maior* or *anathema*) consists of the following: "After due process had been observed, one publicly and by name denounced before the entire church community a public, stubborn, unrepentant sinner or heretic as a scandalous, condemned human being, commended them to the devil, excluded them from the communion of the Christian church, and totally cut them off" (M 794, 42–47). Even this latter case is not an *irrevocable* exclusion from the church.

In configuring church discipline as they do, Calvin and his followers are concerned with the autonomy of ecclesiastical jurisdiction over against civil jurisdiction. It is precisely in this concern that their approaches differ from that of Zwingli, who confers ecclesiastical and moral discipline on the secular authority. Yet this concern on the part of Calvin and his followers does not mean that they separated state and church in the sense that an ecclesiastical excommunication would not entail any civil penalties. Instead the Ecclesiastical Ordinances of Geneva say that one who has been excommunicated and remains unrepentant must "be sent before the Council . . . and be banished from the city for a year as incorrigible" (Ni 62, 9–11). In this case, because of the particular state church constitution, exclusion from the church community is tied to exclusion from the political, civil community (cf. M 795, 24ff.; 798, 21ff.).

THE FORMATION OF THE CHURCH COUNCIL

Spiritual jurisdiction lies in the hands not of an individual person but of the college of elders (*synedrion* or *presbyterion*) (M 444, 47ff.), to which the pastor belongs along with the lay elders. According to the Ecclesiastical Ordinances of Geneva, the pastor's office is "to make fraternal corrections with the elders or others commissioned for this purpose" (Ni 43, 26–27). While in Geneva the consistory comprises pastors and elders, according to the French and Belgic Confessions the church senate is composed of pastors, elders, and deacons. All the offices are related to each other and form a common organ. "The elders and the deacons are the Church Senate, at which the ministers of the word must preside" (Ni 77, 23–24; cf. S 421–22). The leadership of the community is thus constituted in collegial fashion. In the leadership body the different tasks and functions that are necessary for the well-being of the church are not assigned to a single office, but are divided among three or four different offices.

Those who hold the various offices all possess the same authority. None is superior to another in the sense of possessing a greater authority. The French Confession observes "that all true pastors, wherever they may be, have the same authority and equal power" (S 377, cf. 422). Appealing to Jerome, the Second Helvetic Confession says that bishops are placed above pastors "more from custom than from the truth of an arrangement by the Lord," so that the bishops' superiority is a matter of human law and does not rest on divine institution (C 275). "Certainly, in the beginning, the bishops or presbyters governed the Church in common; no man lifted up himself above another, none usurped greater power or authority over his fellow-bishops" (C 274). As a logical consequence the hierarchical Roman understanding of the office of ministry, which was given dogmatic status at the Council of Trent, is rejected (J 150; M 540, 21ff.). The Tridentine view declares anyone anathema who claims "that in the Catholic Church there is no divinely instituted hierarchy consisting of bishops, priests, and ministers," and "that bishops are not superior to priests, or . . . that the power they do have is common both to them and to priests" (DS 1776–77, CT 849–50). However, this rejection of this hierarchical view of the office of ministry applies not only to the office of pastor, but also to the offices of elder and deacon. "No church will obtain primacy or dominion over other churches; no preacher, over other preachers; no elder, over other elders; no deacon, over other deacons" (Ni 279, 1–2; cf. 297, 42–43).

The critique of a hierarchical ordering of the office of ministry is not tantamount, however, to a rejection of a particular order within the church leadership comprised of the officeholders. With explicit reference to Peter's status and function within the early church in Jerusalem, the Hungarian Confession emphasizes the necessity, conditioned by the order of the leadership body, of a "Presider, Elder, Rector, Director or Governor" (*Antistes, Senior, Rector, Director, aut Intendens*) (M 439, 11–12; cf. 438, 40ff.). Yet this position of presiding over the Church Senate, modeled after the example of Peter, does not exist as a divinely instituted "Petrine office," but as a human arrangement solely for the sake of order. It does not provide the basis for any spiritual authority. To be sure—says the Second Helvetic Confession—"for the sake of preserving order some one of the ministers called the assembly together, proposed matters to be laid before it, gathered the opinions of the others, in short, to the best of man's ability took precaution lest any confusion should arise. Thus did St. Peter, as we read in The Acts of the Apostles, who nevertheless was not on that account preferred to the others, nor endowed with greater authority than the rest" (C 274; cf. S 378; M 229, 24ff., 38ff.).

The acceptance of any of the offices of the church presupposes a calling (*vocatio*). To be sure, the confessions of the Reformation period also recognize an *extraordinary* calling as an exception. After all, according to the French Confession it was necessary at that time "for God to raise men in an extraordinary manner to restore the Church which was in ruin and desolation" (S 377; cf. M 435, 31ff.). The acceptance of the Reformation office of ministry by the Reformers was legitimate, even if they were called to it in an extraordinary manner. Yet aside from this kind of exceptional case, in which an extraordinary calling to an office occurs precisely in order to preserve the church, the condition that must be fulfilled in accepting an office is the *regular and orderly* calling of the officeholder. "We believe that no person should undertake to govern the Church upon his own authority," says the French Confession (S 377). Instead, anyone who accepts one of the leadership offices must be called in a regular and orderly manner (*rite vocatus*) (cf. S 374, 501; M 636, 14–15). Insofar as this applies to the office of the public proclamation of the word and administration of the sacraments, we have here the same condition as is put forward in the Augsburg Confession (BC 36). The Irish Articles declare: "It is not lawful for any man to take upon him the office of public preaching or ministering the Sacraments in the Church, unless he be first lawfully called and sent to execute the same" (S 539). However, it remains to be more precisely specified what the detailed shape is of this regular and orderly calling. According to the Ecclesiastical Ordinances of Geneva, "it is necessary to consider three things: namely, the examination—this is the principal matter; then, whose responsibility it is to install ministers; thirdly, what ceremony or manner of action is good to be preserved for inducting them into office" (Ni 43, 29–32).

The examination concerns both the doctrine and the life of the candidate. According to the Second Helvetic Confession, "not any one may be elected, but capable men distinguished by sufficient consecrated learning, pious eloquence, simple wisdom, lastly, by moderation and an honorable reputation, according to that apostolic rule which is compiled by the apostle in 1 Tim., ch. 3, and Titus, ch. 1" (C 271). Examination of doctrine and life is the presupposition of every regular call. According to the Irish Articles, the calling itself is done "by men who have public authority given them in the Church to call and send ministers into the Lord's vineyard" (S 539, cf. 501). Admittedly, the question of who possesses the power to call (*potestas vocandi*) can be answered in very different ways. The Ecclesiastical Ordinances of Geneva give the following description of the act of calling: first, the pastors "elect (*eslisent*) the person who is to be put (*mettre*) in office, having made the person known to our small Council. Then they introduce the person to the Council. If he is found worthy, he is received and accepted there, attesting him in order, finally, to present him to the people during preaching, so that he might be received by the common consent (*consentement commun*) of the company of the faithful" (Ni 43, 50–Ni 44, 4). The fact that the community's consent is of decisive significance is shown by the addition that prohibits the person elected by the pastors and confirmed by the Council as the state authority from being introduced in church without that consent. Otherwise "the people and the entire body of the church [would be] defrauded of their liberty" (Ni 44, 12–13). For this reason the name of the person elected should be made known "together with the notification that anyone who has something to say against that person should come and declare it before the day when the person elected is to be presented, so that, if he is not capable of the office, one may proceed to a new election" (Ni 44, 22–25). Here the regular and orderly call is carried out as an election after prior examination. The election is performed by the college of pastors and confirmed by the state, while the church community is permitted only the right of objection. The election of officeholders takes on an essentially different form where the church is not a state church, but a free one. In this case the power to call lies in the church itself in such a way that the election itself no longer needs to be confirmed by the state. The French Ecclesiastical Discipline provides for the following process: "The ministers [preachers] will be elected in the Consistory [Presbytery] by the elders and deacons, and will be presented to the people for whom they will be ordained. If there is opposition, it will be up to the Consistory to judge it" (Ni 76, 13–15). Unlike the process in Geneva, here no pastors take part in the election. Only the elders and deacons possess the right to elect. The church community again has solely the right to object. By contrast, the Belgic Confession recognizes an actual election by the community. Here the community elects not only pastors but also elders and deacons. The Confession declares "that the Ministers of God's Word, and the Elders and Deacons, ought to be chosen to their respective offices by a lawful election of the Church (*élection légitime de l'Église*)" (S 422; cf. Ni 280, 10–19). It is the individual church community which possesses the power to call: "Every [sc. particular] Church has power in Christ to choose and take into themselves meet and sufficient persons, into the Offices and functions of Pastors, Teachers, Elders, Deacons and Helpers" (M 540, 17–19). According to the Congregationalist Savoy Declaration, the local congregation has the freedom and right to fill the divinely instituted offices of pastor, teacher, elder, and deacon, and to do so "by the *common suffrage* of the Church itself" (S 725).

The regular process of calling is concluded with the introduction (*introduction*) or ordination (*ordinatio*) into office (cf. M 441, 30ff.; N 43, 32). Concerning the form of this introduction, the final form of the Ecclesiastical Ordinances of Geneva states that, "since the ceremonies of past times have been twisted into many superstitions, due to the infirmity of the time, it shall suffice that one of the ministers make a declaration and admonition of the office to which the person elected is being ordained, and then that prayers be made that the Lord give him the grace to carry out that office" (Ni 44, 36–41). In contrast to Calvin's draft, the laying on of hands (*impositio manum*) is eliminated here, while according to the Second Helvetic Confession, elected pastors "are to be ordained by the elders with public prayer and laying on of hands" (C 271). Finally, the Emden Synod leaves the laying on of hands up to the free discretion of each particular church community. "The ministers are examined by those by whom they are elected. If their doctrine and life are approved, they are confirmed with solemn prayers and the laying on of hands—apart, however, from any superstition or necessity" (Ni 280, 24–26). The laying on of hands thus is not part of the essence of the call (S 725). It is a sign of the person called being commended to God (M 441, 32ff.). However, it presents the danger of superstition insofar as one can misinterpret it as the means of a particular communication of grace and of the Spirit, in the sense of the Roman ordination to the priesthood. According to the Roman view of the sacrament of ordination, which sees its material as the laying on of hands and its form as the bishop's words "Receive the Holy Spirit" (DS 1774, CT 847), through this sacrament the Holy Spirit's particular gift of grace is conferred (*gratiam conferri*), and an indelible character (*character indelebilis*) is thereby imprinted on the priest, on the basis of which he cannot become a layperson again by not practicing the office of priest (DS 1766–67). Once a person is ordained as a priest, he always remains a priest. Ordination—which moreover can only be done by a bishop—is thus completely independent of the call (*vocatio*), issued by a particular community, to the particular office of the public proclamation of the word and administration of the sacrament (DS 1769, 1777).

Ordination as the ceremony by which a pastor is introduced into office is not comparable to ordination to the priesthood, insofar as the former presupposes election by a particular church community. Ordination in this sense constitutes the conclusion to the process of being called to the office of the public proclamation of the word and administration of the sacraments in a community. "No one is to be admitted, ordained and appointed to the preaching office of the gospel without a specific church community entrusted to him by his call" (Ni 305, 26–28). This excludes the possibility of an absolute ordination without a call from a particular community. According to the Savoy Declaration, this has the following significance for the validity of the Roman ordination to the priesthood: "Ordination alone, without the Election or precedent consent of the Church, by those who formerly have been Ordained by virtue of that Power they have received by their Ordination, doth not constitute any person a Church-Officer, or communicate Office-power unto him" (S 726). As absolute ordination, the Roman ordination to the priesthood, unlike ordination according to the Reformation understanding, does not confer an office.

THE ORDER OF THE CHURCH
BEYOND THE LOCAL LEVEL

There are considerable differences between the individual Reformed confessions regarding the constitution of the local church. For example, the Second Helvetic Confession recognizes only the one particular office of ministry, while Calvinism divides the functions of that office among three or four offices. However, the differences in the constitution of the church beyond the local level are even greater. The Congregationalist Savoy Declaration propounds the thesis that, besides local congregations as particular churches, "there is not instituted by Christ any Church more extensive or Catholic intrusted with power for the administration of his Ordinances or the execution of any authority in his Name" (S 724). Although the assertion of the complete autonomy of the local church does not imply the rejection of "occasioned Synods or Councils" (S 728), it does imply the rejection of a synodical power overarching the spiritual jurisdiction of the local church: "There is no power given by him [sc. Christ] unto any Synods or Ecclesiastical Assemblies to Excommunicate, or by their public Edicts to threaten Excommunication or other Church Censures against Churches, Magistrates, or their people, upon any account" (S 727, cf. 728).

Therefore, the Savoy Declaration eliminates the article concerning "Synods and Councils" from its adoption of the Westminster Confession, which regards the synods and councils as necessary for the better government of the church (cf. C 178–79). Just as the particular or local churches are governed by a college similar to a senate, the governance of the entire church, which embraces the various particular churches, lies with the synod, for which the biblical model is the apostolic council in Jerusalem. It is the task of the synods, "ministerially, to determine controversies of faith, and cases of conscience; to set down rules and directions for the better ordering of the public worship of God, and government of his Church; to receive complaints in cases of maladministration, and *authoritatively* to determine the same" (S 669). The synod possesses the power to make *authoritative* decisions concerning questions of faith and church order. It is required that these synodical decisions be in accordance with scripture. If—but only if—they are in accordance with scripture, they must be accepted by the particular churches, "not only for their agreement with the Word, but also for the *power* whereby they are made, as being an ordinance of God, appointed thereunto in his Word" (S 669–70). Just as the church senate—that is, the consistory or the presbytery—possesses spiritual jurisdiction for the particular church, the synod possesses such jurisdiction for the church as a whole. To be sure, the presbyteries are subordinate to the synod; but the latter is composed of members of the individual presbyteries. This gives constitutional expression to the basic principle of the French Ecclesiastical Discipline "that no church shall be able to claim primacy or domination over another" (Ni 75, 38–39; cf. S 377; Ni 279, 1–2; 297, 42–43). The synod, like the presbytery of a particular church, is a body of office-holders, for which it is the case that "the ministers shall each bring with them to the synod an elder or deacon of their church, or several" (Ni 76, 5–6). It is true of the conventions of classes (*classis,* presbytery, *colloque*) as well as of the provincial and general synods that each is a body composed of holders of the various offices elected by the specific subordinate body from its midst (cf. Ni 76, 285–86). The Herborn Synod declares: "Let the regular order recognize four types of conventions: (a) conventions of the presytery, (b) conventions of classes, (c) particular or provincial synods, (d) general synods" (Ni 294, 26–27). Their relations are governed by a principle of subsidiary order: "Nothing is to be treated in the larger conventions except matters that could not be handled in the smaller, or that pertain to an entire church, or to several" (Ni 294, 32–34). The constitution of the church in presbyteries and synods is born of necessity as a way of configuring a church that exists independently of the protection of the state authority. "So, if magistrates be open enemies to the Church, the ministers of Christ, of themselves, by virtue of their offices, or they, with other fit persons, upon delegation from their churches, may meet together in such assemblies" (S 669; cf. the alternative wording of the American edition, ibid.).

The organization of the church in presbyteries and synods is primarily directed against the Roman understanding of the church as a hierarchically structured institution culminating in the office of the pope as the universal bishop (cf. S 540). According to the Roman understanding, the one and only church has "one body, one head . . . namely, Christ and his Vicar Peter, and the successor of Peter" (DS 872, CT 153), the Roman bishop, who has "primacy over the whole world" and is "the head of the whole church, the father and teacher of all Christians," and to whom, "in the person of St. Peter, was given by our Lord Jesus Christ the full power of feeding, ruling, and governing the whole Church" (DS 1307, CT 164). By contrast, the French Confession dissolves the hierarchy in the equal authority of all pastors, which it derives from the thesis that they practice their ministry "under one head, one only sovereign and universal bishop, Jesus Christ" (S 377, cf. S 658–59). The title of "universal bishop" belongs only to Christ as head of the church. Christ is "the highest Pontiff before God the Father," and "in the Church he himself performs all the duties of a bishop or pastor, even to the world's end" (C 264). Contrary to the Roman thesis, Christ "does not need a substitute for one who is absent," since "Christ is present with his Church, and is its life-giving Head" (ibid.; cf. C 38; M 50, 20ff.).

CHURCH AND STATE

GOVERNING AUTHORITIES, OBEDIENCE, AND RESISTANCE

When the confessional writings of the Reformation period talk about the state, they mostly talk about the "secular authority." They are not, however, thinking about one specific form of state. Instead they leave unanswered the questions of which form the state must take, and of whether there is a preferred form of state at all. This question does not interest the confessional writings; they assume the multiplicity of actually existing forms of state. Who the state authority is in a specific case depends on the particular form of state. The Geneva Confession speaks of "kings and princes" (*roys et princes*) as well as of "other magistrates and persons of rank" (*autres magistrats et supérieurs*) (M 116, 25–26). The French Confession names as forms of state "kingdoms, republics, and all sorts of principalities, either hereditary or otherwise" (S 382). The secular authorities can be "kings, princes, and magistrates" (S 432) in "empires, kingdoms, dominions, and cities" (C 182). The diversity of forms of state, and thus of forms of governing authority, are explicitly recognized and play no role in the evaluation of secular authority. There is no claim that, from a theological perspective, one form of state is preferable to another or more justifiable than another.

Instead the claim is that the secular authority is divinely instituted, completely regardless of the particular form that authority takes. "I know," declares Zwingli in the Account of Faith, "that the magistrate when lawfully installed, holds God's place no less than the prophet" (Z 57). The secular authority, the magistracy (*magistratum*) is here traced back to God's institution just as much as is prophecy: that is, the spiritual office (*praedicationis munus*). "Magistracy of every kind is instituted by God . . . and thus it should have the chief place in the world," observes the Second Helvetic Confession (C 299). Romans 13:1ff. and 1 Peter 2:13ff. are used to ground the assertion that the secular authority is divinely instituted (cf. C 94). Since "all governmental power is from God" (C 110), the office of the secular authority can be characterized as "the most divine office of all" (M 78, 25). Those who occupy this office are "representatives and lieutenants of God" (*vicaires et lieutenants de Dieu*) (M 116, 34; cf. S 382). The thesis that the "secular authority"—that is, the office of the state—is divinely instituted is directed against the Anabaptist devaluation of the power of the governmental authority. This devaluation results in the view "that Christians cannot occupy the offices of secular authority" (C 96, trans. altered). The Second Helvetic Confession rejects the Anabaptists, who "deny that a Christian may hold the office of a magistrate" (C 300). Since the office of secular authority is a good institution of God, Christians must be allowed to occupy this office.

The question arises, however, concerning the extent to which one can characterize as a good institution of God (*bonne ordonnance de Dieu*) the office of the state and say that those who hold this office serve God and carry out a Christian calling (C 126; M 116, 25ff.). The Second Helvetic Confession declares that "the chief duty of the magistrate is to secure and preserve peace and public tranquillity" (C 299). Its office consists primarily in preserving public order and tranquillity (*reipublicae tranquillitatis conservatio*) (C 116; M 110, 31ff.). The ordered communal life of human beings requires the establishment of particular rules and laws that must be observed. In order to oversee their observance there must also be particular agents who can impose penalties when the laws are not observed. The state's legal order, which enables the ordered communal life of human beings, thus proves to be a coercive order. Since God wills the ordered communal life of human beings, God also wills "to have the world governed by laws and magistrates, so that some restraint may be put upon its disordered appetites" (S 381). For this reason God instituted the state authority and "all that belongs to a just government" (S 382). The office of the state consists, generally speaking, in the task of caring for the common good (*bonum publicum*).

In the words of the Westminster Confession, "God, the Supreme Lord and King of all the world, hath ordained civil magistrates to be under him, over the people, for . . . the *public good*" (S 652). The authority shall be a "minister of goodness and justice" (Z 57). It shall—according to the First Helvetic Confession—rule the people according to just, divine laws. It should sit in judgment and administer justice, preserve the public peace and welfare, guard and defend the public interest, and with fairness punish wrongdoers according to the nature of their crimes against life and property" (C 110–11). The common good, whose preservation is the responsibility of the state, can be characterized by the concepts "justice" and "peace." The state is to maintain "justice, and peace, according to the wholesome laws of each commonwealth" (S 652).

Insofar as the two can only be preserved with the help of a coercive legal order, and since the state is the instrument by which God wills to preserve justice and peace, God has entrusted the state "with the sword and with the highest external power" (C 94) in order to fulfill this purpose. In the view of the Westminster Confession, the state receives from God "the power of the sword, for the defense and encouragement of them that are good, and for the punishment of evil-doers" (S 652, cf. 536–37). Accordingly—in the words of the Second Helvetic Confession—the secular authority is to "draw this sword against all malefactors, seditious persons, thieves, murderers, oppressors, blasphemers, perjured persons, and all those whom God has commanded him to punish and even to execute" (C 300; cf. S 382, 432). Yet the state's penal power, which here includes the death penalty as well, applies not just to retribution for the transgressions of its own citizens; since the state has the task of preserving the common good, its power must extend to defending against external attacks. The state possesses the sword to threaten and use force not only against internal enemies but also against external ones. To be sure, before it in fact uses force against external enemies, it must have "sought peace by all means possible" (C 300). In other words, the use of force against external enemies is allowed only after peace negotiations have failed definitively. Armed conflict—that is, war—is legitimate only as a last resort (*ultima ratio*). "If it is necessary to preserve the safety of the people by war, let him [sc. the authority] wage war in the name of God" (C 300). War as the exercise of the state's power is legitimate when the grounds are just and compelling (M 447, 37ff.). Armed conflicts of this sort are just wars (*iusta bella*) (S 513). The Westminster Confession draws a logical conclusion when, with regard to the participation of Christians in a war that is necessary to preserve the common good, it declares that "for that end, they may lawfully, now under the New Testament, wage war upon just and necessary occasion" (S 652).

Insofar as the office of the state is regarded as divinely instituted and equipped with the power of the sword to preserve the common good, Christians are required to obey the state. Christians possess the moral duty to submit to the laws of the state. The Second Helvetic Confession declares: "For as God wants to effect the safety of his people by the magistrate, whom he has given to the world to be, as it were, a father, so all subjects are commanded to acknowledge this favor of God in the magistrate" (C 300). As citizens, Christians are obligated to honor and respect the state as God's servant. They are obligated not merely to tolerate the secular authority, but to support it actively by, among other things, paying taxes and performing military service. According to the Belgic Confession, one must "supplicate for them in their prayers, that God may rule and guide them in all their ways, and that we may lead a quiet and peaceable life in all godliness and honesty" (S 433, cf. 382).

The Christian duty of obedience to the state is grounded in the view that the state is divinely instituted to maintain justice and freedom. This gives rise to the question of what to do about the duty of obedience when the government of the state is tyrannical. Does the Christian duty of obedience also hold in this case? The Christian's duty of obedience to the state has at any rate a specific limit. Although the duty of obedience to the state applies unconditionally, it does not apply under every circumstance. Zwingli limits his statement concerning the secular authorities: "All Christians, without exception, owe them obedience," by referring to the situation that is the exception: "That is, in so far as they do not require anything contrary to God" (C 40–41). This states an unequivocal limit on the Christian duty of obedience to the state. According to the French Confession, this unconditional duty applies only on the presuppostion "that the sovereign empire of God (*l'empire souverain de Dieu*) remain intact" (S 382). God's sovereignty is not impugned merely by the fact that the secular authority does not adhere to the same confession, or even by the fact that the authority is totally unbelieving. Instead the case of an unbelieving and therefore heathen authority is definitely included. The French Confession declares "that we must obey their laws and statutes, pay customs, taxes, and other dues, and bear the yoke of subjection with a good and free will, *even if they are unbelievers*" (ibid.). The Westminster Confession states: "Infidelity or difference in religion doth not make void the magistrate's just and legal authority, nor free the people from their due obedience to him" (S 654). The Christian duty of obedience to the state does not depend on whether the state is Christian, but results from the legal authority of the government, understood as divinely instituted. The sole ground for refusing Christian obedience to the state—the state's laws being contrary to God—has nothing to do with the state's religiousness or irreligiousness. Instead it is our duty to honor "princes, rulers, and superior powers; to love them, to support them, to obey their orders if they are not contrary to the *commands* of God" (C 173). This means that there is no duty of Christian obedience to the authority if and only if the state's laws are not in agreement with the natural law, but instead contradict it.

But what does it mean to be released in the exceptional case from the duty of obedience? It means, firstly, that one is *permitted* not to obey. A state is tyrannical if its laws and actions contradict the universal standards of human action contained in God's commands and identified with the natural law. Disobedience to a tyrannical state is *permitted* for Christians. But if one *ought* to obey God more than human beings, then in such a case disobedience is not only permitted, but *commanded*. Of course, this civil disobedience can take various forms. While the Geneva Confession says that under no circumstances may one resist (*résister*) the state (C 126, M 116, 33ff.; cf. M 314, 22ff.), the Hungarian Confession interprets the "Petrine conclusion" (*clausula Petri*) as a command to engage in civil disobedience in exceptional cases. In this regard, however, the Hungarian Confession distinguishes between disobedience (*non parere*) and resistance (*resistere*), insofar as it defines resistance as armed—that is, active—resistance (M 448, 25–26). The civil disobedience that is permitted and commanded is thus limited to passive resistance. However, both Zwingli's Theses and the Scottish Confession go beyond this limitation of the right and duty of resistance to civil disobedience in the sense of a merely passive resistance. The Theses consider it necessary that the state's laws "conform to the divine will so that they protect the oppressed, even when he does not complain." If the authority commands something that is "contrary to God," the authority can be "deposed in the name of God." Deposing the authority is permitted in the case where its rule is "unfaithful" and "not according to the rule of Christ": that is, not according to the universal divine law (C 41). This means that in this case there is a *right* to resist. Finally, the Scottish Confession goes even a step further when it not only recognizes a right to resist the power of the state, but declares that resistance to tyranny is a *duty*. To be sure, the Confession regards it as a sin "to disobey or resist any whom God has placed in authority" (C 173, S 455). At the same time, the Confession considers it a commandment belonging to the second table of the Decalogue "to repress tyranny, to defend the oppressed" (C 173). Resistance to a tyrannical state power is thus elevated to the level of a duty that can be deduced from God's universally valid law, summarized in the Decalogue. The right to resist is supplemented by the duty to resist. However, the Scottish Confession leaves open the question of whether this duty is enjoined on all citizens, or only on a specific agent of the state.

When it is said that the secular authority must not transgress God's commands, this does not mean that the authority herself must be *Christian*. The legitimacy of an authority is not measured by the criterion of her being Christian. An unbelieving authority is also divinely instituted. As such, there is a fundamental duty of obedience to her, insofar as her laws and actions do not compel Christians to transgress God's commands. The fact that the authority is a "friend and even a member of the church" (C 299) cannot be the condition for legitimacy and recognition. To be sure, according to the Second Helvetic Confession, "if the magistrate is opposed to the Church, he can hinder and disturb it very much" (ibid.). But that is not yet grounds for refusing to obey the authority. This exceptional case arises only when the authority in no way performs its divinely appointed task of caring for justice and peace—that is, for the common good—by the threat and use of force.

ADMINISTRATION OF BOTH TABLES
(*CURA UTRIUSQUE TABULAE*)
AND THE DOCTRINE OF THE TWO KINGDOMS

The confessional writings do not tie the legitimacy of the secular authorities to the latter's faith. But the confessional writings are of the view that it is part of the specific task of the state to care not only for the second table of the Decalogue, but for the first table as well. This means that the state must focus not only on the observance of laws relating to the welfare of the neighbor but also on the observance of commandments relating to God's

honor. These commandments, summarized in the first table of the Decalogue, oblige us as citizens "to have one God, to worship and honour Him,
to call upon Him in all our troubles, to reverence His holy Name, to hear
His Word and to believe it, and to share in His holy sacraments" (C 173).
The Scottish Confession accordingly confesses "that the preservation and
purification of religion is particularly the duty of kings, princes, rulers, and
magistrates. They are not only appointed for civil government but also to
maintain true religion" (C 183). This view of the office of the secular authorities finds expression in the Appendix to the Scottish Confession,
which articulates the conviction "that the quietness and stability of our religion and church doth depend upon the safety and good behavior of the
king's majesty, as upon a comfortable instrument of God's mercy granted
to this country, for the maintaining of his church and ministration of justice among us." The Appendix binds this conviction with the solemn
promise to "defend his [sc. the king's] person and authority with our
goods, bodies, and lives, in the defence of Christ's gospel" (S 485). The
state's God-given administration of *both* tables of the Decalogue means
that any particular government also possesses the power of the sword to
prevent infractions of the first table of the Decalogue and to visit retribution for such infractions. According to the French Confession, God "has
put the sword into the hands of magistrates to suppress crimes against the
first as well as against the second table of the Commandments of God" (S
382). The power of the sword thus serves to protect not only the common
good but also rightful worship. As a result the Belgic Confession regards
it to be a task of the state to "remove and prevent all idolatry and false
worship; that the kingdom of Antichrist may be thus destroyed, and the
kingdom of Christ promoted." The state authorities "must, therefore,
countenance the preaching of the word of the gospel every where" (S 432;
cf. M 809, 40ff.).

The Old Testament rulers serve as models for the care that is entrusted to
the state for the first table of the Decalogue. The connection between, on the
one hand, care for the common good—that is, for the maintenance of justice
and peace—and, on the other hand, care for right worship of God, is considered a very tight one. Care for right worship is the appropriate and sufficient
means to promote the common good. Concerning promotion of the common
good, the Second Helvetic Confession says that the authority "will never do
this more successfully than when he is truly God-fearing and religious; that
is to say, when, according to the example of the most holy kings and princes
of the people of the Lord, he promotes the preaching of the truth and sincere
faith, roots out lies and all superstition, together with all impiety and idolatry, and defends the Church of God" (C 299–300; cf. M 313, 32ff.; 447, 18ff.).
For the Synodical Declaration of Berne, "Moses and the pious kings of Judah
are the ideal for the behavior of secular authorities" (M 33, 6ff.; C 94). God has

charged the state with the duty of protecting the exercise of true worship, and of preventing and punishing blasphemy (C 110). The Synodical Declaration of Berne states that, "on account of the progress of grace, which a temporal authority should promote as far as that progress consists in external actions," the secular authority will ultimately have to answer, before God's judgment, for its care for the first table of the Decalogue (M 31, 28ff.).

With the extension of the power of the sword to the observance of the first table of the Decalogue, the state is charged with the duty of persecuting heretics. The authorities are to use the sword in cases such as insurrection, murder, perjury, robbery, and extortion. In addition, the Second Helvetic Confession states that the authorities should "suppress stubborn heretics (who are truly heretics), who do not cease to blaspheme the majesty of God and to trouble, and even to destroy the Church of God" (C 300). To be sure, within the framework of Calvinist church orders, proceeding with measures of church discipline against heretics is the task of those ecclesiastical organs which are entrusted with the task of spiritual jurisdiction and are separated from the state. The most stringent measure that can be taken within the framework of discipline internal to the church is exclusion from the church: that is, *excommunicatio maior*. Yet here the cooperation between church and state is conceived as operating in such a way that in a given case the church, after completing the process of ecclesiastical discipline, can hand the heretic over to state jurisdiction (M 313, 11ff.). The state system of justice then proceeds with the heretic in accord with its task of caring for the observance of the first table of the Decalogue. The penalties that it imposes are not ecclesiastical penalties, but secular ones. It is indeed the church that excludes the heretic from the church's communion, thereby carrying out the *excommunicatio maior* as the church's most stringent disciplinary measure. But it is the state which, on the basis of its duty to persecute heretics, contained in the first table of the Decalogue, proscribes the heretic as outside the protection of the law and thus withdraws from him the rights of citizenship (cf. Ni 62).

The separation between the discipline of the church and the jurisdiction of the state in no way means that the state renounces concern for the first table of the Decalogue: that is, the threat and use of force to preserve true worship. The view of the state held by the confessions of the Reformation period are developed on the basis of a doctrine of two kingdoms. The Synodical Declaration of Berne criticizes the Anabaptist view according to which, "since their citizenship is in heaven and they have no abiding dwelling place on earth, but eagerly await the one that is to come, what the temporal authority undertakes does not concern them." The Synodical Declaration characterizes this view as a "separation of God's order . . . which carries out two forms of governance among human beings": spiritual governance, in which Christ governs through his Spirit and his ministers, and temporal governance, in which secular government is instituted by God. "The Christian belongs under both of them. On account of his conscience he belongs under spiritual governance. . . . But on account of his body and goods he belongs under the sword and the external administration" (M 51–37ff.). But this doctrine of two kingdoms or types of governance does not automatically imply that secular rule is to be concerned only with maintaining the order commanded in the second table of the Decalogue. Instead God entrusts it with the administration of both tables of the Decalogue, with the Decalogue being identified with natural law.

Secular authority thus possesses not only the office of holding the Decalogue up to its citizens as the immutable "law of nature," and of holding up to its citizens as positive law those laws which it itself promulgates and which do not contradict the law of nature. It also has the right to punish infractions of *both* tables of the Decalogue.

The Anglican and Irish Articles—the latter being a modification of the former—show what is meant by the distinction between spiritual and secular rule. The Anglican and Irish Articles declare, in agreement with the Zwinglian and Erastian theory of the state church and against the Roman pope's claim of universal jurisdiction, that the English monarch neither is nor ought to be subject to any foreign jurisdiction. To be sure, the English monarch is not—as was still the case in the first version of the Anglican Articles—"the supreme head, after Christ, in the lands of the Anglican and Scottish Church" (*supremum caput in terris, post Christum, Ecclesiae Anglicanae et Hibernicae*) (M 519, 33–35). But the monarch does have "under God . . . the sovereign and chief power within his realms and dominions, over all manner of persons, of what estate, either ecclesiastical or civil, soever they be" (S 536). The monarch is no longer supreme head, but supreme governor "within the said realms and dominions, in all cases, as well ecclesiastical as temporal" (ibid.).

Yet this does not mean that the power of the keys, which is placed in the office of the public preaching of the word and administration of the sacraments, is also given over to the monarch. The Roman episcopacy is reproached for precisely this confusion of this spiritual office with the secular office of the state authorities. According to the papal bull *Unam sanctam*, the church possesses a double power of the sword: namely, a spiritual power and a temporal, earthly power, which is subordinate to the spiritual power and directed by it (DS 873). On this view the pope is the supreme spiritual and secular monarch, for he claims "to be supreme head of the universal Church of Christ, and to be above all emperors, kings, and princes" (S 540). The strict distinction between spiritual and secular power brings with it a contesting of the subordination of the secular authorities, equipped with the temporal, earthly power of the sword, to the pope and the episcopacy. "The Pope, neither of himself, nor by any authority of the

Church or See of Rome, or by any other means with any other, hath any power or authority to depose the King, or dispose of any of his kingdoms or his countries; or to discharge any of his subjects of their allegiance and obedience to his Majesty; or to give license or leave to any of them to bear arms, raise tumult, or to offer any violence or hurt to his royal person, state, or government, or to any of his subjects within his Majesty's dominions" (S 537). The secular authority is not subordinate to the pope, who claims to have been instituted by Christ as the universal spiritual and secular ruler. The secular authority does not receive its authority and the power of the sword from the hands of the pope, but is immediately instituted by God, independently of any ecclesiastical agent. The authority or power of the pope and the episcopacy is strictly distinguished from that of the state authority.

The strict separation between spiritual and secular rule, both of which are immediately instituted by God, means not only that the spiritual office cannot appropriate any functions of the office of the state but also that the state cannot be entrusted with the work of the spiritual office. Even when the monarch is characterized as the supreme governor in all things ecclesiastical and secular, as in the Anglican and Irish Articles, this does not entail handing over to the monarch the administration of word and sacrament. Instead, as supreme governor not only of all state matters, but also of all ecclesiastical matters, the monarch possesses "that prerogative only which we see to have been always given unto all godly princes in holy Scripture by God himself" (S 536, cf. 512–13). The secular authority is not clothed with the spiritual office, but in accordance with the model of Israel's kings the "divine monarch" is granted the prerogative "that he should contain all estates and degree committed to his charge by God, whether they be ecclesiastical or civil, within their duty, and restrain the stubborn and evil-doers with the power of the civil sword" (S 536–37). This also means, however, that it is the monarch's responsibility to care for the first table of the Decalogue: that is, for the maintenance or establishment of right worship. In the monarch's function as supreme *governor* of the church as well, whose supreme *head* is Christ alone, it is within that monarch's purview, among other things, to convoke or approve general councils (S 539–40, cf. 500).

With regard to the civil authorities' care for the first table of the Decalogue, the Westminster Confession follows the Anglican and Irish Articles. The Westminster Confession indeed distinguishes sharply between the church's government and that of the state, between ecclesiastical and state jurisdiction. According to the Confession, the church's government lies exclusively in the hands of the elders, instituted by Christ himself, who form a church council that is distinct from the civil council. "The Lord Jesus, as king and head of his Church, hath therein appointed a government in the hand of Church officers, distinct from the civil magistrate" (S 667). The church's government consists of the church officers, who exist by divine law (*iure divino*). In agreement with the Anglican and Irish Articles, the Westminster Confession says that "the civil magistrate may not assume to himself the administration of the Word and Sacraments, or the power of the keys of the kingdom of heaven" (S 653). But just as it is the task of the "divine monarch" to care for right worship, so the Westminster Confession asserts that the civil magistrate "hath authority, and it is his duty to take order, that unity and peace be preserved in the Church, that the truth of God be kept pure and entire, that all blasphemies and heresies be suppressed, all corruptions and abuses in worship and discipline prevented or reformed, and all the ordinances of God duly settled, administered, and observed" (ibid.). Just as, in the view of the Anglican and Irish Articles, the monarch must convoke and approve synods, so the Westminster Confession grants the magistrate the right "to call synods, to be present at them, and to provide that whatsoever is transacted in them be according to the mind of God" (ibid.). The subject matter of synods, which are necessary to better govern the church and which are composed of pastors and elders, are "matters of religion" (S 669). The resolutions even of synods convoked by the magistrate apply only to ecclesiastical matters and not to civil ones, "unless by way of humble petition in cases extraordinary; or by way of advice for satisfaction of conscience, if they be thereunto required by the civil magistrate" (S 670).

Already in 1532 we find the Synodical Declaration of Berne having to defend itself against the reproach that entrusting the state with care for the first table of the Decalogue "establishes a new papacy" (M 33, 24). The Synodical Declaration means, though, that the state must promote the "free course of grace" (M 32, 23), "as much as it lies in *external* hands" (M 32, 7). But the Synodical Declaration denies the state that *internal, spiritual* sovereignty over the conscience which was illegitimately claimed by the Roman episcopacy. In so doing the Synodical Declaration thinks that it can fend off the reproach that here Christianity is being governed not with the word of God, but with the sword (cf. M 33, 21ff.). Yet the reproach persists at least if the state is to be entrusted with care for the first table of the Decalogue in such a way that the state cannot tolerate any false religion (*religionis falsae toleratio*) (M 627, 34), which according to the Westminster Larger Catechism is prohibited by the second commandment. The task entrusted to the state of using the power of the sword that has been conferred upon it to suppress every false religion implies the uniformity of the church. Furthermore, this task can only be realized when the state is a Christian state that, on the presupposition of confessionalism, conceives itself as the defender and promoter of only one specific Christian confession. The state itself cannot define what counts as the true worship commanded in the first table of the Decalogue, and what counts as false religion, for which the second commandment forbids tolerance. This can only be defined by a church: that is, a particular church or confession. Defining the relation between state and church in such a way that the state is responsible for caring for the first table of the Decalogue thus entails religious intolerance.

Although Congregationalism otherwise recognized the Westminster Confession, it corrected the Confession at precisely this point. The Savoy Declaration eliminated the statement—which manifests religious intolerance—that persons who contradict the "known principles of Christianity . . . may lawfully be called to account, and proceeded against by the censures of the Church, *and by the power of the Civil Magistrate*" (S 645). The Savoy Declaration takes this action because of the way in which the statement connects spiritual and secular power. The Declaration likewise eliminates the article of the Westminster Confession dealing with synodical structure and discipline. Within the article on the civil magistrate, the section defining the relation between church and state is completely changed. It is no longer the state's duty "to take order, that unity and peace be preserved in the Church, that the truth of God be kept pure and entire, that all blasphemies and heresies be suppressed, all corruptions and abuse in worship and discipline prevented or reformed, and all the ordinances of God duly settled, administered, and observed" (S 653).

To be sure, the Savoy Declaration assumes a Christian state. Otherwise it would be impossible to make it the state's task "to encourage, promote, and protect the professors and profession of the gospel, and to manage and order civil administrations in a due subserviency to the interest of Christ in the world" (S 720). The state being discussed here is not entirely neutral with regard to religion. It is a Christian state, which accordingly must take care "that men of corrupt minds and conversations do not licentiously publish and divulge blasphemy and errors, in their own nature subverting the faith and inevitably destroying the souls of them that receive them" (ibid.). Yet although the Savoy Declaration presupposes that the state is Christian and that it has the function, conditioned by its Christian status, of protecting the Christian faith, the Declaration supports the principle that the state is not to interfere in matters of faith. The Declaration abandons the requirement of ecclesiastical uniformity, and regards it as an attack on freedom of belief when the state interferes "in such differences about the doctrines of the gospel, or ways of the worship of God, as may befall men exercising a good conscience, manifesting it in their conversation, and holding the foundation, not disturbing others in their ways or worship that differ from them" (ibid.). The state indeed has the duty of protecting Christian religion as the true religion. But the state is not allowed to interfere when different persons of good conscience advance differing views of doctrine and of worship, as long as such persons do not disturb each other and do not abandon the foundation of the Christian faith.

3.

CONCILIATORY THEOLOGY, TOLERATION, AND THE DEVELOPMENT OF NEO-REFORMED CONFESSIONAL WRITINGS

THE QUESTION OF THE FUNDAMENTAL ARTICLE

Shortly before the Enlightenment's battle against every form of creedal coercion, the Helvetic Consensus Formula appears on the scene. As a testimony to late Reformed Orthodoxy, the Formula brings to a close the development of the old Reformed confessions. The Formula places confessions and doctrinal decrees immediately next to the word of God, which is explicitly identified with the canonical text. The Formula regards the confessional writings as a binding norm of doctrine not only for contemporaries, but for all who will come after. "No one shall put forward either publicly or privately a dubious or new doctrine that has never belonged in our churches, conflicts with God's word, the Helvetic Confession, our symbolic books, and the Canons of the Dordrecht Synod, and has not been proven and confirmed from God's word in a public assembly of the brethren" (M 869, 37ff.). When in Vaud the Formula found only conditional subscription with the caveat "insofar as it agrees with Sacred Scripture" (*quatenus S. Scripturae consentit*), the Berne Council insisted on unconditional subscription. At least in Basle (1686), and in Schaffhausen and Geneva (1706), the Great Elector's critique, made in the interest of his union politics, met with success. Henceforth these cities no longer required subscription to the Orthodox Formula.

The cause of this new turn was a general redirection within theology. Encrusted orthodoxy was opposed both by Pietism, influenced by Dutch precisianism and English Puritanism, and by the Enlightment, which was making its way from Western Europe. The wake of the reception of the new natural sciences washed over and destroyed orthodoxy's old worldview with its belief in miracles and demons. God was no longer experienced in the exceptional case of a miracle, but in the immutability of cosmic laws and of the order of the universe. Cartesianism and Occasionalism led to a heightened idea of omnipotence, thus enabling Reformed theology to be connected to modern philosophy. Angelology and demonology, such as found confessional expression in Article 12 of the Belgic Confession, could not be made compatible with contemporary natural science, and so were dissolved as a pagan remnant by Balthasar Bekker. Philological-historical textual criticism, propagated by Hugo Grotius, Louis Cappel, and Pierre Bayle, replaced the doctrine of inspiration defended in its most pointed formulation by the Helvetic Consensus Formula. An independent exegesis developed, while the viewpoint of covenant theology led to a specifically biblical theology that no longer read scripture from the perspective of the confessional writings. This brought a strengthened critique of dogma, which was directed primarily at the church's doctrine of the Trinity, Christology, the notion of satisfaction, and the idea of predestination. The Enlightenment and Pietism agreed in emphasizing the priority of scripture over the confessional writings and symbolic books. There was a corresponding opposition to the Orthodox "papacy of the confessions," according to which the confessions were understood not as human *testimonies* to faith, applying only to the state of doctrine, but as documents that *grounded* belief. In the new view, a confession could no longer be a *rule of faith*, but only the articulation of a specific *type of doctrine*.

The battle against the "symbololatry" cultivated by Zurich and Berne with regard to the Consensus Formula was initiated by the Lausanne Academy, which was defined by the spirit of the Enlightenment. When the Academy required only a conditional agreement to the Formula, the Berne Council sought to compel the Academy to subscribe "without any reservation or explanation" (1722). At first this gave rise to a compromise, by which the confessional writing was regarded not as a rule of faith but as a norm of doctrine. It was not permitted to teach or preach either publicly or privately anything contrary to this norm. But in the first third of the eighteenth century the Consensus Formula was abandoned without fanfare, bringing Old Reformed Orthodoxy to an end. This took place not only on the basis of interventions by the kings of Prussia and Great Britain, but also because of a unionist policy of conciliation on the part of theology. The Genevan Jean Alphonse Turretini, like the Lutheran Christoph Matthäuus Pfaff, to whom he was connected, dissolved the unity of Orthodox doctrine in favor of a limitation to the articles that were actually fundamental. For Turretini, nothing was fundamental except obedience to the divine commandments and trust in the promises of the gospel. Interested in a union between Reformed Christians and Lutherans, he accordingly entitled his *magnum opus* "A Cloud of Witnesses for a Moderate and Peaceloving Judgment in Things Theological, and for the Unity to be Established among Protestants, Preceded by a Short and Peaceloving Investigation of the Fundamental Articles by Which the Path is Cleared to Peace and Mutual Tolerance among Protestants" (1729). After Geneva under Turretini had removed the strict confessional requirement, its preachers' only obligation was to the teaching of the prophets and apostles, of which the Geneva Catechism was regarded as the summation.

It is characteristic of the early Reformed confessions that, in contrast to the Orthodox doctrinal decrees, they relativize themselves in relation to scripture. Scripture is understood as the sole norm by which a confession must be continually measured. This view anchors in the confessions themselves the possibility of their revision and even abrogation. The First Confession of Basle accordingly states: "Finally, we desire to submit this our confession to the judgment of the divine Biblical Scriptures. And should we be informed from the same Holy Scriptures of a better one, we have thereby expressed our readiness to be willing at any time to obey God and His holy Word with great thanksgiving" (C 96). The Synodical Declaration of Berne expresses itself in similar words: "But where something is presented to us by pastors or others that leads us closer to Christ, and where possible is more favorable than the opinion expressed here to God's word, shared friendship and Christian love, we will gladly accept that, and will not block the course of the Holy Spirit" (M xxi, 30–35). Finally, the Scottish Confession explicitly asks the addressees "that if any man will note in our Confession any chapter or sentence contrary to God's Holy Word, that it would please him of his gentleness and for Christian charity's sake to inform us of it in writing; and we, upon our honour, do promise him that by God's grace we shall give him satisfaction from the mouth of God, that is, from Holy Scripture, or else we shall alter whatever he can prove to be wrong" (C 165). As a consequence of this relativity of the confessions in relation to scripture, which entails the possibility of the confessions being revised or abrogated, they do not as such possess any binding power. They can never have the character of binding, normative interpretations of scripture, but must themselves always be open to being called into question by scripture. Reformed confessions remain open to reform on the basis of better scriptural insight.

As coauthor of the Heidelberg Catechism, Ursinus gave expression to this understanding of the confessions in the following way. "A confessional writing is not a norm or rule by which one can judge and articulate what one believes and affirms, what one rejects and condemns, what is true or mendacious, what is right or heretical. For that which agrees with the confession of a church is not true for all times; nor is that which does not agree with the confession of a church false for all times. Thus one can not demand that all churches subscribe the formula of a particular church. . . . Such formulas are subject to the judgment and examination not only of other churches, but also of the churches that have promulgated the formulas, as well as from those who live and teach in these churches, so that, if mistakes are to be found in them, that might be heard, noted and examined, and if anything is found to be in need of improvement, it be improved or clarified with general agreement and at the command of the church for which it is written. . . . On the other hand, one must guard against too great a bondage and enslavement, so that one church or a few churches not prescribe for all other churches a single formula of unity according to what meets their own approval, and condemn all those who are unwilling to admit this."[1] On this view the church indeed formulates confessions that serve to preserve doctrine. But they are secondary norms of doctrine and not the truth of a particular church. The confessions enable people to ascertain which statements agree with the church's current doctrine and which do not. The confessions can be regarded as binding only for the external community of the church, not for the individual conscience, except insofar as they agree with God's word. Scripture alone is the canon and rule of faith (*canon* and *regula fidei*), while the confessions need continual reform "according to the norm of the word" (*ad verbi normam*).

The Bremen Consensus accordingly understands the word that God "led the prophets and apostles to compose in certain writings" as "an eternal and immoveable ground and certain infallible rules by which all doctrine (of God's essence and will and all other parts of religion) is rightly to be known and to be distinguished from all false and erroneous doctrines" (M 739, 27–31). Scripture "is its own best interpreter," and it is the *doctrine* contained in scripture which functions as "the sole standard by which all doctrines in every time are to be judged, and to which the writings and confessions of all human beings must be and remain subordinate" (M 740, 1–4).

The Sigismund Confession likewise confesses the "true and infallible word of God, in which alone is salvation, as that word is formulated in the writings of the holy prophets and apostles in the holy Bible. This word is and ought to be the sole standard of all pious people (Ps. 119:104). It is complete and sufficient for salvation, as well as for distinguishing what is right in every religious dispute, and it endures forever" (M 836, 21–26). The significance attributed to the confession relativizes it and thereby provides a basis for toleration of a confession pluralism. For ultimately the Sigismund Confession points to the fact that all confessions come from human beings, and "thus can err in many ways" (M 836, 35–36). For this reason "His Electoral Grace [sc. the author] does not wish to bind either himself or his dear subjects by afflicting their consciences, because all matters of faith must be grounded only and solely on God's word. Human writings can and ought to be accepted only to the extent that they agree with God's word, as Herr Luther himself confesses: Scripture alone is the right teacher and master over all writings and teachings on earth. Likewise, this empress, Sacred Scripture, ought to rule and govern, and all others, whatever they might be, ought to be subject and obedient to her. They ought not to be her masters and judges, but only poor witnesses, pupils and confessors, whether they be the Pope, Luther, Augustine, Paul or an angel from heaven. No doctrine should be preached or heard in Christendom other than the pure, unsullied word of God" (M 836, 38–M 37, 1). Of course the author of the Sigismund Confession operates in the firm conviction that his own confession, like the other confessions accepted by him, is "in accord with God's word and upright" (M 842, 35). Yet he denies the confessions in general any binding power, since Christ alone, "who knows the heart," is Lord of the conscience and of faith (M 842, 30ff.). He "does not wish to compel any subject to make this confession either publicly or secretly against his or her will, but to commend the truth's course and career to God alone, because what is important is not running and racing, but God's mercy" (M 842, 44–47).

The Savoy Declaration accordingly distinguishes sharply between shared public confession in the sense of a doctrinal pronouncement and a confession of faith as a private confessional act. The Declaration regards as necessary—because it is among the duties of the first table of the Decalogue—only the actual attestation of one's own faith, not the shared statement of doctrine. This view excludes every confessional requirement in the sense of an obligation, presented as necessary, to a specific symbol. To be sure, the Savoy Declaration says that "Confessions, when made by a company of Professors of Christianity jointly meeting to that end, the most genuine and natural use of such Confessions is, That under the same form of words, they express the substance of the same common salvation or unity of their faith; whereby speaking the same things, they show themselves perfectly joined in the same mind, and in the same judgment" (S 708). But a shared confession of this sort serves exclusively as a testimony to the shared faith of those who freely adopt the confession, not as a binding norm of faith. "And accordingly such a transaction is to be looked upon but as a meet or fit medium or means whereby to express that their common faith and salvation, and no way to be made use of as an imposition upon any: Whatever is of force or constraint in matters of this nature, causeth them to degenerate from the name and nature of Confessions, and turns them from being Confessions of Faith, into Exactions and Impositions of Faith" (ibid.).

Insofar as Reformed confessions regard themselves as open to revision on the basis of better scriptural insight, they are testimonies of faith that articulate the doctrine of a specific time. Moreover, the earliest confessions are confessions of particular cities. For example, the First Confession of Basle is the "confession of our sacred Christian faith, as held by the church of Basle" (M 95, 3–4). The unity of faith of different particular churches can be manifested in diverse ways. The development within Switzerland led first to the Reformation-minded Swiss German cities accepting the First Helvetic Confession, which was later replaced by the Second Helvetic Confession, which was also accepted by the church of Geneva as a common confession. The Second Helvetic Confession understands itself as a "confession and simple exposition of the Christian faith and of the universal dogma of the pure Christian religion, edited in a spirit of concord by ministers of the church of Christ in Switzerland: in Zurich, Berne, Schaffhausen, St. Gall, Chur and Dreibünden, as well as in Mühlhausen and Biel, to whom the ministers of the church of Geneva have also joined themselves" (J 177). The purpose of this exposition of the faith is to give public testimony—and therefore testimony that is open to criticism—to the fact "that they persist in the unity of the true and ancient church of Christ, are not disseminating any new and erroneous doctrines, and thus have nothing in common with any sort of sect or heresy" (ibid.). In this way the signatories to the confession confirm that, despite differences in the linguistic formulation and structure of doctrine, and in rites and ceremonies that could never call into question the unity of Christ's church, in the individual local churches there is a God-given "mutual consensus in the primary dogmas of the faith" (*mutuus in praecipuis fidei dogmatibus consensus*) (Ni 221). However, this consensus need not find expression in the presentation of a unitary confession. Unity of faith does not require unity of confession. It is instead possible that different particular churches demonstrate their unity of faith by recognizing their particular confessions as testimonies to the common faith. The Emden Synod states: "In order to testify to the consensus of doctrine among the churches of the Netherlands, it appeared good to the brethren to subscribe the confession of the churches of the Netherlands. And in order to testify to the consensus and communion of these churches with the churches of France, it seemed good to the brethren to subscribe in the same way the confession of faith of the French churches, in sure trust that the ministers of those churches would in turn subscribe the confession of faith of the churches of the Netherlands in order to testify to the mutual consensus" (Ni 279, 4–10). Communion of faith is not constituted by the mutual recognition of confessions, but is solely attested as a presupposition. Because the particular churches agree as to faith, so that there is a consensus, they can give expression to this consensus by mutually recognizing each other's confessions.

The recognition of other confessions thus presupposes agreement in the foundation of faith. The Bremen Consensus explicitly observes that, "according to the Harmony of Evangelical Confessions (*Harmonia Confessionum Evangelicarum*), the publicly disseminated and approved confessions of the other Evangelical Reformed churches outside Germany agree concerning the foundation and chief principle of the Christian religion" with the Augsburg Confession, "the first and oldest evangelical confession" (M 740, 28ff.). The First Helvetic and the Sigismund Confessions explicitly specify the content of this foundation of faith. The prior confession states that "in all evangelical teaching the most sublime and the principal article and the one which should be expressly set forth in every sermon and impressed upon the hearts of men should be that we are preserved and saved solely by the one mercy of God and by the merit of Christ" (C 104). The fact of God's free grace is here the foundation of faith. The Sigismund Confession instead regards the article concerning God's gracious eternal election as that foundation "on which not only all other articles are primarily grounded, but also our salvation" (M 841, 22ff.). But this is not to contradict the First Helvetic Confession. The Sigismund Confession considers election solely as the necessary presupposition of justification. Understood in this way, the article concerning God's gracious election says that "before the foundation of the world was laid, God the omnipotent ordained to eternal life and elected all who steadfastly believe in Christ, out of pure grace and mercy, without any regard for human worthiness and without any merit or works" (M 841, 23–28).

Because they felt that they agreed in the foundation of faith, Reformed Christians, Lutherans, and Bohemian Brethren were able to subscribe the Sendomir Consensus as the first step to a Polish national church. The mutual recognition here of the various confessions—the Second Helvetic Confession, the Augsburg Confession, and the Confession of the Bohemian Brethren—presupposed agreement in the "necessary principles of faith" (*Capitibus Fidei necessariis*): that is, in the "foundation of our faith and salvation" (*fundamentum fidei ac salutis nostrae*) (N 559, 670). The Palatine practitioner of irenic theology David Pareus could thus regard the Sendomir Consensus as a model for union between the Reformation confessions. The Heidelberg theologian Franz Junius had given Palatine irenics its theoretical grounding. Referring to the foundation mentioned in 1 Cor. 3:11, in the interests of interconfessional union Junius developed the doctrine of the fundamental articles of faith, the affirmation of which was necessary for salvation. The Leipzig Colloquy between Lutheran and Reformed Christians accordingly granted "toleration" on the presupposition of consensus in the "principal matters" of faith (N 664), and the Huguenot National Synod of Charenton (1631) declared: "Since the churches of the Augsburg Confession otherwise agreed with the Reformed churches in the fundamental articles of the true religion . . . believers of that confession could . . . be admitted to the Lord's Table in common with us, without making any sort of renunciation."[2] The distinction between those articles of faith which are fundamental and those which are not thus led to the recognition of a theologically justified pluralism and paved the way theologically for the idea of toleration. The Savoy Declaration characterizes it as a "great principle of these times, That amongst all Christian States and Churches, there ought to be vouchsafed a forbearance and mutual indulgence unto Saints of all persuasions, that keep unto, and hold fast the necessary foundations of faith and holiness, in all other matters extra fundamental, whether of Faith or Order" (S 710).

CONFESSIONALISM AND THE
IDEA OF TOLERATION

An officially received confessional writing serves as a norm for the proclamation and teaching of an ecclesiastical community. However, the status
of the Reformed confessional writings shifted increasingly on the path
from the Reformation to Orthodoxy. Initially they were expositions of the
faith that were to ground and justify the reformation of the church. But
they increasingly attained the status of a doctrinal law, which not only
served as a norm of proclamation and teaching in the church, but also defined the territorial unity of doctrine from the top down. This completed
the move from the age of the Reformation, which was still bound to the
medieval idea of the Christian body politic (*Corpus christianum*), to the age
of confessionalism. The confessions were no longer understood as expositions of the teachings of specific local churches or congregations (*ecclesiae
apud nos*) that belonged to the one church, but as normative unitary confessions of particular churches. Where these were not minority churches,
but territorial or state churches, these confessions of the state authority
served to preserve the confessional unity of the authority's territory.

The Augsburg Confession played a particular role within the German
development, insofar as the Peace of Augsburg granted imperial peace
only to those estates which made the Augsburg Confession their own. For
this reason the Augsburg Confession was also the confessional foundation
in those territories which, following the model of the Palatinate, switched
from the Lutheran to the Reformed camp. The introduction of other
doctrinal norms as well does nothing to alter the fact that they either explicitly or implicitly presuppose their agreement with the Augsburg Confession. When Frederick III of the Palatinate was threatened with exclusion
from the Peace of Augsburg, he appealed to his subscription to the Augsburg Confession. Those lands which with the help of the Cryptocalvinists
carried out a "second Reformation" explicitly adopted reference to the
Augsburg Confession in their own confessions. Thus the Bremen Consensus concludes that "according to the Harmony of Evangelical Confessions,
the publicly disseminated and approved confessions of the other Evangelical Reformed churches outside Germany" agree on the chief matter
with the Augsburg Confession as the first and oldest Evangelical confession (M 740, 33–34). Precisely in the face of Concordistic Lutheranism, the
Bremen Consensus presents itself as a "confession that we hold to be in accord with the word of God and the testimonies of the ancient orthodox
churches, as well as with the scripturally appropriate understanding of the
Confession of Augsburg and of other churches, Reformed by the word of
God" (M 741, 27–30). Like the Formula of Concord, the Bremen Consensus

sees itself as an accurate interpretation of that confession whose "religious relatives" alone were granted imperial peace. The nature of the Peace of Augsburg thus defined the confessional development in the German Empire. What triumphed in that Peace was not the principle of freedom of religion, desired by the Evangelical side, but the Catholic idea that the ruler of a particular land determines the confessional status of his territory (*cuius regio, eius religio*). The idea of a Christian body politic was replaced by the idea of territorial states whose "religion" or "religious party"—that is, confession—could ultimately be determined only by their rulers, while the right of emigration (*ius emigrandi*) was nevertheless conceded to the subjects, provided they belonged to one of the two religious parties taken into consideration. The Peace of Augsburg extended neither to the Zwinglian "Sacramentarians" nor to the Anabaptists, Spiritualists, and Antitrinitarians, who were instead handed over to the law concerning heretics. In German-speaking Switzerland the Second Peace of Kappel (1531) had already led to the solidification of the confessional stalemate and thus to the construction of confessionally homogeneous territories—later followed by Geneva. As was demonstrated by the execution of Manz in Zurich, Servetus in Geneva, and Gentile in Berne, heresy laws were applied against Anabaptists and Antitrinitarians here in the same way as in the German territories, where the Elector Palatine condemned the Antitrinitarian Silvanus to death.

Where the secular authority promoted the Reformed confession as the pure doctrine in a territory, that confession assumed the form of a state or territorial church. The confession accepted by the authority not only served as an ecclesiastical norm of doctrine but also defined the public religion of the land. This was the case not only in the German territories but also in the city-states of German-speaking Switzerland and in Geneva. The only difference was that the relation between church and state was variously organized. While Zwingli propagated a state church in which the secular authority governed the church, Calvin insisted on the church's relative independence in relation to the state. Germany saw the development of mixed forms, such as in the Palatinate or in Nassau-Dillenburg, where with the Herborn Church Order (1586) Wilhelm Zepper tied the presbyterial-synodical organization to the already existing institution of superintendants or inspectors acting on behalf of the ruler of the land. In the Palatinate, by contrast, the Calvinist constitution of the church existed only at the congregational level, and thus was clearly subordinated to the secular ruler's governance of the church. The theological grounding for this governance came by reference to the "care of both tables" (*custodia utriusque tabulae*), insofar as the administration of religion (*cura religionis*) as the duty to preserve the purity of church doctrine was counted as part of the first table of the Decalogue, and was assigned to the ruler of the land as the "pre-eminent member of the church" (*praecipuum membrum ecclesiae*). On this view the ruler of the land also had the duty and the right to care for the confessional uniformity of his territory by combating the public spread of doctrines that did not agree with the officially received confession.

Besides this specifically theological grounding, the governance of the church by the ruler of the land also was grounded purely in terms of civil law. The Peace of Augsburg interprets this latter grounding in such a way that, with the extinguishing of episcopal jurisdiction in the Evangelical territories, governance of the church was conferred upon—or reverted to—the ruler of the land. This latter idea provided the bridge from an episcopal system to a territorial one. Steps in that direction were already present in the thought of Zwinglian proponents of a state church like Thomas Erastus. Erastus had developed a doctrine of sovereignty, according to which the church is completely subordinate to the state's legal power. Erastianism exercised its greatest influence on the shaping of the Anglican state church, in which the king or queen functions as the supreme governor of the church. Supported by Jean Bodin's early absolutistic theory of sovereignty, the territorial system also exercised heightened influence in Germany. Under the impression made by the French confessional wars, Bodin sought to remove the government from the influence of the confessions and to develop it into a neutral agent capable of ensuring peace. To this end Bodin defined sovereignty as the absolute and enduring power of a state—that is, as the supreme power to command. The only figure who counts as an earthly sovereign is the one who recognizes God alone as greater than himself, and who is subject only to the divine command and natural law.

By applying this concept of sovereignty to the monarch, Bodin opposed the monarchomachic theory of the state supported by Calvinists under the impression made by the St. Bartholomew's Day Massacre. In the context of the discussion concerning the Huguenots' right to resist a monarchy that was tyrannical in its confessional suppression, Beza, Daneau, Hotoman, and Duplessis-Mornay had advanced the thesis that the people, represented by their estates, were the actual sovereign, while the ruler was tied to the power accorded him by the people. In Bodin's eyes, under the conditions of confessionalism such a theory, which entails the people's active right to resist, could lead only to never-ending civil war. The territorial system picked up on Bodin to the extent that: (1) it no longer regarded the ruler as the subject of two systems of governance—the state and the church—but as absolute sovereign, and (2) it derived the church's governance from the ruler's territorial sovereignty. If the governance of the church under the ruler of the land were not to destroy the church's freedom completely, that governance would have to be limited. This limitation was carried out by the Heidelberg theologian David Pareus, who distinguished between ecclesiastical power (*potestas ecclesiastica*) in the narrower sense—that is, the church's internal governance, encompassing the office of preaching and the administration of the sacraments—and the "royal power concerning the church" (*potestas regia circa ecclesiastica*)—that is, the external governance of the church, exercised only by the ruler of the land. The ruler possessed as a consequence of his sovereignty only the right of law concerning sacred matters (*ius circa sacra*), not the right of law in sacred matters (*ius in sacris*).

The Herborn theoretician of the state Johannes Alsthusius brought to its conclusion the monarchomachic doctrine of the sovereignty that the people cannot surrender, but can only allow to be administered on their behalf. By contrast, Arminianism hearkens back to territorialism. For reasons similar to those which brought Bodin to his absolutistic doctrine of sovereignty, Hugo Grotius borrowed from the Zwinglian-Erastian view of a state church, in which Grotius saw the best guarantee of peace and confessional toleration. Grounded purely in natural law, the state seemed to him to be beyond the reach of confessions striving against one another. Finally, under the influence made by the English Civil War, territorialism found its classic expression in the thought of Thomas Hobbes. He saw confessional civil war as the state of nature consisting of the war of all against all, without either state or security. This condition of war can only be resolved by a social contract in which all surrender their right once and for all to the sovereign. This is the birth of the state as a "mortal god." For Hobbes this entails the total subordination of the churches and confessions to the state. Insofar as he does not identify particular confessions with the sole article of faith necessary for salvation—namely, that Jesus is the Christ—Hobbes does not allow any resistance to the state's imposition of confessions. He regards as absolute the divine command of obedience to the state authority. After all, it is solely the absolute sovereignty of the ruler that is able to prevent confessional civil war.

In Germany the territorial viewpoint already underlay the Peace of Augsburg with its assignment of the right to execute reform (*ius reformandi*) to the ruler of the land. But the territorial system found actual recognition in the Peace of Westphalia (1648). Religious peace was now also extended to the "Reformed," who were now "tolerated." However, a limitation was also imposed on the confessional supremacy of the ruler of the land. The principle of *cuius regio, eius religio* (the ruler of a region determines its religion) no longer applied to the religion or confession itself, but only to the forms in which the religion or confession was practiced. Moreover, the confessional status was temporally fixed at the condition obtaining in the normative year of 1624. Finally, a Protestant ruler's switching from the Lutheran to the Reformed confession could no longer affect the public practice of religion in his territory. Already in 1613, the

Elector of Brandenburg had in moving to the Reformed camp explicitly refused to determine as ruler the confession of his subjects. The Sigismund Confession accordingly states: "His Grace the Elector is sufficiently assured in his heart and conscience that this confession is right and in accord with God's word, and could wish for no better experience than that the Lord God, out of pure grace and mercy, would bless and illuminate his true subjects with the light of infallible truth. Nevertheless, since faith does not belong to everyone . . . but is God's work and gift . . . and since no one is allowed to rule over consciences . . . His Grace the Elector does not wish to compel any of his subjects either publicly or privately to this confession" (M 842). Here for the first time, above and beyond the right of emigration, a German ruler connects faith and freedom of conscience, and thereby does away with territorial confessional unity.

In the Reformation period, the first apologists for a fundamental tolerance, grounded in an individualistic understanding of faith or in a skeptical critique of dogma, were the Anabaptists and the Antitrinitarians. Because of their partial rejection of the authorities—that is, because of their political position—the Anabaptists were condemned from the Reformed side as well, so that Zwingli, unlike Bucer and Calvin, could even argue for the death penalty. By contrast, the Antitrinitarians were considered atheists, against whom Calvin sought to apply the heresy laws anchored in imperial law. It was precisely the burning of Servetus that led Sebastian Castellio to the thesis of a fundamental freedom of belief which, although it presupposed recognition of the triune God and observance of the commandments, permitted the authority to punish only immorality, not heresy. A limited freedom of religion was first realized in Transylvania, then in Poland, where it extended to Reformed, Lutherans, Catholics, and Socinians. In France the Reformed were recognized alongside the Catholic state church. In the States General of the Netherlands, Calvinism could not enforce its requirement of uniformity over against the strong elements of Anabaptism and of the humanists gathered within Arminianism. As a result Socinianism, driven out of Poland, ultimately found a reception here. However, the decisive influence for the ultimate victory of the idea of toleration emanated from the solution of the conflict between both Anglican and Presbyterian insistence on uniformity and Congregational-Independent pluralism. The various versions of the proposed Independent constitution, the "Agreement of the People" (1647), clarify the way from a state-sanctioned confessional uniformity, as demanded by Episcopalians and Presbyterians, to a state recognition of many confessions. The last version of the proposed constitution assumes that Christianity is to be the public national religion, and must be reformed in doctrine, worship, and discipline in accordance with God's word. But with the exception of Papism and Episcopalism, confessions that are not identical with the public national confession are now also to be protected by the state. Toleration extends to "such as profess Faith in God by Jesus Christ (however differing in judgement from the Doctrine, Worship or Discipline publicly held forth)."[3]

The state is thus freed of the task, also assigned to it by Presbyterianism, of insisting on confessional uniformity to the exclusion of all other confessions. John Milton, who himself belonged to the Independent circle around Cromwell, attempted to give a theological grounding to this state-protected relative freedom of religion by pointing to scripture as the sole external judge in religious matters, according to the Reformation. In Milton's view, insofar as personal conviction of the truth of scripture is effected by the divine Spirit, and the Spirit is thus the sole internal judge in matters of religion, religious conviction is an issue of conscience, which cannot be decided by any state or church authority. Contrary to the Presbyterian idea of uniformity, for Milton church discipline extends exclusively to those persons who have voluntarily joined themselves to a specific covenant of union. The local church community as the circle (*coetus*) or assembly (*congregatio*) of the faithful who regularly gather for worship is the result of a voluntary covenant. If the sole agent of decision in religious matters is the personal conviction gained with the help of scripture and wrought by the Spirit, then there can be no superindividual decisions that bind the conscience in such questions. "For Protestants, whose common rule and touchstone is Scripture, there is nothing that can be permitted with a better conscience, more properly and in a more Protestant sense than a free and lawful debate—at any time, in written form, in negotiations or in disputations—of any opinion whatsoever that can be defended on the basis of Scripture."[4] Insofar as neither a single individual nor an ecclesiastical figure or body is accorded an interpretive monopoly, the return to scripture leads to a confessional freedom. Milton wants only the Roman church to be excluded from this freedom. The reasoning is that the Roman church excludes itself from this freedom by its claim to be the ultimate court of authority in deciding religious matters.

This Independent confessional understanding itself found confessional expression in the Savoy Declaration (1658). To be sure, the Declaration adopted the Westminster Confession (1647), but altered it in the article concerning the state. The Declaration no longer considered it the task of the state to concern itself with uniformity of religion in its territory, with actions that ran counter to the uniformity requirement being subject to the state's penal law. The Savoy Declaration continued to regard it as a function of the state not only to protect adherents of the Christian religion, but also to support them and to suppress public heresies. Yet the Declaration could declare that "in such differences about the doctrines of the gospel, or ways of the worship of God, as may befall men exercising a good conscience, manifesting it in their conversation, and ever holding the foundation, not disturbing others in their ways of worship that differ from them, there is no warrant for the magistrate under the gospel to abridge them of their liberty" (S 720). The fact of confessional diversity does not necessarily imply a difference of faith. Instead the Preface to the Savoy Declaration emphasizes that confessional freedom needs to extend to all persons who hold to the foundation of the Christian faith despite their differences in confessional status. The Declaration thus characterizes it as a "great principle of these times, That amongst all Christian States and Churches, there ought to be vouchsafed a forbearance and mutual indulgence unto Saints of all persuasions, that keep unto, and hold fast the necessary foundations of faith and holiness, in all other matters extra fundamental, whether of Faith or Order" (S 710).

This thesis of religious toleration received its most influential theological grounding from John Locke, who is himself to be counted among Independent circles. In his first Letter on Toleration (1689), Locke declares that toleration is nothing less than the chief mark of the true Christian church. In order to banish confessional wars in the name of the public good, he draws a strict distinction between the state's care for the commonwealth as a society of human beings, the constitution of which concerns only the satisfaction of their civil interests—life, liberty, property, and so on—and the church's care for individual salvation of the soul. This latter care cannot be given over to the state, particularly since the state's power consists only of external coercion, while the power of religion consists of internal certainty, so that no one can be compelled to believe by the threat of force. Instead faith rests solely on a conviction wrought by "light and evidence." The church is accordingly defined as a "voluntary society of men" who meet by their own agreement in a worshiping assembly, which seems to them to be effective for the salvation of their souls. The church is thus a free society. Its power is defined on that basis. Like any other society, the church needs certain laws and ordinances.

Yet due to the church's voluntary character, ecclesiastical legislation can lie only in the hands of the church's members or of their elected representatives. This excludes the possibility of tying the legislative power to a particular class. Since the purpose of a church community is the public adoration of God and the mediation of salvation, its ordinances, unlike those of the state, cannot be coercive. The observance of its laws can only be attained through admonition and, as a last resort (*ultima ratio*), through excommunication. Toleration does not entail a renunciation of excommunication, since otherwise church communities would dissolve themselves. Toleration does, however, entail a renunciation of civil penalties following excommunication. Church discipline and civil penal law are strictly separated. Moreover, no civil disadvantage can arise on the basis of differences in confession, so that the relation of churches to one another corresponds to that of private persons who belong to different confessions. Along the same lines, the authority of the so-called clergy extends solely to their own confessional community. The state must tolerate the various confessions, since individual salvation of the soul, which is found only by the decision of one's own conscience and not on the path of coercive legal measures, cannot be the state's concern. State toleration extends to the individual church communities' discipline and cultic life, as well as to their doctrines and confessions.

However, there is a limit to toleration of doctrine. The state cannot tolerate any doctrine that contradicts the laws necessary to maintain civil society or that grants its adherents a dispensation from civil law while preserving the appearance of conformity with that law. For this reason Locke excludes from toleration the Roman church, which holds to the jurisdictional primacy of the pope. Locke also excludes atheists insofar as they undermine the religious foundation of the state's judicial system. Aside from these exceptions Locke, unlike Hobbes and the defenders of the state church concept, regards the separation of state and confession, and thus confessional toleration, as the appropriate means of solidifying the security of the state, since the tolerated confessions could have no interest in abandoning the condition of their own existence. The Dutch first edition of the Letter on Toleration still names Remonstrants, Antiremonstrants, Lutherans, Anabaptists, and Socinians as confessions to be tolerated. The English translation, though, having removed the Lutherans, who were not present in England, and the Socinians, who were suppressed there, accommodates itself to the state of affairs there: "Thus if solemn assemblies, observations of festivals, public worship be permitted to any one sort of professors, all these things ought to be permitted to the Presbyterians, Independents, Anabaptists, Arminians, Quakers, and others, with the same liberty."[5]

It was Locke's idea of toleration, which also met with agreement among the Anglican Latitudinarians, which ultimately—with strong restrictions—found expression in the Acts of Toleration (1689) promulgated by William III after the Glorious Revolution. These acts conceded to the Nonconformists and Dissenters the right to practice their religion freely, but did not grant them full civil equality. Antitrinitarians and Papists continued to be excluded from toleration, but the Acts themselves in no way entailed equality among the Protestant confessions. The Acts in fact granted the Anglican state church privilege that was withdrawn from the Presbyterianism both of the period of the Revolution and of the high church restoration of the Stuarts. The toleration that was granted presupposed confession of the triune God and of the inspiration of the biblical scriptures. Toleration was enjoyed not only by the Congregationalists, but also by the Quakers and the Baptists, whose roots were in Reformed Congregationalism. The Particular Baptists, who merely mitigated the Calvinist doctrine of predestination, had at any rate received most of the Westminster Confession in their Second London Confession, the Assembly Confession (1667), merely supplementing the Westminster Confession with the Congregational Points of Difference as well as with statements on believers' baptism. While the Baptists had already come forward as proponents of an unlimited confessional freedom, the Quakers' Fifteen Articles (1678), authored by George Fox's student Robert Barclay, finally declare that the sole limit to freedom of conscience is the Golden Rule as the principle that makes it possible to live together in society in the first place.

In view of the toleration granted even in absolutist states, when Ludwig XIV revoked the Edict of Nantes (1685) and the freedom of religion proclaimed therein for adherents of the Reformed confession, it could only appear as an anachronism, particularly since the Huguenots were not even granted the general right of emigration. As one who was himself affected by the revocation, Pierre Bayle argues for a fundamental toleration on the basis of the difference between universal rational insight and the revealed content of faith, the truth of which could not be decided by any human authority. Bayle rejected the literal interpretation of Luke 14:23—"compel them to come in" (*cogitare intrare*)—which supposedly legitimated the coerced reintegration of heretics into the Roman church, and was also applied to the Huguenots. Bayle rejected this interpretation as not being in harmony with the spirit of the gospel as a matter of conscience. It is in accordance with this spirit, Bayle argued, that all of scripture is to be interpreted. When in the Edict of Potsdam (1685) the Great Elector of Brandenburg-Prussia granted asylum to the Huguenot refugees, he took a further step in the direction of freedom of religion. He explicitly went beyond the Peace of Westphalia and permitted Reformed Christians who, unlike their German coreligionists, did not make the Augsburg Confession their own, to practice their religion publicly. The religious politics of Brandenburg-Prussia found its theological legitimation in the systems of ecclesiastical law advanced by Samuel Pufendorf and Christian Thomasius, and shaped by the natural law of Western Europe. As an adherent of the territorial system, Thomasius vigorously opposed the episcopal system's sovereignty of the consistories and theological faculties: that is, of the *magisterium*, to whom the ruler of the land, as protector of the one true church, delegates the care for internal affairs of the church. For Thomasius, insofar as the right of law concerning sacred matters is a component of the ruler's sovereign rights, it cannot be limited by councils, synods, clerical ministries, or theological faculties. But this opens to the territorial ruler the possibility of both tolerating and uniting various confessions. And it then happened in the interest both of toleration and of the union of Lutherans and Reformed that the Great Elector addressed the Swiss cantons when they demanded that the exiled Huguenots subscribe the Helvetic Formula of Consensus.

CHANGES IN OLD REFORMED AND
THE DEVELOPMENT OF NEO-REFORMED
CONFESSIONAL WRITINGS

ENGLAND AND NORTH AMERICA

The development of the modern idea of toleration is connected to: (1) the spread of the Independent ideal of freedom of religion in the American colonies; (2) those colonies' dissolution of their ties to the motherland in the name of freedom and independence; (3) the repercussions of the ideals of the American Revolution for the collapse of the *ancien régime* in France. Besides the influence of antiquity's natural law, an essential source of the modern understanding of freedom lies in the insight that religion, as a matter of personal conscience, cannot be regimented and compelled by state legislation. This insight, which acquired effective power through the Independent protest, formed the presupposition for the modern separation of church and state, which is in turn a condition of religious freedom.

The understanding of the state held by the leaders of the American Revolution is shaped by Locke's political theory. Although Locke picks up on Hobbes's concept of the state, formed with the help of the idea of a contract, Locke does not understand the contract itself as a contract of subjugation that would legitimate absolute monarchy. Instead Locke wishes to use the idea of a contract to justify the Glorious Revolution, thereby avoiding absolutism and grounding constitutionalism. To this end Locke, unlike Hobbes, starts from a conception of the state of nature, according to which natural freedom was already limited by a natural law or law of reason prior to the existence of the state. This law of reason forbade injury to the life, property, health, and freedom of one's fellow human beings. In the state of nature all human beings are equal and free: that is, independent of the power of other individuals. The only sense the social contract can have is to make it easier for individuals to live together. It does this by establishing and implementing norms that serve the general welfare: that is, by means of legislative and executive power. The state does not annul the freedom that exists under natural law, so that the social contract is not a contract of subjugation. Instead the natural rights are inalienable, and the state's power is limited by natural law. For this reason when the people are faced with a threat to natural rights by the state, whose sole task is to better protect these rights, they can cancel the social contract and temporarily return to the state of nature.

Drawing upon Locke's view of the social contract, the Virginia Declaration of Rights written by George Mason and James Madison (1776) states "that all men are by nature equally free and independent, and have certain inherent rights, of which, when they enter into a state of society, they cannot, by any compact, deprive or divest their posterity; namely, the enjoyment of life and liberty, with the means of acquiring and possessing property, and pursuing and obtaining happiness and safety."[6] The Declaration of Independence authored by Jefferson grounded natural law in a Deistic theology of creation insofar as, according to the Declaration, God created all human beings free: that is, independent of any higher earthly power. Finally, the sixteenth article of the Virginia Declaration of Rights proclaims that freedom of religion is a natural right: "That religion, or the duty which we owe to our Creator, and the manner of discharging it, can be directed only by reason and conviction, not by force or violence; and, therefore, all men are equally entitled to the free exercise of religion, according to the dictates of conscience; and that it is the mutual duty of all to practise Christian forbearance, love, and charity, toward each other."[7] Freedom of religion is thus regarded as an innate natural or human right: that is, a right that is granted by God the Creator and is thus inalienable. This right cannot be annulled by the power of the state, which in any case is established on the basis of a social contract solely for the purpose of better procuring the general welfare. In this sense human rights always also entail the people's right to resist a state power that undermines their basis in natural law.

As a consequence of religious freedom, the United States Constitution (1787) declared the state's religious neutrality, and thus the strict separation of church and state. Presbyterians saw themseves compelled by this development to accommodate the Westminster Confession to the changed political relations. This modification affected primarily the articles concerning the state and synods. The revised version of the Confession adopted by the Synods of Philadelphia and New York (1788) considers the only task of the state to be "to protect the Church of our common Lord, without giving preference to any denomination of Christians above the rest" (S 653). Presupposing toleration of the various Christian denominations, the revision makes it the state's duty to protect the entirety of these denominations as the visible church of Christ, without privileging any of them. The state is to treat the diverse Christian confessions as equal members of the one Christian church, and to grant freedom of religion on this basis. This also means that the church is no longer conceived as the secular organ for carrying out church discipline. Instead the separation of state and church jurisdiction is now implemented in a truly strict manner: "As Jesus Christ hath appointed a regular government and discipline in his Church, no law of any commonwealth should interfere with, let, or hinder, the due exercise thereof, among the voluntary members of any denomination of Christians, according to their own profession and belief " (S 654). The state also loses the right to convene synods (cf. S 669), so that the only task remaining for the state with regard to the church is to ensure the free exercise of the Christian religion.

Presbyterian influence made itself felt not only in the War of Independence, but also in the revivalism or Great Awakening of the eighteenth century. A fruit of this revival is the Cumberland Presbyterian Church that arose in Kentucky and Tennessee. On the basis of its rejection of particularism with regard to predestination, the Cumberland Presbyterian Church broke off from the Presbyterian Church (1806) and presented its own confession, the Cumberland Presbyterian Confession (1829). The Confession corresponds in most parts to the American revision of the Westminster Confession, but deviates from the latter in the third article. The first two paragraphs of this article are changed so that the doctrine of divine decrees is conceived exclusively a posteriori on the basis of God's revealed will: "God has not decreed any thing respecting his creature man, contrary to his revealed will or written word" (S 771). According to the Cumberland Confession, God's revealed will applies to: (1) election to eternal life on the condition of true faith, and (2) rejection of those who remain unrepentant to the end. This means that conditional predestination replaces unconditional predestination. For this reason all further paragraphs of the third article of the Westminster Confession are excised. A footnote giving the reason for this step rejects both the Calvinist doctrine of unconditional predestination and the Arminian counterposition. Fatalism and Pelagianism are to be avoided by a middle position that understands reprobation not as an eternal reprobation of specific individuals, arising from an immutable decree. "That all mankind become legally reprobated by transgression is undeniable, and continue so until they embrace Christ" (S 772). In this case reprobation applies equally to all sinners and characterizes the condition of the subject prior to faith. "Reprobation is not what some have supposed it to be, viz., a sovereign determination of God to create millions of rational beings, and for his own glory damn them eternally in hell, without regard to moral rectitude or sin in the creature" (ibid.). In this way reprobation is distinguished from damnation. To identify them, as does the Calvinist particularism of predestination, is illegitimate because it does not do justice to the eternal election of humankind in Christ or to God's offer of grace to sinners. "God offered, and does offer, the law-condemned sinner mercy in the gospel, he having from the foundation of the world so far chosen mankind in Christ" (ibid.). Election applies to those who are in Christ: that is, exclusively to believers. There is no unconditional election, but only an election that occurs on the condition of faith. In the view of the Cumberland Confession, an unconditional election, to which would correspond an unconditional reprobation in the sense of a damnation, contradicts the universalism of grace. "For God declares in his Word that Christ died for the whole world; that he offers pardon to all; that the Spirit operates on all; confirming by an oath that he has no pleasure in the death of sinners" (S 773).

FRENCH REVOLUTION, AWAKENING (*RÉVEIL*), AND THE DEVELOPMENT OF FREE CHURCHES

Under the influence of the ideals of the American Revolution, a revolution of social relations was also brewing in continental Europe. In the wake of this revolution the relation between church and state came to be organized in a new way. While Voltaire had already protested the persecution of Reformed Christians under Louis XV, Lafayette's support of the movement for independence in America played a key role in popularizing the idea of toleration, which found its expression in Louis XVI's Edict of Toleration (1787). The Edict granted non-Catholics the right to register publicly their civil status. But it was only with the Declaration of Human and Civil Rights (1789) that fundamental freedom of religion was defended.

Unlike the American Revolution, the French Revolution lacked religious roots. It was instead a revolution of the liberal bourgeoisie, which, supported by the enlightened nobility and clergy, wished primarily to ensure the natural right to private property. If on the one hand Lockean ideas made their imprint on the French Declaration of Human Rights, on the other hand Rousseau's influence was felt, primarily in the theory of the general will (*volonté générale*). For Rousseau the state is founded by a social contract, whose basic condition is that all partners to the contract divest themselves of all their rights and turn them over to the community. By giving up their natural freedom, individuals attain their judicial freedom as citizens of the state. Arbitrary freedom is surrendered in favor of a freedom that is autonomy, in the sense of obedience to self-imposed laws: that is, to universal norms. In this way the union of individual wills gives rise to a general will of the whole. This will must be distinguished from the sum of individual wills (*volonté de tous*). According to Rousseau, all individual wills can together be different from the general will without the latter thereby losing its normative power. Since by definition the general will is concerned with the common good and the welfare of the whole, it is itself infallible. Insofar as judicial freedom exists exclusively in agreement with the general will, and the state as representative of the sovereign embodies the general will, the state can use coercive measures to bring about conformity between individual wills and the general will. To be sure, the state is tolerant toward the various private religious opinions, so that the possibility of an intolerant confession is excluded. But in Rousseau's view, the state must also practice a fundamental religious coercion with regard to the civil religion that is necessary to preserve morality and duty. Insofar as this religion is prescribed by the state, it is a state religion as an expression of the general will, and thus of the autonomy of the citizens.

While Rousseau's idea of a Deistic state religion was given a short-lived realization by decision of the National Convention (1794), freedom of religion was anchored in the basic law of the land by the Declaration of Human Rights adopted by the constituting National Assembly (1789) "in the presence and under the auspices of the Supreme Being (*Être suprême*)." However, freedom of religion is here only a particular case of the universal freedom of opinion, which moreover is restricted with regard to the law: "No one ought to be disturbed on account of his opinions, even religious, provided their manifestation does not derange the public order established by law." The law itself is regarded as "the expression of the general will": that is, of the autonomy of the citizens of the state. Citizens are "born and remain free and equal in rights," and united politically for "the preservation of the natural and imprescriptible rights of man":[8] that is, in Locke's sense, liberty, property, security and—as a French supplement—resistance against oppression. The source of state sovereignty thus lies with the people, who found the state with the help of a contract. The declaration of liberty and equality as inalienable human rights led to the dissolution of the estates of the nobility and the clergy. In addition, the relation between church and state was ordered in a new way in the sense that, after church property was expropriated, the state assumed the duty of providing for worship, payment of the clergy, and ecclesiastical care for the poor. Only after the end of the Reign of Terror was the state church founded by the Civil Constitution of the Clergy (1790) removed in favor of a strict separation of church and state (1795). The failure of the religious politics of the Reign of Terror, with its anarchical cult of reason and its official cult of the Supreme Being institutionalized by Robespierre, led to the state's declaring neutrality in things religious and its granting a limited freedom of worship. Admittedly the Organic Articles (1802), which the Consul Bonaparte had published together with the Concordat agreed upon with the Holy See (1801), again annexed the churches to the realm of state power. But the limited freedom of religion for the Reformed confession was not again withdrawn. Catholicism did not regain its place as the sole state religion, but sank to the level of the "religion of the great majority of French citizens."

The conquests of the French revolutionary armies during the civil republic also reordered the relation between church and state in France's sister republics. In the United Netherlands the Reformed church lost its privileged status. The constitution now granted equal protection to all confessions (1801). In the Helvetic Republic the Reformed theologian Philipp

Albert Stapfer labored as minister of culture to found an interconfessional national church. The events in France also gave strength in England to the call for a separation of church and state, which had already been demanded by the Dissenters. However, Reformed churches not tied to the state were first formed in the context of the European revival movement or "Awakening" (*Réveil*). In Scotland Thomas Chalmers carred out the Disruption (1843) of the Free Church from the Presbyterian state church. The catalyst for the break was the question whether the patrons could impose on their communities clergy that the communities had rejected. In the Netherlands William I had completely subjected the Reformed church to the influence of the Restoration state (1816), and had replaced the presyterial-synodical system with a consistorial one. Here the revival led to renewed reflection on the confessional foundations—that is, the Belgic Confession and the Canons of Dordrecht—which had in fact lost their operative authority under the influence of the Enlightenment Rationalism that ruled the restored state church. The dispute about the obligatory character of the confessional writings finally brought the separation (*Afscheiding*) (1834) of the free *Gereformeerden* church from the *Hervormden* state church. In French-speaking Switzerland the Awakening led to the formation of free Reformed congregations, and ultimately to the founding of the Free Church (*Église libre*) in Geneva (1849) and in Vaud (1847). A similar development occurred in France where, after the National Synod decided to disregard every specific confession, free congregations split off and joined in a union (1849).

The decisive role in the formation of the Free Church in Vaud was assumed by Alexandre Vinet. In the context of the discussion of the constitution, the question also arose concerning the validity of the Second Helvetic Confession as the norm of doctrine and proclamation in the state church of Vaud. While the state Council, in an official proposal (1838), had argued for retaining the Confession, the Great Council of the canton adopted an article that advocated giving up the Confession, and recognized the Old and New Testaments as the sole rule of faith. In opposition Vinet advanced the thesis that the territorial church of Vaud was necessarily a confessional church, and that a church without a confession was a self-contradiction. The Bible cannot take the place of a confession precisely because, in the face of the plurality of interpretations of the Bible, a confession prescribes a specific interpretation or a specific principle of interpretation. In Vinet's view, the elimination of a confession would mean that, in the absence of an independent administration of the church, there would no longer be any authority at all to decide religious differences of opinion, and religion would degenerate to a mere department of the state administration. The result is "that the suppression of the confession legally entails the dissolution of the contract that connects church and state, indeed entails the rapid collapse of the church, and that as long as the church exists, one can not require this suppression in the name of liberty."[9] This does not mean that for a confession one would be compelled to retain the Second Helvetic. Vinet explicitly considers the possibility of a new confession being produced. "One can thus propose that the old confession be subjected to the formality of official affirmation—this old confession, which ultimately could be the one that you prefer, and of which you only wish that its sovereignty be legally renewed. Or one could propose that this confession would be replaced by another for an indefinite time. But if one can not create a confession that pleases all, one must create a confession that pleases the greatest number."[10] Here Vinet explicitly recurs to the democratic procedure of a free and general election to legitimate the introduction of a confession. In the case of a state church represented by the Council, the Council cannot impose a confession on the people. A confession can be accepted by the people only through their majority decision.

After the Free Church was founded on the basis of the exertion of pressure by the state government on the Awakening, the Free Church undertook the development of a confession of faith. Vinet's draft of the pertinent constitutional article ran as follows: "The Free Church, connected by the bonds of a common faith to all evangelical churches that proceeded from the Reformation, confesses with them and with their ancestors . . . the divinity of the Scriptures of the Old and New Testament, and proclaims as the sole and sure means of salvation for penitent sinners faith in Jesus Christ, Son of God and Son of Humanity, mediator between God and human beings, and high priest of the New Covenant, who was handed over on behalf of our sins, who arose for our justification, who effects our sanctification by God's Holy Spirit, whom he sends us from his Father, and who, finally, is capable, worthy and determined to save completely all those who draw near to God through him."[11] The commission's draft supplemented Vinet's brief confession at several points. The former mentions at the outset the fact that the Free Church belongs to the evangelical churches who have proclaimed their faith "with such marvelous agreement in their symbolic books, and in particular in the Helvetic Confession of Faith." Along with the divinity of the biblical scriptures, the commission's draft emphasizes their "complete sufficiency," and makes unessential alterations to the Christocentric main statement. The version that was ultimately adopted again expands the main statement by means of a Trinitarian and christological formula, adheres more closely to the Apostles' Creed, and proclaims the Free Church's ties to the apostolic church and the churches of all times who "have confessed the doctrine of salvation by grace through the blood of Jesus Christ."[12]

In his proposed draft of the confession, Vinet characterized the particular existence of the Free Church by three marks: the formation of the

church according to the principle of voluntary membership, the proclamation of the principle of freedom, and the immediate participation of
congregations or of simple believers in church administration. On the basis of its constitution as a sovereign free church, separated from the state,
the Free Church has the right to confess its faith in its own words in a manner that is appropriate to the particular time. In this way it takes account
of the changed position of the church in the modern period. Given the con-
frontation with atheism in the modern period, what is important is not so
much drawing boundaries over against Catholicism, but testifying to
Christianity. Even if one is in fundamental agreement with the Second
Helvetic Confession, one cannot simply repeat it. In contrast to the Reformation confessions, the subject of the confession is now the entirety of the
voluntary members of a church community, which with the confession attests its faith and states the principles by which that faith is to be taught.
The confession thus has the function of a rule of doctrine, but one that is
freely accepted, rather than imposed by the state church. Although the
new confession adopts the principles and spirit of the Second Helvetic
Confession, for Vinet it is unlike the latter in that it is a law with exclusively
foundational articles. It has the character of a constitution. "As author of a
confession intended for the people, we wanted to know nothing other than
Jesus Christ: specifically, Jesus Christ crucified. He is truly the actual object of our confession. It is him we confess."[13] The new confession chose
not the path of enumeration, but the principle of concentration, which se-
lected only the basic conditions of Christianity and of salvation, and
thereby exclusively truths of the first order. Specifically, along with the divinity and sufficiency of scripture, the confession highlighted the Protestant character of the Free Church and, with the confession of Jesus Christ
as the sole ground and mediator of salvation, the Free Church's evangelical essence.

GERMAN UNION MOVEMENT

In the course of the French Republic's politics of conquest, in Germany
a new ordering of religious relations came about in the occupied territories on the left side of the Rhine. Here the parity of confessions replaced
the imperial law, arising from the Peace of Westphalia, that prescribed
confessional status. The ties between church and state were loosened, and
the restrictions on worship and civil activity gradually disappeared. The
Final Recess (1803) was followed by the secularization of the majority of
the lands under church sovereignty—which were perceived as anachro-
nisms anyway—and by the annulment of most of the economically bank-
rupt imperial cities in order to compensate the large and middle-sized

states for their loss of territory on the left side of the Rhine. Through the necessary change in the imperial constitution, the proportion of voices with regard to confession shifted in favor of the Protestants in both the Electoral College and the Council of Princes. The Final Recess specified that, while the previous religious practice of every land should be protected against annulment and injury, the ruler of the land was free to tolerate other coreligionists and to grant them the full enjoyment of civil rights. After the dissolution of the old Reich (1806) and after the ultimate victory over Napoleon, Germany was reorganized at the Vienna Congress (1815). The Acts of Confederation, conceived as the treaty that set the framework for the newly founded German Confederation, took confessional difference in the new states into account. The variety of Christian religious parties in the territories of the German Federation could no longer provide the basis for a difference in the enjoyment of civil and political rights. Confessional parity was thus anchored in law.

However, the specification of the ruler of the land as the supreme bishop (*summus episcopus*) went hand in hand with a strengthening of the state's influence on the individual territorial churches. This influence was promoted by the definition of the relation between state and church in the collegial system, which in Enlightenment absolutism had replaced the territorial system. The collegial system was initially favored by those Dutch Calvinists who, in opposition to a territorial state church, wanted to emphasize the independence of a church directing itself on the basis of its presbyterial-synodical constitution. They viewed the church as an independent association (*collegium*), while granting to the state the right of law concerning sacred matters, in the sense of sovereignty in the church: that is, the right of overseeing a particular association. But the collegial system separated the ruler's rights of oversight, which were grounded in the power of the state, from the association's internal power, which belonged to the church as a public corporation and society. The internal power of the association as the actual power of the church belongs not to the state but to the church. That power thus cannot be understood as flowing out of the power of the state. But within the framework of Enlightenment contractualism, one conceived the relation between church association and ruler in such a way that the church supposedly had, on the basis of a contract, transferred its internal power as an association to the ruler of the land. In this way rights pertaining to church governance were granted to the ruler, along with the ruler's inherent rights pertaining to state governance. Besides the general oversight of the church, church governance also lay in the ruler's hands. The ruler possessed not only the right of law concerning sacred matters, but likewise, as the supreme bishop of the territorial church, the right of law in sacred matters. This collegialistic description of the relation between church and state found lasting expression in the Prussian

Territorial Law (1794). At the same time this made it apparent that the collegial system, understood in this way, led to a complete surrender of the church's independence. It is true that the ruler of the land could permit his episcopal rights to be exercised by consistories, but the latter were in turn merely auxiliaries to the ministries of the state. In any case they were shortly removed during the Prussian Reform in favor of a total state church.

On the occasion of the 300th anniversary of the Reformation (1817), there were increased exertions, especially in those territories which had experienced a "second Reformation," to bring about a union of Lutherans and Reformed. The greatest success in this direction was enjoyed by the reflections in Prussia, where there had indeed been unionistic efforts ever since the ruling house switched to Calvinism. The ruler, by virtue of his episcopal rights or the right of law in sacred matters, acted on the concern for union. The first of these unions ordained by the state authority was in Nassau. There the Edict of Union (1817) stated as the essential character of the Protestant church inner freedom of belief and religious reverence for the teachings of the gospel, along with complete independence from human opinions. The Edict also announced the founding of an evangelical Christian territorial church. In the Palatinate the Document of Union (1818) approved by the General Synod in Kaiserslauthern resulted in the two separate Protestant confessions being reunited in the Protestant Evangelical Christian Church. Although the Document shows the appropriate respect for both the common symbols and the particular confessions, it names scripture as the sole ground of faith and the only norm of doctrine. Articles are appended that describe the consensus in the disputed questions of doctrine. The Lord's Supper is now understood as a feast of remembrance and of union with the Redeemer; confession, as preparation for the Supper. Emergency baptism is rejected, and universal election is taught with regard to predestination. Unlike the Palatine Document of Union, the Baden Act of Union (1821) did not proceed without any confessional writing, but recognized the Augsburg Confession as a common confession, and Luther's Catechism and the Heidelberg Catechism as particular confessions. In the question of the Lord's Supper, the Act of Union emphasized that the mode of Christ's presence was not essential. In the conviction that Lutherans and Reformed were united by belief in the reconciling love of Christ and by the spirit of free investigation of scripture as the sole source of faith, the parties joined together to form an Evangelical Protestant territorial church. All Union churches eventually agreed in recognizing the Augsburg Confession as a confessional foundation. The Palatinate also adopted this position by recognizing the altered Augsburg Confession as a consensus document.

In calling for the formation of the Union (1817), Friedrich Wilhelm III held that, in view of the fact that Lutherans and Reformed were one in the "chief matter of Christianity," "the true religious union of the two Protestant churches, which remain separated only by external differences . . . is in accordance with the great purposes of Christianity. This union corresponds to the primary intentions of the Reformers; it belongs to the spirit of Protestantism; it promotes the sense of the church; it is salutary for household piety; it becomes the source of many useful improvements in churches and schools—improvements that have often been inhibited previously only by confessional difference." Neither of the confessions is to merge into the other, but both together are to form "a new, revitalized evangelical Christian church in the Spirit of their holy Founder." After the broad-based resistance to the compulsory introduction of his Romantic and restorationist agenda of union and of the accompanying move from a merely administrative union to a cultic union, Friedrich Wilhelm III felt himself compelled to emphasize in a cabinet order (1834) that the previous confessions of faith and the authority of the confessional writings would continue. He insisted that the goal of the Union was the spread of the insight that diversity in individual points of doctrine was no reason for failing to enact external ecclesiastical communion.

Unlike Nassau, the Palatinate, Baden, and other regions in which there were Union churches, in Prussia a consensus for union did not occur, since the attempt of the Prussian General Synod (1846) to produce a Union confession ultimately failed. Nor did Prussia succeed in forming a unitary ecclesiastical constitution. Schleiermacher indeed emerged as the proponent of collegialism; he saw the introduction of the presbyterial-synodical system as the best way of preserving collegialism's original interest in the separation of church and state for the sake of the church's independence. But only the Church Ordinance of Rhine-Westphalia (1835) adopted the decisive principles of this system, while retaining consistorial elements. In the rest of Prussia the failure of the revolution in 1848 also meant the end of the discussion of a synodical order. Admittedly, the Evangelical Church Council was introduced (1850) as the highest administrative authority, existing independently of the state, of the Prussian territorial church. But only after the founding of the Reich did the liberal cultural politics lead to the adoption of the presbyterial-synodical system, and thus to the restriction of the ruler's power to act as supreme bishop.

Large parts of Neo-Lutheran confessionalism agreed with the representatives of the presbyterial-synodical constitution of the church with regard to their interest in a separation of church and state, and in thereby ceasing to have the ruler act as supreme bishop, instead entrusting the secular authorities with a responsibility for caring for the church. They did not agree, however, in their solutions to the problem of the right constitution of the church. For these Neo-Lutherans a collegial understanding

of the church was replaced by an institutional understanding, which
assigned the governance of the church to the official ministers as the apostles' successors. These ministers were distanced from the church community. Under the influence of Friedrich Julius Stahl, parts of Neo-
Lutheranism thus arrived at a Catholicizing hierarchical concept of the
church, and thereby at the episcopal system. In the wake of this restorationist ecclesiology, the confession regained its function of setting the law
for doctrine. In spite of the protest even within Neo-Lutheranism against
the thesis that the Lutheran confessional writings of the Book of Concord
were finished and sufficient, the entire confession, and not just its spirit or
principle, was now declared to be the binding norm of faith and doctrine.
This stood in decisive opposition to the leading Union theologians, who
were interested only in the spirit of the symbols. With this position the
Union theologians were continuing the Enlightenment's tradition of re-
placing the confessions' status as doctrinal law with an obligation only to
their meaning. Precisely the symbolic books' status as doctrinal law was
seen as nothing less than a transgression against the Protestant scriptural
principle. To be sure, Schleiermacher explicitly objected to getting rid of
the confessional writings in favor of the sole validity of scripture, insofar
as he thought that scripture could only demonstrate that a doctrinal statement was Christian, not that it was Protestant. But at the same time he re-
marked with regard to the Reformed and Lutheran confessions "that only
that part of the confessional documents in which they all agree can be really essential to Protestantism."[14] Schleiermacher further specifies that attention must be directed more to the "spirit" than to the "letter." Insofar as
the decisive symbolic books, on the one hand, are the first public exposition of Protestant doctrine and, on the other hand, delineate the opposition
to Catholic doctrine, only that which corresponds to the spirit of these
books can count as Protestant. For this reason Schleiermacher recom-
mends the following as the correct formula for ministers' ordination vows:
"I declare that I find to be in full agreement with Holy Scripture and with
the original teaching of the church all that is taught in our symbolic books
against the errors and abuses of the Roman church—especially in the articles concerning justification and good works, the church and ecclesiastical
power, the Mass, the ministry of the saints, and oaths. I further declare that
as long as the office of teaching is entrusted to me, I will not cease to present these doctrines, and to observe the ordinances appropriate to them."[15]
Since the obligation is to the spirit and not to the letter of the confessions,
and this spirit is the spirit of Protestantism, only those teachers are Protestant who do not restrict this obligation by means of an "insofar" (*quatenus*),
rather than confessing a "because" (*quia*). This view prevailed in Mediating Theology, so that the Reformed theologian Carl Ullmann could declare: "If we can not find in the words of the confessions that which

constitutes the Protestant character, we must turn to their principle and their spirit. Formally, their principle is the return to Scripture as the ultimate basis for deciding what is Christianly true. This return is tied to the rejection of the tradition as dogmatic authority. Materially, their principle is the derivation of salvation from the redeeming and reconciling activity of Christ, which is to be appropriated by each individual through faith. This derivation is tied to the rejection of all human merit."[16] In this way the unionistic Mediating Theology arrived at the thesis of the two principles of Protestantism. In this view Lutherans and Reformed agree on the doctrine of justification by faith ("faith alone"—*sola fide*) as the material principle, and the principle of scripture ("scripture alone"—*sola scriptura*) as the formal principle. However, a hermeneutical priority is granted to the material principle, insofar as it is the key to the interpretation of scripture and is meant to guard against a legalistic—that is, fundamentalist—application of the formal principle.

The specific difference between Reformed and Lutheran Protestantism could then be specified against the background of this general distinction between the two principles of Protestantism. K. B. Hundeshagen characterizes Reformed piety as predominantly active, with Lutheran piety being predominantly resting. The Zurich theologians A. Schweizer and A. E. Biedermann—the one a disciple of Schleiermacher, the other a Hegelian—see Lutheran Protestantism directed against the "Judaizing" works righteousness of the Catholic church, and Reformed Protestantism directed against Catholicism's paganizing divinization of the creature. For Biedermann these are two moments, inseparable from each other, "of the one foundational Protestant principle: to maintain the purity of the freedom, opened up in Christ, that is attendant on being God's children."[17] But since the way in which this principle found expression in confessional writings in the Reformation period and in old Protestant Orthodoxy does not stand up to criticism, for Biedermann the old Reformed confessional writings lose binding validity. The fact that the Swiss Reformed territorial churches ultimately no longer acknowledge any binding confessional foundation, and thus are without any confession, can be traced back to Biedermann and Swiss theological liberalism.

WEIMAR, THE GERMAN CHURCH STRUGGLE, AND THE BARMEN THEOLOGICAL DECLARATION

The end of the monarchy in Germany also spelled the end of governance of the church by the ruler of the land. Unlike the strong separation of church and state in France, or the situation in Bolshevik Russia, the relation between church and state after the Revolution of 1918 was defined not in the sense of a strict separation with the withdrawal of all the public privileges that the church had previously enjoyed, or even in the sense of a baldly antireligious posture. Instead the Constitution of the Weimar Republic (1919) adopted the basic principles of the Constitution of 1848. Churches received the status of public and legal corporations to which specific privileges were granted and which were legally protected. The more detailed regulation of the relation between churches and individual lands of the Reich occurred through concordats or church treaties. The constitution of the Reich guaranteed full freedom of belief and of conscience, as well as the undisturbed exercise of religion. Belonging to a particular confession did not give rise to civil advantages or disadvantages. There was no longer a state church. Instead the freedom to unite in religious societies, and for religious societies to combine, was confirmed throughout the territory of the Reich. "Each religious society orders and administers its affairs independently within the limits of the law that holds for all. Each religious society confers its offers without the involvement of the state or the civil community" (Weimar Constitution).

Although the Weimar Constitution did not bring the end of the state's sovereignty in the church, it did put an end to church governance being exercised by those who held state power. Unlike the conservative circles, both liberalism and religious socialism welcomed the separation of throne and altar. Here the Revolution led to a movement for a "people's church" (*Volkskirche*). This movement, in part in the form of people's church councils, called for a general German ecclesiastical assembly to provide a constitution, as well as for a free electoral system, based on the sovereignty of the people, in all ecclesiastical offices and church councils. The goal was a Free Evangelical People's Church in Germany. However, the transfer of actual ecclesiastical power to the territorial churches themselves at first led only to the individual territorial churches providing themselves with their own constitutions, which in the main took account of the model of parliamentary democracy by strengthening the synods. In most of the churches, the ruler of the land as the supreme bishop was replaced by a collegial governing board, which was composed of members of the synods and consistories, the latter now being formally active as actual ecclesiastical administrative authorities. The unity of the territorial churches increasingly found expression in some form of "territorial episcopal" office. The constitutions of the Weimar Republic fundamentally retained the collegial system, with the only difference being that now the elements of a constitutional monarchy were replaced by those of a parliamentary democracy. A direct connection between the constitution and the confession of the church was not established—if the territorial church attached any importance at all to its confessional status. Instead specific elements of the state's constitution were transferred to the church as external to the latter's essence. In accord with Rudolf Sohm's thesis of the contradiction between ecclesiastical law and the essence of the church, the presbyterial-synodical constitution could be adopted as a system of order that most readily expressed the parliamentary representation of the people of the church, and the legislative power that lay in their hands.

The gradual erosion of the Weimar democracy together with its parliamentary system by radicalism of the Left and especially of the Right was decisive for the further development of the relation between church and state in Germany. Elements of the conservative revolution and of social nationalism were picked up from the church's side by German Christian movements. Among the latter, Hossenfelder's Faith Movement of German Christians met with the support of National Socialism. The party platform of the National Socialists had already assumed the position of a "positive Christianity" without any confessional ties, but had extended freedom of confession only to those confessions which did not offend the ethical and moral sensibility of the German race. The Guiding Principles of the Faith Movement of German Christians (1932) then explicitly adopted the racist elements. Understood not as a replacement for a confession of faith, but as a "confession of life," the Principles argue for a people's Reich church that abandons the parliamentary system of ecclesiastical politics. This church is to be based on a belief in Christ in accord with the German spirit of Luther and with heroic piety—a belief that regards race, people, and nation as God-given orders of life, and thus forbids any mixing of races. The German Christians' condemnation of Judaism, Marxism, pacifism, and internationalism enabled the German Christians to acquire the majority of seats in the Prussian ecclesiastical elections. After the victory of National Socialism the Principles of the German Christians were initially moderated to be more appealing to the electorate. They called for a new church constitution that would replace the democratic right of election with the principle of suitability, and for a spiritual head of the Reich church, constructed in accordance with the Führer principle. The Principles also argue "for the full preservation of the confessional position of the Reformation, but demand a further development of the confession in the sense of a sharp rejection of all modern heresies, of Mammonism, Bolshevism, and of unchristian pacifism," as well as of a recognition of the divinely willed diversity of races and peoples. After the constitution of the German Evangelical Church (1933), which arose from the German Evangelical Federation of Churches (1922), was declared a law of the Reich and was adopted by the individual territorial churches, the German Christians emerged victorious in Prussia as in most of the other territorial churches. Moreover, the state-legislated Aryan Paragraph was applied to the church: that is, non-Aryan ministers and officials were excluded from ecclesiastical service, and church officials were unqualifiedly obligated to the national state.

At the Wittenberg National Synod Ludwig Müller, as patron of the German Christians, was elected Bishop of the federated Reich church. But the introduction of the Aryan Paragraph also signified the beginning of the German church struggle (*Kirchenkampf*), introduced by Niemöller's founding of the Pastors' Emergency League. The constitution of the German Evangelical Church had characterized as the church's unquestionable foundation "the gospel of Jesus Christ, as it is attested for us in Holy Scripture, and again found the light of day in the confessions of the Reformation." In this way the constitution defined and limited the church's authority by that gospel. On this basis the declaration of obligation of the Pastors' Emergency League could regard the application of the Aryan Paragraph as an offense to the confessional status: that is, to the "bond to Holy Scripture and to the Reformation confessions as the correct interpretation of Holy Scripture." The founding of the Pastors' Emergency League led to the formation of Councils of Brethren, free synods, and ultimately to the Confessional Communion of the German Evangelical Church. This Confessional Communion, which also included "intact" churches, designated itself as the rightful evangelical church in Germany, and rejected the official government of the Reich church as illegitimate and confessionally destructive. Legitimated by emergency ecclesiastical law, the "Confessing Church" constituted itself, with the Reich Council of Brethren as its executive branch, at the first Confessional Synod in Barmen. As the theological grounding for its actions, the Synod adopted the Theological Declaration on the Current Position of the German Evangelical Church. After World War II both Reformed and United churches of the Evangelical Church of Germany incorporated this Declaration, of which Karl Barth was the primary author, into the ordination vows alongside the respective Reformation confessions.

The Barmen Theological Declaration (1934) formed the preliminary culmination of a development that had led to an increasing concentration on church and confession within Dialectical Theology. The theology of revelation and of God's word was now developed as dogmatics, which presented itself as reflection on the Credo publicly spoken and affirmed by the church, and thus as "Church Dogmatics." Since the visible church was not at one with itself, Church Dogmatics had to take account of confessional difference. In this manner Barth came to a renewed reflection on the Reformed confession. He insisted above all on the confession's being relativized by scripture and the Spirit as the two sole doctrinal authorities. In his view, this relativity allowed both the repristination of Reformation confessions and the establishment of new ones. The Reformed World Federation had raised the question of the desirability and possibility of a universal Reformed confession of faith (1925). Employing a definition that highlighted the relativity of the Reformed confession, Barth answered the question in the negative. "A Reformed Creed is the statement, sponta-neously and publicly formulated by a Christian community within a geo-graphically limited area, which, until further action, defines its character to outsiders; and which, until further action, gives guidance for its own doctrine and life; it is a formulation of the insight currently given to the whole Christian Church by the revelation of God in Jesus Christ, witnessed to by the Holy Scriptures alone."[18] On this view, the confession's contents relate exclusively to God's revelation in Jesus Christ, which is attested nei-ther by church tradition nor by significant historical phenomena, but only by scripture. Insight into this revelation is wrought by the Holy Spirit. As the exposition of this insight, the confession is dogma, and as such stands between the word of God attested in scripture and a merely human word. But Reformed dogma possesses only a relative validity: "'We, here, now, confess faith in this!' Certainly we are conscious of speaking in the name of the one Holy Church (*Una Sancta*), conscious of speaking the truth—but we, here, now speak."[19]

The subject of the confession is in this case the sovereign Christian community, represented if need be by synods in the sense of a representa-tive Christian democracy. This sovereign Christian community knows no office over it, but only Christ, ruling as king. The presupposition of the spontaneous confession of a particular church or a local congregation is al-ways that there is something present that concretely drives the church to confess something that is to be known and to be willed. Until new devel-opments arise, the confession thus points the way not only for the teach-ing of the community, but also for its life. In this sense one would expect from a confession spoken not "between the times," but at the future "turn-ing-point," both the church's rejection of the Neo-Protestant "heresy" that began with Schleiermacher and the condemnation of "fascist, racialist na-tionalism," anti-Semitism, and war.[20] Insofar as the church at any particu-lar time is summoned by concrete circumstances to a new confession, the church understands itself as essentially "a church confessing its faith."[21] Barth ultimately developed the relation between confession interpreted as dogma, scripture, and the revelation in Jesus Christ within the framework of his doctrine of the threefold form of the word of God. Confessions rep-resent the attempt, repeatedly renewed to meet differing situations, to ex-plicate the insight into the revelation attested by scripture. The confession thus relates by means of God's written word to Jesus Christ as God's word become flesh. These points delineate an approach that not only takes its methodological starting point with ecclesiastical doctrine, but also takes its starting point in terms of content with the revelation in Christ alone. The latter then found its confessional expression in the Barmen Theological Declaration and its precursors.

The Düsseldorf Theses (1933), composed by the Reformed professors, pastors, elders, and deacons of the Rhineland, are to be regarded as one such precursor. The Theses ushered in a new consideration of the essence of the church at the time when the constitution of the German Evangelical Church was being elaborated. The first of the Düsseldorf Theses cites the first of the Berne Theses (1528), thereby establishing an explicit relation to the Reformation confessions. But the Reformation confession is interpreted completely along the lines of Barth's dogmatic approach. When the Düsseldorf Theses say that "the holy, Christian church, whose only head is Christ, is born of the Word of God," they mean by "Word of God" the word of God spoken through the scriptures of the Old and New Testaments, which the third thesis identifies exclusively with Jesus Christ. "The Word of God spoken to us is our Lord Jesus Christ." Christ's regency in the church is implemented "through carrying out the ministry of preachers, teachers, elders, and deacons instituted and ordered by Jesus Christ" (CC 229). In this way the order of the church is regarded not as a constitution that is external to the church's essence and that corresponds to the political order of the state, but as grounded christologically. This provides a specifically theological legitimation of the Calvinist order of four offices of ministry. Each of the offices has a different function, and each receives its promise and authority directly from Christ as the Lord of the church. This excludes the possibility of an office of spiritual leader in the sense of an episcopal office oriented according to the Führer principle. "Jesus Christ is the only 'spiritual leader' of the Church. He is its heavenly King who lives on earth through his Spirit in every one who is obedient to his commission in serving him in the Church." It is not "the dominion of a single congregation over others or the dominion of an episcopal office over other offices" that corresponds on earth to Christ's dominion over his church, "but rather the service that congregations mutually owe one another and which they seek to render to one another in the form of synods composed of servants appointed thereto" (CC 229). The Düsseldorf Theses oppose the organization of a Reich church analogously to the state's Führer principle, with a bishop at its head, distinguished by special authority. In opposition the Theses advance as christocratically grounded the presbyterial-synodical order of the church in the sense of a representative Christian democracy.

Unlike the Düsseldorf Theses, which merely ground the order of the church christocratically, the Declaration Concerning the Right Understanding of the Reformation Confessions of Faith in the German Evangelical Church of the Present (1934), which was written by Barth and adopted by the Free Reformed Synod in Barmen, begins with a fundamental rejection of Neo-Protestantism and its theological roots. This condemnation is legitimated by the thesis that in the theology of the Faith Movement of German Christians "an error has become ripe and visible, which has had a devastating effect upon the Evangelical church for centuries." This error "consists in the opinion that besides God's revelation, God's grace, and God's glory, a justifiable human arbitrariness also has to determine the message and form of the Church, that is to say, the temporal way to eternal salvation" (CC 230). The Declaration disputes the normalcy of the post-Reformation development of the church and identifies Neo-Protestantism with "the error of the papal Church and of the fanatics," which must be countered anew with "the old Confession" (ibid., trans. altered). The point is not to set up a new confession that would *supplant* the Reformation confessions, but to *attest* those confessions today. In view of the unity of the error, what is called for is a *common* evangelical confession and action against the error and for the truth, despite confessional differences. This common evangelical confession is possible on the basis of the essential unity of faith, love, and hope, as well as of the proclamation through preaching and sacrament and of the confession of the confessionally diverse churches of the German Evangelical Church.

The fundamental rejection of Neo-Protestantism leads to the thesis of God's exclusive revelation in God's word, spoken through Jesus Christ in the power of the Spirit, and thus to the rejection of any "divine revelation in nature and history accessible to man in spite of the Fall" (CC 231). In opposition to every attempt to level the Old Testament, the Declaration decidedly understands the entire scripture as testimony to Christ and not as, for instance, a document of piety. The church's task is to continue this testimony to Christ, the exclusivity of which excludes giving attention to God's activity in the events of each particular present. It also excludes an unreserved obedience to a supposed "autonomy of this world" (CC 232, trans. altered). Instead the Declaration grounds the church's action in exclusively christocratic terms. In this world, which although it was created good is fallen in sin, not only the church's trust but also its obedience stands in exclusive relation to the revelation in Christ. The Declaration rejects every recourse to a supposed "order of creation" (ibid.). To be sure, the Declaration recognizes that the political, philosophical, and cultural attempts of human beings, like all twists and turns of the history of peoples and humanity, stand under the order of God's command and thus need the church's intercessory prayer. But the Declaration characterizes those attempts as temporal, defined, and limited, so that the intercession must be supplemented by pointing to the relativity of these human attempts: that is, by "recalling God's Kingdom, law, and judgment" (ibid.).

The last two sections of the Barmen Declaration articulate the message and form of the church on the basis of these fundamental determinations concerning the church in the present, under Holy Scripture, and in the world. The church's message relates exclusively to God's free grace, present in Jesus Christ, through which we are justified and sanctified. Justification and sanctification are, like gospel and law, both regarded as the work of the one grace of Jesus Christ. The relation of the law exclusively to sanctification, and thus the reduction of the law to the third use (*tertius usus*), grounds the sequence of gospel and law, as well as a purely christocratic ethics. Finally, as in the Düsseldorf Theses, the form of the church is conceived on the basis of Christ's sovereignty. The Declaration does not understand the church in a collegialistic manner as a religious association that could organize itself arbitrarily. Instead the four offices that characterize the church's external order, which are defined as ministries, are grounded in Christ's commission, for the fulfillment of which the individual church communities, and not an ecclesiastical office of Führer, carry the responsibility. The message and form of Christ's church are identical "in different times, races, peoples, states, and cultures." This is a rejection of the theses that "the justification for temporal, national, and local differences in Church forms is to be derived from special revelations of God in history," and that "it is consistent with the unity of the message and form of the Church to limit membership and qualification for service in the Church to those who belong to a particular race" (CC 234). The Declaration rejects a specifically German Christian theology as well as the application of the Aryan Paragraph to the church. The state cannot define the message and form of the church. The state is instead an independent ordinance of the divine command, in the framework of which human beings can find justice and can maintain it by force. However, this also entails a limitation of the state's sphere of influence, insofar as the Declaration denies the view that "the State is the highest or even the only ('totalitarian') form of a historical reality visibly and temporally fashioned to which therefore the Church with its message and form also has to submit and conform and into which it has to be integrated" (ibid.).

The Theological Declaration Concerning the Contemporary Situation of the German Evangelical Church, adopted at the first Confessional Synod in Barmen, picks up on the first Barmen Declaration. The difference is that the second Declaration is a declaration of Lutheran, United, and Reformed representatives of intact churches or free synods, who met on the territory of the German Evangelical Church as a federation of confessional churches in confession to the one Lord of the church. These churches saw the commonality of this confession and thus the unity of the German Evangelical Church threatened by the ecclesiastical governance of the German Christians. Out of faithfulness to their various confessions, they believed themselves justified in pronouncing a "common message," leaving open "what this may mean for the interrelations of the Confessional Churches" (C 334). However, the confessional diversity did nothing to alter the fact that the Theological Declaration, as a common word in the face of the church-destroying errors of the German Christians, is a common confession of "evangelical truths" equally recognized by all participants (ibid.).

The first of the Barmen theses adopts Barth's exclusively christological theology of revelation insofar as the first thesis characterizes the Christ attested by the entire scripture as the sole Word of God, requiring trust and obedience, and contests the recognition of other events, powers, figures, and truths as divine revelation. Following the very language of the Synodical Declaration of Berne (1532), the thesis of the one word of God contests the distinction drawn by the other old Reformed confessions between general and special revelation, or between law and gospel. Insofar as the second thesis characterizes this one word not only as God's promise of forgiveness of all our sins, but at the same time as God's claim on our entire life, both gospel and law are placed in exclusive relation to Christ— as in the first Barmen Declaration—so that the law is merely subordinated to the gospel and is enlisted in the service of sanctification. Christologically anchored in this way, the law extends not merely to specific areas of our life, but to all areas, so that Christian ethics in its entirety is conceived christocratically. Insofar as the traditional doctrine of offices is reinterpreted by virtue of Christ's sovereignty no longer extending only to the church, but to all areas of life, all action is subjected to the law of Christ's sovereignty and is drawn into the process of sanctification.

To counteract the thesis that the natural world and its order of creation are autonomous, the universalization of Christ's sovereignty brings with it—again in contrast to the old Reformed confessions—the abandonment of the traditional doctrine of the two kingdoms. The tension between this second thesis, which grounds a christocratic ethics, and the fifth thesis is mere appearance. Like the first Barmen Declaration, the fifth thesis sees the state as having the divinely ordained "task of providing for justice and peace . . . by means of the threat and exercise of force, according to the measure of human judgment and human ability" (C 336). The state's relative autonomy is recognized as resting on divine ordinance, and the church is assigned the task of calling to remembrance the reign, commandment, and righteousness of God: that is, of calling to remembrance the responsibility not only of those who rule, but also of those who are ruled. The autonomy and freedom of church and state thus lead to the rejection of the absolute state as well as of the state church, or of the church assuming the mode of the state. The church has the specific task, which the state cannot fulfill, of proclaiming as Christ's ambassador through preaching and sacrament the message of God's free grace.

As the church differs from the state in its message, so too does it differ from the state in its form, insofar as the church is regarded as "the congregation of the brethren in which Jesus Christ acts presently as the Lord in Word and sacrament through the Holy Spirit" (C 335). In agreement with the Reformed tradition, the order of the church defined in this way is no longer something external to the church itself, which could change

NOTES

PREFACE

1. The English-speaking reader will find important confessional collections edited and translated by Cochrane and Torrance (see Abbreviations)—translator's note.

PART 1

1. English has the two words *justice* and *righteousness,* where German uses only the one word *Gerechtigkeit* (corresponding to the one Greek word *dikaiosunē*)—translator's note.

PART 3

1. P. Jacobs, *Theologie reformierter Bekenntnisschriften in Grundzügen* (Neukirchen: Neukirchener, 1959), 16.
2. E. Hirsch, *Hilfsbuch zum Studium der Dogmatik,* 4th ed. (Berlin: Walter de Gruyter, 1964), 387.
3. D. M. Wolfe, *Leveller Manifestoes of the Puritan Revolution* (New York: Thomas Nelson, 1967), 348–49.
4. Hirsch, *Hilfsbuch zum Studium der Dogmatik,* 441.
5. J. Locke, *A Letter Concerning Toleration,* ed. M. Montuori (The Hague: Nijhoff, 1963), 103.
6. "The Virginia Declaration of Rights," in *The First Amendment: The Legacy of George Mason,* ed. T. D. Shumate (Fairfax, Va.: George Mason University Press, 1985), 186.
7. Ibid., 188–89.
8. "The Declaration of the Rights of Man and Citizen," in *Great Expressions of Human Rights,* ed. R. M. MacIver (Port Washington, N.Y.: Kennikat, 1969), 255–56.
9. A. Vinet, *Ausgewählte Werke,* ed. E. Staehelin, vol. 3 (Zurich: 1944), 163.
10. Ibid., 164.
11. Vinet, *Ausgewählte Werke,* vol. 4 (1945), 304–5.
12. Ibid., 338.

13. Ibid., 332.

14. F. D. E. Schleiermacher, *The Christian Faith,* trans. D. M. Baillie et al., ed. H. R. Mackintosh and J. S. Stewart (Edinburgh: T. & T. Clark, 1928), 114.

15. F. D. E. Schleiermacher, "Üuber den eigentümlichen Werth und das bindende Ansehen symbolischer Bücher," in *Sämtliche Werke* sec. 1, vol. 5 (Berlin: G. Reimer, 1846), 451.

16. C. Ullmann, "Vierzig Sätze, die theologische Lehrfreiheit innerhalb der evangelisch-protestantischen Kirche betreffend," *Theologische Studien und Kritiken* 16 (1843): 14–15.

17. A. E. Biedermann, *Christliche Dogmatik,* vol. 1, 2d ed. (1884), 339.

18. K. Barth, "The Desirability and Possibility of a Universal Reformed Creed," in *Theology and Church: Shorter Writings, 1920–1928,* trans. L. P. Smith (New York: Harper & Row, 1962), 112.

19. Ibid., 116.

20. Ibid., 131, 133.

21. Ibid., 129.

FOR FURTHER READING

This list contains only works to which the text itself does not refer. The following abbreviations are used:

ET   English translation
*RE*³   *Realenzyklopädie für protestantische Theologie und Kirche,* 3d ed.
*RGG*³ *Die Religion in Geschichte und Gegenwart,* 3d ed.
TRE   *Theologische Realenzyklopädie*
ZKG   *Zeitschrift für Kirchengeschichte*

Althaus, P. *Die Prinzipien der reformierten Dogmatik im Zeitalter der aristotelischen Scholastik.* Leipzig, 1914.

Armstrong, B. G. *Calvinism and the Amyraut Heresy.* London, 1969.

Bangs, C. *Arminius: A Study in the Dutch Reformation.* Nashville, 1971.

Barth, Chr. *Bekenntnis im Werden. Neue Quellen zur Entstehung der Barmer Erklärung.* Neukirchen, 1979.

Barth, K. *Die christliche Lehre nach dem Heidelberger Katechismus.* Munich, 1949. ET by S. C. Guthrie, Jr., *The Heidelberg Catechism for Today.* Richmond, 1964.

———. *Texte zur Barmer Theologischen Erklärung.* Zurich, 1984.

Baur, J. *Gott, Recht und weltliches Regiment im Werk Calvins.* Bonn, 1965.

Beyer, U. *Abendmahl und Messe. Sinn und Recht der 80. Frage des Heidelberger Katechismus.* Neukirchen, 1965.

Bizer, E. *Studien zur Geschichte des Abendmahlsstreits im 16. Jahrhundert.* Gütersloh, 1940.

———. "Die reformierte Orthodoxie und der Cartesianismus." *Zeitschrift für Theologie und Kirche* 55 (1958).

———. *Frühorthodoxie und Pietismus.* Theologische Studien 71 (1963).

Blösch, E. "Berner Synodus." *RE*³ IX (1897).

Bohatec, J. *Calvins Lehre von Staat und Kirche.* Breslau, 1937.

———. *Budé und Calvin.* Graz, 1950.

Bos, F. L. *Johann Piscator.* Kampen, 1932.

Brunner, P. *Vom Glauben bei Calvin.* Tübingen, 1925.

———. "Allgemeine und besondere Offenbarung in Calvins Institutio." *Evangelische Theologie* 1 (1934).

Brunotte, H. "Die Theologische Erklärung von Barmen 1934 und ihr Verhältnis zum lutherischen Bekenntnis." *Luthertum* 18 (1955).

Burgsmüller, A., ed. *Zum politischen Auftrag der christlichen Gemeinde (Barmen II)*. Gütersloh, 1974.

———, ed. *Kirche als Gemeinde von Brüdern (Barmen III)*. Vol. I. Gütersloh, 1986.

Campenhausen, H. von. "Die Bilderfrage in der Reformation." *ZKG* 68 (1957).

Cardauns, L. *Die Lehre vom Widerstandsrecht des Volkes gegen die rechtmässige Obrigkeit im Luthertum und Calvinismus des 16. Jahrhunderts*. Bonn, 1903.

Dantine, J. "Das christologische Problem im Rahmen der Prädestinationslehre von Th. Beza." *ZKG* 78 (1967).

D'Assonville, V. E. *John Knox and the Institutes of Calvin*. Durban, 1968.

Dooren, J. P. van. "Dordrechter Synode." *TRE* IX (1981).

Erbkam, W. H. "Konsensus von Sendomir." *RE*³ XVIII (1906).

Fahlbusch, E. "Monarchomachen." *RGG*³ IV (1960).

Farner, A. *Die Lehre von Kirche und Staat bei Zwingli*. Tübingen, 1930.

Faulenbach, H. "Coccejus, Johannes." *TRE* VIII (1981).

Fister, E. *Die Seligkeit erwählter Heiden bei Zwingli*. Zurich, 1952.

Gäbler, U., and E. Herkenrath, eds. *Heinrich Bullinger, 1504–1575. Gesammelte Aufsätze zum 400. Todestag*. Zurich, 1975.

Ganoczy, A. *Ecclesia militans. Dienende Kirche und kirchlicher Dienst bei Calvin*. Freiburg, 1968.

Geiger, M. "Evangelische Theologie im Zeitalter der Hochorthodoxie." *Evangelische Theologie* 9 (1949/50).

Gestrich, Chr. *Zwingli als Theologe*. Zurich, 1967.

Gierke, O. *Johannes Althusius und die Entwicklung der naturrechtlichen Staatstheorien*. Breslau, 1880.

Grass, H. *Die Abendmahlslehre bei Luther und Calvin*. Gütersloh, 1940.

Greschat, M. "Der Ansatz der Theologie Martin Bucers." *Theologische Literaturzeitung* 103 (1978).

Gründler, O. *Die Gotteslehre Girolami Zanchis und ihre Bedeutung für seine Lehre von der Prädestination*. Neukirchen, 1965.

Hagenbach, K. R. *Kritische Geschichte der Entstehung und Schicksale der ersten Basler Konfession*. Basel, 1827.

———. *Encyklopädie und Methodologie der theologischen Wissenschaften*. Leipzig, ⁵1857. ET (adapted), *Theological Encyclopedia and Methodology*, 1884.

Heppe, H. *Geschichte des deutschen Protestantismus in den Jahren 1555–1581*. 4 vols. Marburg, 1852–59.

Hollweg, W. *Neue Untersuchungen zur Geschichte und Lehre des Heidelberger Katechismus*. Neukirchen, 1961; vol. 2, 1968.

———. *Der Augsburger Reichstag von 1566 und seine Bedeutung für die Entstehung der Reformierten Kirche und ihres Bekenntnisses*. Neukirchen, 1964.

Hundeshagen, K. B. *Beiträge zur Kirchenverfassungsgeschichte und Kirchenpolitik insbesondere des Protestantismus*. Vol. I, no. 3. Wiesbaden, 1864.

Jacobs, M. "Das Bekenntnisverständnis des theologischen Liberalismus im 19. Jahrhundert." In *Bekenntnis und Einheit der Kirche*, ed. M. Brecht and R. Schwarz. Stuttgart, 1980.

Jacobs, P. *Prädestination und Verantwortlichkeit bei Calvin*. Neukirchen, 1937.

———. *Das Schottische Bekenntnis*. Witten, 1960.

Kamen, H. *Intoleranz und Toleranz zwischen Reformation und Aufklärung*. Munich, 1967.

Kickel, W. *Vernunft und Offenbarung bei Theodor Beza*. Neukirchen, 1967.

Kittelson, J. M. *Wolfgang Capito: From Humanist to Reformer*. Leiden, 1975.

Koch, E. *Die Theologie der Confessio Helvetica Posterior*. Neukirchen, 1968.

Köhler, W. *Zwingli und Luther. Ihr Streit über das Abendmahl nach seinen politischen und religiösen Beziehungen*. Vol. 1, Leipzig, 1929. Vol. 2, Gütersloh, 1953.

———. *Zürcher Ehegericht und Genfer Konsistorium*. Vol. 1. Leipzig, 1938–.

———. *Dogmengeschichte als Geschichte des christlichen Selbstbewusstseins*. Vol. 2. Zurich, 1951.

———. *Huldrych Zwingli*. Stuttgart, ²1952.

Koopmanns, J. *De Nederlandse geloofsbelijdenis*. Leiden, 1939.

Krusche, W. *Das Wirken des Heiligen Geistes nach Calvin*. Göttingen, 1957.

Kruske, R. *Johannes a Lasco und der Sakramentsstreit*. Leipzig, 1901.

Landerer, M. A. von, and G. Kawerau. "Philippisten." *RE*³ XV (1900).

Lang, A. *Der Heidelberger Katechismus und vier verwandte Katechismen*. Leipzig, 1907.

Lechter, G. V. *Geschichte der Presbyterial-Synodalverfassung seit der Reformation*. Leiden, 1854.

Leith, J. H. *Assembly at Westminster: Reformed Theology in the Making*. Richmond, 1973.

Locher, G. W. *Die Theologie Huldrych Zwinglis im Lichte seiner Christologie*. Part 1. Zurich, 1952.

———. "Die Prädestinationslehre Huldrych Zwinglis." *Theologische Zeitschrift* 12 (1956).

———. "Die theologische Bedeutung der Confessio Helvetica Posterior." In *Vierhundert Jahre Confessio Helvetica Posterior*. Bern, 1967.

———. *Die Zwinglianische Reformation im Rahmen der europäischen Kirchengeschichte*. Göttingen, 1979.

McLelland, J. C. "The Reformed Doctrine of Predestination according to Peter Martyr." *Scottish Journal of Theology* 8 (1955).

Meyer, W. E. "Soteriologie, Eschatologie und Christologie in der Confessio Helvetica Posterior." *Zwingliana* 12 (1966).

Moltmann, J. "Prädestination und Heilsgeschichte bei Moyse Amyraut," *ZKG* 65 (1953/54).

———. "Reformierte Orthodoxie." *Evangelisches Kirchenlexikon*, 2d ed., II (1956/57).

———. "Zur Bedeutung des Petrus Ramus für Philosophie und Theologie im Calvinismus." *ZKG* 68 (1957).

———. *Christoph Pezel und der Calvinismus in Bremen*. Bremen, 1958.

———. *Prädestination und Perseverenz*. Neukirchen, 1961.

Müller, E. F. K. "Coccejus und seine Schule." *RE*³ IV (1898).

———. "Erste helvetische Konfession." *RE*³ VII (1899).

———. "Das dreifache Amt Christi." *RE*³ VIII (1900).

———. "Kirchenzucht in der reformierten Kirche." *RE*³ X (1901).

———. "Presbyterialverfassung." *RE*³ XVI (1905).

Müller, J. *Die Vorgeschichte der pfälzischen Union*. Witten, 1967.

Neuser, W. H. "Die Erwählungslehre im Heidelberger Katechismus." *ZKG* 75 (1964).

———. *Die Tauflehre des Heidelberger Katechismus*. Theologische Existenz heute, n.s., 139. Munich, 1967.

———. "Melanchthons Abendmahlslehre und ihre Auswirkung im unteren Donauraum." *ZKG* 84 (1973).

Niemöller, G. *Die erste Bekenntnissynode der Deutschen Evangelischen Kirche zu Barmen*. 2 vols. Göttingen, 1959.

Niesel, W. *Calvins Lehre vom Abendmahl*. Munich, 1930.

———. *Die Theologie Calvins*. Munich, 1938. ET by H. Knight, *The Theology of Calvin*. Grand Rapids, 1980.

Pfister, E. *Das Problem der Erbsünde bei Zwingli*. Leipzig, 1939.

Pollet, J. V. "Zwinglianisme." *Dictionnaire de théologie catholique* 15 (1950).

Raitt, J. *The Eucharistic Theology of Theodore Beza*. London, 1972.

Ritschl, A. "Ueber die beiden Principien des Protestantismus." *ZKG* 1 (1876).

———. "Geschichtliche Studien zur christlichen Lehre von Gott." In idem, *Gesammelte Aufsätze*. Tübingen, 1896.

———. *Dogmengeschichte des Protestantismus*. Vol. III. Göttingen, 1926.

Ruhbach, G., ed. *Kirchenunionen im 19. Jahrhundert*. Gütersloh, [2]1968.

Scholder, K. *Ursprünge und Probleme der Bibelkritik im 17. Jahrhundert*. Munich, 1966.

———. "Die Bedeutung des Barmer Bekenntnisses für die evangelische Theologie und Kirche." *Evangelische Theologie* 22 (1967).

Schrenk, G. *Gottesreich und Bund im älteren Protestantismus*. Gütersloh, 1923.

Seeberg, R. *Lehrbuch der Dogmengeschichte*. Leipzig, [3]1920. ET, *Textbook of the History of Doctrines*. Grand Rapids.

Seils, M. "Der 'Stellenwert' der Bekenntnisse in den unierten und reformierten Kirchen." In *Theologische Versuche*, vol. XI, ed. J. Rogge and G. Schille. Berlin, 1979.

Staedtke, J., ed. *Heinrich Bullinger. Das höchste Gut*. Zurich, 1955.

———, ed. *Glaube und Bekennen. 400 Jahre Confessio Helvetica posterior*. Zurich, 1966.

———. "Die Lehre von der Königsherrschaft Christi und den zwei Reichen bei Calvin." *Kerygma und Dogma* 18 (1972).

Staehelin, E. *Das theologische Lebenswerk Johannes Oekolampads*. Leipzig, 1939.

Torrance, T. F. *Calvin's Doctrine of Man*. Reprint, London, 1977.

Troeltsch, E. *Die Soziallehren der christlichen Kirchen und Gruppen*. Tübingen, 1922. ET by O. Wyon, *The Social Teaching of the Christian Churches*. Louisville, 1992.

Tschackert, P. "Thorn, Religionsgespräch." *RE*[3] XIX (1907).

———. *Die Entstehung der lutherischen und reformierten Kirchenlehre samt ihren innerprotestantischen Gegensätzen*. Göttingen, 1910.

Usteri, J. M. "Vertiefung der Zwinglischen Sakraments- und Tauflehre bei Bullinger." *Theologische Studien und Kritiken* 56 (1883).

Vischer, L., ed. *Reformed Witness Today*. Bern, 1982.

Walser, P. *Die Prädestination bei Heinrich Bullinger im Zusammenhang mit seiner Gotteslehre*. Zurich, 1957.

Weber, H. E. *Reformation, Orthodoxie und Rationalismus*. 2 vols. Gütersloh, 1937–51.

Weber, O. "Vorerwägungen zu einer neuen Ausgabe reformierter Bekenntnisschriften." In *Hören und Handeln. Festschrift für E. Wolf*. Munich, 1962.

Weerda, J. "Reformierte Kirche." *RGG*[3] V (1961).

Wendel, F. *Calvin*. ET by P. Mairet, *Calvin: The Origins and Development of His Religious Thought*. New York, 1963.

Wesel-Roth, R. *Thomas Erastus. Ein Beitrag zur Geschichte der reformierten Kirche und zur Lehre von der Staatssouveränität*. Lahr, 1954.

Willis, E. D. *Calvin's Catholic Christology*. Leiden, 1966.

INDEX OF SUBJECTS